CONCERNING THE SPIRITUAL **AND THE CONCRETE** IN KANDINSKY'S ART

CONCERNING THE SPIRITUAL **AND**

THE **CONCRETE** IN KANDINSKY'S ART

LISA FLORMAN

STANFORD **UNIVERSITY PRESS**   **STANFORD** CALIFORNIA

Stanford University Press
Stanford, California

Printed in the United States of America on acid-free, archival-quality paper

Library of Congress Cataloging-in-Publication Data

Florman, Lisa Carol, author.
  Concerning the spiritual and the concrete in Kandinsky's art / Lisa Florman.
      pages cm
  Contains an English translation of Les Peintures concrètes de Kandinsky by Alexandre Kojève.
  Includes bibliographical references and index.
  ISBN 978-0-8047-8483-2 (cloth : alk. paper) — ISBN 978-0-8047-8484-9 (pbk. : alk. paper)
  1. Kandinsky, Wassily, 1866-1944—Criticism and interpretation. 2. Hegel, Georg Wilhelm
Friedrich, 1770-1831. Ästhetik. 3. Painting, Abstract. 4. Painting, Modern—20th century. 5. Art—
Philosophy. 6. Aesthetics. I. Kojève, Alexandre, 1902-1968. Peintures concrètes de Kandinsky.
English. II. Title.
  ND699.K3F59 2014
  759.7—dc23
                              2013021476
ISBN 978-0-8047-8923-3 (electronic)

Designed by Bruce Lundquist
Typeset at Stanford University Press in 10/15 Adobe Garamond Pro

For Ellie

CONTENTS

ILLUSTRATIONS

PLATES

The Plates appear in a separate full-color section.

FIGURES

ACKNOWLEDGMENTS

A book this long in the making incurs many debts on the way to completion. To begin with those of the longest standing: An early version of some of this material was presented in 2004 at the annual meeting of the College Art Association, in a session on "Modernist Abstraction across the Disciplines." I'd like to thank the two session chairs, Marek Wieczorek and Marshall Brown, for the invitation to participate and for their feedback at that time.

The project began to take shape in earnest during the autumn of 2006, when I was fortunate enough to have held the Agnes Gund and Daniel Shapiro Membership at the Institute for Advanced Study in Princeton. My deepest appreciation goes not only to Agnes Gund and Daniel Shapiro, whose support made my stay there possible, but also to everyone at the School of Historical Studies who commented on the work in progress, especially Yve-Alain Bois, Bettina Gockel, Cordula Grewe, Christopher Hailey, and Avishai Margalit. A return visit to the IAS during the 2009–2010 academic year—this time as a "trailing spouse"—advanced the manuscript even further. The conversations I had then (and have continued to have since), on matters both related to the book and not, with Yve-Alain Bois, Susan Laxton, Eric Michaud, and Maria Stavrinaki, have sustained me throughout the process. The opportunity to discuss my work with members of the Princeton University faculty was equally valuable. I'm deeply grateful to Brigid Doherty, Hal Foster, Michael Koortbojian, Esther da Costa Meyer, Spyros Papapetros, and Molly Warnock (then at Princeton) for their interest in the project. Brigid in particular helped me to see several important aspects of my argument whose full weight I had not quite caught, and Hal pointed me to the essay on Hegel and Kandinsky by Jean-Joseph Goux that importantly shaped my conclusion.

A number of colleagues at Ohio State University, both past and present, also contributed enormously to this book, often in ways difficult to measure. No doubt my deepest debt is to Stephen Melville, whose frequent talks with me about Hegel (and all manner of other things) I miss more than I can say. For their general encouragement, and friendship, I also want to thank Judy Andrews, Philip Armstrong,

Amanda Boetzkes, Gwyn Dalton, Mark Fullerton, Amanda Gluibizzi, Ron Green, Barbara Groseclose, Barbara Haeger, Byron Hamann, Mary Jones, Youn-mi Kim, Christian Kleinbub, Namiko Kunimoto, Laura Lisbon, Tim McNiven, Myroslava Mudrak, Kris Paulsen, Andrew Shelton, Aron Vinegar, and Karl Whittington, as well as all of the other faculty and students, both within the History of Art Department and across the university, with whom I've spent the better part of two decades. An invitation from Graeme Boone to present the portion of the text concerning Kandinsky and Schoenberg to the OSU musicologists helped to reassure me, at a crucial moment, that I was not wholly out of my depth.

Scholars who read all or part of the manuscript and generously offered their thoughts include Warren Breckmann, Jason Gaiger, and Bibiana Obler. To Jason in particular—who, heroically, read and provided commentary on the work in its entirety—I am grateful. (Whatever mistakes remain I have to acknowledge, stubbornly, as my own.) Thanks are due as well to Todd Cronan for organizing the Modernism seminar at Emory University where I was able to present the chapter on Kojève's "Les Peintures concrètes." To Todd, Nell Andrew, Liz Goodstein, Sarah Hamill, Gordon Hughes, Dalia Judowitz, Andrew Mitchell, Charles Palermo, and Michael Schreyach: thank you for your careful reading and perceptive questions.

For their help with obtaining the many images required for this book, I'm indebted to Stephanie Bernhardt, Kristin Brockman, Mary-Allen Johnson, Michelle Maguire, Predrag Matejic, Romain Paumard, MaryBeth Robinson, and Catherine Walworth. Tracey Bashkoff and Gillian McMillan gave generously of their time, providing me access to many of the works by Kandinsky in the Guggenheim Collection that were not on display when I needed to see them. The opportunity to examine *Painting with White Border* in the conservation lab, and to ask questions of those who knew the work so well, remains for me one of the highlights of the entire project.

Alexandre Kojève's essay on Kandinsky has been central to my conception of this book from the beginning. Permission to publish a translation of "Les Peintures concrètes de Kandinsky" was kindly granted by Madame Nina Kousnetzoff. I am enormously grateful to her, and to Michael S. Roth for his communications with me about that text. The entire staff of the Bibliothèque Kandinsky in Paris, where the manuscript is housed—from Didier Schulmann, the director, to Véronique Borgeaud and Brigitte Vincens—could not have been more helpful.

To my editor, Emily-Jane Cohen, at Stanford University Press: thank you for your patience and for your commitment to the project. I know it's been a much longer haul than you originally anticipated.

Valuable funding for some of the research and images for the book came from the Ohio State University College of the Arts and Sciences, and the Virginia Hull

Research Award, as well as from the OSU History of Art Department. The support of all three was and is much appreciated.

Over the decade or so that I've been working on this project, numerous family members and friends (in addition to those already mentioned) served as interlocutors or, just as importantly, offered their moral support. Among them I'd like to mention Michele Acker, Trisha Craig, Susan Dackerman, Susan Glaser, Ann Hamilton, Josiah McElheny, Ruth Melville, Michael Mercil, Ara Merjian, Helen Molesworth, Tom Nelson, Frank and Kathy Richardson, Hans-Walter Rix, Sarah Rogers, Birgitte Søland, Bob and Wendy Weinberg, and pretty much the entire staff of the Northstar Café in the Short North.

Finally, there are two people who deserve more credit than any of the others for the appearance of this book: they have lived with it, quite literally, every step of the way. David Weinberg has been, throughout, as supportive as any (equally busy) partner ever was; and Ellie Weinberg managed to tolerate what undoubtedly felt to her like my near-constant state of preoccupation. The project is as old as she is. And although she's always said she wanted a sibling—a twin, even—its rivalry for my attention was plainly more than she had bargained for. Because of her patience—and the joy that she has brought to my life—I dedicate this book to her.

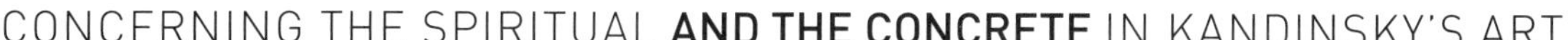

CONCERNING THE SPIRITUAL **AND THE CONCRETE** IN KANDINSKY'S ART

ALTHOUGH HE DID WRITE AN EARLY DRAFT in his native Russian, Wassily Kandinsky (1866–1944) chose to publish his first major theoretical statement on painting in German.[1] The statement appeared, consequently, as *Über das Geistige in der Kunst*, a title typically translated into English as *On* [or *Concerning*] *the Spiritual in Art*. Most Anglophone scholars have tended to hear in that title (and in the text's other, frequent references to "spirit") the root of something like "spiritualist," with the result that over the last half century or so we have been asked to see Kandinsky's work in light of Theosophy and Eastern mysticism and various obscure forms of the occult.[2] I don't want to deny the significance of such things to the development of Kandinsky's thinking and writing about art—or, rather, even though I *want* to deny their significance, I find I can't entirely. Yet I can and will insist that for many of the early German readers of Kandinsky's text the term "Geistige" would have evoked above all the philosophy of Hegel, and most especially Hegel's *Aesthetics*, in which art had similarly been presented as a vehicle for the developing self-consciousness of spirit or *Geist*. In fact, I suspect that one of Kandinsky's principal motives for writing in German was that he wanted to use the same language—in many passages, even precisely the same phrasing—that Hegel himself had employed. In any case I'm convinced that he intended *Über das Geistige* as a fairly direct response to the *Aesthetics*—a revision of its historical account that would culminate not in the end of art proclaimed by Hegel, but rather in something on the order of Kandinsky's own abstract paintings.

I am convinced, too, that Kandinsky's later writings are every bit as fully, and perhaps even more successfully, engaged with Hegel's philosophy—a fact no doubt connected to the artist's regular communication, beginning in 1929, with his nephew, Alexandre Kojève (1902–1968).[3] From 1933 (the year Kandinsky settled in Paris) until the outbreak of war in 1939, Kojève led a seminar on Hegel's *Phenomenology of Spirit* at the École des hautes études that was attended by a veritable who's who of French intellectuals, including Jacques Lacan, Georges Bataille, Maurice Merleau-Ponty, and André Breton.[4] In 1936—presumably after having had various conversations on the subject with Kojève—Kandinsky asked his nephew to write an essay about painting, focusing particularly on his own. Unfortunately, Kojève's essay, "Les Peintures concrètes de Kandinsky," was published only in 1985. A shorter, revised version appeared in 1966, but even that was already twenty-two years after Kandinsky's death, and just two years before Kojève's.[5] Had the piece found its way into print when written, in 1936, we might have been left with a very different understanding of both Kandinsky's art and its philosophical implications.[6] This book is intended, however belatedly (and incompletely), to effect that understanding now. It sets out to reexamine Kandinsky's writings and paintings alike within what I believe is their proper and by far most interesting context: as part of an extended, three-way exchange among Hegel, Kandinsky, and Kojève.[7]

PART I

PAINTING IN THEORY

FIRST MOMENT
HEGEL'S *AESTHETICS*

KANDINSKY DECLARED the fundamentally Hegelian nature of his views in the very first lines of *Über das Geistige*, its opening phrase—"Every work of art is the child of its time"—having been lifted almost verbatim from the *Aesthetics*.[1] In fact, Kandinsky's entire first paragraph reads largely as a précis of a key passage in Hegel—though, significantly, one that appears at the end of the *Aesthetics*'s historical narrative, in the section that lays out the dissolution of the romantic arts, and so the decline of art *tout court*. Here is the relevant passage from Hegel:

Now just as every man is a child of his time in every activity, whether political, religious, or scientific, and just as he has the task of bringing out the essential content and the therefore necessary form of that time, so it is the vocation of art to find for the spirit of a people the artistic expression corresponding to it. Now so long as the artist is bound up with the specific character of such a world-view and religion, in immediate identity with it and with firm faith in it, so long is he genuinely in earnest with this material and its representation . . . only in that event is the artist completely inspired by his material and its presentation; and his inventions are no product of caprice, they originate in him, out of him, out of his substantial ground, this stock, this content of which is not at rest until through the artist it acquires an individual shape adequate to its inner essence. If, on the other hand, we nowadays propose to make the subject of a statue or painting a Greek god, or, Protestants as we are today, the Virgin Mary, we are not seriously in earnest with this material. It is the innermost faith that we lack here.[2]

Although Kandinsky simplified both the *Aesthetics*'s grammar and its argument, Hegel's basic claims persist:

Every work of art is the child of its time, often it is the mother of our emotions. Thus, every period of culture produces its own art, which can never be repeated. Any attempt to give new life to the artistic principles of the past can at best only result in a work of art that resembles a stillborn child. For example, it is impossible for our inner lives, our feelings, to be like those of the ancient Greeks. Efforts, therefore, to apply Greek principles, e.g., to sculpture, can only produce forms similar to those employed by the Greeks, resulting in a work that remains soulless for all time.[3]

Kandinsky's decision to begin his text with a passage drawn from the end of the *Aesthetics* might easily be seen as part of a larger effort to reopen the latter's closure and thereby revise its historical trajectory. Certainly it was the ending of Hegel's narrative that posed the greatest challenge to artists of Kandinsky's generation. In order to understand why Hegel saw it as the necessary conclusion to his story, and also how Kandinsky might have seen things otherwise, we will need to sketch out the general shape and sweep of the *Aesthetics*'s highly nuanced history of art. It would also be useful to review, however briefly, the structure of Hegel's larger philosophical system, so as to better grasp the crucial but limited place that art occupies within it.

The idea of spirit (*Geist*) is the central motif of both the *Aesthetics* and the Hegelian system at large. By "spirit," Hegel intended a collective human subjectivity or consciousness, whose development over time could be seen to account for all significant—his phrase is "world-historical"—political, religious, intellectual, and artistic change. The 1807 *Phenomenology of Spirit* was the first of Hegel's books to try to describe at least a portion of the circuitous route that spirit had traveled on its path to the present. The text has therefore occasionally been regarded as a sort of *Bildungsroman*, recounting the growth and maturation of its protagonist over the course and as a result of its various, frequently harrowing experiences. Indeed, that latter term, experience (*Erfahrung*), is also an important one for Hegel, and is intimately bound up with his conception of the dialectical structure of history. As Frederick Beiser explains,

> Hegel is . . . reviving the original sense of the term, according to which '*Erfahrung*' is anything one learns through experiment, through trial and error, or through enquiry about what appears to be the case. . . . [It] is therefore to be taken in its literal meaning: a journey or adventure (*fahren*), which arrives at a result (*er-fahren*), so that '*Erfahrung*' is quite literally '*das Ergebnis des Fahrens*.' The journey undertaken by consciousness [or spirit] in the *Phenomenology* is that of its own dialectic, and what it lives through as a result of this dialectic is its experience.[4]

Crucial to Hegel's conception of experience is his assertion that spirit never ends its journey in quite the same state or place from which it set off. The dialectic entails a movement outside into otherness, followed by reflection, and then a "return" to a self that has been substantially changed through the process. Of the several means by which spirit has externalized or stepped outside itself, art, according to Hegel, was initially the most important.[5] Historically, works of art were above all a way that spirit took sensuous, material form, and so brought itself before itself, for the specific purpose of its conscious self-reflection. Humanity's increasing self-awareness—and more, its realization of freedom—has come in no small measure, Hegel says, through the experience of art.

The freedom at issue here is principally a freedom from nature's determinacy.[6] In the *Aesthetics*, Hegel argues that the earliest works of art gave form to a consciousness or spirit that was still trying to extricate itself from its subservience to nature, and so was not to be fully reconciled with sensuous materiality. As yet vague and undeveloped, with no sense of its own autonomy, spirit could express itself only indirectly; works of art could do nothing more than point to their spiritual content *through* their obdurate material form. This is presumably what Hegel has in mind when he refers to art's earliest period as symbolic,[7] and designates architecture as its predominant and most characteristic form. Hegel argues that the material used in these early works was inherently non-spiritual—mostly heavy stone whose shape was limited by the law of gravity—and that whatever meaning the works themselves may have had was carried by, or in some cases merely stamped onto, their external surfaces (see Figure 1).[8]

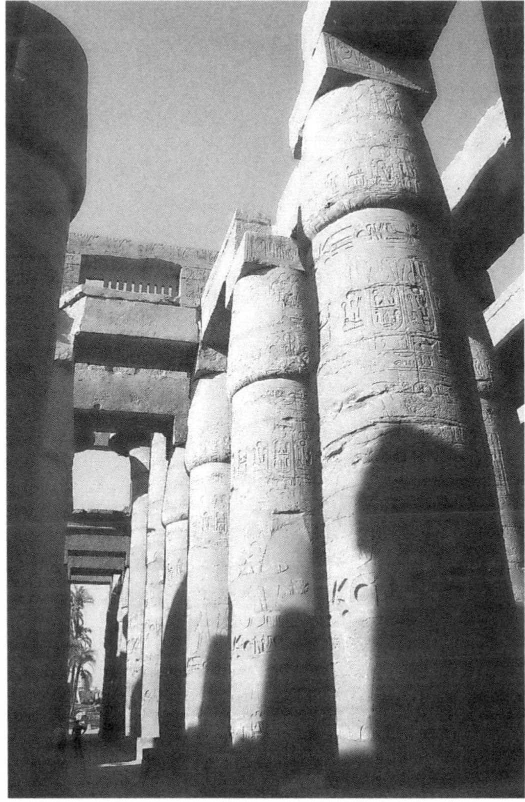

FIGURE 1. Temple of Amen-Re, Karnak, Egypt, Dynasty XIX, ca. 1290–1224 BCE.
© 2013 Robert Harding Picture Library Ltd.

During the ensuing classical period, by contrast, sculpture became the predominant form of art. Classical sculptures were still produced out of heavy matter, of course, but now with little regard for its weight and natural properties (Figure 2). Each work's form was determined solely by its chosen subject matter, which in this period, Hegel observes, was almost always the human form. The *Aesthetics* emphasizes that the cultural beliefs of ancient Greece were perfectly suited to sensuous embodiment—witness the anthropomorphism of its gods—so that the figures of classical Greek sculpture seemed thoroughly pervaded by spirit, their form and content fused in an indissoluble unity. In this sense the classical work of art didn't so much *mean* (in the way that either a sign or symbol might) as simply exist: a pure self-showing.

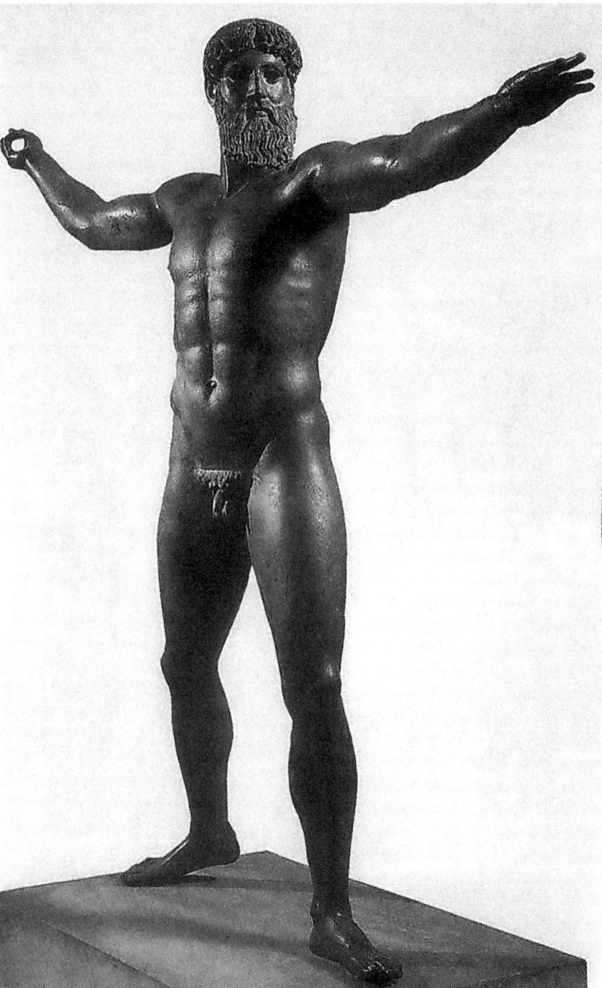

FIGURE 2. Artemision Zeus, ca. 460 BCE. Bronze, approx. 6′10″ high. National Archaeological Museum, Athens. © Jack Balcer Image Archive, Ohio State University.

Yet the introduction of subjectivity into both the content of the work and the form of its presentation signaled the demise of the classical era. According to Hegel, in the ensuing romantic period, which arose with the advent of Christianity, spirit came to be characterized by a profound and ever-growing inwardness that, unlike the spirituality of the ancient Greeks, was only imperfectly expressed in the sensuous externality of art. Clearly sculpture was no longer up to the task, as it was unable to present consciousness as something withdrawn *out of* the sphere of material embodiment into self-reflection. It was instead in the painting of the romantic era (Figure 3) that inner subjectivity first found its adequate expression. Painting accomplished this by presenting its subjects in an artificial or "unnatural" space, one that had been created by subjectivity itself, for the purpose of its own self-contemplation. This was the space of visual illusion—the term Hegel uses is *Schein*—and it effectively dissolved the sense that what one beheld in the work was something objective, independent, and solidly material.

The work of sculpture has to retain [its independence] because its content is what it is, within and without, self-reposing, self-complete, and objective. Whereas in painting

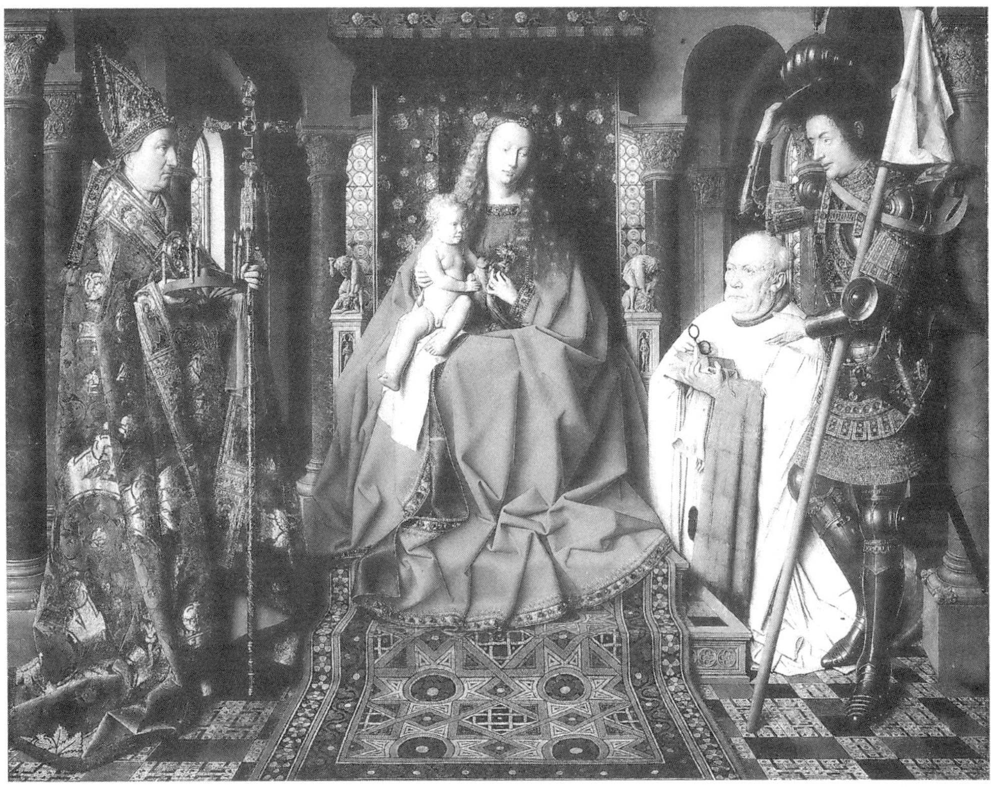

FIGURE 3. Jan van Eyck, *Madonna with Canon van der Paele*, 1436. Oil and tempera on wood, 122.1 × 157.8 cm. Groeninge Museum, Bruges. The Art Archive at Art Resource, New York.

the content is subjectivity, more precisely the inner life inwardly particularized, and for this very reason the separation in the work of art between its subject and the spectator must emerge and yet must immediately be dissipated because, by displaying what is subjective, the work, in its whole mode of presentation, reveals its purpose as existing not independently on its own account but for subjective apprehension, for the spectator. The spectator is, as it were, in it from the beginning . . . and the work exists only for this fixed point, i.e. for the individual apprehending it.[9]

In its presentation of a space that was only *apparently* three-dimensional—that existed only through and for human consciousness—romantic painting was to be seen, Hegel argued, as a direct manifestation of spirit's increasing inwardness and autonomy. Painting's illusionistic space was one, moreover, in which human drama could unfold, and during the romantic era gesture and facial expression—along with other means for suggesting the interior life of the figures portrayed—were similarly perfected over time (see Figure 4).

The romantic era differed from its predecessors, however, in that no single art form could be seen to predominate over its entire duration. At a certain moment, as Hegel tells it, spirit achieved a state of subjective inwardness no longer suited

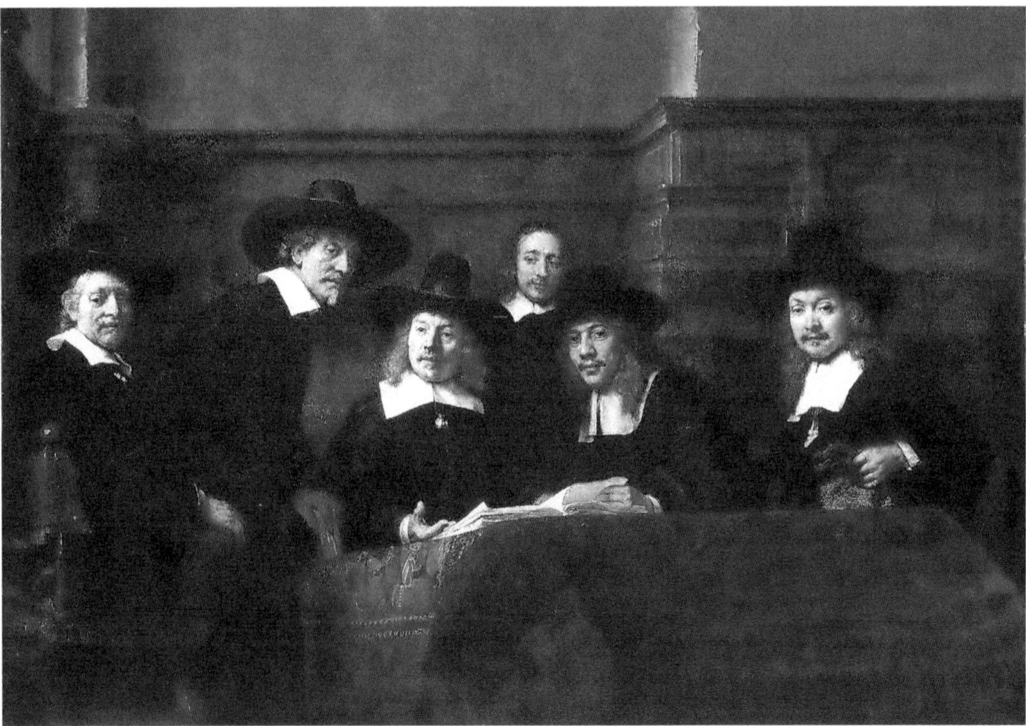

FIGURE 4. Rembrandt van Rijn, *Syndics of the Cloth Guild*, 1662. Oil on canvas, 185 × 274 cm. Rijksmuseum, Amsterdam. bpk, Berlin / Rijksmuseum Amsterdam / Hermann Buresch / Art Resource, New York.

to even the most subtle of paintings, at which point first music and then poetry (with their still greater immateriality) rose to prominence among the arts. Already with the romantic era, then, we witness the dissolution, and so the beginning of the end, of art. Not that buildings, sculptures, paintings, musical compositions, and poems wouldn't continue to be produced. They would, but they would no longer function as the primary vehicle of spirit—which is to say that they would no longer serve as the place where humanity realized its deepest and most meaningful truths. That role was given over first to religion and finally to philosophy, from whose vantage point it could be seen that the history of art belonged not, ultimately, to art itself; instead it constituted only a moment (now passed) within the larger history of spirit.

Because the story the *Aesthetics* has to tell is not in the end its own, it doesn't follow the same dialectical structure of other Hegelian narratives.[10] In both the *Phenomenology of Spirit* and the *Science of Logic*, for example, thought is seen to progress through three interrelated stages: from the universal (characterized by an inchoate unity), to the particular (in which energies are directed toward the differentiation of parts), and finally to an integration of those two earlier moments in a concrete individuality able to comprehend not only the whole but also the place of the parts within it. If the larger movement from art through religion to philosophy generally follows this pattern, the specifically art-historical narrative of the *Aesthetics* does not. We are instead presented with an inverted dialectic, an "unhappy" turn of events: art reaches its apex in the second (classical) moment, and then ends its story in the dispersion of its particular forms. The task of gathering those pieces together and reintegrating them into a meaningful whole is left to philosophy—more precisely, to the comprehensive system that Hegel himself articulated in the *Aesthetics* and elsewhere.

KANDINSKY'S *ÜBER DAS GEISTIGE IN DER KUNST*

ÜBER DAS GEISTIGE IN DER KUNST is aimed above all at restoring a properly progressive shape to the dialectic of art's history, so as to assert the continuing relevance of painting and the other romantic arts. Admittedly, Kandinsky doesn't use exactly those terms. We hear nothing of the "romantic" nomenclature—in fact, the contemporary forms that Kandinsky singles out for attention are painting, music, and (in the place of poetry) *dance*[1]—and the text surprisingly avoids any reference to "dialectic." Still, Kandinsky does clearly state that art is a "powerful agent" of spirit, whose trajectory describes "a complex but definite movement forward and upward—a progress, moreover, that can be translated into simple terms."[2] More importantly, his subsequent characterizations of art's past, present, and future— and the relationships pertaining among them—are plainly dialectical.

As we've already seen, including in our discussion of "experience," the Hegelian dialectic is comprised of three "moments." The first two of these stand (or at least appear to stand) in radical opposition to each other. The third is the critical one, the moment of sublation, when that initial contradiction is overcome—without, however, being entirely abolished. "Sublation" is an awkward translation of the term, *Aufhebung*, that Hegel most often uses in describing the work of the dialectic. The German word has three distinct and appropriately contradictory senses: both to preserve and to cancel, as well as to raise up to a higher level.[3] As will become apparent, Kandinsky regarded the past and present as being wholly at odds with one another. At the same time, he contended that the future (the first stirrings of which were, in 1911, already beginning to be felt) would be a period of integration and uplift: the epoch, he called it, of the great Spiritual (*der Epoche des großen Geistigen*).[4]

If Hegel, speaking from the vantage point of the early nineteenth century, had argued that the present period was distinctly non-conducive to the achievement of great art, Kandinsky, for his part, could only agree. There is a sense, in fact, in which Kandinsky's assessment is the more severe of the two. Hegel had seen at least some advantage in art's current divorce from spirit. He had pointed out that the modern artist possessed a certain autonomy; painters could now take up any material whatsoever, as there was no longer any content or form immediately identical with (and so prescribed by) *Geist*.[5] In contrast, Kandinsky saw in these same circumstances only crass superficiality:

Art, which at such times [as these] leads a degraded life, is used exclusively for material ends. It seeks its content [*inhaltlichen Stoff*] in hard matter, for it knows nothing finer. Thus objects, whose portrayal it regards as its only purpose, remain the same, unaltered [*unverändert diesselben*, i.e., not transformed or animated by spirit]. The question "What?" in art disappears *eo ipso*. Only the question of "How?"—that is, how those same corporeal objects should be represented by the artist—remains.[6]

In this regard, Kandinsky considered modern art to be the antithesis of the work produced by those he referred to as "primitives." Illustrating the point with an image of the Theodora mosaic from San Vitale (Figure 5), Kandinsky argued that, in complete contrast to artists of the more recent past, the primitives "wanted to capture in their works the inner essence of things, which of itself brought about the relinquishing of external contingency [*der Verzicht auf äußerliche Zufälligkeit*]."[7] Despite having asserted the futility of trying "to give

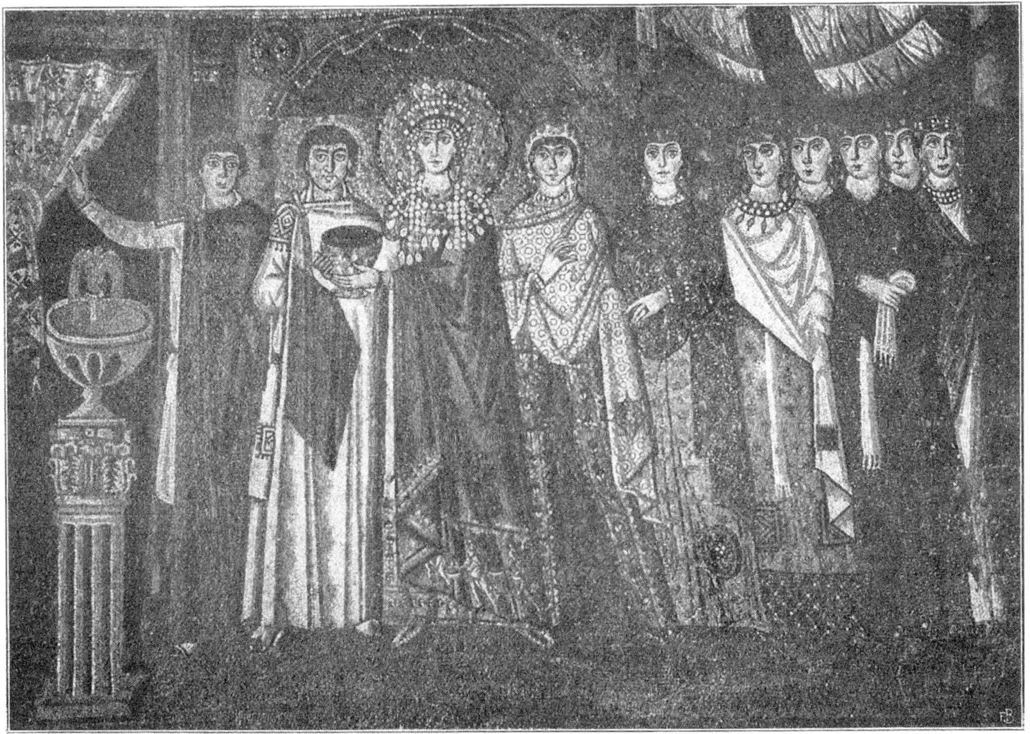

FIGURE 5. Mosaic from San Vitale, Ravenna, ca. 546. Plate 1 in Wassily Kandinsky's *Über das Geistige in der Kunst*.

new life to the artistic principles of the past," Kandinsky expressed optimism over the fact that contemporary artists were taking an interest in the work of earlier, "primitive" periods. He himself was basing many of his pictorial compositions at this time on Russian *lubki* and other centuries-old popular prints, particularly those depicting scenes of the Apocalypse (see Figures 6 and 7).[8] Presumably he wanted those images to be seen as anticipating his own, and to be read, in quasi-typological fashion, as forecasting the new spiritual age he believed was imminent. The text is clear, however: "the movement toward the primitive, . . . with its present borrowed forms, can only be of short duration."[9]

It seems it was chiefly the *lubki*'s (and the other "primitive" images') fore-grounding of spiritual content that Kandinsky regarded as exemplary. That content could testify, in effect, to the former ambition of art—to the role it had once played in satisfying what Hegel called the "highest needs of human spirit"—and in that sense could perhaps reawaken present audiences to the enormous potential of art.

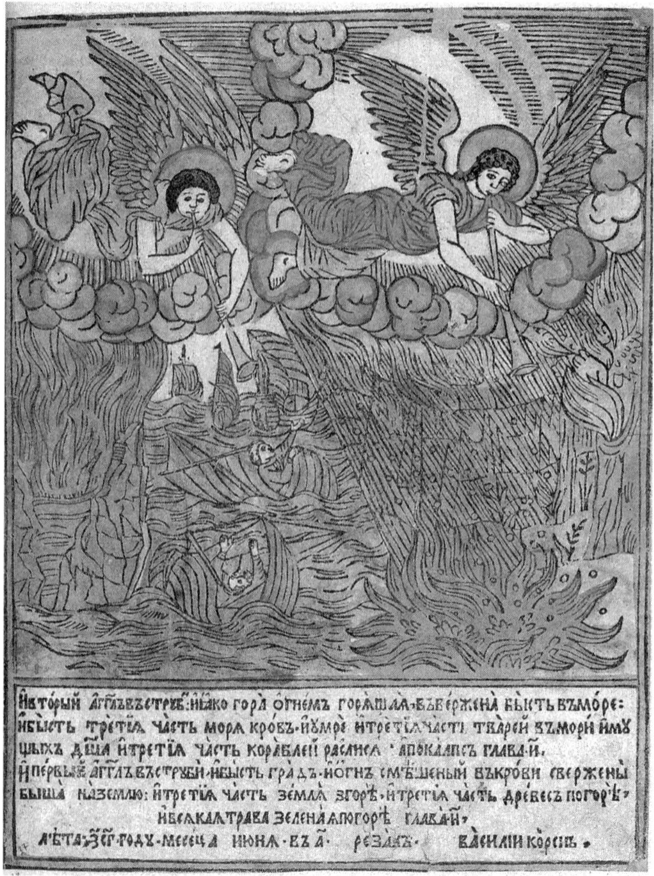

FIGURE 6. Vasilii Koren, woodcut from the *Koren Picture-Bible*, 1696, GPB V 4.2, f. 7(27). Russian National Library, Saint Petersburg.

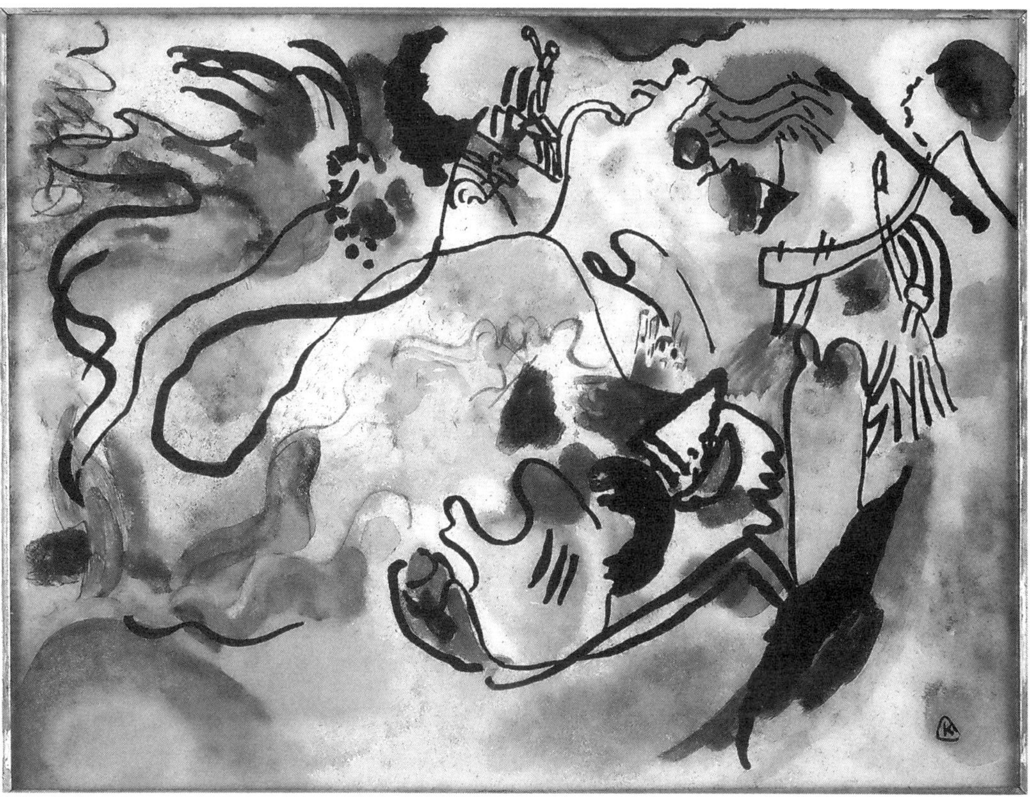

FIGURE 7. Wassily Kandinsky, *Last Judgment*, 1912. Painting on glass with ink and color, 33.6 × 44.3 cm. Musée national d'art moderne, Centre Georges Pompidou, Paris. CNAC/MNAM/Dist. RMN–Grand Palais/Art Resource, New York. © Artists Rights Society (ARS), New York.

Even so, there was to be no going back. If spirit were to develop further, the content or subject matter of art would have to progress well beyond the *lubki*'s primitive articulations. And form would necessarily have to follow suit, transforming itself beyond recognition from anything that was familiar to audiences of centuries past. It is at precisely this point in Kandinsky's narrative of art's progress that we encounter the dialectical turn. Artistic forms adequate to the coming spiritual epoch were beginning to be found, Kandinsky contended, just where they might have been least expected: in the empty, materialist art of the recent past and present. In an essay titled "Kuda idet 'novoe' iskusstvo?" (Whither the "New" Art?), which appeared just before the publication of *Über das Geistige*, Kandinsky offered perhaps his fullest explanation to date of these developments. Speaking of "Russian artists during the World of Art [*Mir Iskusstva*] period," and other second- and third-generation "impressionists," he lamented the relative impoverishment of their vision:

While rejecting any material, tangible "content," these artists could neither see nor find a new "content" (i.e., an immaterial one, possessed only by art and effused by it).

Hence, they declared any content to be unartistic and alien to art. Art does not have an aim, they said; it has an aim unto itself. *L'art pour l'art!*

Immediately, though, Kandinsky reversed course:

This very statement [*L'art pour l'art!*] contained the seedling [*rostok*] of the salvation and liberation of art from its servility to material: once art is self-sufficient, it must concentrate on itself and, above all, must attend to itself and its own means of expression.[10]

The claim is that artists, having become indifferent to content, trained their attention instead on purely formal matters. However intellectually or spiritually shallow the resulting work, its formal experimentation had nonetheless provided the necessary means (had emerged, in effect, as the "seedling") for art's further advance.

A similar claim is repeated in *Über das Geistige*. Before taking up the relevant passages of that text, however, we might want to linger a bit over Kandinsky's image of the "seedling." Not the *seed*, mind you; evidently Kandinsky wanted to emphasize that the moment in question was continuous with the past, an outgrowth or offshoot of it, rather than an absolute beginning. He makes the point even more explicitly later in the essay, when he asserts that the changes now taking place will appear in retrospect to be the "natural continuation" of earlier trends: "So the new branch is the continuation of the same tree. And the leaf is the continuation of the same branch."[11] Implicit in all of these metaphors is an assertion of organic development—of a process that is internally driven rather than the product of forces imposing themselves from outside.[12] In *Über das Geistige* and elsewhere, Kandinsky would repeatedly describe art's recent developments as compelled by an "inner necessity" (*innere Notwendigkeit*), thereby underscoring essentially the same point.[13] But the tree and "seedling" imagery of "Whither the 'New' Art?" also carries with it allusions to a well-known passage from the *Phenomenology of Spirit* in which Hegel suggests that successive philosophical viewpoints should be regarded not as simple disagreements but rather as manifestations (or moments) of the progressive unfolding of truth:

The bud disappears in the bursting forth of the blossom, and one might say that the former is refuted by the latter; similarly, when the fruit appears, the blossom is shown up in its turn as a false manifestation of the plant, and the fruit now emerges as the truth of it instead. These forms are not just distinguished from one another, they also supplant one another as mutually incompatible. Yet at the same time their fluid nature makes them moments of an organic unity in which they not only do not conflict, but in which each is as necessary as the other; and this mutual necessity alone constitutes the life of the whole.[14]

Similarly, Kandinsky's Russian essay suggests that earlier artistic styles, no matter how apparently antithetical to the forms that would succeed them, were as integral to the development of art (and so also of spirit) as the seedling was to the tree. As he says in *Über das Geistige*: "New principles do not . . . come down from heaven, but rather stand in a causal relationship to the past and the future."[15]

Earlier in that essay, in the section titled "Movement" (*Die Bewegung*), Kandinsky attempted to outline the specific processes by which such "new principles" were currently developing, and to explain their "causal relationship" to both past and future. The argument there recalls the one laid out in "Whither the 'New' Art?," except that now it is couched in the "What?"/"How?" terminology that Kandinsky had already used to differentiate content from form. Having declared that, for most artists of the recent past, "only the question of 'How?' remained," he added:

Art moves forward on the path of "How?" It becomes specialized, comprehensible only to artists, who begin to complain about the indifference the public shows toward their work. . . . [But already] in that same question "How?" lies a hidden kernel of recuperation. Even if in general this "How?" remains barren, nevertheless in that same "idiosyncrasy" (which today we call "personality") exists the possibility of seeing in the object not only the pure hard material, but also something less physical than the object itself. . . .

Moreover, if this "How?" includes the artist's inner emotion and is capable of disseminating his finer experiences, then art already stands on the threshold of the path by which it will inevitably find again the lost "What?"—the same "What?" that constitutes the spiritual bread for the spiritual awakening now beginning. This "What?" will no longer be the material, objective "What?" of the period left behind, but rather an artistic content, the soul of art, without which its body (the "How?") can never lead a full healthy life.[16]

In other words, although art's earlier orientation toward spiritual content (toward the question of "What?") had given way in the modern era to narrow, formalist concerns (i.e., to an *art-pour-l'art* attention to "How?"), the two moments were actually to be seen as existing in dialectical relation to one another. In the third moment, Kandinsky insists, during "the spiritual awakening now beginning," the apparent contradiction would be sublated, its terms at once cancelled and preserved. The question of spiritual content would return but at a higher level: integrated with recent formal developments, it would "no longer be the material, objective 'What?' of the period left behind," but would instead constitute a true advance, a realization of greater freedom for art and spirit alike.[17]

Kandinsky believed, with Hegel, that the history of art revealed spirit's progressive liberation from the coarse materiality of nature. There was, however, one important difference between them: whereas Hegel took it as given that painting was representational (and thus tied to a kind of pictorial thinking ultimately limiting to spirit), Kandinsky insisted that painting's movement away from representation was the means by which it would at last free itself from the constraints of nature's mere materiality. As he saw it, in the increasingly abstracted forms of late-nineteenth- and early-twentieth-century art, painting had finally found the means by which it could again become adequate to spirit in spirit's present, advanced stage of development.

We first glimpse this association of naturalistic representation with materiality (and the concomitant opposition of both to spirit) fairly early in the introduction to *Über das Geistige*. Discussing a hypothetical work, though one that we might easily associate with some of Kandinsky's own early landscapes (see Figure 8)—a painting in which "some inner feeling [is] expressed in terms of natural form (a picture, as we say, with *Stimmung*)"[18]—Kandinsky conceded that its spiritual potential was limited. Such works, grounded as they were in the representation

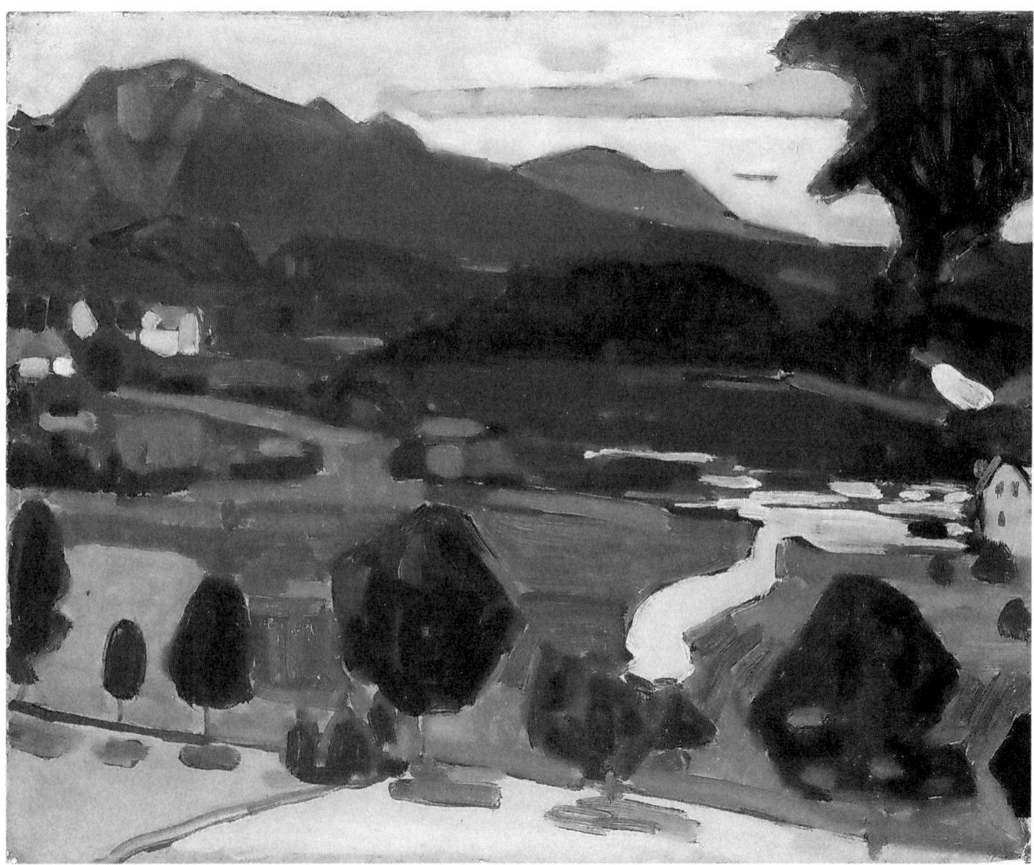

FIGURE 8. Wassily Kandinsky, *Murnau—View of the Staffelsee in Summer*, 1908. Oil on cardboard, 32.7 × 40.5 cm. Städtische Galerie im Lenbachhaus, Munich. © Artists Rights Society (ARS), New York.

of nature, could "prevent the soul from being coarsened," he said; but they were at best "one-sided [*einseitig*], and by no means exhaust[ed] the possible effects of art."[19] Kandinsky's characterization of this hypothetical painting as "one-sided" is particularly significant, as *einseitig* was a key term in the Hegelian lexicon. There it served as a synonym for "abstract," which is to say, "unrealized" or "underdeveloped"—the reverse of what Hegel termed the "concrete." If Kandinsky employed *einseitig* in his discussion of the picture with *Stimmung*, it was no doubt because he felt that the Hegelian alternative, *abstrakt*, was unavailable to him in this context. Not only did "abstract" carry very different connotations within the field of painting, but it was specifically via abstraction (now in the painterly sense of the term) that Kandinsky saw the potential for art's development beyond the mere one-sidedness attributed to it by Hegel.

In fact, a bit later in *Über das Geistige*, Kandinsky suggests that the processes of abstraction might also enable a rapprochement of the various arts, thus counteracting the dispersal that Hegel had declared characteristic of the romantic period:

And so, gradually, the different arts have set forth on the path of saying what they are best able to say, through means that are peculiar to each.

And in spite of, or thanks to, this differentiation, the arts as such have in recent times never been closer to one another than in this latest period of spiritual development.

In every manifestation are the seeds of a striving toward the nonnaturalistic, the abstract, *toward inner nature* [*zu innerer Natur*]. Consciously or unconsciously, they obey the words of Socrates: "Know thyself!" Consciously or unconsciously, artists are gradually focusing on and proving [*prüfen*] their material, placing in the balance the spiritual value of those elements out of which it is suitable to create their art.[20]

Once again, Kandinsky's specific language—in this case, both the phrase *zu innerer Natur* and the verb *prüfen*—insinuates the generally Hegelian context in which his argument is framed.[21] Early in the *Aesthetics*, Hegel had stated that any "science" worthy of the name, including the scientific study of art that he himself was in the process of writing, necessarily had to *prove* its object.

Philosophy has to consider an object in its necessity, not merely according to subjective necessity or external ordering, classification, etc.; it has to unfold and prove the object, according to the necessity of its own inner nature [*nach der Notwendigkeit seiner eigenen inneren Natur*]. It is only this unfolding which constitutes the scientific element in the treatment of a subject.[22]

Said differently, we cannot simply assume an object's givenness. This is true even when we're dealing with material things like seedlings and acorns, Hegel suggests, but it is all the more imperative when the matter at hand is of an intellectual or *geistige* nature. The object must be demonstrated—must be shown to show itself—to be the thing that it in fact is.[23] Philosophy, or any other comparably "scientific" discipline, is thus charged with articulating the relationship between its object and the principles that both derive from and explain it. Of course, in Hegel's understanding of these things, it is entirely possible that the attempt to prove an object will culminate instead in its dissolution; in fact for him, as we've seen, art is an object of exactly this sort.

No less obviously, Kandinsky hoped to disprove Hegel on just that count. His argument in *Über das Geistige* is that contemporary artists—or at least the few world-historical individuals at the forefront—were at that very moment in the process of proving the object of art. Even if painting was not yet in a position to forego all representational content, the path toward nonrepresentation was still clearly the one along which art would—of its own necessity—eventually unfold. For the moment, Kandinsky argued, music was leading the way in this drive toward the nonnaturalistic. Because, historically, it had been the form least concerned with representation of the natural or material world, Kandinsky extolled music as "the least material of the arts."[24] In making that claim, he was pointedly challenging the Hegelian hierarchy, which held poetry to be the most immaterial form. The underlying rationale in Hegel's scheme is that the poem's letters rest weightlessly on the page, certainly in comparison with the pigments and glazes that are the painter's stock in trade. Moreover, as Hegel explains in the *Aesthetics*, sound, that other "external material" that yet clings to the poem, is "in poetry [unlike in music] but a *sign*, by itself void of significance."[25] And it is those arbitrary or unmotivated signs, according to Hegel, that allow poetry to possess a content far more determinate than anything music might ever achieve. Poetry, therefore, was for him the form of art closest to philosophy, to thought simply thinking itself.

Kandinsky, for his part, not only sought to dissociate "materiality" from the physical heft of the artist's medium, and to tie it instead to notions of representation; he also argued, in a move equally upsetting to the Hegelian hierarchy, that color tones, "like those of music, are of a much subtler nature . . . than can be described in words."[26] The implication is clearly of an insufficiency in language. Although Kandinsky never really presses the point, the inevitable—and radically anti-Hegelian—conclusion is that painting and music afford insights otherwise inaccessible, even to philosophy. Something of this suggestion had arisen, too, in his remarks on the spiritual content of the painting to come. It would be, he said, "that content which only art can contain, and to which only art can give clear expression through the means available to it."[27] Such work would be possessed of a kind of *indeterminate* content, whose very existence would cast into doubt philosophy's ability to articulate humanity's highest truths. Spirit could never pass beyond painting or music, on this account, without excluding dimensions of our being that were simply irreducible to cognitive terms.[28] Those arts were not to be understood, then, as things of the past, but rather as vital organs of spirit, indispensable to its continuing realization of freedom.

Having displaced poetry from the privileged position accorded it in the *Aesthetics*, Kandinsky then set about eliding the differences that Hegel had drawn between painting and music. According to Hegel, music had succeeded painting during the romantic era because painting was inadequate to "object-free inner life, to abstract subjectivity as such."[29] To this Kandinsky replied, in effect, that inner subjectivity would, however, find its adequate form in an *object-free, abstract painting*—one, that is, that had finally overcome the limitations imposed by the representation of material things. Painting of this sort, Kandinsky held, would in every way be music's equal where the expression of subjective inwardness was concerned.

Interestingly, his argument seems in many ways anticipated by a passage in the *Aesthetics* where Hegel discusses the development of painterly sfumato:

This magic of the pure appearance of color has in the main only appeared when the substance and spirit of objects has evaporated and what now enters is spirit in the treatment and handling of color. In general, it may be said that the magic consists in so handling all the colors that what is produced is an objectless play of pure appearance which forms the extreme soaring pinnacle of coloring, a fusion of colors, a shining of reflections upon one another which becomes so fine, so fleeting, so expressive of the soul that they begin to pass over into the sphere of music.[30]

No doubt, in saying as much, Hegel hoped to prepare the next transition in his narrative of the romantic arts by suggesting that the use of sfumato by Leonardo and his contemporaries reflected painting's own aspirations toward the condition of music. It's tempting to think of Kandinsky as latching on to that passage, and using it as the basis for his own, rather different account of modern art. This much at least is certain: Kandinsky's discussions of painting both revolve around color and resonate deeply with the characterizations of music found in the *Aesthetics*. "What [music] claims as its own," Hegel had written, "is the depth of a person's inner life as such; it is the art of the soul and is directly addressed to the soul."[31] Kandinsky's parallel assertion—that "color is a means of exerting a direct influence upon the soul"—is echoed and extended in the piano analogy that follows it: "Color is the keyboard. The eye is the hammer. The soul is the piano, with its many strings. The artist is the hand that purposefully sets the soul vibrating through means of this or that key."[32] Such analogies—and there are many throughout the text—serve not only to establish a close connection between painting and music, but to do so precisely on (and in) Hegel's own terms.[33]

It has frequently been pointed out, including by Hegel himself, that his understanding and appreciation of music were considerably weaker than his grasp of the other arts.[34] The complete absence of any reference to Beethoven—Hegel's exact contemporary—has seemed to many an especially telling, and egregious, omission. T. M. Knox, for example, felt compelled to add a footnote to his 1975 English translation of the *Aesthetics*, speculating that "if [Hegel] ever heard Beethoven's music, he probably regarded it . . . as restless and incoherent."[35] It may be too much to imagine that Kandinsky's own mention of Beethoven as the prime example of a world-historical individual ignored or derided during his lifetime is a direct response to the composer's omission from the *Aesthetics*.[36] It seems somewhat less fanciful, though, to regard Kandinsky's enthusiastic references to Arnold Schoenberg, his own contemporary, as deeply colored by his understanding of Hegel's work. A brief digression is required to make the case convincingly.

AT SEVERAL PLACES WITHIN THE *AESTHETICS*, Hegel draws explicit comparisons between musical composition and his idea of the "Concept," with its distinctively dialectical unfolding.[37] In one instance, Hegel argues that the major triad (for example, the chord CEG), which is the basic unit of consonance in diatonic music, expresses the "Concept of harmony in its simplest form, indeed [it expresses] the very nature of the Concept. For we have a totality of different notes before us which shows this difference just as much as undisturbed unity."[38] The claim is that, although the single note C may be unified, it is indeterminate and one-sided compared with the unity of *different* notes in the triad CEG. This is not the end of the matter for Hegel, either. He also argues that the significance of diatonic music doesn't depend only (or even primarily) on consonance—just as scientific progress isn't driven simply by agreement.[39] Dissonance, he says,

constitutes the real depth of notes [*Tönen*] in that it also progresses to essential oppositions and is not afraid of their severity and disunity. For the true is admittedly unity in itself but this subjectivity negates itself [Hegel uses the verb *aufheben* with its triple meaning of negation, preservation, and raising up] as ideal transparent unity into its opposite, into objectivity, indeed it is as the simply ideal itself only a one-sidedness and particularity . . . and only truly subjectivity when it goes into this opposition and overcomes and dissolves it. . . . Consequently along with the contradiction there is immediately given the necessity for a resolution of the discords and a return to the triad.[40]

The implied comparison here, between the thematic development of a musical composition and the historical development of the Concept, is one that has been taken up and itself interestingly developed by philosophers and musicians alike. Somewhat ironically, given Hegel's own silence on the subject, it is Beethoven's music that has seemed to lend itself most naturally to this particular comparison. Theodor Adorno repeatedly linked Beethoven's sonata movements to the Concept as articulated by Hegel, claiming that the sonatas' triumphant resolution of the contradictions introduced in their opening material mirrored the course and conclusion of Hegel's *Logic*.[41] By the same token, like the tension in Beethoven's music between thematic development and the systematic impulse to return to the tonal center, the traditional sonata form and the composer's inventiveness within that form were seen by Adorno to exist in dialectical relation.

An interestingly analogous argument was made by Schoenberg in his 1911 *Harmonielehre* (Theory of Harmony). The essential claim of that book is that the development of the Western harmonic technique can be analyzed in terms of music's increasing ability to incorporate contradiction or dissonance into itself. In fact, Schoenberg asserted that dissonance was but a consonance more remote from the fundamental tone, so that it was possible to see the evolution of Western harmony as an apparently endless climb up the overtone series.[42] He suggested that even atonal music, of the sort he himself was then producing, would eventually be folded into this developmental scheme.

It is clear that, just as the overtones led to the 12-part division of the simplest consonance, the octave, so they will eventually bring about the further differentiation of this interval. To future generations music like ours will seem incomplete, since it has not yet fully exploited everything latent in sound, just as a sort of music that did not yet differentiate within the octave would seem incomplete to us. . . . [Change] will come, if not in the manner that some believe, and if not as soon. It will not come through reasoning, but from elemental sources; it will not come from without, but from within. It will not come through imitation of some prototype, and not as technical accomplishment; for it is far more a matter of mind and spirit [*Geist*] than of material, and the *Geist* must be ready.[43]

It is not difficult to understand why passages such as this struck a particular chord with Kandinsky. Reading the *Harmonielehre* as he was revising his own theoretical treatise on art, he found confirmation in Schoenberg's text—as in his music—that he himself was on the right (dialectical) path.[44] Moreover, despite Schoenberg's occasional equivocation on the matter, Kandinsky clearly saw atonal composition as defiantly avoiding the "natural harmonies" of the diatonic scale— and so also as moving away from the authority of nature in the direction of increasing *self*-legislation.[45] "Schoenberg's music leads us into a new realm, where musical experiences are no longer acoustic, but purely spiritual [*geistige*]. Here,"

Kandinsky declared, "begins the 'music of the future.'"[46] For Kandinsky, the lesson of atonality was the same as that of nonrepresentational painting. The history of art and music alike revealed (or at least soon would reveal) the achievement of absolute freedom, of a mode of self-determination no longer set or in any way limited by nature.

The trick, of course, was to convince people that if music and painting were both in the process of overcoming nature's normative authority, they were not, for all that, descending into normlessness. Kandinsky underscored the point in *Über das Geistige* via a direct quotation from the *Harmonielehre*: "Every combination of notes, every progression is possible. And yet," Schoenberg had added, "I feel already today that . . . there are certain conditions that govern whether I choose this or that dissonance."[47] What needed to be proven was that these "conditions" were neither naturally given nor arbitrary—that they were instead the necessary result of art's internal development up to that point.[48] Again, this sort of proof was the principal raison d'être of Schoenberg's text; and Kandinsky seems to have wanted *Über das Geistige* to play the same role for painting that he saw the *Harmonielehre* performing for music. In fact, in the foreword to the second edition of his book, published in 1912, Kandinsky explicitly stated that he hoped its text would form the basis for a *Harmonielehre der Malerei* (Theory of Painting-Harmony) that he intended some day to write.[49]

The key for painting, no less than for music, Kandinsky felt, was contradiction, dissonance. In his letter to Schoenberg dated January 18, 1911, Kandinsky wrote of recent developments in painting "of a constructive or geometric nature"; he seems to have had in mind specifically French cubism. As interesting as these experiments were, Kandinsky suggested, they were too "logical"—by which he seems to have meant too consciously calculated and too insufficiently dialectical—to hold out any real promise for the future. "I am certain that our own modern harmony is not to be found in the 'geometric way,'" he wrote, but rather via "'dissonances in *art*,' in painting, therefore, just as much as in music." "'Today's' dissonance," he added, in language remarkably similar to Schoenberg's own, "is merely the consonance of 'tomorrow.'"[50]

That same claim was taken up and more fully elaborated—as well as made more fully Hegelian—in "Whither the 'New' Art?," the essay Kandinsky wrote later that year for *Odesskie novosti* (and from which we have already quoted):

The Viennese composer Professor Schoenberg, one of the few radical reformers in music, writes in his *Theory of Harmony*, "In order not to look back, you must always be contemporary." I would add, however, that some people should look back—not we artists and not you the public, but art historians—but only after the new harmony, the new law, the new beauty has been found, and after it has flowered at the end of our epoch (a long and great one because it is the epoch of the Spiritual). And when that day comes (which will also be the end of our era), the historian will see that our ugliness was harmony; he will see that it was in no way the rejection of all previous kinds of harmony and beauty, but was their organic, immutable, and natural continuation. So the new branch is the continuation of the same tree. And the leaf is the continuation of the same branch.[51]

In *Über das Geistige* itself, the language may be less overtly Hegelian, but the underlying dialectical nature of the Concept is still plainly evident. At one point Kandinsky declares: "Clashing discords, loss of equilibrium, 'principles' overthrown, . . . *opposites and contradictions—this is our harmony.*"[52] And much as Schoenberg had argued in the *Harmonielehre* that calling a certain combination of notes "bad, harsh, not beautiful, etc." was tantamount simply to saying that it was "*not [in] common usage*," so Kandinsky insisted that the distinction between pictorial consonance and dissonance, or indeed that between beauty and ugliness, was "wholly relative and conventional."[53] Implicit in all these claims is the belief that dissonance and contradiction should structure the individual composition every bit as much as they ought to characterize the new work's relation to the past. It's tempting to think of this as a lesson Kandinsky derived from Schoenberg—to imagine, in other words, that it was via Schoenberg's music (and music theory) that Kandinsky began to see dissonance within the individual work on analogy with the dialectical unfolding of the Concept and so also with the historical development of art. After all, that analogy seems infinitely better suited to music than it does to painting, insofar as musical compositions have a much more clearly articulated temporal dimension; something like "development" is built into their very structure. If Kandinsky's claims to have written most of *Über das Geistige* before 1911 are true, however, he must have arrived at the analogy largely on his own.[54] His discovery of Schoenberg's theory would simply have provided strong, independent confirmation of views he already held. In any case, it's clear that, by the time Kandinsky published the first edition of *Über das Geistige*, he had already fully assimilated the lessons of the analogy. Paintings are presented in that work not as static objects but, rather, as *processes* oriented toward significant historical change. And "dissonance" is seen as integral to that progress, just as progress, according to the text, will make what had once seemed dissonant resolve itself into a new, higher-level harmony.

EVEN BEFORE 1911, opposition and contradiction were evident in Kandinsky's art, but they played increasingly important roles thereafter—at first, particularly where color was concerned. In *Über das Geistige* Kandinsky repeatedly asserted the current necessity of chromatic dissonance, and so also the inappropriateness of apparently more "harmonious" color combinations. In the chapter on "The Language of Forms and Colors," for example, he dismissed as outmoded the practice of keying a painting to a particular color or, more commonly, to a certain, narrowly delimited section of the color wheel:

There are pictures . . . that are executed throughout in a particular local color, chosen according to artistic feeling. The permeation of a specific color tone, the joining together of two contiguous colors by a mixture of one with the other, is the basis upon which the harmony of colors is often constructed. From what has been said about the effects of color, and from the fact that we live in a time full of premonitions and omens—hence full of contradictions . . . —we can easily conclude that harmonization on the basis of a single color [*der einzelnen Farbe*] is precisely the least suitable for our time.[55]

Kandinsky even went so far as to devise his own color wheel (Figure 9), which was subtly if significantly different from the one advanced by Goethe and still widely used by practicing painters. Perhaps the most intriguing deviation in Kandinsky's version occurs in the lower right quadrant, where the normal positions

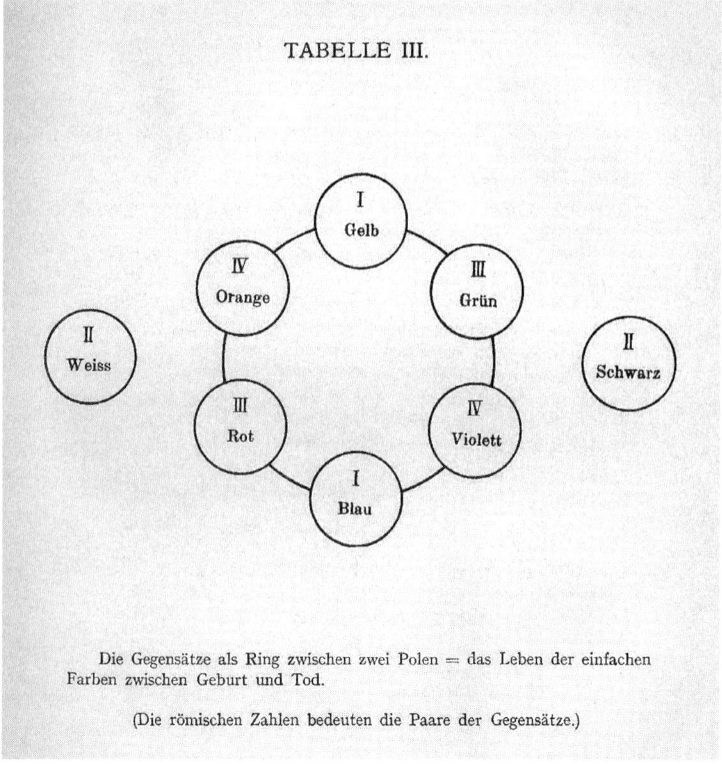

FIGURE 9. Color chart from Kandinsky's *Über das Geistige in der Kunst*.

of blue (*Blau*) and violet (*Violett*) have been reversed. As we'll see, the reasons underlying this reversal were several, though chief among them was almost certainly a desire to discourage artists from thinking in terms of the color contiguities emphasized by the more traditional arrangement. The separated, self-enclosed circles around every individual hue of Kandinsky's chart also work toward that same end. Indeed, as the caption and Roman numerals indicate, his chart is oriented far more toward oppositions than adjacencies. Kandinsky seems, in fact, to have based his views of color on what was then known as the "opponent-process" theory of vision, first advanced in the 1870s—and passionately championed for several decades thereafter—by the Viennese physiologist Ewald Hering.[56] Hering's theory represented a radical challenge to the reigning orthodoxy of the views espoused by Hermann von Helmholtz and Thomas Young.[57] In contrast to the trichromatic Young-Helmholtz model, Hering's opponent-process theory suggested that there were *four* primary colors: green, red, blue, and yellow. Moreover, Hering argued that in perception those colors exist as oppositional pairs (green versus red, blue versus yellow), sensory responses to one hue of the pair being antagonistic with— or inhibitory to—those of the other. According to his model, in other words, the output of retinal receptors was encoded as either red *or* green, blue *or* yellow, but never both simultaneously. The same was true, Hering asserted, of light and dark, black and white.

Kandinsky's color wheel is constructed, as the accompanying text makes clear, around precisely the oppositions identified by Hering. Unlike Hering, however, Kandinsky established a hierarchy among his antagonistic pairs. Yellow and blue represented the primary antithesis, he said, as they epitomized the most fundamental distinction, between warm and cold colors.[58] He regarded white and black as only slightly less important, as they determined the relative lightness or darkness of any given shade. Plainly enough, these first two oppositions (marked by the Roman numerals I and II) form the horizontal and vertical axes of Kandinsky's revised color chart. Hering's third oppositional pair, red-green, is joined on the circle by the two hues—orange and violet—that had also been part of Goethe's schema and that had, largely as a result, become traditional for every color wheel since.[59]

With the aid of his revised, antagonistically arranged wheel, Kandinsky had a means of *systematically* producing color dissonance. As he wrote in *Über das Geistige*: "The incompatibility of certain forms and colors should be regarded not as something 'disharmonious,' but conversely, as a new possibility—and therefore also [as a new] harmony."[60] Again, however, those juxtapositions had to appear other than merely arbitrary. Like Schoenberg, Kandinsky seems to have felt that there were or ought to be "certain conditions" that governed whether one chose this or that dissonance. The color wheel that appeared in *Über das Geistige* provided him with precisely those conditions. As a result, it guided the color selection in many of his most important works from the years both immediately before and following its publication in 1911.

WE CAN GET A FAIRLY CLEAR PICTURE of how Kandinsky employed color dissonance in his early paintings by looking to the highly finished sketch for *Composition II* that is now in the collection of the Guggenheim Museum, New York (Figure 10 / Plate 1). Kandinsky included an illustration of the finished painting (along with several others) in *Über das Geistige*, presumably to help illuminate particular aspects of his theory, and vice versa. Although *Composition II* itself was destroyed during the Second World War, the Guggenheim sketch appears to correspond closely enough in its distribution of colors and forms to adequately substitute for that no-longer-extant final version.

Before analyzing its color, it may be worth mentioning the consensus among Kandinsky scholars that the sketch is—as *Composition II* was—an inherently divided (and, in that sense, dissonant) work, its left half suggesting the Deluge or

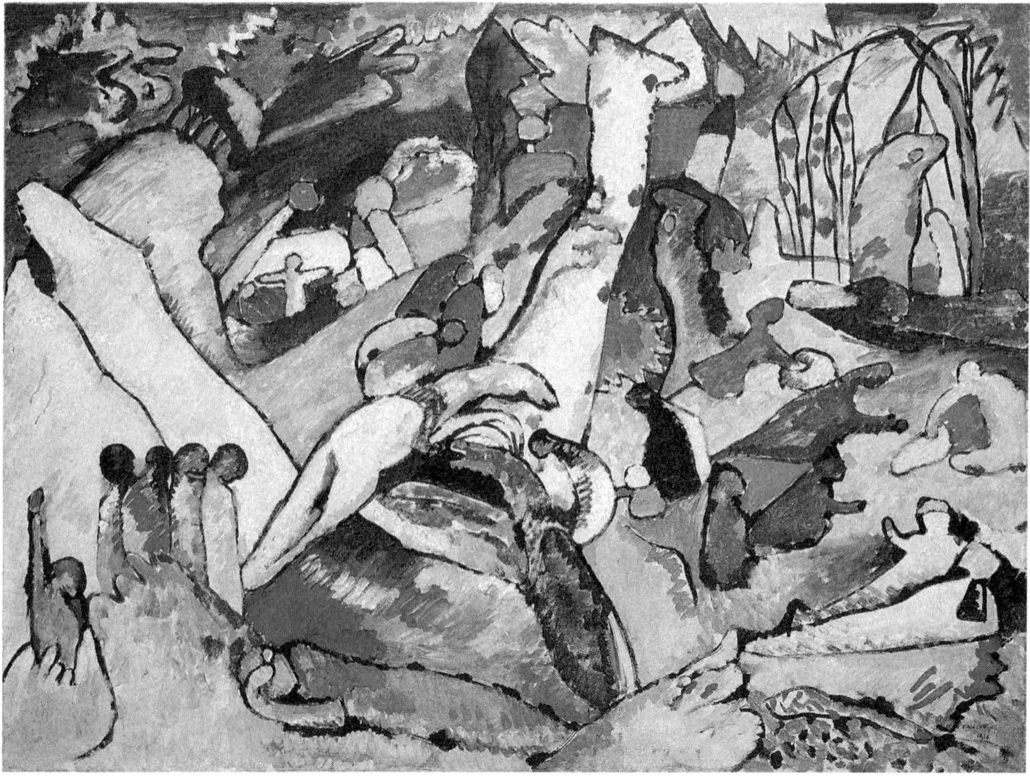

FIGURE 10. Wassily Kandinsky, Sketch for *Composition II*, 1909–1910. Oil on canvas, 97.5 × 131.2 cm. Solomon R. Guggenheim Museum, New York, Solomon R. Guggenheim Founding Collection 45.961. © Artists Rights Society (ARS), New York.

some other Apocalyptic scene, the right appearing more paradisal, a variation on the Garden of Love.[61] It has also been widely accepted that the painting—perhaps the right side in particular—bears a resemblance to Matisse's *Bonheur de vivre* (Figure 11 / Plate 2), which Kandinsky may have seen at the 1906 Salon des Indépendants or, more likely, later, at the home of Gertrude and Leo Stein.[62] Certainly the two paintings' palettes are similar in their audacity. Confronted with the broad planes of color in *Le Bonheur de vivre*, and the startling and seemingly artless or arbitrary juxtapositions of those hues, the painter Paul Signac likened it to the "multicolored shop fronts of the merchants of paints, varnishes, and household goods."[63] The critic Jean Tavernier similarly found the painting's color combinations "disconcerting": "violent at the right, calmer on the left."[64] Presumably what disturbed Tavernier most in that right-hand side was not simply its departure from anything one might describe as "local color," but also the unexpected pairings of pale yellow and violet, red-orange, and a faintly bluish green. *Le Bonheur*'s left-hand side undoubtedly seemed tame in comparison, because it was dominated by a narrower and, significantly, more continuous spectral range—roughly equivalent to that half

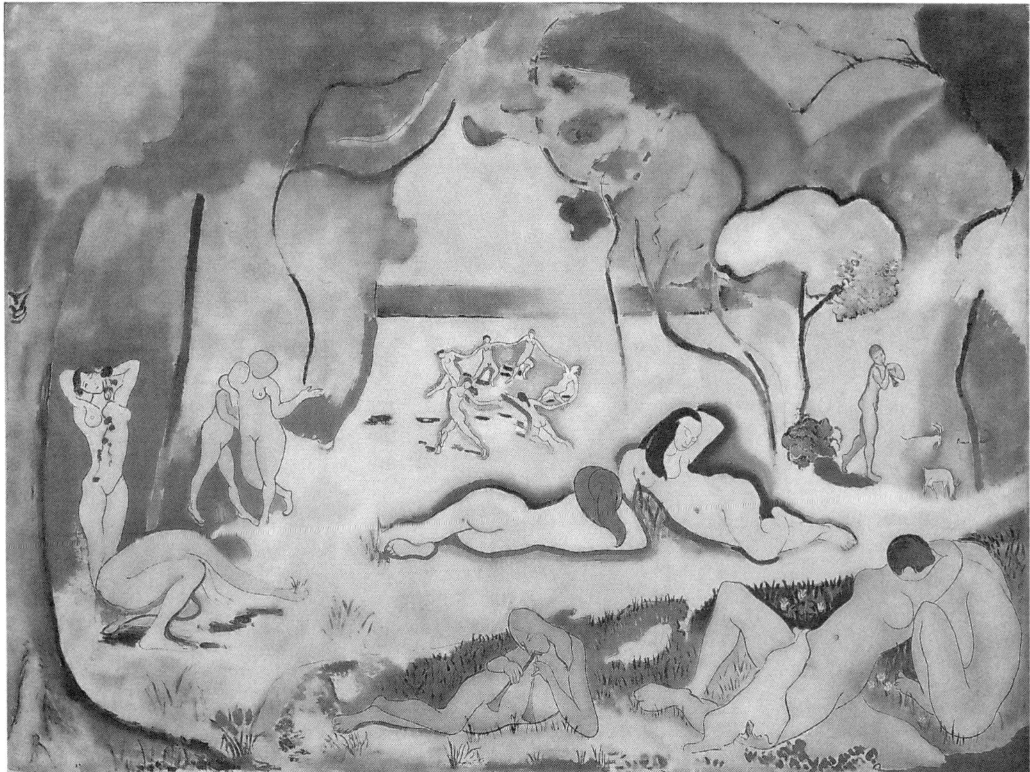

FIGURE 11. Henri Matisse, *Le Bonheur de vivre*, 1905–1906. Oil on canvas, 176.5 × 240.7 cm. The Barnes Foundation. Image © 2013 The Barnes Foundation. Art © 2013 Succession H. Matisse/Artists Rights Society (ARS), New York.

of the color wheel running from yellow through orange and red to violet. (Only the bluish green of, for example, the near tree trunk sounds a discordant note, and that discord is precisely what enables the trunk to stand out as a foreground object against the left side's otherwise chromatically continuous landscape.)

Kandinsky, in contrast to either Signac or Tavernier, seems to have admired *Le Bonheur de vivre*, and principally *because of* its disjunctiveness. He invoked the difference between its right and left halves in the iconographic division of *Composition II* and, more importantly, acknowledged the right's violent color combinations in the overall dissonance of his own palette. Nevertheless, the dissonance of *Composition II* differs noticeably from that of *Le Bonheur*, as quickly becomes evident in a comparison of the two paintings. Kandinsky achieved his particular brand of "discord" with the aid of even more highly saturated colors and the careful distribution of those colors according to the principles laid out in *Über das Geistige*. He seems to have been particularly keen to avoid analogous harmonies (that is, harmonies of the sort produced when a painting or portion thereof is keyed to a specific segment of the standard color wheel), as well as to balance the opposed-primary pairs enumerated in his own chart (see Figure 9). As a result, if yellow appears almost as frequently in *Composition II* as in *Le Bonheur de vivre*, it nearly always appears there in close proximity to blue (which had played a conspicuously minor—in fact, all but nonexistent—role in Matisse's painting). In Kandinsky's work, blue and yellow exist in nearly equal measure. Similarly, although the white shapes outnumber the black ones in *Composition II*, the presence of black *lines* at any number of places throughout effectively redresses the balance, so that neither seems dominant.[65] Red and green, the artist's third opposed-primary pair (marked on his color chart with the Roman numeral III), are likewise both repeatedly juxtaposed and weighted one against the other— though now in somewhat smaller quantities than either blue and yellow or black and white, reflecting, one assumes, their lesser place in Kandinsky's color hierarchy. His designated fourth pair, orange and violet, is present too, but plays a role more subsidiary than any of the others'.

Although based in physiology (i.e., in Hering's opponent-process model of vision), Kandinsky's system was designed to flout every norm prescribed by that model—to give us in the repeated juxtapositions of yellow and blue, green and red, compositions whose color pairings would seem wholly "unnatural," and so answerable only to spirit. By repeatedly juxtaposing each of these saturated primaries with its antagonistic "partner"—and by doing so in a manner that spreads their occurrence across the breadth of the composition—Kandinsky was able to completely avoid the contiguous-color harmonies that had been made especially popular by late impressionism. *Composition II* is, as a result, not only coloristically dissonant; its every patch of color seems to sound a distinctly separate note. In this sense, the painting is an even better accompaniment to Schoenberg's music than is the more illustrational *Concert* (Figure 12), which Kandinsky actually produced after first hearing the composer's work. Franz Marc, who attended the Schoenberg recital that January evening with Kandinsky, was quick to appreciate the similarities between atonal music and the palette of *Composition II*. In a letter to August Macke written immediately following, he asked:

Can you imagine a music in which tonality (that is, conformity to a given key) is entirely suspended? When listening to this music, I was constantly thinking of Kandinsky's large Composition, which disavows any trace of tonality . . . and also of Kandinsky's "jumping spots" [*springende Flecke*], which permit each tone sounded to stand by itself (a sort of white canvas between the specks of color!).[66]

Kandinsky, if he knew of the letter, was undoubtedly gratified. For him, Schoenberg's music was the model of a modern, progressive, *geistige* art—one

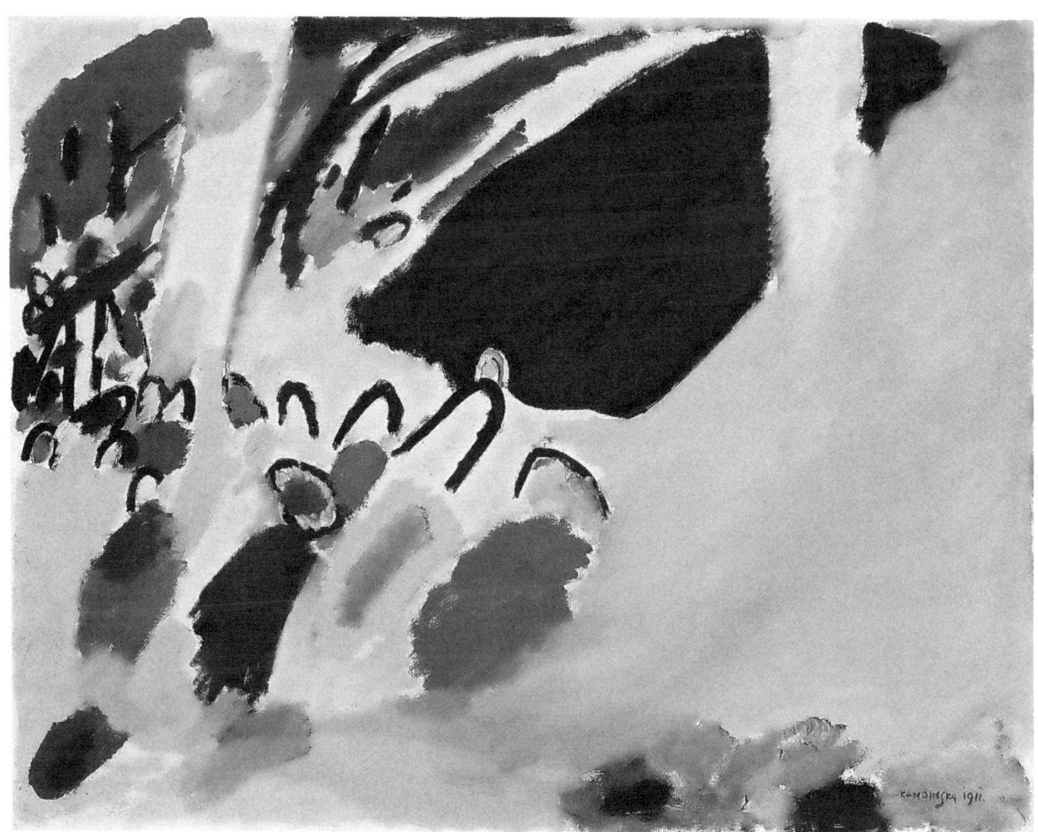

FIGURE 12. Wassily Kandinsky, *Impression III (Concert)*, 1911. Oil on canvas, 77.5 × 100 cm. Städtische Galerie im Lenbachhaus, Munich. © Artists Rights Society (ARS), New York.

that, in its conscious avoidance of "natural" harmonies, appeared responsive to the demands of Spirit alone. For Marc to recognize his own *Composition* as similar was a corroboration of sorts. It proved—Hegel's *Aesthetics* to the contrary—that painting had ceded nothing to music, and that in fact both remained vital, each in its own way pointing toward future development.

KANDINSKY'S *PUNKT UND LINIE ZU FLÄCHE* AND RELATED ESSAYS

ALTHOUGH IT REMAINS IN MANY WAYS his most important statement on the subject, *Über das Geistige* is far from the only text in which Kandinsky indicated his generally Hegelian-dialectical views on art.[1] In his "Rückblicke" (Reminiscences) of 1913, we find a concise summary of several Hegelian themes:

The progress of truth is extremely complex: the untrue becomes true, the true untrue. . . . Art in many respects resembles religion. Its development consists not of new discoveries that obliterate old truths and stamp them as false (as is apparently the case in science). Its development consists in moments of sudden illumination . . . that are in essence nothing other than organic development, the continuing organic growth of earlier wisdom. . . . The new branch does not render the tree trunk superfluous: the trunk determines the possibility of the branch.[2]

Still more succinct is a phrasing that took its initial form in an essay Kandinsky wrote for the catalogue of a 1922 exhibition of his work in Stockholm, and then used repeatedly thereafter: "The worn-out words of yesterday, 'either-or,' will be replaced by the one word of tomorrow, 'and.'"[3] In fact, two of the essays in which Kandinsky employed this aphorism bear titles—"And, Some Remarks on Synthetic Art" (1927) and "Yesterday-Today-Tomorrow" (1925)—that read as their own, even pithier encapsulations of the shape and movement of the Hegelian dialectic.[4]

Kandinsky's second book, *Punkt und Linie zu Fläche* (Point and Line to Plane), published in 1926 as the ninth volume in Gropius and Moholy-Nagy's Bauhaus series, also contains a number of suggestive parallels with works in Hegel's corpus.[5] In the forward to the book, Kandinsky asserted that the ideas developed in it were an "organic continuation" of those laid out in *Über das Geistige*.[6] He didn't add, perhaps regarding it as self-evident, that such organic continuity in no way precluded (and, in a Hegelian universe, actually necessitated) significant, dialectical change. The differences between the two texts are in fact striking. True to its title, *Über das Geistige* had concerned itself with art's intellectual or spiritual dimension. *Punkt und Linie*, by contrast, says precious little about spirit. The text is offered instead as "a precise, purely scientific examination of pictorial means" at once "theoretical" and "analytic."[7] We are even warned near the beginning of *Punkt und Linie* that its account "will proceed with painful, pedantic precision," for only "by a process of microscopic analysis will the science of art lead to an all-embracing synthesis."[8] *Über das Geistige* had argued almost exactly the opposite: "Theory is never in advance of practice in art, never drags practice in its train, but vice versa. Everything depends on feeling, especially at first. What is right artistically can only be attained through feeling, particularly at the outset."[9] Plainly the intuitive method, guided by "feeling," that had directed Kandinsky's artistic explorations "at the outset" had given way by 1926 to antithetical practices. More than simply reflecting a change of heart, the new approach was necessitated, *Punkt und Linie* suggests, by wholly new circumstances—above all that the nonrepresentational painting that remained only *in potentia* when *Über das Geistige* was written had become in the years following a well-established reality.[10]

Kandinsky's Bauhaus book also differs significantly from its predecessor in regard to the particular formal elements on which it focuses. Where *Über das Geistige* had attended to color—as if in affirmation of Hegel's dictum that "color is the element of painting"—*Punkt und Linie* concentrates instead on linear and geometric form.[11] Ever since he began writing about art, Kandinsky, like Hegel before him, had drawn a distinction between "form" and "content," even as he insisted on their adequation. In great works of art, spirit found its proper form, and form was, by definition, whatever gave shape to that (otherwise insensible) spiritual content. As he wrote in his 1913 essay "Painting as Pure Art" ("Malerei als reine Kunst"): "For the content, which exists first of all only '*in abstracto*' to become a work of art, the second element—the external—must serve as its embodiment. Thus content seeks a means of expression, a 'material' form."[12]

Following his arrival at the Bauhaus, however, Kandinsky introduced a distinction within that earlier conception of "form." If in its larger or more general sense it was still to be understood in opposition to "content," there was also, he said, a narrower definition of the term that explicitly excluded color.[13] "Form" in this more limited sense designated all of painting's *other* elements—lines, shapes, and their distribution in space—that contributed to the work's overall composition. In introducing this new distinction, Kandinsky also suggested a parallel between the two senses of "form," which, had he written it out in its simplest terms, would have looked roughly as follows:

$$\text{form}^1 \text{ (i.e., form in its broader sense) : content :: form}^2 \text{ : color}$$

By rendering the analogy in this fashion, we're able to see that for Kandinsky "form," in either of its senses, was always the more material of the paired terms in question. Just as form at large embodied or *gave form to* content, so lines and shapes served to incarnate color, which, in their absence, would be without extension and so wholly immaterial, the mere *idea* of this or that hue.

It's worth pausing here long enough to appreciate what a radical inversion of traditional art theory Kandinsky's argument represents. In most of the accounts preexisting his own, color was considered merely secondary to the primary elements of form (i.e., contour and shape), since color was seen as being not only sensuously material but also subject to the vagaries of perception—this in contrast to the objective intelligibility of line. Repeatedly in Kandinsky's writings, however, color is presented as the more absolute or ideal element, an element which in some sense is only "subsequently" embodied in material form.[14]

Again, although color and *geistige* content, and the affinity between them, had been the main subjects of *Über das Geistige*, Kandinsky turned his attention in *Punkt und Linie* to the explicitly material elements of form, that is, to "form" in its more limited, linear-geometric sense. The underlying rationale for this change—as well as for a whole series of future developments—had already been sketched out in Kandinsky's 1925 essay "Yesterday-Today-Tomorrow." That essay unfolds through a series of eight antithetical terms, each pair of which represents something like a turn of the dialectical "wheel." From the most general or universal statement of the fundamental opposition, between "the materialistic movement" and its "spiritual" counterpart, we pass on to more particular concerns with the actual making of art. At this level, Kandinsky opposes an "intuitive method," linked to the spiritual (and so also, one infers, to his work from the period of *Über das Geistige*), with a more recent "theoretical method" that has its roots in overtly material concerns.[15] "Yesterday-Today-Tomorrow" links this theoretical method in turn to an "analytical movement," which is described as "within sight of its final conclusion"—and which we might therefore take to be more or less synonymous with Kandinsky's own nearly completed work on the manuscript for *Punkt und Linie zu Fläche*. Beyond this analytic "conclusion" lies a contrary synthetic movement, "gathering its strength for tomorrow," as well as that movement's own projected results: both a "synthetic, 'monumental' art" and a fully fleshed out "science of art" (a pair that might itself one day be reconciled, the text speculates, in some still greater unity).

Although there is a good deal of overlap among them, and a certain mixing of the chronological ("movements") with the technical ("methods"), the terms enumerated in the essay are evidently meant to suggest a more or less continuous development, reaching from the relatively recent past into what Kandinsky hopes is the not-too-distant future. The engine driving things forward is the fundamental dialectical opposition between matter and thought, nature and spirit. Kandinsky clearly regarded *Punkt und Linie zu Fläche* as itself one moment in this development, though, again, a moment belonging to the more *material* side of things.[16] To couch this in the language of "Yesterday-Today-Tomorrow," we might say that *Punkt und Linie* draws on Kandinsky's (INKhUK and Bauhaus) experience with the "theoretical method of constructing a work"—a method that derives, once more, from the earlier "materialistic movement"—and points toward a future, more fully worked-out "science of art."[17]

Given its materialistic orientation, we might compare *Punkt und Linie zu Fläche* to the *Philosophy of Nature*, the second of the three books that constitute Hegel's *Encyclopedia of the Philosophical Sciences*. In the *Encyclopedia*, the *Philosophy of Nature* comes between the *Logic* and the *Philosophy of Spirit*, occupying, then, the "antithetical" position that precedes and prepares the way for an eventual synthesis. Whereas, in the *Logic*, Hegel sought to reconstruct the self-determining development of rational thought (what he referred to there as "the Idea in and for itself"), in the second book he turned to "external" nature, to "the Idea in the form of its otherness."[18] Ultimately that opposition between "pure thought" and nature—or inner and outer, ideal and real—would be sublated (shown, that is, to have been only an apparent opposition) in the final book of his encyclopedic trilogy, the *Philosophy of Spirit*.

As "Yesterday-Today-Tomorrow" attests, Kandinsky's ambition was comparably "encyclopedic," in the sense that he too sought to develop a complete and holistic system. *Punkt und Linie* clearly belongs to that system's second moment. It prepares, in effect, for the eventual embodiment of abstract color—color "as such" or in and for itself—in visible form, as part of a concrete composition. Like Hegel's *Philosophy of Nature* before it, Kandinsky's *Punkt und Linie zu Fläche* was meant to take its place within a larger, unfolding narrative aimed at the sublation of "inner" and "outer." Its ultimate purpose was to show how nature's materiality was related to *Geist* and, conversely, how *Geist*'s "being-within-itself" actually "comport[ed] [with] 'externality,'" with nature (or matter) conceived of as its "other."[19]

My own sense is that Kandinsky had the *Philosophy of Nature* specifically in view when composing *Punkt und Linie zu Fläche*. His very title invokes the first section of Hegel's text, which opens with a discussion of, precisely, the point, the line, and the plane, and their logical developments out of one another. As I read it, Kandinsky's title was intended to serve as a reference for the knowing reader to the *Philosophy of Nature*. It also sets the terms for the (tripartite) structure of *Punkt und Linie zu Fläche*, which itself closely resembles the structure of its Hegelian predecessor.

Before turning to those structural similarities, it might be helpful to discuss, however briefly, Hegel's stated purpose in the *Philosophy of Nature*; if nothing else, it will help to illuminate later Kandinsky's parallel comments regarding the goals of his own theoretical project. With the *Philosophy of Nature* Hegel sought to provide a systematic ordering of scientific knowledge (as it existed in the early nineteenth century), beginning with its most abstract and undifferentiated components—space and time—and working toward the vastly greater complexity of organic life.[20] His intention was to translate the findings of empirical science into a conceptual form or structure that could then be viewed in terms of its nonempirical, "internal" necessity. Early in the introduction to the *Philosophy of Nature* Hegel contrasted his own speculative method with the method of the empirical sciences, as well as with "man's *practical* approach to Nature." Both of these, he argued, considered nature as "something immediate and external," and man himself as an "external and therefore [merely] sensuous individual."[21]

Echoing Hegel, Kandinsky opened *Punkt und Linie zu Fläche* by drawing his own firm distinction between external and internal approaches: "Every phenomenon can be experienced in two ways. These two ways are not random, but bound up with the phenomena—they are derived from the nature of the phenomena, from two characteristics of the same: External—Internal."[22] In the paragraphs following, Kandinsky asserted that his would be an *internal* examination of the "material" elements of painting, even though part of his project "—the analytic part—verges on the tasks of 'positive' science."[23] That is, because no real science of art yet existed, *Punkt und Linie zu Fläche* would have to establish, in quasi-positivistic fashion, the basic principles of that science, even as it also sought to analyze them (à la Hegel) in relation to their underlying conceptual structure.

As already mentioned, Hegel began the first section of the *Philosophy of Nature*, on "Space and Time," with a discussion of the point, the line, and the plane, and of their successive developments out of one another. At the start of the text's narrative, nature is presented as purely external, wholly other to logic or reason. In its most abstract or universal form, Hegel says, it exists simply as space, completely undifferentiated (and, in that sense, external even to itself). He then identifies the point as the negation of space's differencelessness, so a negation actually posited *in* space. The line, in turn, is described as the "the point existing *outside* of itself, i.e. *relating* itself to space [thereby also generating the concepts of time and motion] . . . , and the plane, similarly, is the sublated line existing outside of itself."[24]

Much the same continuous, dialectical development structures *Punkt und Linie zu Fläche*. Kandinsky explicitly says in the introduction that "it is necessary to organize [the pictorial elements] into an organic series of gradations"[25]—and then attempts to follow that logic throughout the remainder of the text. The line is accordingly described as "the trail left by the point in motion": "It comes about through movement—indeed, by destroying the ultimately self-contained repose of the point. Here we have a leap from the static to the dynamic."[26] The plane is similarly characterized as the result of a line that, responding to the "generative force" of "inner tensions," expands to become a plane. The final section of the book then broaches the nearly infinite complexity of composition on "that material plane . . . called upon to accommodate the content of the work of art"[27]—the picture plane.

The title of Kandinsky's text—*Punkt und Linie zu Fläche*—signals both this developmental progression driving its analysis forward and, as I asserted previously, the tripartite, characteristically Hegelian structure of the book. The three separate sections of the *Philosophy of Nature* had dealt with Mechanics, Physics, and Organics, in that order. (And that order, once more, is clearly "ascending," the complex organisms of the final chapter being presented as decidedly more sophisticated, and infinitely more self-aware, than the elementary particles discussed nearer the beginning of the book.)[28] Although *Punkt und Linie*'s chapters can't be mapped directly on to Hegel's—if they could, all that talk of internal necessity would have to be regarded as wholly disingenuous—there are enough correspondences between them to suggest that the *Philosophy of Nature* served as a frame of reference for Kandinsky's study. Until that time when the science of art could establish itself as a mature and more fully independent discipline, it would evidently have to progress in part through analogical thinking, by drawing comparisons between pictorial elements and other, "lower" forms of matter. It's not particularly surprising, then, to discover that Kandinsky's various descriptions of the graphic point, for example—as an entity "in repose, absorbed in itself" or subject to a "tension [that] is ultimately always concentric"—recall any number of passages in the Mechanics that treat of statics (i.e., the equilibrium of bodies) and gravitational force.[29] The content of Hegel's chapter on Physics, which includes, among other things, an extended discussion of chemistry, likewise resonates with the characterization of line in *Punkt und Linie zu Fläche*. Throughout we find parallels, such as in Kandinsky's observation that pictorial elements in conjunction behave quite differently than they do in isolation. "Comparable facts are not unknown in other sciences," he remarks, including "chemistry: the sum of component elements when separated is not the same as the total produced by their combination."[30]

Perhaps the most Hegelian aspect of this middle chapter, however, is its contention that matter is inherently dynamic. "Quite apart from differences in character determined by inner tensions," Kandinsky writes, "and quite apart from any generative processes, the fundamental source of every line remains the same—force [*Kraft*]."[31] Hegel, having rejected what he regarded as the outworn explanations of mechanism or atomism, argued that the essence of matter consists not in mere extension but rather in power or force (*Kraft*), which expresses itself as motion.[32] That Kandinsky also subscribed to this view—at least where painting's formal or "material" elements were concerned—was already made evident (if not yet quite explained) in our analysis of *Über das Geistige*.[33] There it was argued that Kandinsky conceived of the individual composition on analogy with the dialectical unfolding of the Concept and so also with the historical development of art. Of course, composition in *Über das Geistige* was presented as almost entirely a matter of color; in *Punkt und Linie* the discussion turns to graphic lines and shapes, and neither are seen as static:

Tensions, for their part, give expression to the inner aspect of the given element. The element is the concrete result produced by the force operating upon the material. Line is the most distinct and simplest instance of this formative process, which occurs every time with logical precision. . . . Thus, composition is nothing other than the logically precise organization of those living forces encapsulated within elements in the guise of tensions.[34]

Already here we begin to sense what will become even more apparent in the following chapter of *Punkt und Linie*: namely, that for Kandinsky the successful, unified composition is composed not of inherently harmonious or quiescent forms but rather of carefully balanced *tensions*, each often straining against the others. Pictorial elements—lines and shapes—were for him simply external manifestations of the otherwise unseen "internal" forces that produced them. Consequently, a certain restlessness animates even the simplest of pictorial configurations. Kandinsky clearly felt that if abstract composition were to progress beyond a rudimentary, intuitive level, a careful calibration of the tensions in play would be required. *Punkt und Linie* was meant as a first stab in that direction. Eventually, Kandinsky hoped, it would lead to something much more systematic—something roughly analogous to the system of opposed-primaries outlined in *Über das Geistige* but that, in this case, would facilitate the careful counterbalancing of lines and shapes or, rather, of the tensions to which they gave visible expression.

The final chapter of *Punkt und Linie* addresses composition on the picture plane and, even more than the preceding two chapters, does so in terms highly evocative of the *Philosophy of Nature*. This time the parallels are specifically with Hegel's third section ("Organics"), which concerns complex organic systems such as plants and animals. "Systems" of this type, Hegel emphasized, possess a special kind of unity. They are not to be understood as comprising merely *parts* defined in relation to one other; rather, an organism's constituents are *members* that could not exist in isolation from the whole. As he argued in both the Encyclopedia *Logic* and then again in the *Aesthetics*, a hand severed from the body is no longer a hand: it "loses its independent subsistence; it does not remain what it was in the organism; its mobility, agility, shape, color, etc., are changed; indeed it decomposes and perishes altogether."[35] Kandinsky, already in his 1913 essay "Painting as Pure Art," had defined the work of art as a "spiritual organism," and directly evoked Hegel's understanding of the special unity thereby implied:

In isolation, [its] individual parts are lifeless, like a chopped-off finger. The life of the finger, its effectiveness, is determined by its ordered juxtaposition with other parts of the body. This ordered juxtaposition is called construction. Like the work of nature, the work of art is subordinated to the same law, that of construction. The individual parts have life only by virtue of the whole.[36]

In *Punkt und Linie zu Fläche*, Kandinsky would assert that not just the painting but the picture plane itself possessed this kind of integrated unity. The picture plane is an "admittedly primitive but living organism," he wrote, yet one that, "if correctly treated, [will be] transformed into a new, living organism that is no longer primitive but manifests all the characteristics of a developed organism."[37] Most of the chapter focuses on the lower, "primitive" end of this hierarchy; it analyzes the tensions inherent in different quadrants of the picture plane, for example, or how those of a rectangular canvas oriented horizontally differ from the tensions in a canvas of the same dimensions turned to the vertical. The twenty-five black-and-white drawings and one color reproduction that make up the book's appendix are the closest we come within *Punkt und Linie* itself to anything approaching the complexity of a fully "developed organism." For precisely that reason, I'm inclined to regard the appendix as absolutely integral, rather than extraneous, to the text. It serves as the proper *conclusion* to *Punkt und Linie zu Fläche*, the place where the elements isolated and analyzed in the preceding chapters are brought together in the context of individual, "synthetic" compositions.[38] Near the beginning of the text, Kandinsky had described "his idea of the concept 'composition' [*des Begriffes "Komposition"*]" as

the internally purposive [*innerlich-zweckmäßige*] subordination of
    1. individual elements [and]
    2. the structure (construction)
to a concrete pictorial goal.[39]

Again, I take it that the drawings of the appendix are compositions of this sort, lacking color, to be sure, but otherwise "manifest[ing] all the characteristics of a developed organism." (Such self-sustaining, "organic" functioning presumably *is* their pictorial purposiveness or goal.) But Kandinsky would also have us see that "organic unity" is often achieved through the coordinated interaction of extremely diverse—perhaps even antithetical—elements:

The overall harmony of a composition can . . . reside in a number of complexes that themselves scale the heights of contrast. These contrasts can even have a disharmonious character; nonetheless, if correctly used they will affect the overall harmony not in a negative, but in a positive way, lifting the work to the highest level of harmonic being.[40]

To the extent that the drawings of the appendix are meant to put into practice the principles articulated in the text, it might behoove us at this point to look closely at one of those drawings in particular. No doubt all of them would reward our attention in one way or another. Yet given the constraints of time and attention, I've chosen to focus on plate 20 (Figure 13); if it is more involved than many of the appendix's other compositions, it is not yet so complicated as to pose a serious challenge to verbal description. My aim is to discuss the drawing exclusively in the terms used in *Punkt und Linie zu Fläche*, so that what follows is, quite literally, a by-the-book analysis.

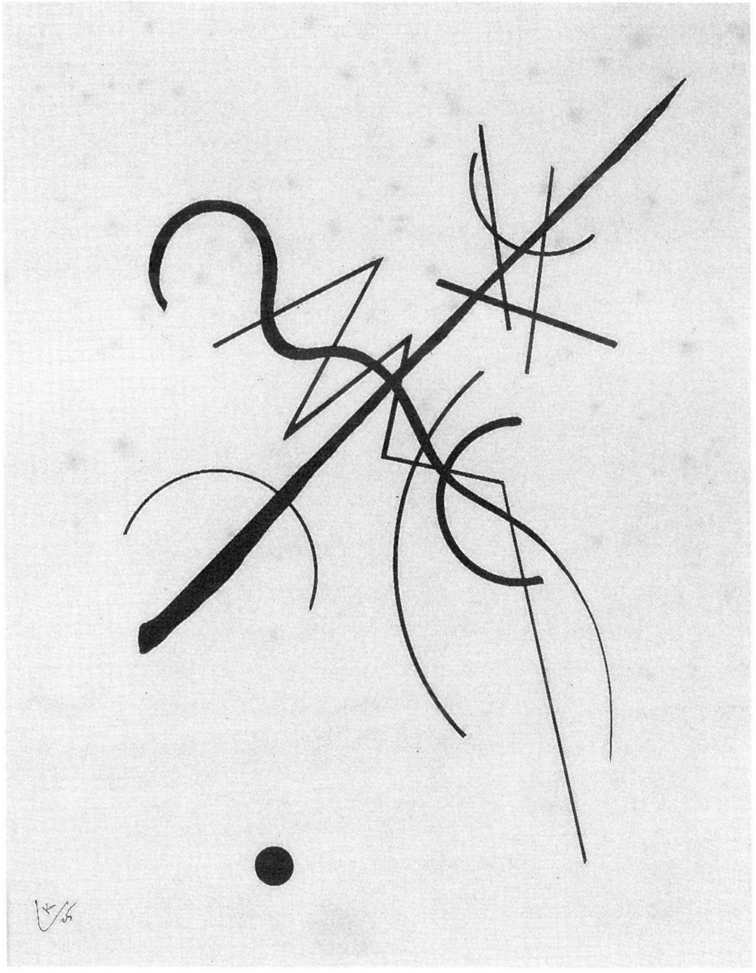

FIGURE 13. Wassily Kandinsky, Drawing for plate 20 of the appendix to *Punkt und Linie zu Fläche*, 1926. © Christie's Images Limited, 2013. © Artists Rights Society (ARS), New York.

THE MAIN LINES OF ACTION in the composition are laid down by the two counter-thrusting diagonals that cross above and ever so slightly to the right of the center of the picture plane.[41] One of these, the one descending from upper left to lower right, is what Kandinsky described as an "unharmonic diagonal," in that it joins together the two most disparately weighted quadrants of the picture plane.[42] Appropriately enough, then, that diagonal appears not as a single line but rather as the "conflicting combination" of an independently undulating curve with a "colder" but still "dramatic" zigzag.[43] The other ("harmonic") diagonal, rising in the opposite direction, is in itself a combination of contrasts, in that its uneven, obviously hand-drawn external limits suggest qualities very different (in tactility and "sound") from the utterly straight line we sense existing at its core.[44] The entire X-shaped configuration is rounded out by a collection of arcs and short, straight lines that both articulate the pull exerted by the corners of the page and serve as counterweights to one another.[45] The tautness of the arrangement turns on the presence of these marks; were it not for them, the energy of the major diagonals would have dissipated a short distance from their crossing. Similarly, the composition as a whole, which might otherwise appear to be drifting toward the upper right-hand corner, is pulled back by the circular "point" along the picture plane's lower edge.[46] That concentric point, "burrowing into the surface," anchors itself to the page—but only so that the other elements, despite their much greater size and "mass," might seem to float freely from it.[47]

In all, the drawing exemplifies three of the most important principles advanced in *Punkt und Linie zu Fläche*. First, no single element dominates the composition, and all seem integral to the organic functioning or "inner purposiveness" of the whole. Second, many of those elements are nonetheless antithetical to one another; they generate "disharmonious contrasts" that still manage, in the context of the work, to reach a kind of harmonic reconciliation. Finally, even the fundamental opposition between materiality and *im*materiality is at least provisionally overcome—principally via that "point" which, in adhering so firmly to the lower edge of the picture plane, produces the illusion of the plane's derealization above. "The practiced eye," Kandinsky wrote near the end of *Punkt und Linie*, "must possess the ability to see that plane which is necessary for the work of art . . . [and] to ignore it when it dons the guise of space."[48]

If such an analysis rings at all true to our experience of the drawing, we may be tempted to see *Punkt und Linie zu Fläche* along lines similar to those used to characterize the *Philosophy of Nature* and any number of other Hegelian texts (save, of course, the anomalous *Aesthetics*). The book might be said to take us from an initial, undifferentiated unity (the point) through a second moment of particularity, in which individual elements (lines and the various shapes they engender) are finely differentiated from one another, and then finally to a concrete individuality (the developed composition on the picture plane) that manages to integrate those earlier, antithetical moments so as to achieve a complex (and no longer merely "material") unity-in-difference. If that account in turn rings true, we may also be inclined to see the dialectical rhyme between the point and the composition on the plane as significant—the self-supporting, organic unity of the latter marking a return "at a higher level" of the former's "self-absorbed repose." In itself, there's nothing particularly surprising in this; the movement of the dialectic periodically produces such recurrences. (Indeed that sort of recurrence is precisely what allows Hegel to break up the continuity of history into distinct chronological "periods.") Less expected, however, is that the language Kandinsky uses to describe the point—as "an introverted entity pregnant with possibilities" or, again, an element "in repose, absorbed in itself"—very closely approximates the phrasing Hegel had used to describe the work of classical sculpture.[49]

Once more, it's an important feature of the *Aesthetics* that the unity characteristic of the classical does not recur at a later moment within the text. The classical may be the apex of art, but it arises in the middle of Hegel's historical narrative, after which point we witness gradual dissolution and dispersal. Never again, Hegel claims, does art attain the plenitude it enjoyed in classical Greece. When *Geist* does eventually realize a totality rivaling and even surpassing that of Greek sculpture—such that that sculpture can be seen, in some sense, to have "prefigured" the later moment—it does so not as art but as philosophy. More specifically, it does so in the form of the Hegelian system of "absolute knowing."[50] By extension, if the similarities between Kandinsky's description of the point and Hegel's characterization of classical sculpture are not mere coincidence, they invest the realized composition on the plane with a profound significance. The internally purposive, organic totality that, according to *Punkt und Linie*, the successful composition ultimately *is* might then also be regarded as the pictorial equivalent of Hegel's philosophical system, with its complex, self-supporting structure.[51]

At best this is a thought that remains only nascent or inchoate in Kandinsky's text. To the extent that he was aware of it at all, he may have imagined a fuller articulation in some future book—perhaps one belonging to the still-to-come "synthetic movement" forecast in "Yesterday-Today-Tomorrow." Had that book been written, it might also have provided the opportunity to synthesize, and so advance beyond, the particular arguments of *Über das Geistige* and *Punkt und Linie zu Fläche*. Unfortunately (perhaps), there was no subsequent book—nor even any extended essay in which that thought was again taken up and developed. Or, rather, there was no subsequent essay *by Kandinsky*. One might regard "Les Peintures concrètes," which was written by Kojève at the explicit request of his uncle, as fulfilling exactly that role.[52] As we'll see, there is a real sense in which it can be said to reconcile not only Kandinsky's own two previous texts but also *both* of them with the larger argument of Hegel's *Aesthetics*. In any case, it is to "Les Peintures concrètes" that we now turn.

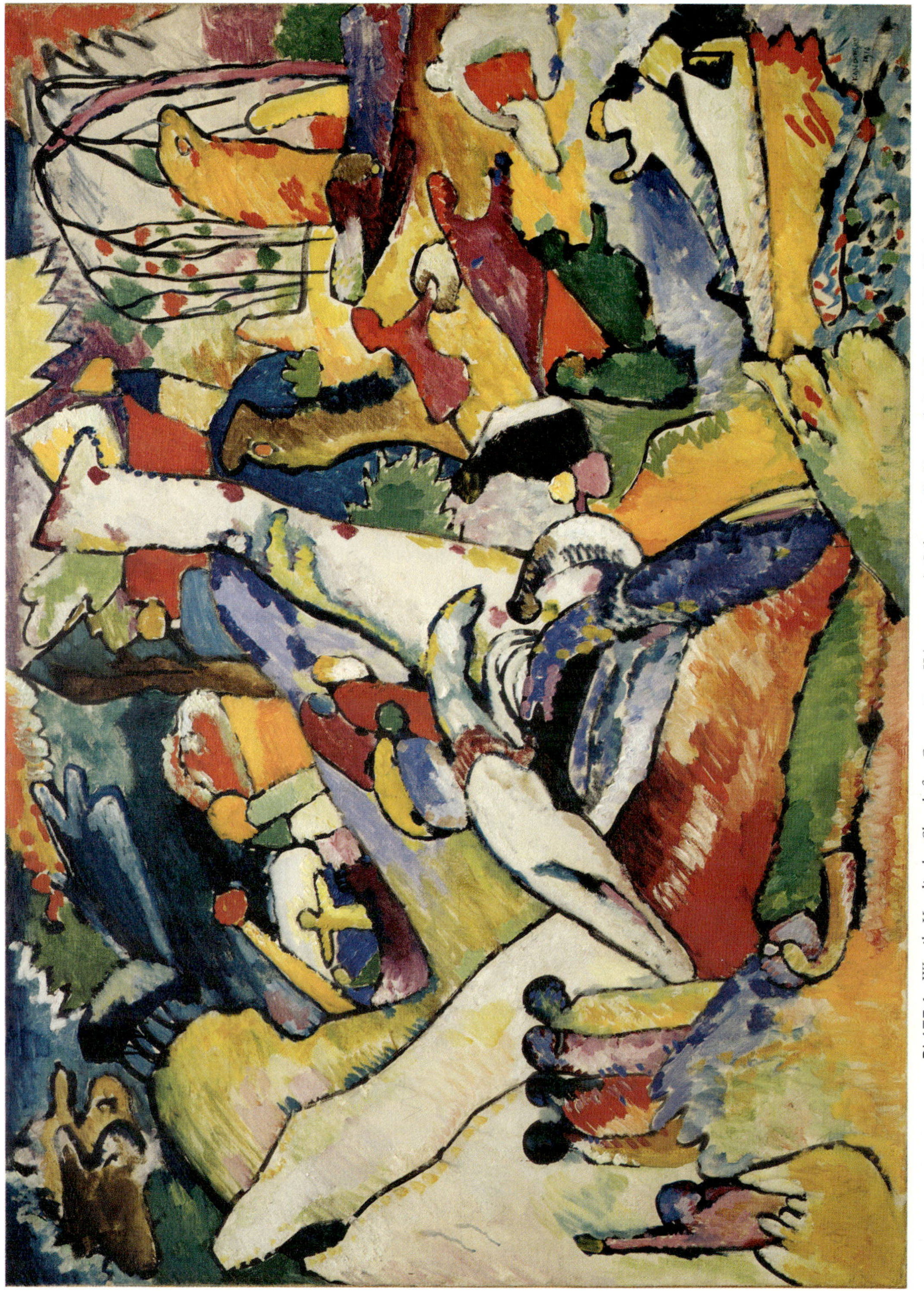

PLATE 1. Wassily Kandinsky, Sketch for *Composition II* (1909–1910), Solomon R. Guggenheim Museum, New York

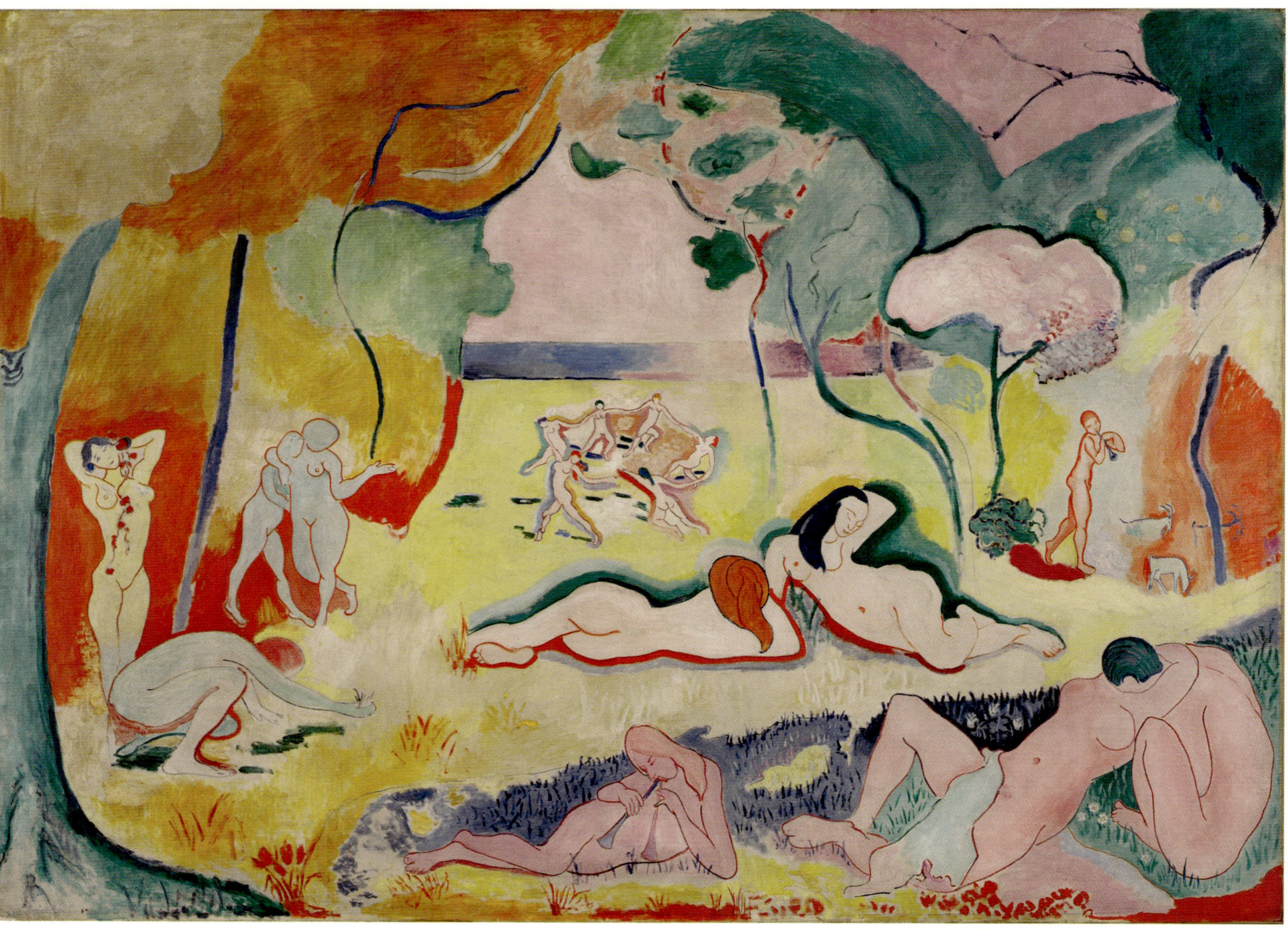

PLATE 2. Henri Matisse, *Le Bonheur de vivre* (1905–1906), Barnes Foundation

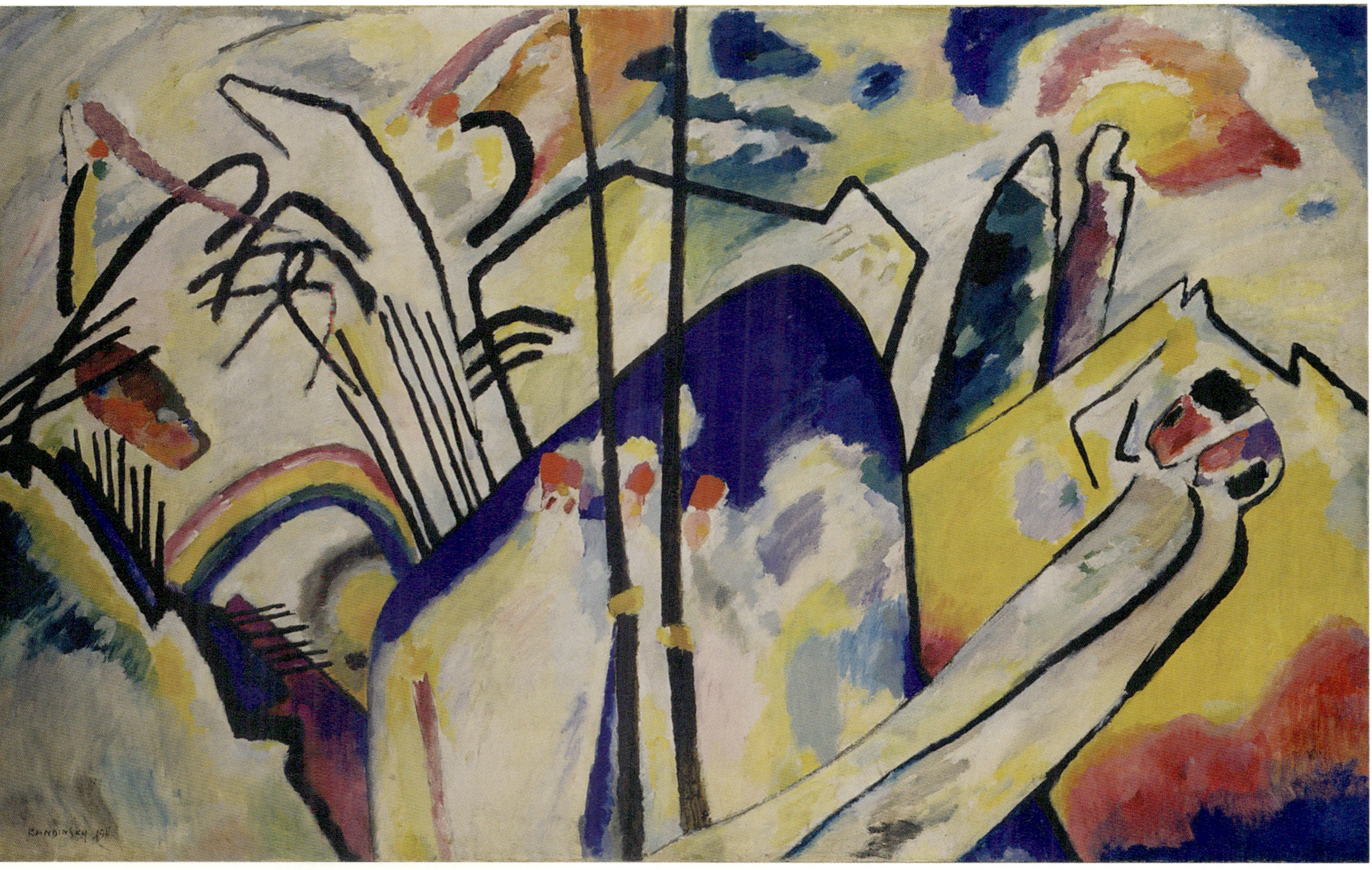

PLATE 3. Wassily Kandinsky, *Composition IV* (1911), Kunstsammlung Nordrhein-Westfalen, Düsseldorf

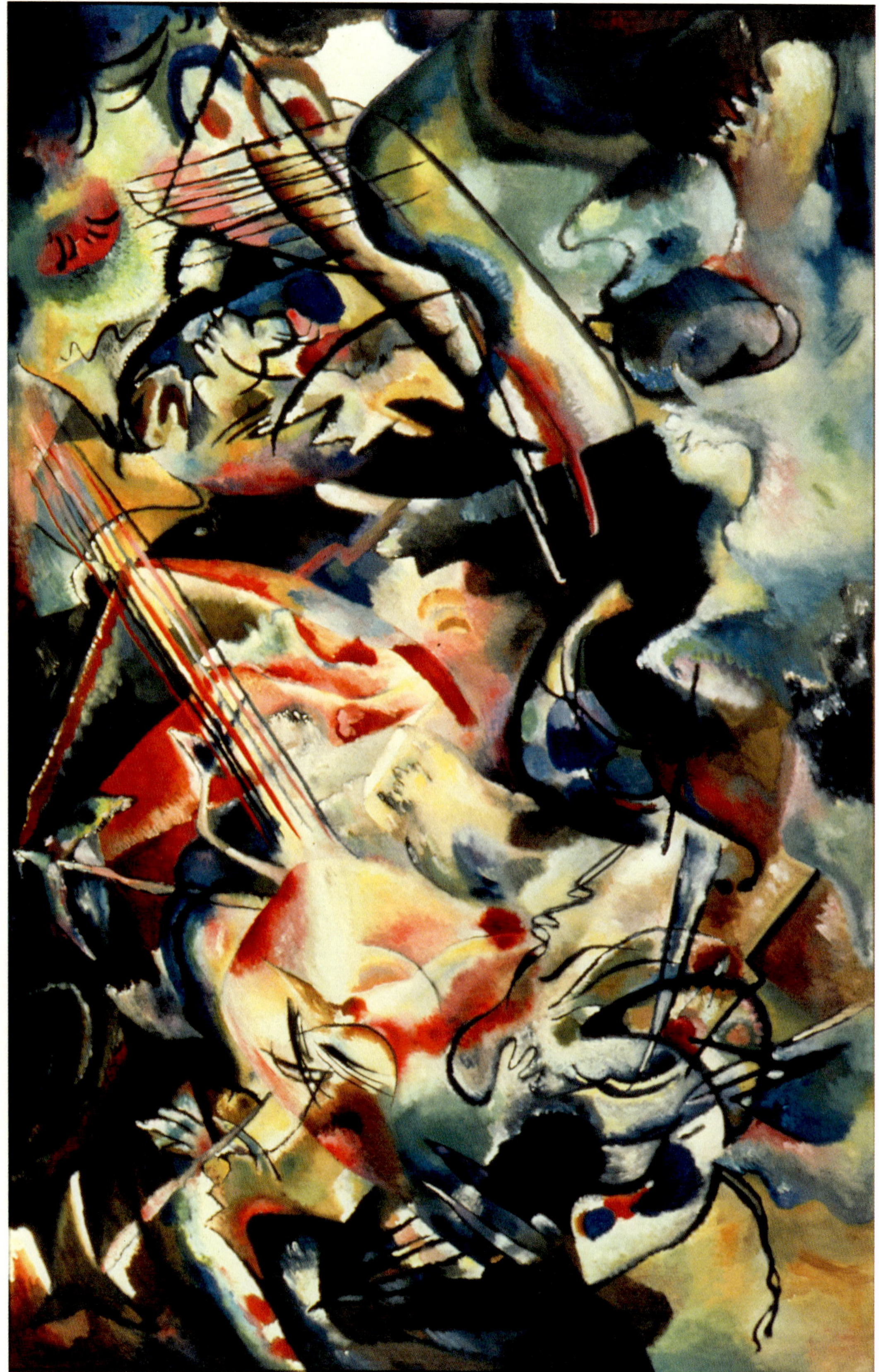

PLATE 4. Wassily Kandinsky, *Composition VI* (1913), Hermitage, Saint Petersburg

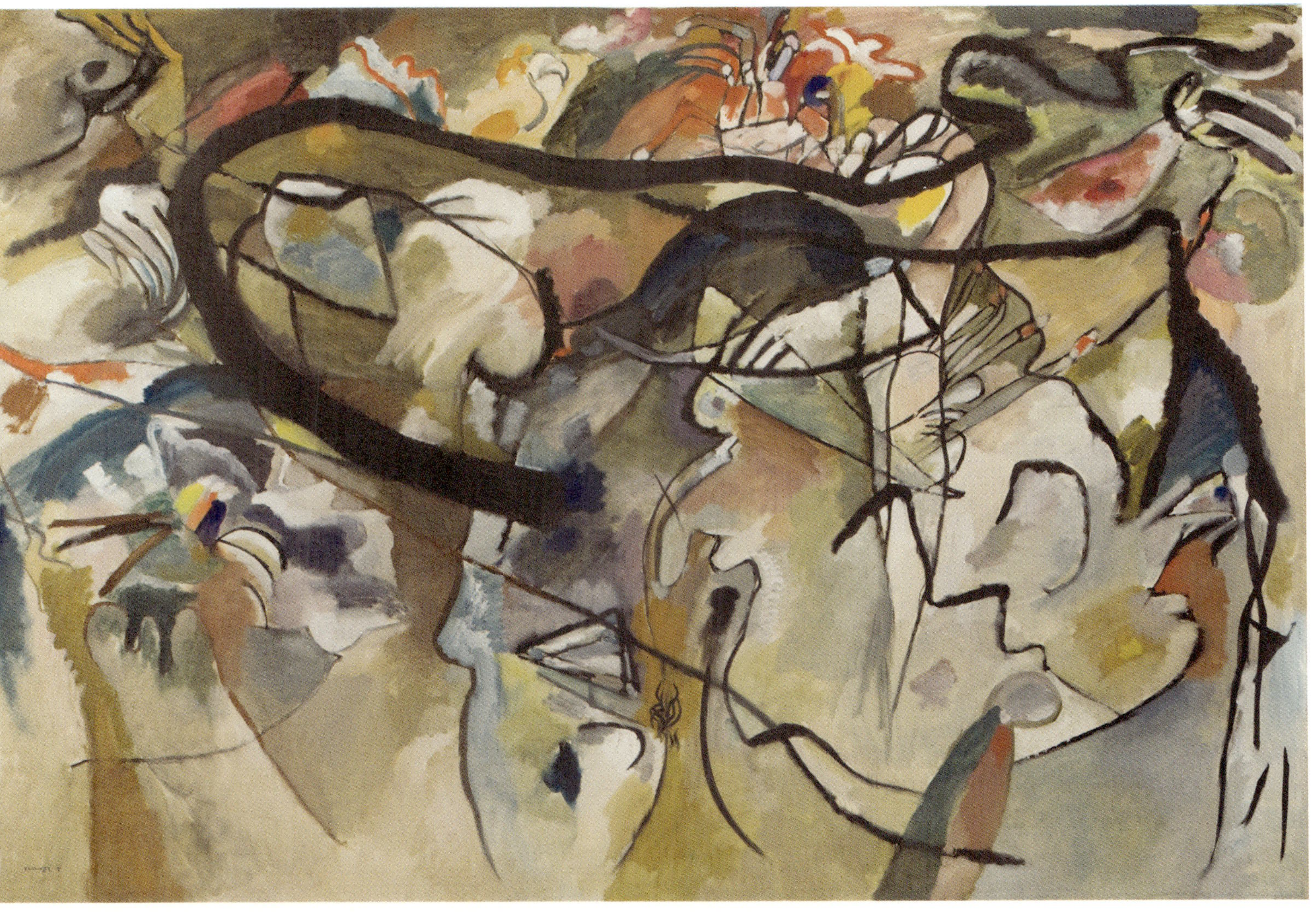

PLATE 5. Wassily Kandinsky, *Composition V* (1911), private collection

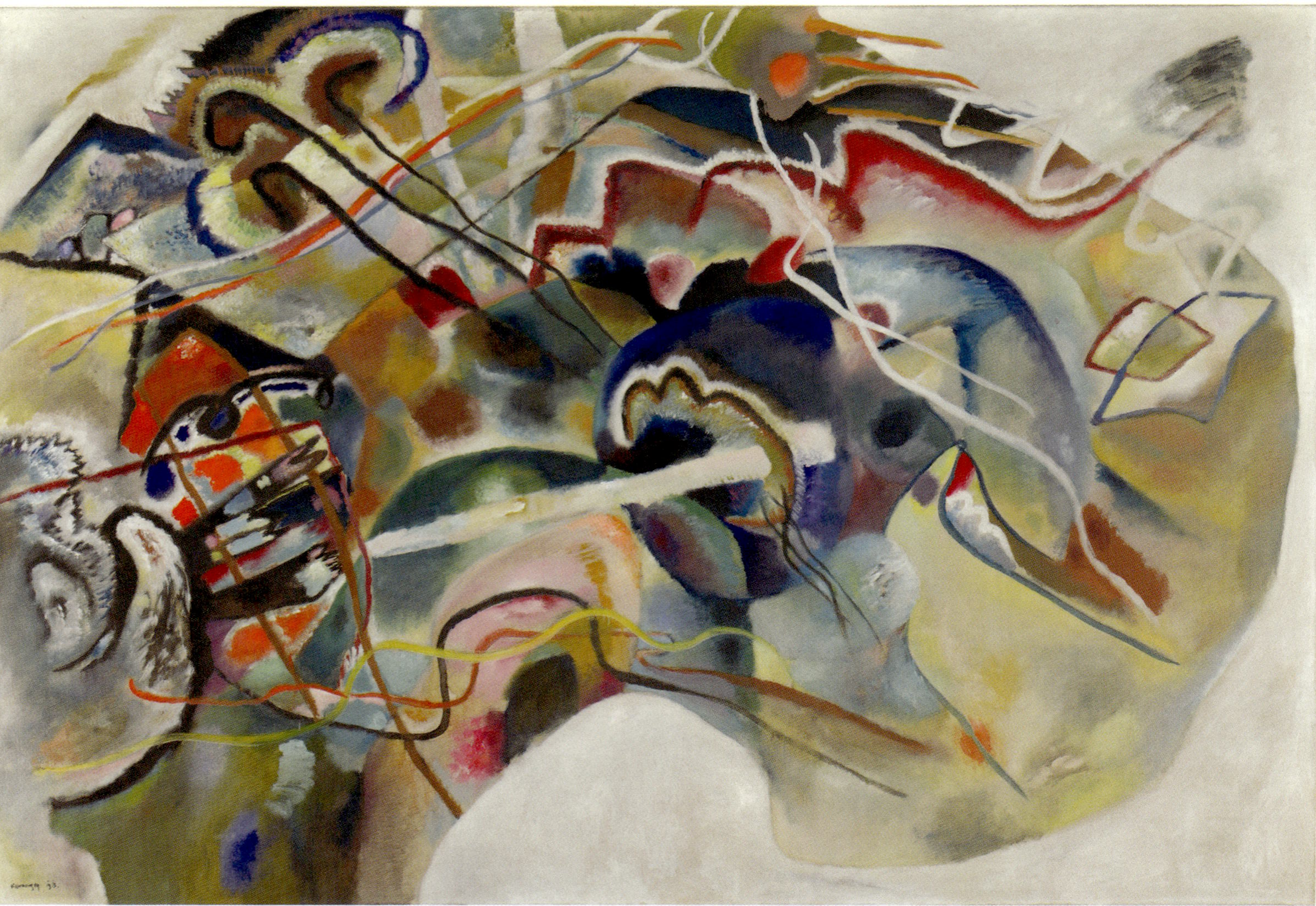

PLATE 6. Wassily Kandinsky, *Painting with White Border* (1913), Solomon R. Guggenheim Museum, New York

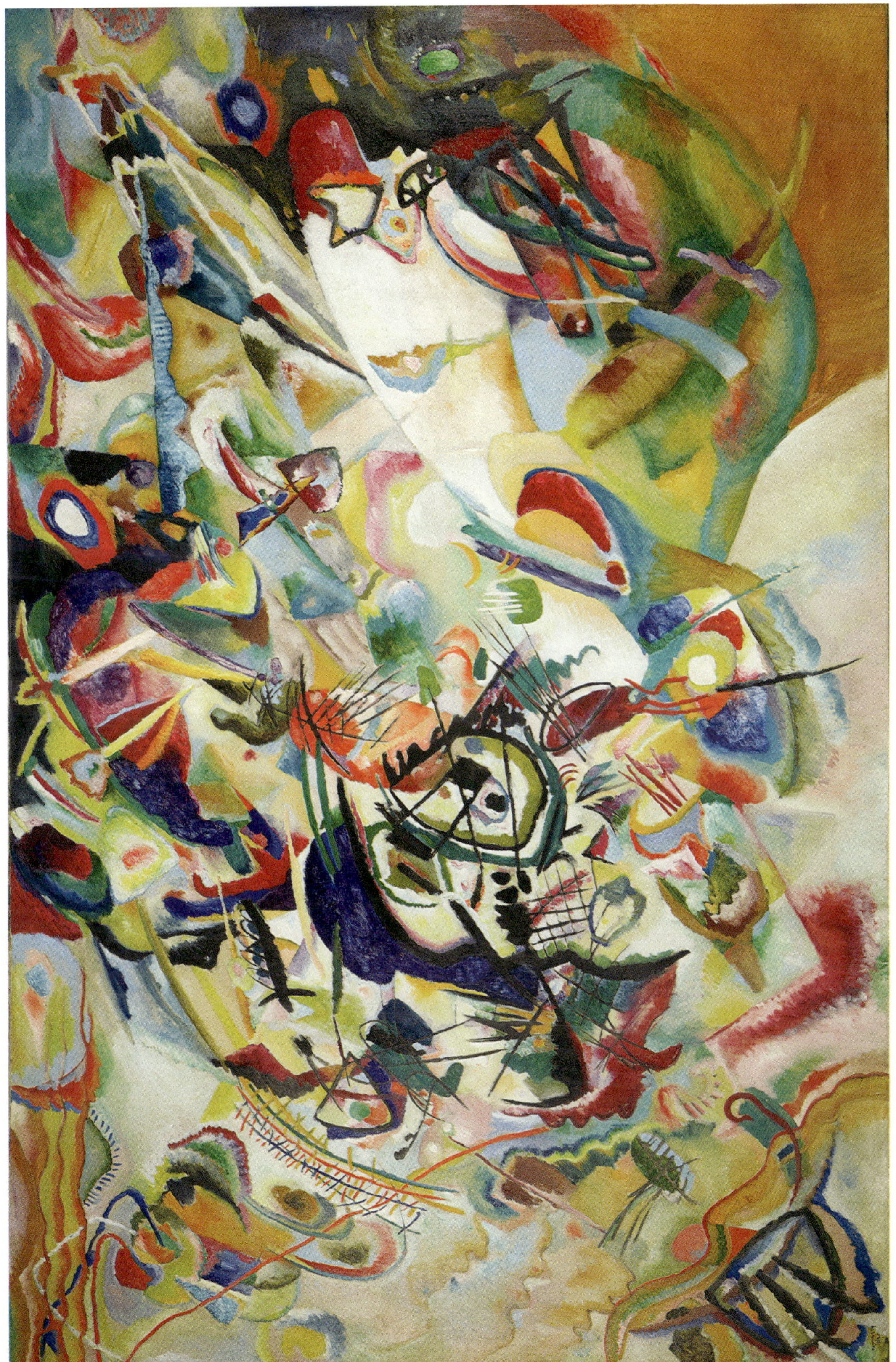

PLATE 7. Wassily Kandinsky, *Composition VII* (1913), Tretyakov Gallery, Moscow

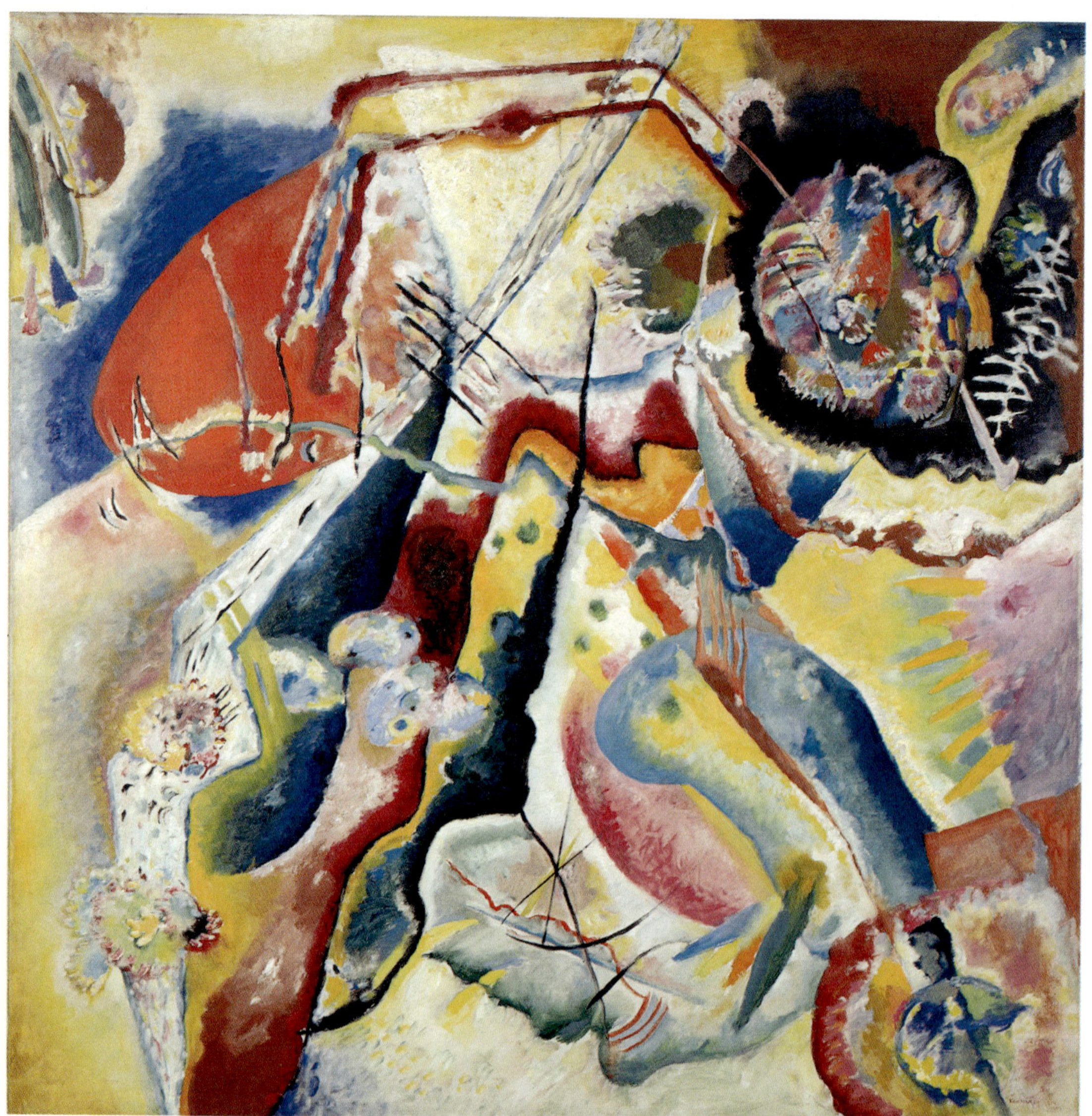

PLATE 8. Wassily Kandinsky, *Picture with Red Spot* (1914), Musée nationale d'art moderne, Paris

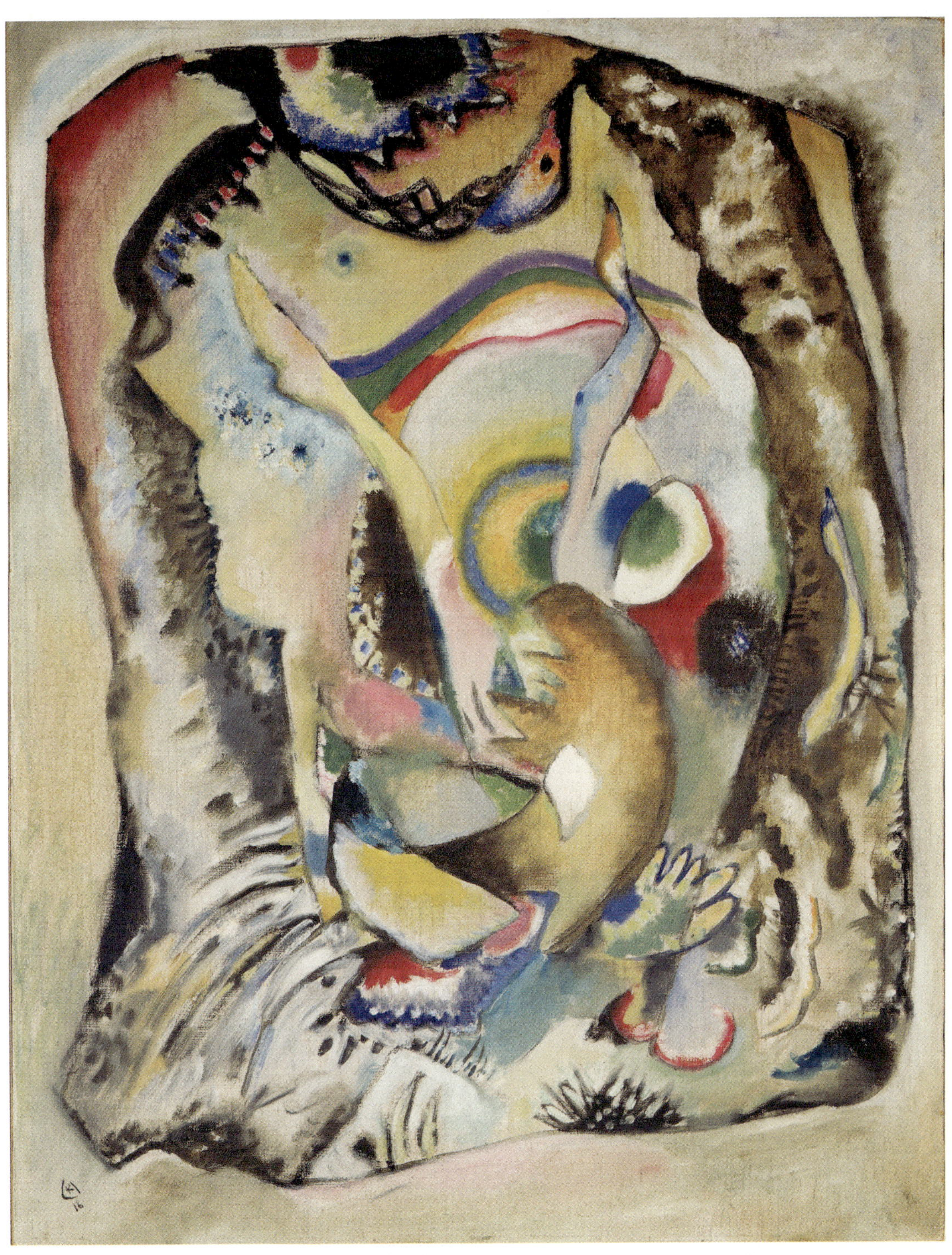

PLATE 9. Wassily Kandinsky, *Picture on Light Ground* (1916), Musée nationale d'art moderne, Paris

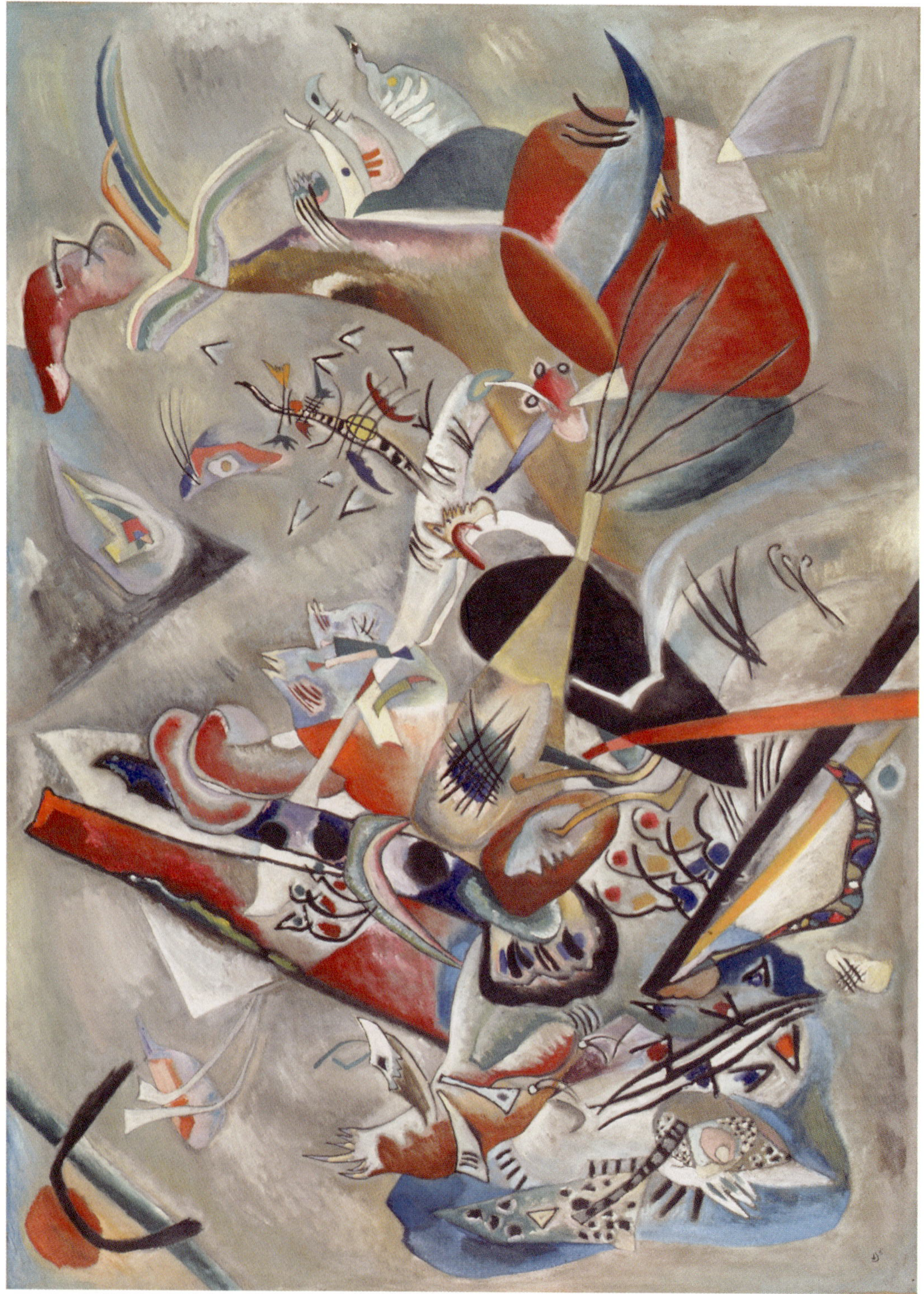

PLATE 10. Wassily Kandinsky, *In Gray* (1919), Musée nationale d'art moderne, Paris

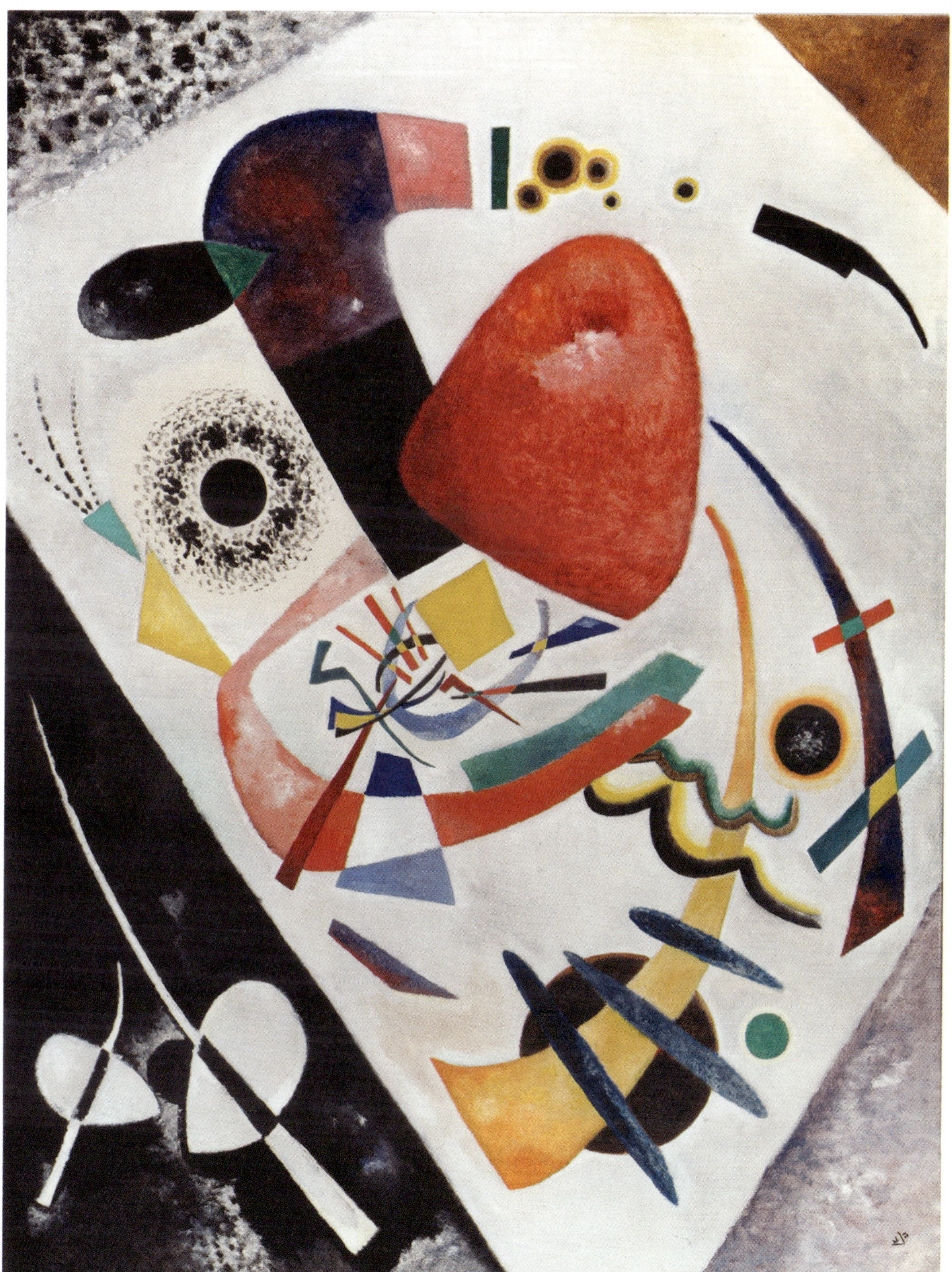

PLATE 11. Wassily Kandinsky, *Red Spot II* (1921), Lenbachhaus, Munich

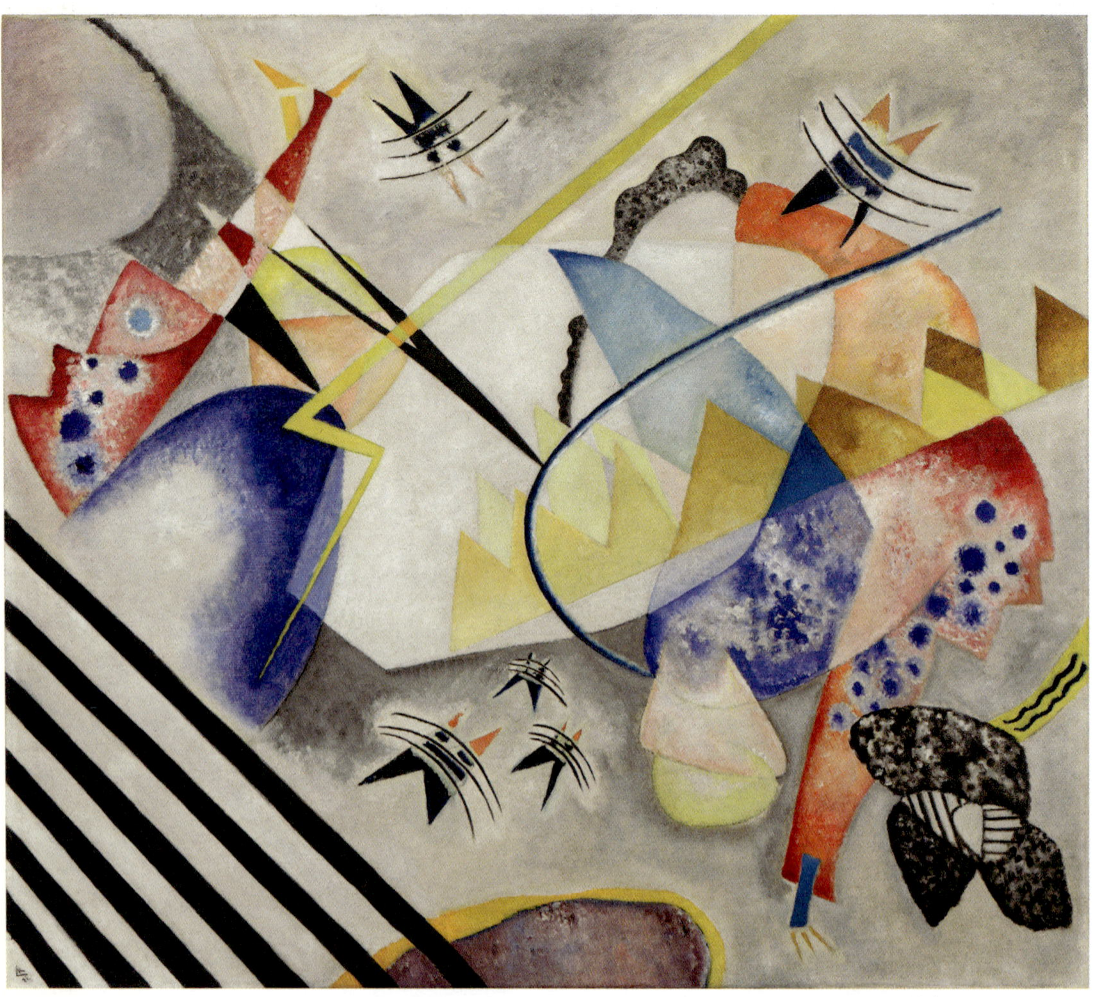

PLATE 12. Wassily Kandinsky, *White Center* (1921), Solomon R. Guggenheim Museum, New York

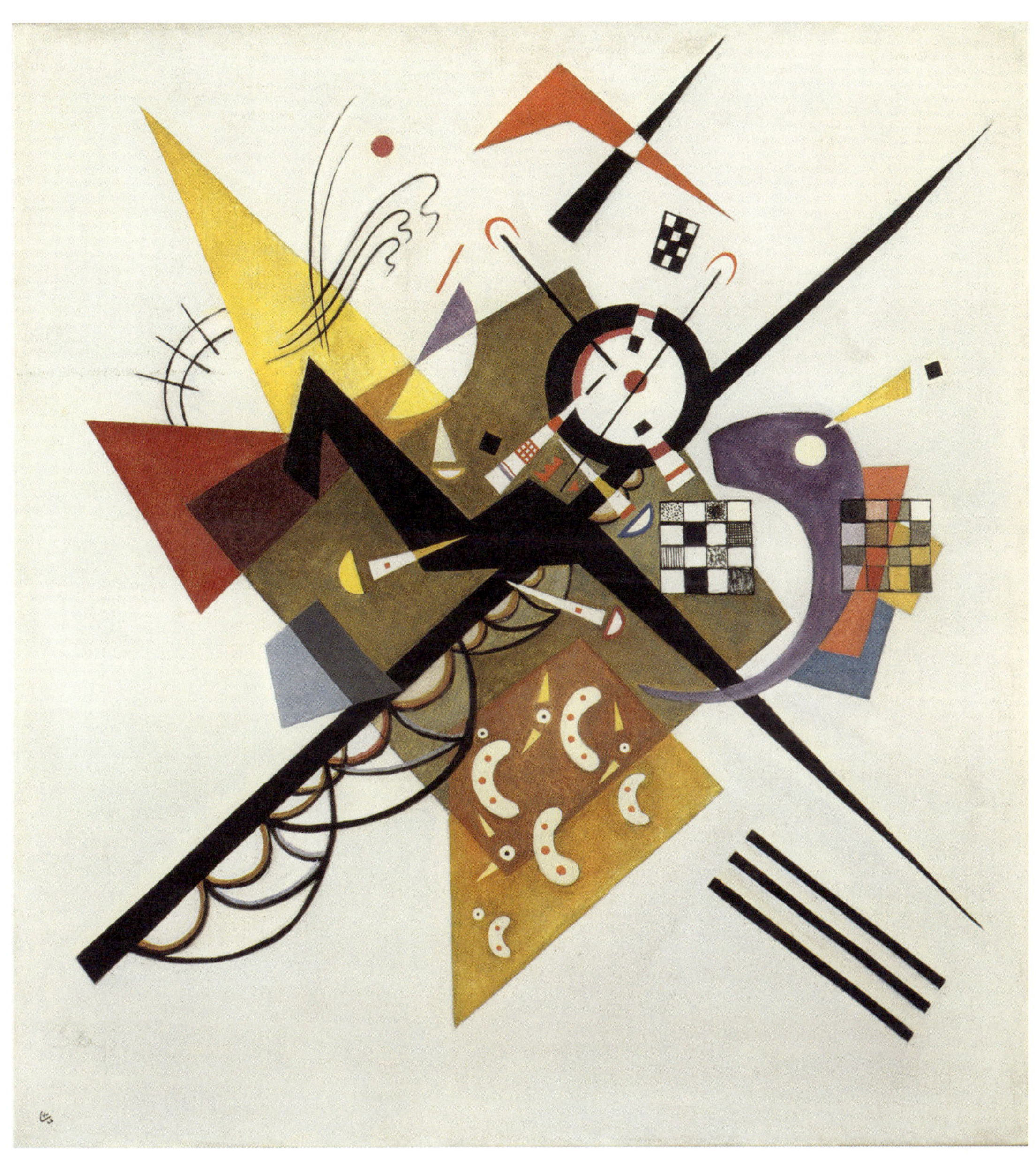

PLATE 13. Wassily Kandinsky, *On White II* (1923), Musée nationale d'art moderne, Paris

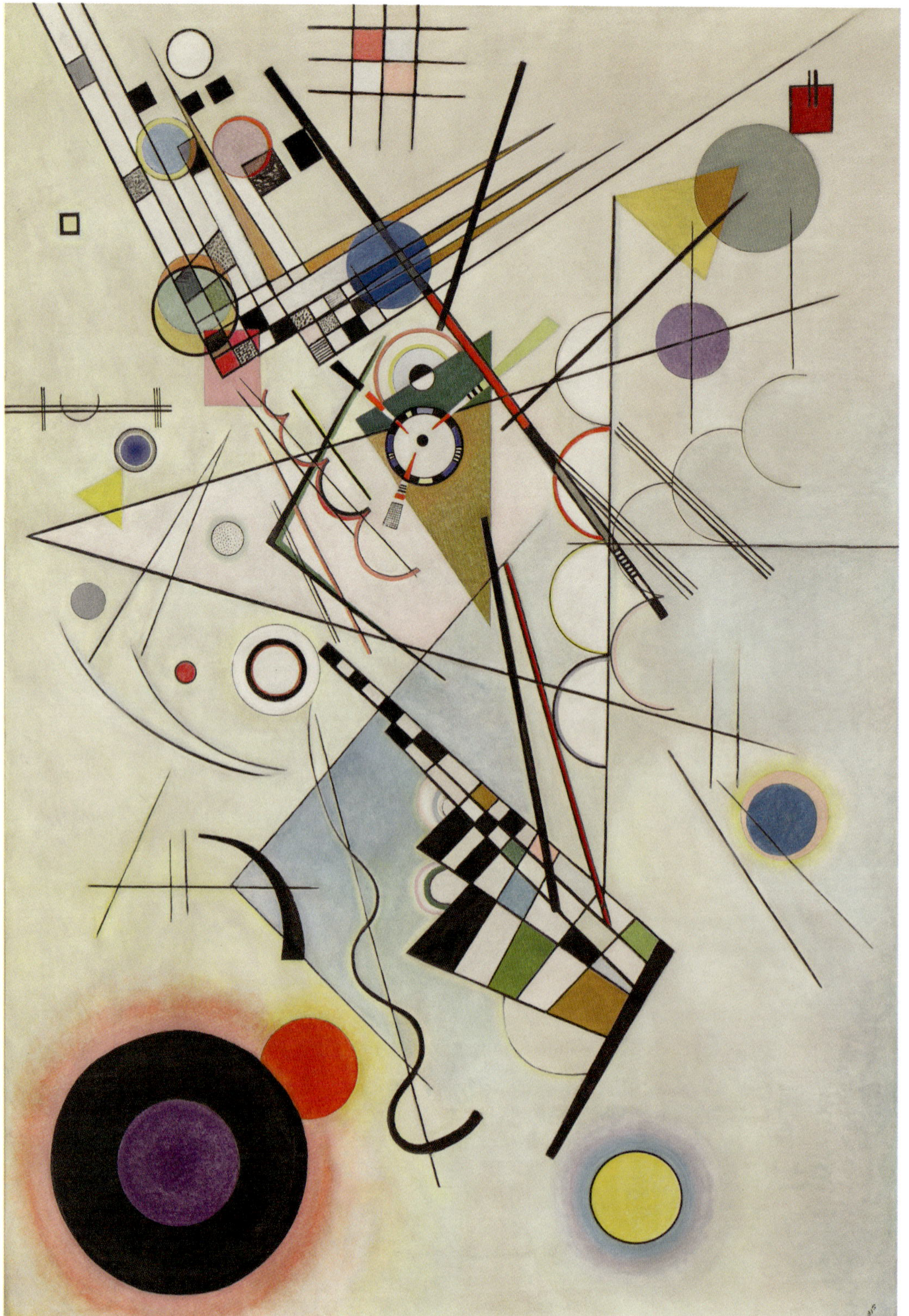

PLATE 14. Wassily Kandinsky, *Composition VIII* (1923), Solomon R. Guggenheim Museum, New York

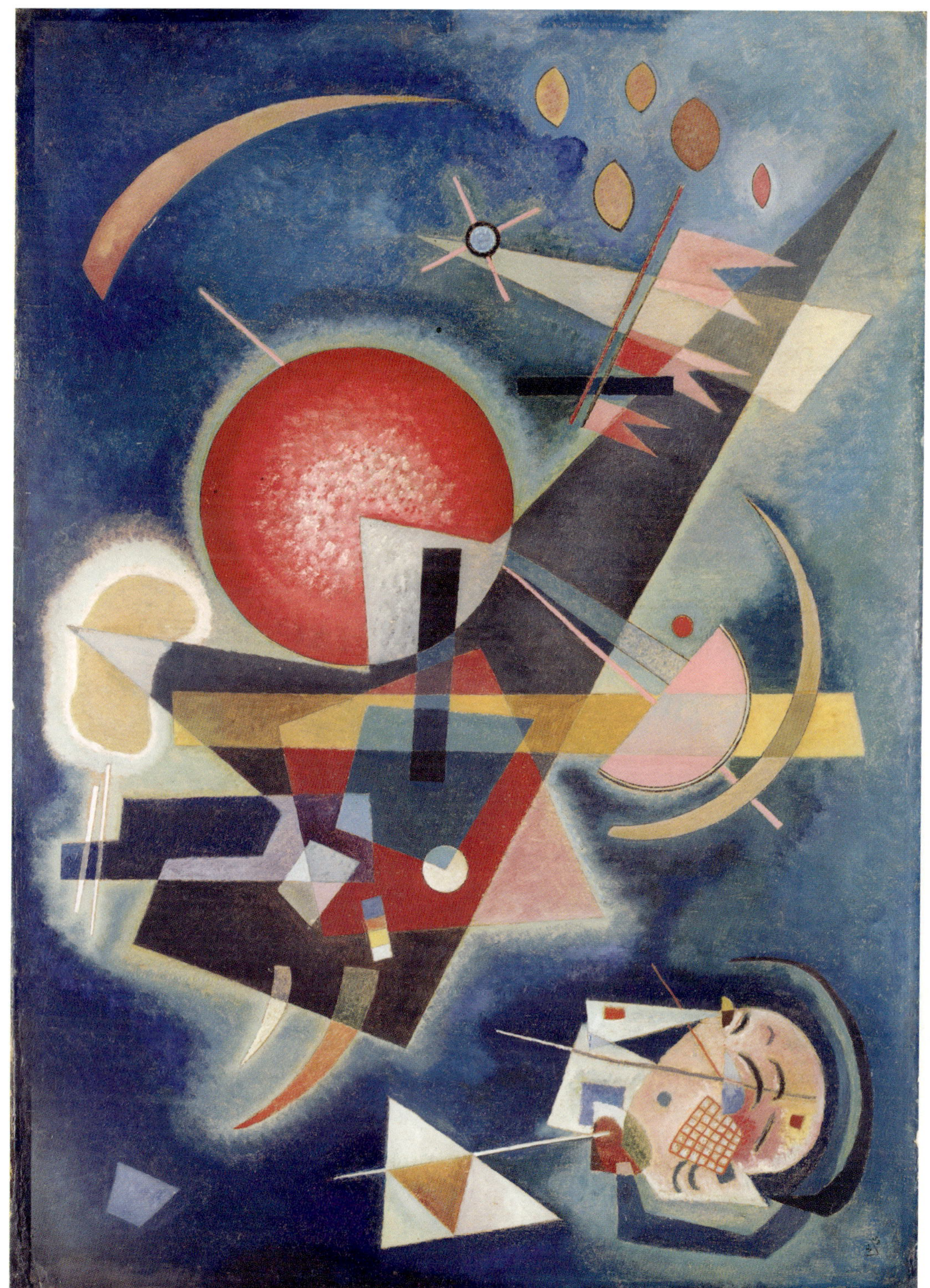

PLATE 15. Wassily Kandinsky, *In Blue* (1925), Kunstsammlung Nordrhein-Westfalen, Düsseldorf

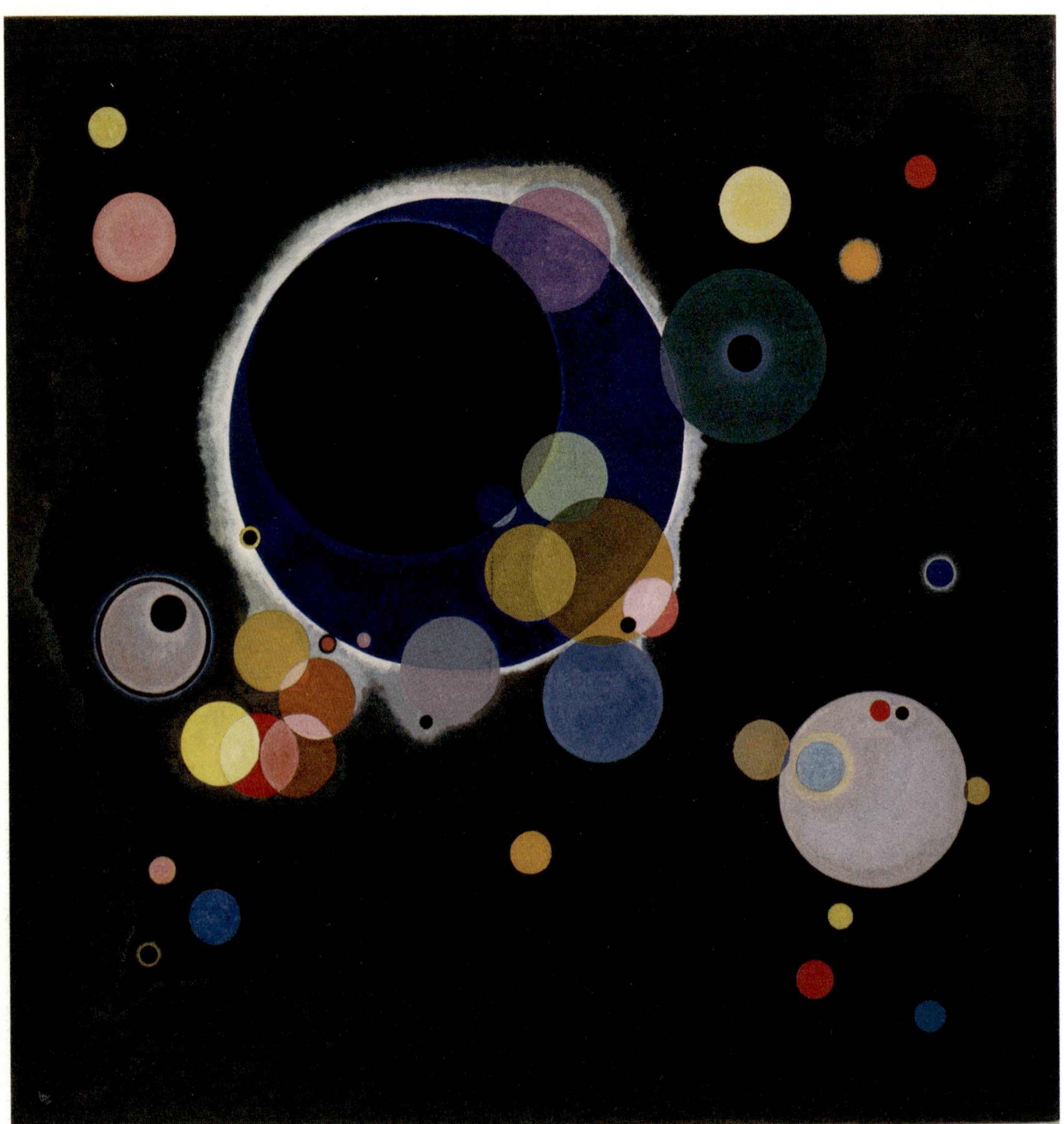

PLATE 16. Wassily Kandinsky, *Several Circles* (1926), Solomon R. Guggenheim Museum, New York

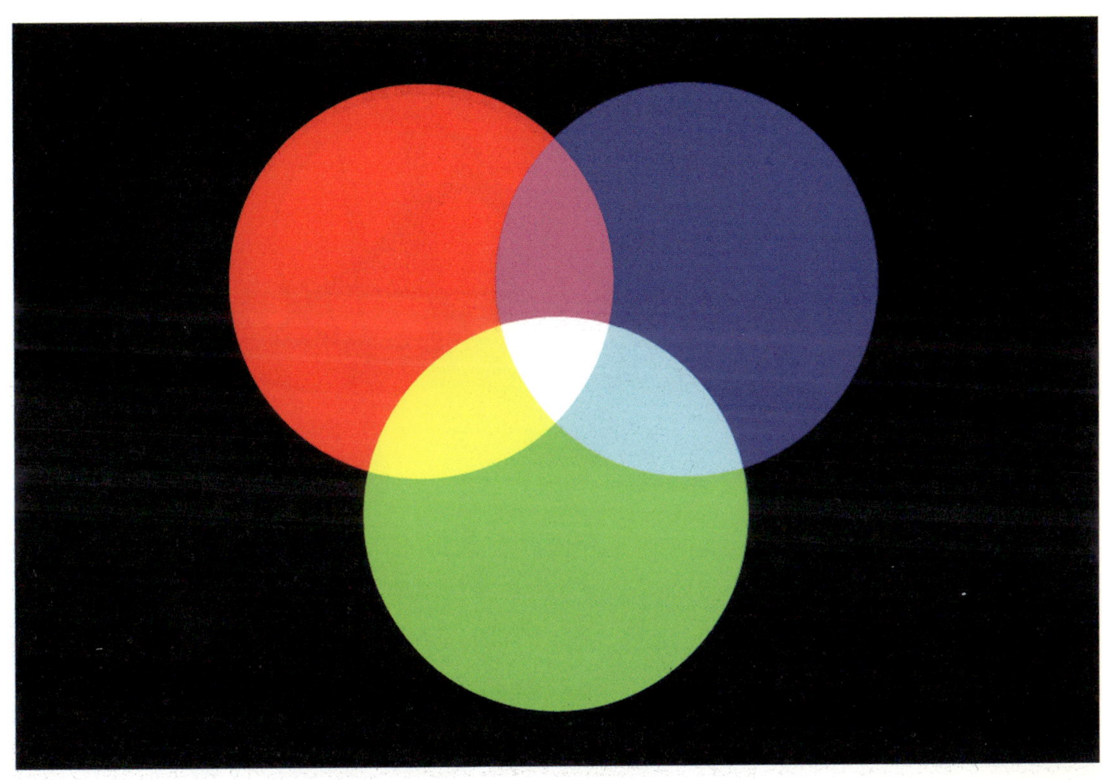

PLATE 17. Diagram of projected light / additive color mixing

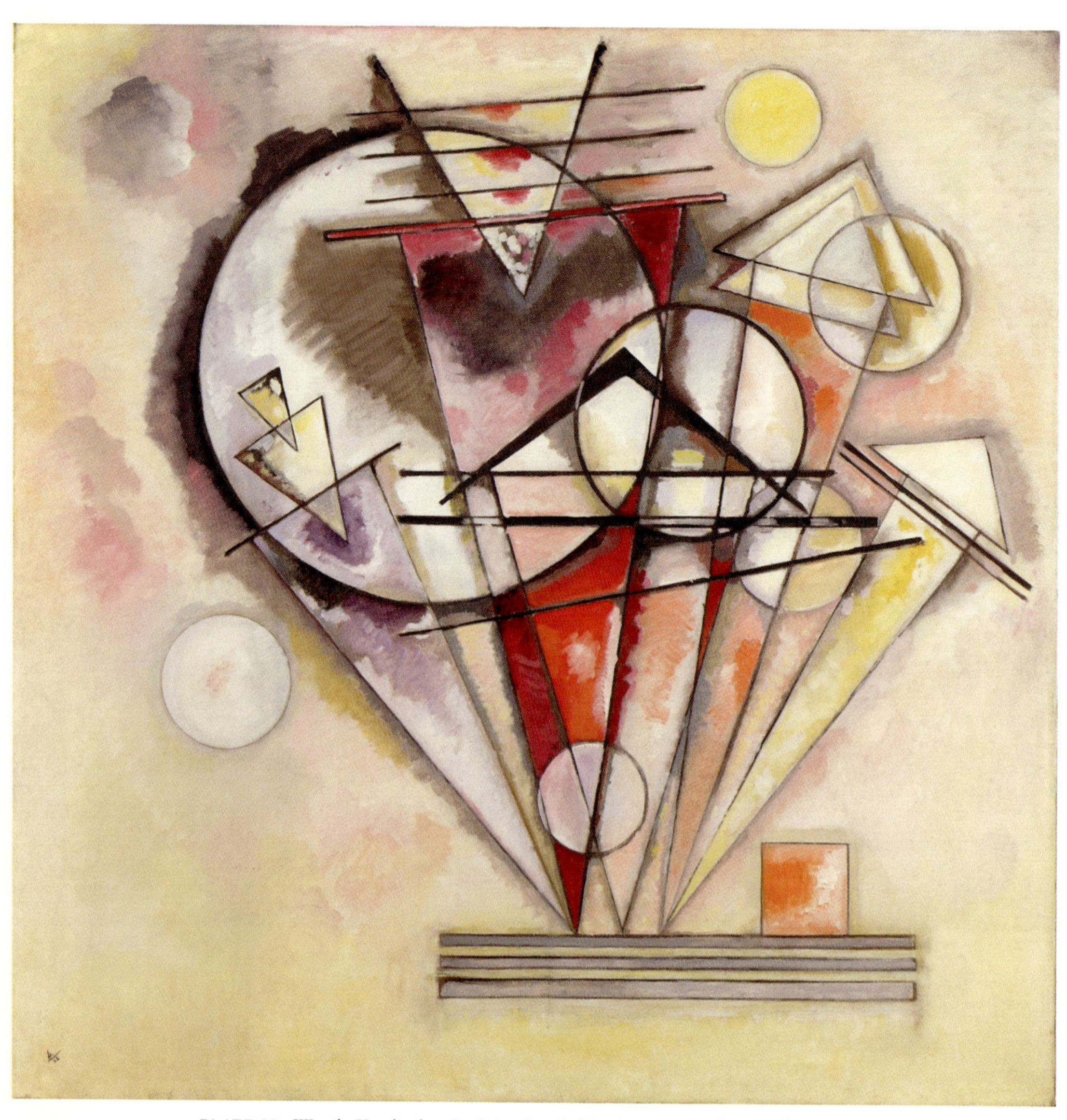

PLATE 18. Wassily Kandinsky, *On Points* (1928), Musée nationale d'art moderne, Paris

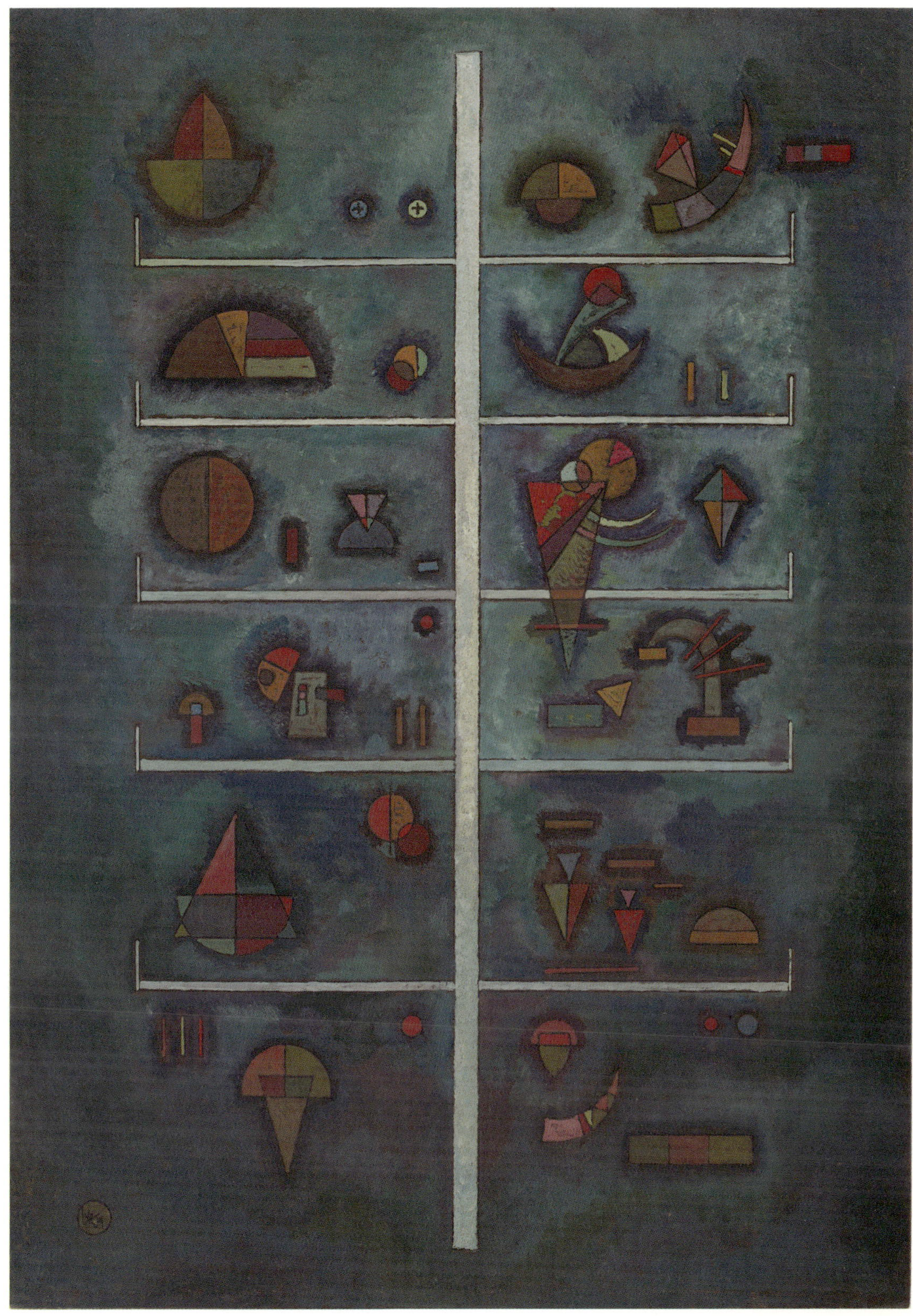

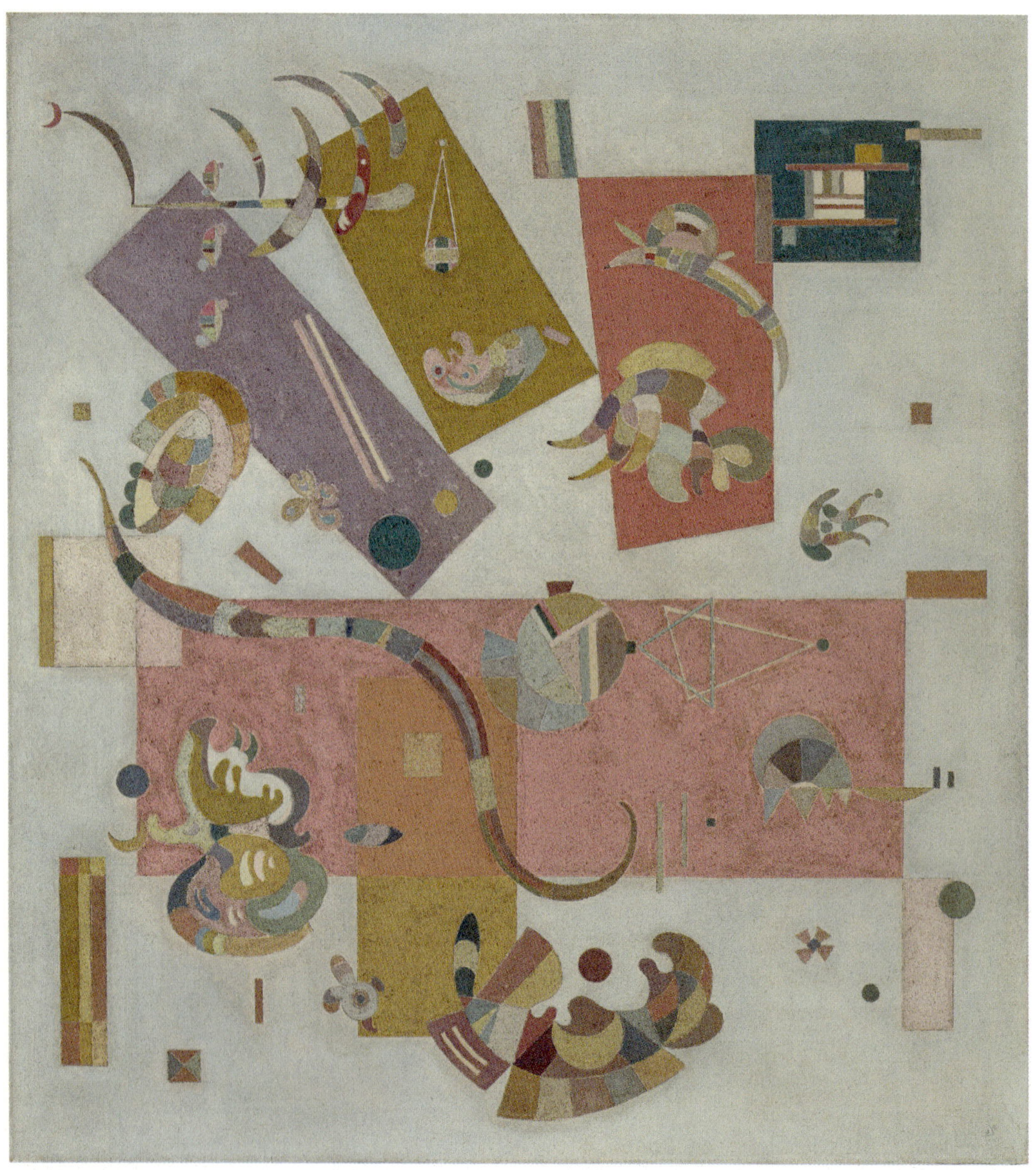

PLATE 20. Wassily Kandinsky, *Blue World* (1934), Solomon R. Guggenheim Museum, New York

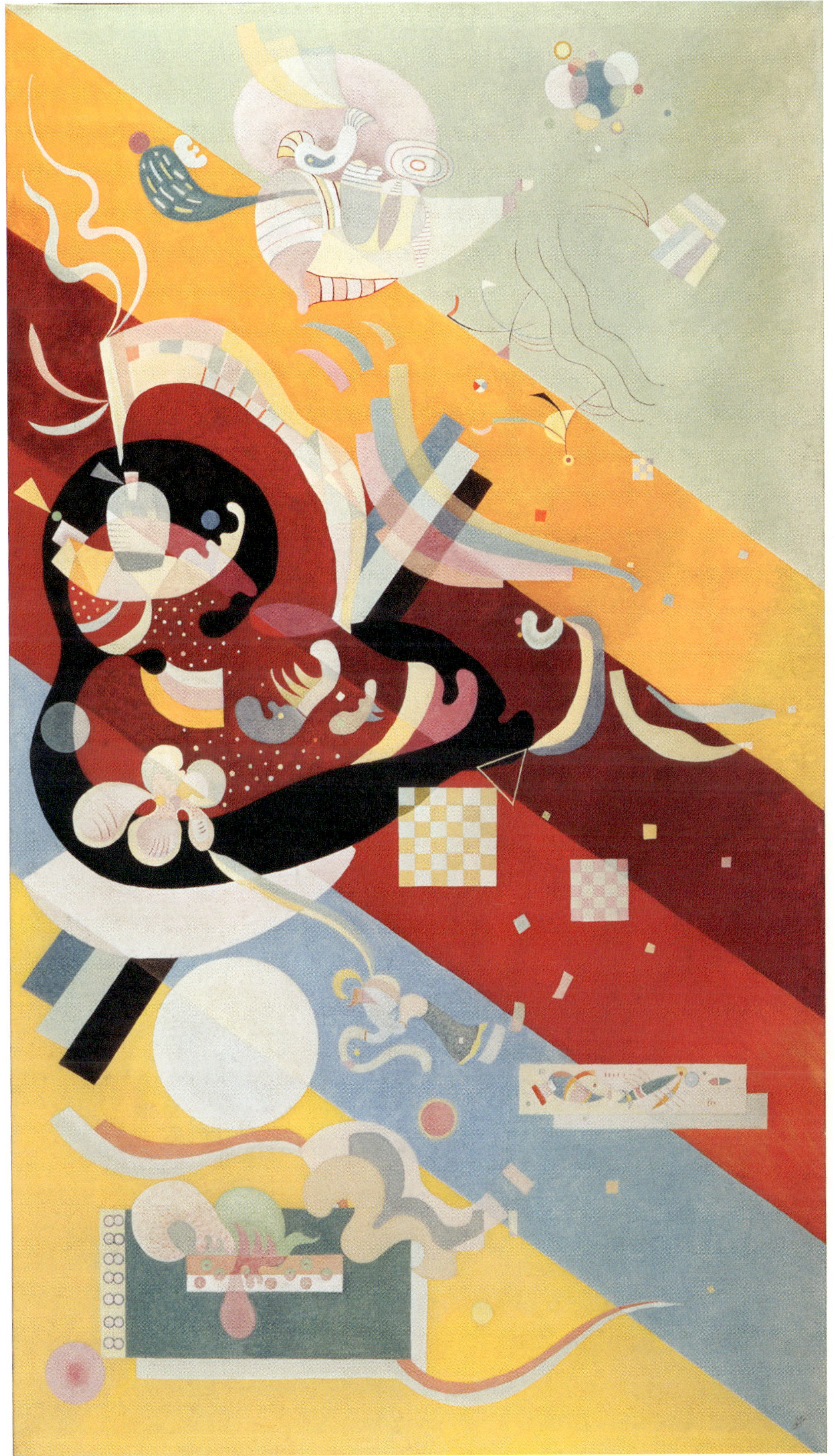

PLATE 21. Wassily Kandinsky, *Composition IX* (1936), Musée nationale d'art moderne, Paris

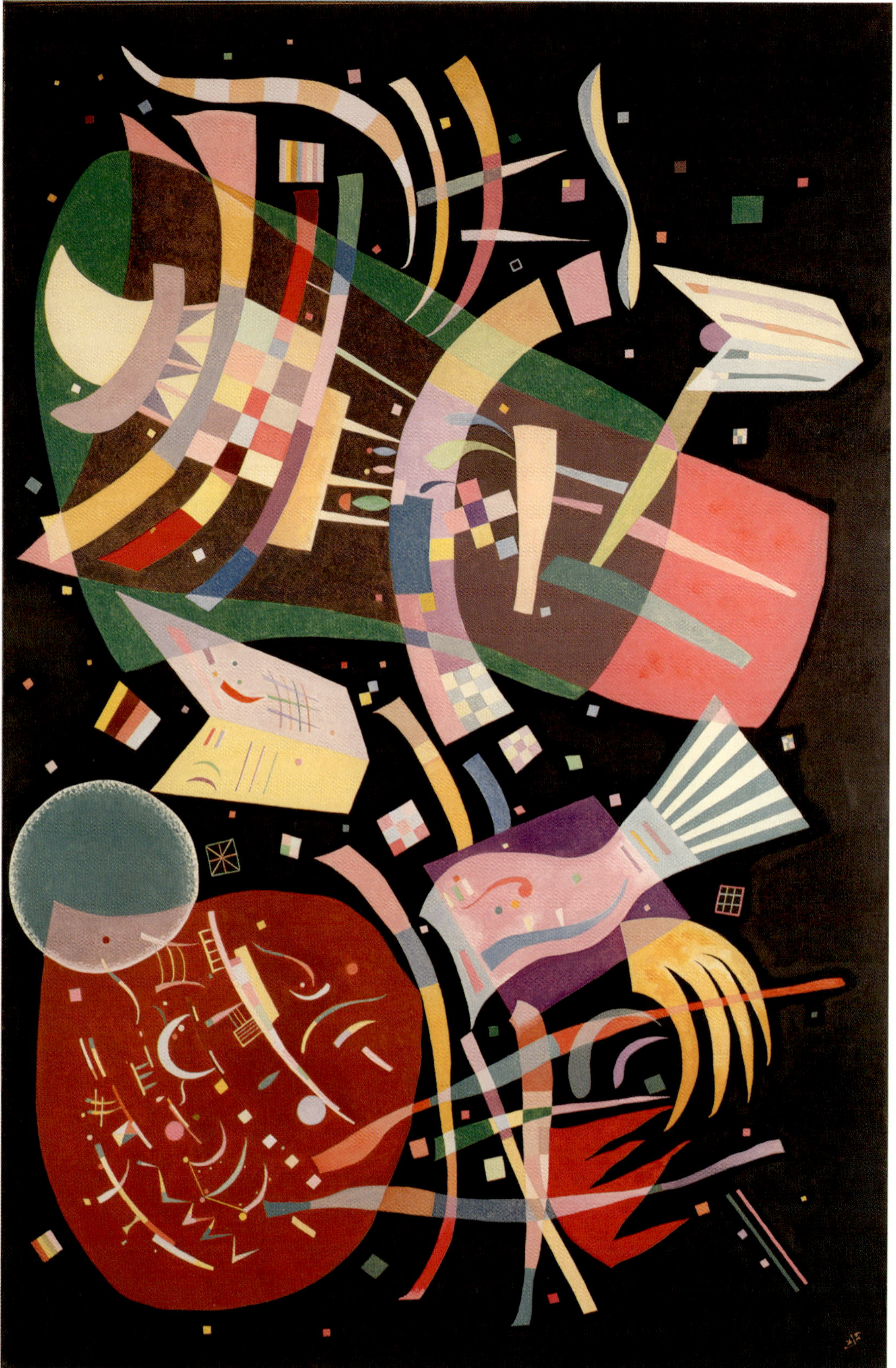

PLATE 22. Wassily Kandinsky, *Composition X* (1938–1939), Kunstsammlung Nordrhein-Westfalen, Düsseldorf

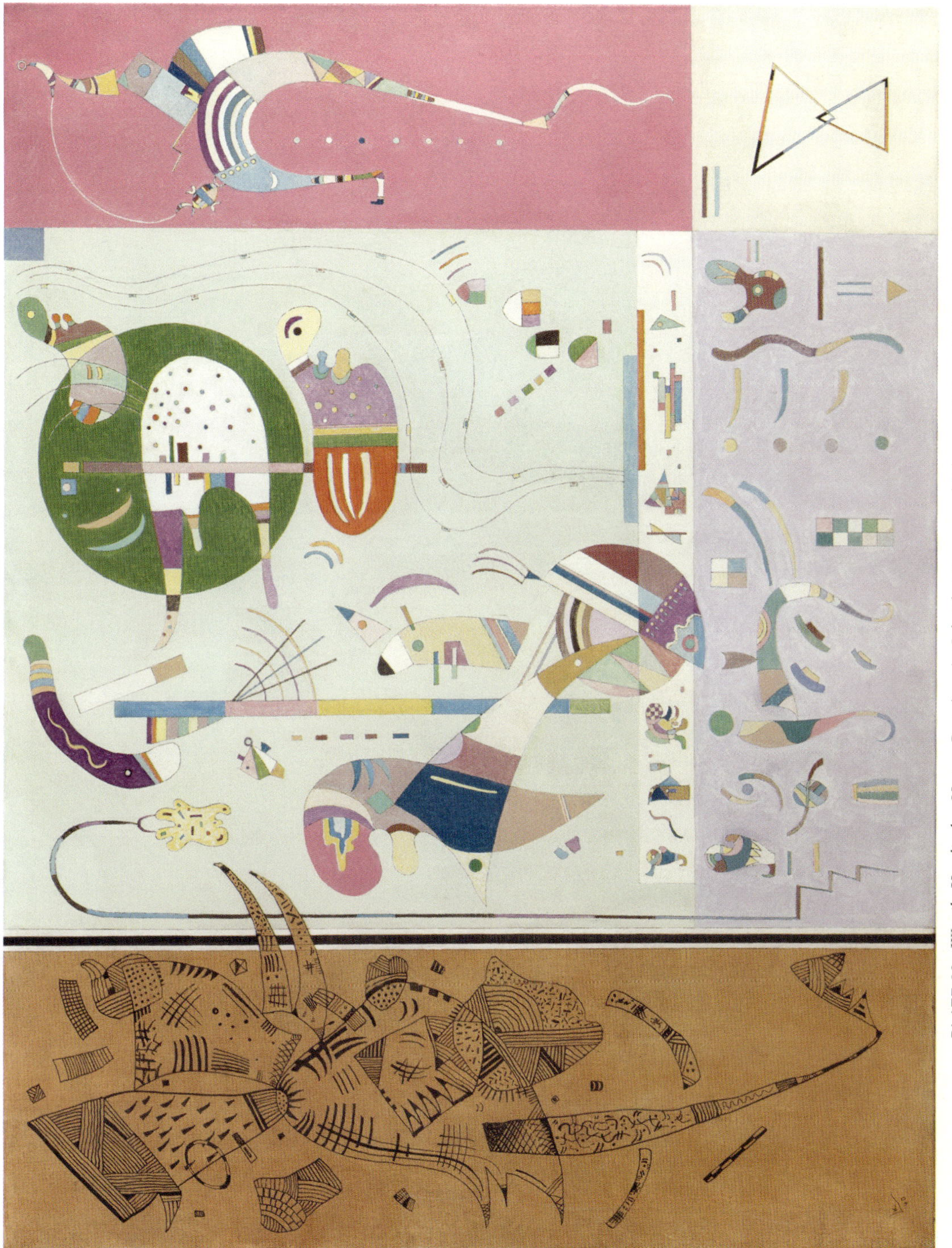

PLATE 23. Wassily Kandinsky, *Various Parts* (1940), Gabriele Münter- und Johannes Eichner-Stiftung, Munich

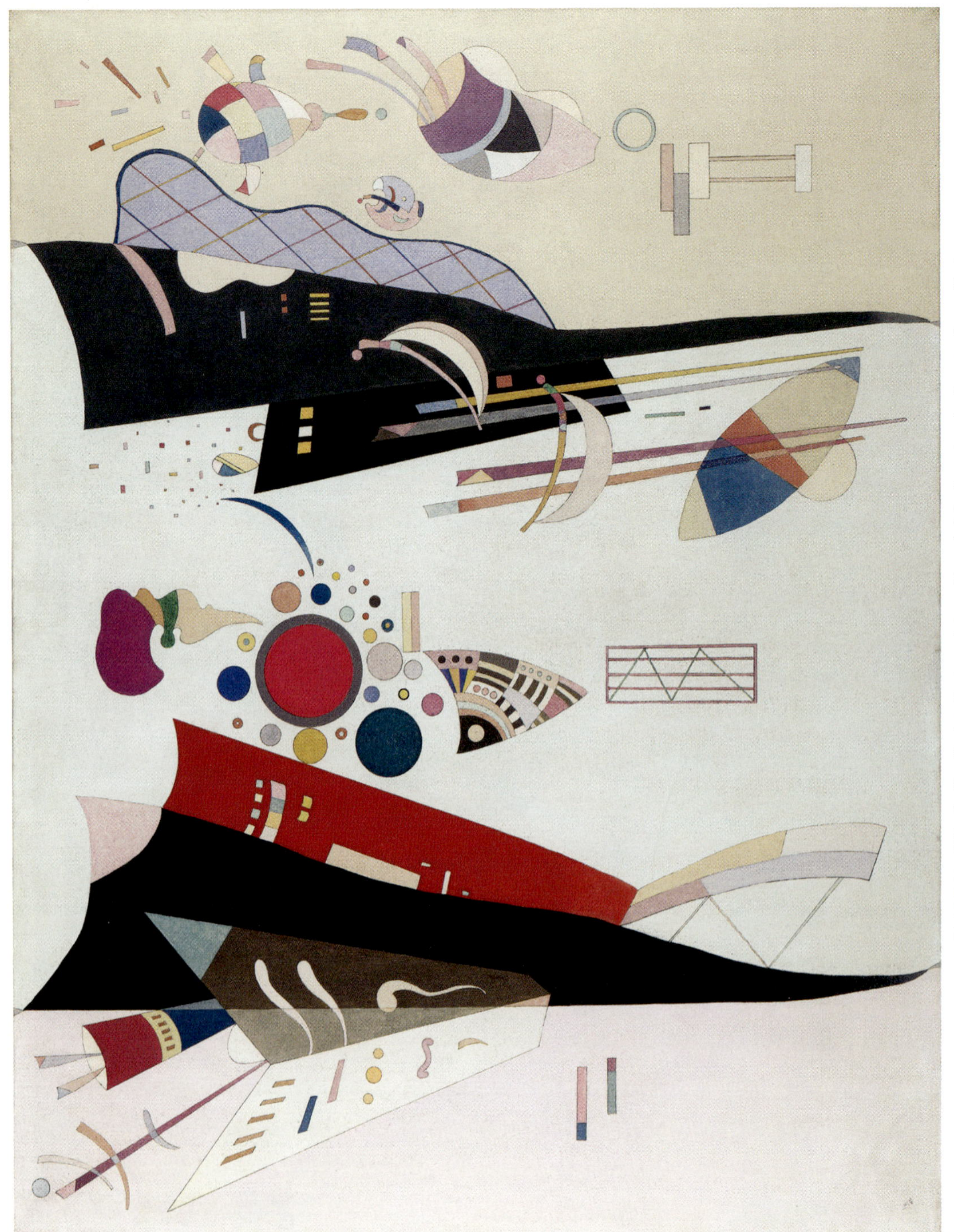

PLATE 24. Wassily Kandinsky, *Reciprocal Accord* (1942), Musée nationale d'art moderne, Paris

KOJÈVE'S *"LES PEINTURES CONCRÈTES DE KANDINSKY"*

ALEXANDRE KOJÈVE'S ESSAY on Kandinsky is markedly different from his other work of the period—from either his *Introduction to the Reading of Hegel* (the published version of which was actually assembled from notes by Raymond Queneau) or the two-part article derived from his dissertation on the nineteenth-century Russian philosopher Vladimir Soloviev.[1] In contrast to the relatively dense prose of those texts, "Les Peintures concrètes de Kandinsky" treads lightly, assuming no particular familiarity with aesthetics or philosophy more broadly. Like both *Über das Geistige* and *Punkt und Linie zu Fläche*, it avoids any direct mention of Hegel or dialectic (however much they are indirectly present) and, equally unusual for a work by Kojève, it includes no reference at all to Desire. Clearly the essay was aimed not at those following the seminar on Hegel's *Phenomenology of Spirit* at the École des hautes études but instead at a wider, less philosophically oriented audience—Kandinsky's audience. "Les Peintures concrètes" is perhaps best seen as a kind of "corrective" to Kandinsky's earlier texts. It attempts to reconcile some of the inconsistencies or contradictions in those works, to make their arguments more conceptually coherent, and so also to produce a more fully realized (if still accessibly written) response to Hegel's *Aesthetics*.[2]

It is this function as "corrective" that also explains what is by far the text's most unexpected omission. Very much unlike *Über das Geistige* (not to mention Kojève's own other writings of the period), "Les Peintures concrètes" avoids any and all reference to Spirit. It is not posited as the essence of art, not the motor driving historical change. In "Les Peintures concrètes de Kandinsky," those roles have been assumed instead by the Beautiful (*Le Beau*).

It will take us a while to sort out the various motives and implications of that substitution. Plainly not the least of them, though, is that it seems to open for art the possibility of a history that would not simply be a chapter (relatively brief and long since concluded) within the larger history of spirit. Presumably Kojève felt that, so long as *Geist* continued to be held up as the essence of art, art would necessarily seem an historical also-ran, outdistanced by philosophy on the road to concrete universality. No doubt he saw *Über das Geistige* as simply being confused on this point. One of the real shortcomings of Kandinsky's essay is in fact that it never pushes beyond an alignment of (nonrepresentational) painting with music—as if, in demonstrating that the one art form could yet be the other's equal, the *Aesthetics*'s entire argument would thereby somehow be dismantled. In essence, Kandinsky was so focused on that moment in Hegel's account when painting ceded its spiritual dominance to music that he lost sight of the subsequent turns in the narrative. As a result, his text never really answers to the Hegelian contention that all of the arts had now outlived their spiritual relevance, their role in the development of *Geist* having been taken over by, first, religion and, more recently, philosophy. According to Hegel, philosophy is "the highest form of inwardness," because "it brings to our minds the same content [as art and religion] . . . but makes its own and knows conceptually what otherwise is only the content of subjective feeling or pictorial thinking."[3] Although *Über das Geistige* had successfully defended painting against accusations of pictorial thinking, it had still left it wide open to—even courted—the charge of "subjective feeling." Not so "Les Peintures concrètes de Kandinsky." As we will see, Kojève's essay provides the basis for a history of painting that is not only entirely its own but that also culminates in the concrete objectivity of Kandinsky's art. Even if its account is not primarily a historical one, it nonetheless manages to present the medium as having, precisely, unfolded and "prove[n] its object, according to the necessity of its own inner nature."[4]

That Kojève chose to assert the autonomy of art by identifying the Beautiful as its object or essence might seem to suggest a reversion to the principles of Kant's third *Critique*.[5] Yet "Les Peintures concrètes" remains Hegelian (and so resolutely un-Kantian) in fundamental respects, not only in its devaluation of the subjective—and its concomitant assumption of the wholly objective basis of beauty—but, equally, in its contention that the beauty of art is superior to the beauty of nature. For Kant, art manifested only a dependent beauty, in contrast to the free beauty of the natural world. The view held by Hegel was almost the reverse. "The beauty of art is beauty born of the spirit and born again," he famously stated, "and the higher the spirit and its productions stand above nature and its phenomena, the higher too is the beauty of art above that of nature."[6] Although Kojève pointedly uncoupled art from any direct connection to *Geist*, he would still adhere to the Hegelian view that natural beauty was inferior to the beauty of art precisely because, and to the extent that, in art the Beautiful manifested a certain freedom from nature.

Rather than from Kant, Kojève appears to have derived his argument regarding art's relation to the Beautiful from a source much less well known in the West but still deeply familiar to Kojève: the writings of Vladimir Soloviev. Not only had

Kojève written his dissertation on Soloviev at the University of Heidelberg under the supervision of Karl Jaspers, he had also completed, just before beginning his essay on Kandinsky, a two-part summary of Soloviev's work for the *Revue d'histoire et de philosophie religieuses*.[7] As Kojève explained there, in Soloviev's philosophical system the Absolute was not the singular achievement of spirit or *Geist*, but rather the collective aim of three interrelated "hypostases"—Feeling, Willing, and Thinking—each of which had its own guiding essence or object. These were the Beautiful, the Good, and the True, respectively.[8] To a certain extent, we can see this hypostatic trinity as aligned with the three "moments" of spirit identified by Hegel as art, religion, and philosophy, albeit with this one crucial difference: according to Soloviev, they were not successive phases in a now largely completed development but, rather, three equally vital aspects of an Absolute toward which humanity was still striving.[9] Although the "contents" of these hypostases were held to be different, Soloviev maintained that all three were the same in *substance*, the Beautiful being, then, "simply an embodiment in sensuous form of that very ideal content which, prior to such embodiment, is called the True and the Good."[10]

In "Les Peintures concrètes de Kandinsky," Kojève avoided the religious connotations of Soloviev's argument; in fact, neither "the Good" nor "the True" are mentioned. Not surprisingly, Kojève also worked to dissociate the Beautiful from "feeling," claiming instead that the Beautiful is only fully realized, only made "concrete," when it has been completely divested of subjectivity. Despite all of this, however, Kojève's account clearly encourages us to regard the Beautiful as had Soloviev, as a facet of the Absolute—something on par with *Geist* but possessing its own distinct, sensuous content.

If Kojève looked to Soloviev's conception of the Beautiful for a means to address some of the deficiencies of *Über das Geistige*, he may well have been prompted by the fact that, in his own writings on art and aesthetics, Soloviev had explicitly contested Hegel's claim that art was now a thing of the past. According to Soloviev, that claim amounted to an underestimation of the sensuous—to declarations of its sublation by spirit that were wholly premature—and so also to an undervaluation of art's role in attaining concrete universality or (to use his preferred term once again) the Absolute. Soloviev admitted that "sculpture [had been] brought to its final perfection by the ancient Greeks," and that it was unlikely that "further progress [would] be made in heroic epic and pure tragedy" either. He even conceded that "modern European nations [had] exhausted all species of art" theretofore known, and yet he refused to admit that art had no future. "Separate branches [of art] attain their perfection and develop no more," it was true; but "to make up for this, other branches come into being." It only stood to reason, therefore, that if art had a future, it would lie "in quite a new sphere of activity."[11] In short, Soloviev already offered something like a variation on the core argument of *Über das Geistige*, even if, in 1890, he had failed to identify nonrepresentational painting as the "new sphere" of art that would eventually emerge.

Kojève, though he never directly acknowledged this debt to Soloviev, nonetheless paid indirect tribute by beginning "Les Peintures concrètes" with virtually the same opening that Soloviev had used in his essay "The Meaning of Art." "A tree growing beautifully in the open and a tree beautifully painted on canvas produce the same kind of aesthetic impression," Soloviev had written, "—it is not for nothing that in both instances the same word is used to express it."[12] In Soloviev's essay, as would also be the case in Kojève's, the comparison of the two "beautiful" trees serves both to highlight similarities between art and nature and to throw their differences into relief. Soloviev, however, placed rather more emphasis on the similarities or contiguities, insisting that art "consists not in the repetition [or imitation of nature], but in the continuation of the artistic work begun by nature—in a further and more complete solution of the same artistic task."[13] That task, he argued, was the promulgation and increasing perfection of the Beautiful. And just as man—*human* being—was nature become self-conscious, so the work of art was an extension of nature's work at a higher, more fully reflexive level.[14]

Although similar notions are implicit in Kojève's reuse of Soloviev's arboreal comparison, "Les Peintures concrètes" places much greater weight on the *differences* between the real and represented trees. One of the more curious consequences of this emphasis is that Kojève neglects to define the Beautiful, despite its absolute centrality to his argument; nor does he even identify which specific characteristics the two trees have in common that qualify them both as "beautiful." Presumably he felt he was adhering to a given or preexisting understanding of the term, which therefore required no further elaboration on his part. Under the circumstances, I think we have to assume that the understanding in question was *Hegel's*, and that "Les Peintures concrètes" adheres fairly closely to its terms. Before turning to an analysis of Kojève's essay, then, we might do well to look briefly first at how the Beautiful is characterized in the *Aesthetics*, as well as at the relation between natural beauty and artistic beauty as it is presented there.

In the opening of the *Aesthetics's* first chapter, concerning the "Concept of the Beautiful as Such," Hegel insisted that "the beautiful must be grasped as Idea, in particular as Idea in a determinate form, i.e. as Ideal."[15] He followed immediately thereafter with the claim that "the Idea as such is nothing but the Concept, the real existence of the Concept, and the unity of the two."[16] Already here he would have us understand that the Beautiful entails the concrete appearance of the Concept (this is what "real existence" seems to imply)—of its diversification into particular manifestations, as well as their unity under or within the Concept itself.

Hegel would go on to argue, as would Soloviev in turn, that nature "foreshadows" (*geahnt*) the Concept of beauty as it appears in art. But he also insisted (in a manner akin to that later taken up by Kojève) that no natural thing could be *fully* beautiful—this, even though the Idea of beauty entailed a specifically "organic" unity. In a natural organism, Hegel asserted, the (inner) soul was to be regarded as the Concept that was realized in the (external) body: "we must regard the body and its members," he wrote, "as the existence of the systematic articulation of the Concept itself."[17] Despite the diversity of its individual members, the organism was unified by the simple self-identity of the soul. And this is the crux of the matter for Hegel: the living thing fails to be truly beautiful because its (external) members do not make the (inner) soul fully manifest. Insofar as the soul is some inner, hidden principle of unity, the body whose unifying organs are internal and hidden is an adequate expression of it, and nature is (partially or imperfectly) beautiful. Yet to the extent that the soul remains hidden, the organic unity of the body fails to be fully apparent, and so the organism fails to be fully beautiful.[18] To be sure, this is not quite the argument that Kojève will make. Even so, as we will see throughout the present chapter, his conception of the Beautiful—indeed, his veritable equation of the Beautiful with the structure of the Hegelian Concept—turns precisely on the kind of self-sustaining, "organic" unity that the Concept is understood to possess.

Again, in his discussion of the real and represented trees, Kojève attends primarily to their differences, to both the distinctions between the trees themselves and the relative purity and primacy of the beauty they body forth:

One and the same Beautiful is incarnated in the real tree and the painted tree. But the incarnation of the Beautiful in the real tree—that is to say, the beauty of this tree, the Beautiful in the tree or of the tree—differs from the Beautiful in the painted tree. The real tree is "in the first place" a tree; it is only following—"in the second place"—that it is beautiful, that it is an incarnation of the Beautiful. . . . The real tree is beautiful "in addition," "also," and it remains a tree even if it is not beautiful or ceases to be beautiful. Things are completely different with the painted tree, the painting "Tree". . . . It is not beautiful "also" and "in addition": it is only beautiful—or nothing at all.[19]

—In any case, Kojève declares in the next line, it is not *un tableau*. Admittedly, we discover shortly thereafter that even the tableau could in some sense be regarded as "nothing at all." Wholly weightless, intangible, it has few of the characteristics we typically associate with *things*: "It wouldn't weigh down the pan of a scale," Kojève insists, "wouldn't alter the needle of a galvanometer. . . . It would do nothing to avoid a blow, but the blow would be able to do nothing to it."[20] Indeed Kojève claims that the tableau, as distinct from the painting (*la peinture*), doesn't even belong to the universe of real things—"there it exists not as a tableau, but only as canvas, oil, etc."[21] The tableau, we are left to infer, is simply the Beautiful in the painting, or the painting insofar as it is beautiful. On the heels of this recognition it becomes increasingly apparent that, even if Kojève's argument revolves crucially around the art of painting, he cares very little about paintings; his interest is almost exclusively in tableaux.

However audacious it may seem, Kojève's assertion of the wholly immaterial nature of the tableau actually takes its cue from arguments advanced in Hegel's *Aesthetics*. According to Hegel, works of art in general, and paintings in particular, display a distinct form of "sensuousness," one that has been "liberated from the scaffolding of mere materiality."[22] What is sensible in the work of art—what "shines forth" (*herausscheinen*) or makes its appearance (*Erscheinung*) there—is a presence specifically to *Geist*.[23] In contrast to what Hegel describes as an *appetitive* relation to things, in which, driven by desire, "man maintains himself in [those things] by using and consuming them," in his relation to works of art, the object is left free to exist on its own account: "[man] relates himself to it without desire, as to an object which is for the contemplative side of spirit alone."[24] In this sense, the work's material presence is a matter of indifference, if not complete irrelevance, because the work isn't there to be either used or consumed. Nor, Hegel adds, is it to be touched, smelled, or tasted. Those senses are all far too involved with sensuous immediacy for them to properly take in things that are fundamentally *geistige* in nature. Almost by definition, then, works of art appeal exclusively to our hearing or our sight. And where sight is concerned, Hegel insists, it is enough that they should "appear only as the surface and as a pure appearance of the sensuous [*Schein des Sinnlichen*]."[25]

This reference to "surface" (*Oberfläche*) reminds us that, although Hegel intends his description to pertain to all the visual arts, it has a special purchase on the art of painting. (Painting is the "shining" example, as it were, of the phenomenon in question.) For painting—and, again, Hegel knew only the representational kind—contracts the solid, three-dimensionality of the natural world onto a single plane, effectively de-realizing space, de-materializing objects, turning everything represented into pure appearance, or *Schein*. The things depicted become in the process *vergeistigt*, remade exclusively for the purpose of spirit's self-reflection.[26] Simultaneously they suggest, precisely because of their withdrawal from three-dimensionality, a deficiency in tangible, external form—its inadequacy, in other words, to the depiction of subjective inner life. As Hegel says, the "reduction of the three dimensions to a level surface is implicit in the [romantic] principle of *interiorization*."[27] Nature's loss, he would have us see, is wholly to the gain of spirit.

That Kojève was looking specifically to the precedent of Hegel's *Schein* in his characterization of the tableau is indicated by his own repeated assertions that painting is an art of *surfaces*, yet surfaces that are wholly immaterial. Such intangible "superficiality," he suggests, is what finally distinguishes painting from either sculpture or architecture, both of which remain fundamentally rooted in literal, physical space. Kojève even goes so far as to describe painting's pictorial illusionism as, precisely, a transformation wrought on those other, three-dimensional forms of art: "the tableau," he says, "'represents' a space, that is, a statue (living or not) or a building (artificial or natural)."[28] Implicit in that description, I would argue, is a very Hegelian conception of the arts *as system*, with painting marking a passage beyond the other visual forms. It's clear, in any case, that what is won in painting—or, rather, in the tableau—is a freedom from both materiality and natural, three-dimensional space. "The tableau," Kojève declares, "is *only* surface. That's why the tableau is essentially *flat*. Not the canvas (which can be concave or convex, etc.), but the tableau as tableau."[29]

In taking this tack, Kojève effectively sidesteps the worry expressed by Kandinsky that the suppression of pictorial illusionism, so crucial to many early twentieth-century movements toward abstraction, might bring unwanted attention to the material plane of the canvas. In *Über das Geistige* that fear had been couched as follows:

As far as drawing and painting are concerned, the turn away from the representational—and one of the first steps into the realm of the abstract—was the exclusion of the third dimension, i.e., the attempt to keep the "picture" as painting upon a flat surface. Modeling was abandoned. In this way, the real object was moved nearer to the abstract, a move that indicated a certain progress. As an immediate consequence, however, one's possibilities became pinned down to the real surface of the canvas, so that painting took on new, purely material overtones. This pinning down was at the same time a limitation of possibilities.[30]

For Kandinsky's argument in *Über das Geistige*, the merest suggestion that the painting was to be identified with—or simply seen as adhering to—the literal surface of the canvas would have spelled its complete undoing. His entire case depended on linking representation to materiality, and then suggesting that, by getting rid of all representational content, matter could finally be transcended. Yet the materiality of the *canvas*—touted in most modernist accounts of painting—threatened to trouble that argument by constantly resurfacing in critics' and viewers' awareness. Kojève did much to neutralize the issue by locating the moment of matter's sublation considerably earlier, with the rise of easel painting as a medium. The tableau's pictorial illusionism, he claimed, had already effected the dematerialization of three-dimensional space and tangible form. Kandinsky's turn to nonrepresentational painting was then left to play a very different role in

Kojève's revised history of the medium. In "Les Peintures concrètes" that move becomes important because it marks a turn, specifically *not* toward abstraction, but rather toward what Kojève described as concrete and fully objective painting. His argument unfolds roughly as follows.

On the basis of his comparison of the two exemplary trees, Kojève had defined representational painting as "the art of extracting the Beautiful from its concrete incarnation, from this 'other thing,' which is—'also'—beautiful, and of preserving it [*de le maintenir*] in its purity."[31] That process of extraction entailed, he said, a certain degree of abstraction as well, in that the artist could never reproduce the Beautiful-of-the-tree in its entirety, but necessarily had to accommodate it to the planarity of the tableau.

The Beautiful-of-the-real-tree is not only in the Beautiful of the flat visual aspect of this tree but also the Beautiful of the entire concrete, real tree: the Beautiful of the tree is also the Beautiful of its depth, of its sounds, of its smell, of its rough trunk, etc. Just like the tree itself, the Beautiful-of-the-tree is a Beautiful in three dimensions: tall, wide, and deep. The Beautiful-of-the-painted-tree, by contrast, is only the Beautiful of the *flat* surface of the tableau. Besides, the tree doesn't exist in a vacuum: it is on earth, under a sky, etc., etc.—in short, it is part of the *Universe*, and it cannot be isolated from this universe, from the concrete world of real things. Accordingly, the Beautiful-of-the-real-tree is also a non-isolated Beautiful, not withdrawn into itself, but a Beautiful inserted into the Beautiful of the Universe and, above all, into the Beautiful of the "landscape" of which it is a part.[32]

Here, too, Kojève is clearly following Hegel, who likewise regarded "abstraction" as synonymous with "extraction" and viewed both as processes enacted upon the "concrete." Etymology supports this understanding: the German verb *abstrahieren* derives from the Latin *abstrahere*, meaning "to draw away" or "remove something (from something else)." *Konkret*, by contrast, from the Latin *concrescere*, implies things grown together. Thus, for Hegel, "concrete" referred to anything—whether a tree or a philosophical system—that constituted a whole whose parts, having developed together over time, were mutually adapted and internally related. *Abstraktion*, Hegel wrote, was "a *sundering* of the concrete and an *isolating* of its determinations; through it only *single* properties and moments are seized."[33] To "extract" the Beautiful-of-the-real-tree would thus be to "abstract" it from that concrete entity that was the tree itself and to regard that single, "one-sided" (*einseitig*) aspect apart from its connection to the larger whole.

Kojève additionally argued that, because both the extraction of the Beautiful and its abstraction had to be carried out by a particular individual (namely, the artist), the resulting image was always also to some extent subjective, affected by the artist's mood and temperament, physical vantage point, and previous experiences. Again, Kojève insisted, this was true of all representational paintings, which is to say, all paintings prior to Kandinsky's. "Every tableau that incarnates a Beautiful already incarnated first in a real, nonartistic object," he wrote, "is necessarily and essentially an *abstract* and *subjective* tableau."[34] Kojève did concede, however, that the degree of abstraction and subjectivity could vary widely from tableau to tableau. In fact he proceeded to divide the field of representational painting into four general types—symbolic, realist, impressionist, and expressionist—based precisely on the ratio of abstraction to subjectivity present in the image.

Expressionist painting, Kojève explained, is the most subjective in that its aim is to reproduce less the tree, or the Beautiful within that tree, than the artist's attitude (itself in some sense beautiful) toward the tree and its beauty. Despite being the most subjective, such works are simultaneously the least abstract, in that it is *his* attitude that the artist attempts to visually reproduce. His viewpoint, while singular (and strongly colored by emotion), in no way limits his access to his subject. Instead, it is wholly integral to it.

Impressionist paintings, by contrast, embody the Beautiful of the visual impression that the object made on the artist. "There is therefore less subjectivism than in the expressionist painting," Kojève stated, adding that "if—in this case again— the painter paints less the object than himself, he is now absorbed by the object, whereas before it was the object that was absorbed by him."[35]

The *realist* painting is distinguished from either its expressionist or impressionist counterparts in that, there, the artist aims at an "in-depth ocular study" of the object in question. Accordingly the subjective elements of the composition will be substantially reduced, potentially even limited to the particular vantage point from which the object was observed. But the degree of abstraction will have concomitantly increased, and for all of the reasons already mentioned: everything exceeding the flat visual aspect of the (three-dimensional) object and its beauty will have to have been suppressed.

Symbolic paintings, finally, are the least subjective of all in that in them the object is represented schematically, the schema referring "neither to the personal 'attitude' of the painter nor to the visual impression that the object produces in him."[36] Kojève holds up as an example Egyptian painting, in which single, frontal eyes inhabit profile faces. In such images subjectivity is at a minimum—much less even than in realist paintings—though the level of abstraction is correspondingly much greater.

Rather curiously for an essay by Kojève, "Les Peintures concrètes" leaves the potential historical dimension of these distinctions largely unremarked. Given the reference to Egyptian art, however, and Kojève's (re)use of the term "symbolic" to designate that work, little imagination is required on the part of the reader to conjecture how that history would have gone: from an early period dominated by the symbolic, through realist and then impressionist phases, and finally to expressionism. Indeed, when Kojève summarized his essay in 1966 for publication in the journal *XXe Siècle*, he added a footnote charting precisely this course. "Just as with animal species," he wrote, "pictorial species evolve over time. Historical evolution has generally occurred in the sense of a progressive augmentation of the subjective element and a diminution in the degree of abstraction: symbolism→realism→impressionism→expressionism."[37] Still, both in that summary and in "Les Peintures concrètes" itself, Kojève, when laying out the four different types of painting and describing their characteristics, proceeded in reverse order, beginning with the expressionist and concluding with the symbolic. Certainly one advantage of this reversal is that it encourages any reader who might be so inclined to recognize in recent artistic developments—above all, in the work of the two specific artists subsequently discussed by Kojève—a dialectical or quasi-dialectical return to aspects of painting's symbolic past.

Picasso's work is the first held up in this light. His, we are told, is a hybrid art, a kind of expressionist symbolism or symbolic expressionism: "That combination is carried out in such a way that this painting is at once the most *abstract* and the most *subjective* of all possible representational paintings: the *abstraction* of the objective symbol serves to 'represent' the *subjectivism* of the painter's personal attitude."[38]

Within the field of representational painting, the symbolic and the expressionist appear to be wholly antithetical modes, the ratio of abstraction to subjectivism in the one being the inverse of their proportion in the other. Picasso's "genius," Kojève says, is to have attempted a synthesis of the two—bringing into conjunction the poles around which the entire field had been structured, effectively enfolding the whole. But even an artist as great as Picasso could pull off such a feat only occasionally. The symbolic-expressionist combination is so volatile, Kojève implies, that the majority of attempts simply annihilate themselves "in the void of absolute abstraction and pure subjectivism."[39] One needn't read too carefully between the lines to gather that Kojève regards Picasso's art as achieving only a failed or false sublation. For all its "genius," his work is unable to reconcile the symbolic with the expressionist in a productive, elevating way. Too much of its energy is simply spent in vain.[40]

Kojève presents Kandinsky's nonrepresentational paintings, by contrast, as both fully successful and fully resolved. Never having existed outside of or apart from the tableau, the Beautiful embodied there, he says, was never extracted from anything, and so ought not to be described (whatever our previous inclinations) as "abstract." Neither, obviously, was that Beautiful abstracted or extracted *by anyone*.

In that sense, Kojève declares, Kandinsky's tableaux are wholly objective, wholly impersonal.

For if every "representational" tableau is [an image of] a thing seen by . . . , in such a way that it is relevant to know *by whom* the thing is seen, that is, *whom* the tableau is *by*, the [nonrepresentational] tableau is the thing itself, and it is just as irrelevant to know who saw or sees that thing as it is to know if a real tree is seen by someone and by whom it is seen, if it is seen. If—for those who don't know Kandinsky personally—he is nothing without "his" tableaux, those tableaux are *everything* they are *without* Kandinsky.[41]

We will refrain for the moment from assessing the accuracy of this characterization of Kandinsky's work. For now it may be enough to say that our judgment will ultimately turn on whether the compositions of individual tableaux seem to have been generated out of a logic internal to painting or whether they appear instead as largely arbitrary or idiosyncratic. Kojève's conviction, in any case, is clear: Kandinsky's tableaux are neither abstract nor subjective, and in that sense ought to be seen as both the antithesis of Picasso's work and, even more importantly, the overcoming or sublation of the symbolic-expressionist opposition in which that work was rooted. (Had Kojève diagrammed his argument, it undoubtedly would have looked much like the schematic rendering of Figure 14.) Although it is never phrased it in quite this way, the entire essay encourages us to conclude that Kandinsky's tableaux constitute a determinate negation of representational—which is to say, of all previous—painting.

Of course, up until 1936, when Kojève wrote the essay, even Kandinsky had been accustomed to referring to his nonrepresentational paintings as "abstract."

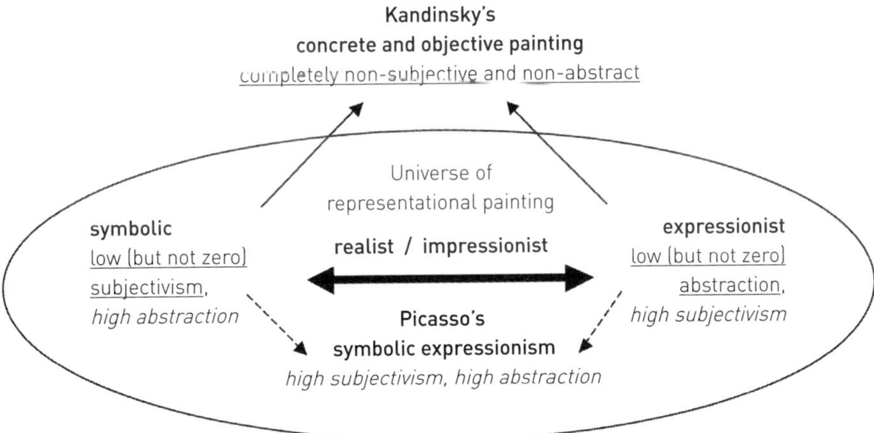

FIGURE 14. Diagram of Alexandre Kojève's argument in the last two sections of "Les Peintures concrètes de Kandinsky."

A significant portion of the last section of "Les Peintures concrètes" is devoted to correcting what Kojève regarded as this widespread misconception, and to re-designating those tableaux as wholly "concrete." His argument revolves around the completeness and integrity of the individual work:

Now, if the Beautiful was not *extracted* or *abstracted* but created whole cloth, it is—in its very *being*—not *abstract* but *concrete*. Being created whole cloth, that is entirely, it is as whole: nothing is missing from it, nothing was removed from it, since this Beautiful—nonexistent outside of the tableau—cannot be richer and more real than it is in the tableau or as the tableau. The Beautiful is thus in the tableau in the full plenitude of its being, which is to say, it is there in all its concretion; the Beautiful of the tableau is a real and concrete Beautiful, the tableau is a real and concrete Beautiful; the real tableau is concrete.[42]

Kandinsky's tableaux are to be understood as concrete, in other words, precisely because they are integral—organically unified and therefore self-sustaining—wholes. No part of them has been extracted or abstracted from anything, and that includes the Beautiful that they (therefore wholly) embody. Consequently, we might with equal accuracy refer to such paintings as "total" or "absolute," Kojève says.[43] And, in phrasing things this way, he clearly means to remind us that there is yet another, related—but even more fully Hegelian—sense in which those tableaux might be regarded as "concrete." This is a sense left largely unarticulated by Kojève, though it is everywhere implicit in the larger argument of "Les Peintures concrètes." "The truth is the whole," Hegel tells us in the *Phenomenology*. But the whole is not what it is "in truth" until the dialectical process of self-becoming has arrived at its conclusion: "The whole . . . is merely the essential nature reaching its completeness through the process of its own development. Of the Absolute it must be said that it is essentially a *result*."[44] Again, although Kojève nowhere explicitly makes this case, being Kojève, he still undoubtedly wants us to see that the totality or wholeness of Kandinsky's tableaux—that is, their very status *as concrete*—is the culmination of a particular history, one in which painting's "essential nature" has at last been realized.[45] It is only at this point, at the end of the process of its self-development, that, according to Kojève, we are finally able to make out the "self" in question and to discern what its "essential nature" in fact is. It is only in the concrete tableaux of Kandinsky that painting at last *proves its object*; and it is only in them as well that the Beautiful, as the object or essence of painting, finally wins its freedom from nature. Looking backward from the vantage point opened up by Kandinsky's *peintures concrètes*, Kojève would have us see that an entire history comes into view—a history whose protagonist, the Beautiful, begins its existence within the totality of nature, then is extracted and abstracted in representational painting, and finally emerges as itself a totality, wholly self-sufficient (having shed its earlier dependence upon nature), in the nonrepresentational art of Kandinsky. Kojève summarizes the claim this way:

Each of Kandinsky's tableaux is a real, complete, and therefore concrete universe, self-contained and self-sufficient: a universe that, just like the nonartistic Universe, the uni-totality of real things, is only in itself, by itself, and for itself. One cannot say that these tableaux "represent" fragments of that nonartistic Universe. One can say at the very most that they *are* fragments of that Universe: Kandinsky's tableaux belong to the Universe in the same way as do trees, animals, rocks, men, States, clouds ..., as does everything real that belongs to (is in) the Universe while constituting this Universe. But where the *Beautiful* of Kandinsky's tableaux are concerned, it is more accurate to say that it is independent of the Beautiful of the Universe and of the Beautiful of the things that belong to this Universe: the Beautiful of each tableau by Kandinsky is the Beautiful of a complete universe, and these artistic Beautifuls come to stand alongside—in a sense—the unique and artistic Beautiful of the real Universe.[46]

It seems important to note that portions of this passage closely echo ideas that Kandinsky himself had expressed much earlier. In a footnote to his "Rückblicke" (Reminiscences) of 1913, for example, Kandinsky had written: "In this respect [that is, in respect of movement away from the imitation of nature], painting has caught up with music, and both assume an ever-increasing tendency to create 'absolute' works, i.e., completely 'objective' works that, like the works of nature, come into existence 'of their own accord,' . . . as independent beings."[47] Indeed we might regard the entirety of the argument of "Les Peintures concrètes" as having been similarly presaged in a brief and rather anomalous section of *Über das Geistige*—one where Kandinsky identifies and differentiates among three distinct "internal necessities," none of which is directly correlated with spirit, even as all are held to shape the nature of art at any given moment.[48] The first, as Kandinsky enumerates them, is the element of personality, the artist's own need to express what is peculiar to him- or herself. The second "necessity," by contrast, is suprapersonal, embodying not what is unique to the artist but what is peculiar to the age—what makes the work, in other words, "the child of its time." The most important, Kandinsky says, is the third: "the pure and eternally artistic . . . which is to be seen in the works of every artist, of every nation, and of every period." "The development of art," Kandinsky writes, "consists to a certain extent in the ability of the pure and eternally artistic [here Kojève would say "the Beautiful"] to free itself from the elements of personality and temporal style. . . . Thus . . . the struggle of the objective against the subjective."[49] For better or worse, this line of thought was soon dropped. Coming as it did in the section of *Über das Geistige* on "The Language of Forms and Colors," it quickly gave way to a much more extended discussion of light and dark and the complexities of differing hues. And Kandinsky never returned to pick up the thread—with the result that his claim for art's growing freedom from subjectivity never got linked to the larger argument about painting's increasing emancipation from nature's materiality via its turn to nonrepresentational forms. One suspects that the argument lingered a bit longer with Kojève, however, and that in his reading of *Über das Geistige* it became not an anomalous or peripheral claim but something much more central. It may well have been what planted the seedling for "Les Peintures concrètes." In any event, it's clear from these textual similarities that Kojève's essay should be seen as continuing or developing from Kandinsky's own earlier theoretical writings—resolving in the process some of those writings' internal contradictions, as well as the inadequacies of their response to Hegel, but not striking out into wholly new territory of its own. Kojève conceived of the text, I'm convinced, as bringing to a close an argument whose earlier moments (constituted by Hegel's *Aesthetics* and Kandinsky's writings, respectively) had each proven inconsistent or incomplete and therefore still "abstract." No doubt he regarded "Les Peintures concrètes," in contrast, as fully concrete—above all because it had shown that Kandinsky's tableaux were themselves the concrete culmination of a historical development specific to painting.

AND WHAT OF KANDINSKY? What, we ought to ask, did he make of the argument of "Les Peintures concrètes"? And what difference, if any, did that argument make to Kandinsky's art? To address the simpler question first: I'm inclined to think that, in many crucial respects at least, Kandinsky accepted the essay's claims. For one thing, we have Kojève's testimony to that effect. In a prefatory statement appended to his 1966 article, "Pourquoi concret," Kojève explained that that publication summarized a longer essay he had written at the express request of his uncle, that the two men had discussed its argument on multiple occasions, and that Kandinsky, having read and annotated the manuscript, had "declared himself in accord with its essential content."[50] Further evidence of Kandinsky's approval can be found in the artist's own writings—above all in his adoption, after 1936, of the term "concrete" to refer to paintings he had previously regarded as "abstract."[51]

The story told by the paintings themselves is similar, though also somewhat more complicated. Before turning to look at them, we should first register the fact that "Les Peintures concrètes" never differentiates among Kandinsky's nonrepresentational tableaux. All of them—the entirety of Kandinsky's output from 1910 onward[52]—is regarded by Kojève as being of a piece. It's true that, whenever his argument demands a specific case, he turns to the example of *Circle-Triangle*—a work that, although only hypothetical, must belong (given its geometric "subject matter") to Kandinsky's Bauhaus period. Presumably the paintings of that era held a kind of normative status for Kojève.[53] Even so, the world-historical moment, in his view, the event that concluded (and so made "concrete") art's developing relation to the Beautiful, occurred much earlier, when painting first cut its ties to the representation of nature. Any subsequent changes were comparatively minor refinements to that already achieved end.[54]

I have no intention of challenging the significance of Kandinsky's turn to non-representation; that was a world-(art-)historical event no matter how one reckons such things. And yet, it also seems to me that the changes in Kandinsky's oeuvre—not only in the years just after 1910, but also following the appearance of "Les Peintures concrètes"—are more sustained and more substantial than mere tinkering would suggest. Throughout his career, Kandinsky remained invested in the ongoing development of his art. Evidently he didn't share Kojève's conviction that history had come to an end.[55] Certainly not *art*'s history. If Kandinsky's writings leave open the possibility that that end might yet be realized, they assert with far greater conviction that it will not be anytime soon. Indeed Kandinsky's oeuvre is exceptional in its commitment to a paradigm of continual transformation. Even among other avowedly modernist practices (Mondrian's being the most obvious case in point), Kandinsky's stands out for its incessant unsettledness.[56] In Part II, we will examine the extent to which the development of his work can be seen as dialectical; for the moment, I simply want to look at a single painting produced in the wake of "Les Peintures concrètes," so as to gauge the immediate impact of its argument on Kandinsky's artistic production.

The painting in question, *Thirty* (Figure 15), was completed in January 1937, roughly six months after Kojève signed and dated his manuscript. I've chosen to focus on this particular work not only because of its chronological proximity to "Les Peintures concrètes," but also because it seems so relatively unanticipated by the paintings that preceded it. Its composition is as surprising as anything in Kandinsky's oeuvre.[57] In that sense, *Thirty* appears to be responding to a new, or perhaps only newly clarified, impetus; something happened toward the end of 1936 to quicken the pace of "development" within Kandinsky's practice.

Two features of the painting especially stand out. First, the palette is restricted to a simple pairing of black and white.[58] In Kandinsky's early color theory (as in Hering's opponent-process model of vision) and again in *Punkt und Linie zu Fläche*, black and white were presented as both primary colors and the poles of a diametric opposition. By restricting its palette to them, *Thirty* achieves maximum dissonance by the most minimal of means. Moreover, in the context of this particular composition, the pair is fully dialectical: black only appears in any given

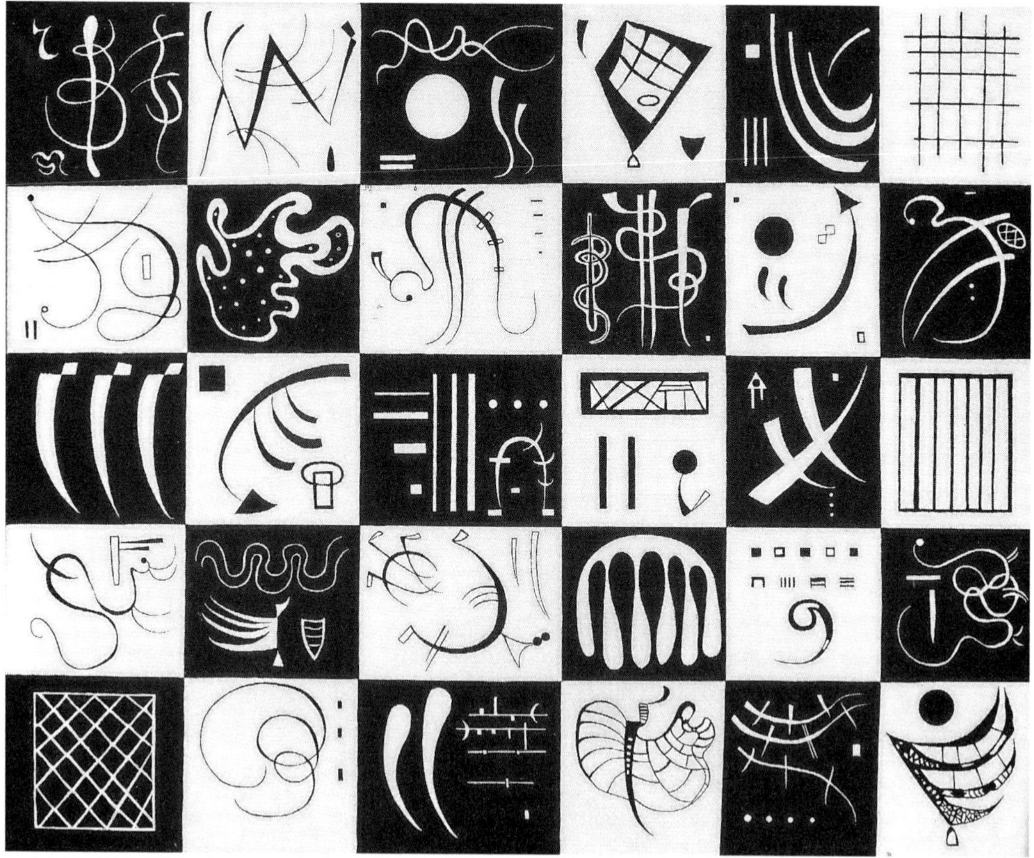

FIGURE 15. Wassily Kandinsky, *Thirty*, 1937. Oil on canvas, 81 × 100 cm. Musée national d'art moderne, Centre Georges Pompidou, Paris. CNAC/MNAM/Dist. RMN–Grand Palais/Art Resource, New York. © Artists Rights Society (ARS), New York.

place to the extent that white does not, and vice versa. Each is in that regard the negation of the other, just as every shape within the composition exists (and so can be grasped) only in relation to the whole.

The second striking feature of *Thirty* is, of course, its subdivision into thirty discrete units. One consequence of that arrangement is the profound decentering of the composition. Rather than a painting with one or two focal points, we are given a highly ordered proliferation: 5×6 individual units, each of which could reasonably stand as a coherent (if still largely decentered) composition on its own. One might even say that the whole of *Thirty* consists of thirty units that are themselves each provisional wholes. In fact, each of them, in its internal counterbalancing of forces and diagrammatic black-and-whiteness, recalls the individual plates of the appendix to *Punkt und Linie zu Fläche*. (Remember, too, that some of those plates had been designed specifically to demonstrate the effects of black/white reversal.) In fact we may be tempted to imagine *Thirty* as having, in some sense, made itself out of the appendix's separate, successive images. It's as if those compositions—which had been revealed, one by one, only after the preceding page had physically been turned—were now able to make their simultaneous appearance as part of a single, comprehensive totality. We witness in *Thirty*, too, the same ambition to dematerialize form that we saw in the plates of *Punkt und Linie* (see Figure 13), in this instance carried out on an even larger scale. Here the illusion is produced by the checkerboard-like alternation of black and white grounds. Scanning across the surface of the painting, we experience a continual figure-ground reversal that effectively disrupts our perception of a level picture plane. Shapes seem to float in an indeterminate "somewhere," their distance from or proximity to us varying with our breadth of focus. The composition, even as it abjures all modeling and so also any reference whatsoever to volumetric form, plainly aims at a high degree of spatial illusion. Said differently, despite the absence within it of represented objects (hence the elimination of any need to illusionistically re-create their three-dimensionality), *Thirty* nonetheless continues to insist on painting's condition as *Schein* or—to use the language favored by Kojève—its status as tableau.

We ought to notice, too, that the individual units of the composition vary considerably in size. Although the lines of the "checkerboard" are more or less straight, they are unevenly spaced, with the result that the thirty "squares" (or, more properly, rectangles) appear commensurate—that is, approximately equal—but by no means uniform.[59] The grid thereby loses any sense it might otherwise have had of being an immutable, a priori structure. Instead we are encouraged to see it as responsive to the various tensions active across the picture plane—tensions that also give shape to the myriad lines and forms of the smaller compositions. The impression, again, is of a careful counterbalancing of forces pulling in any number of directions. This, the work would have us see, is its inner purposiveness: its composition is built of individual units that are (or are meant to appear) not only *self*-sustaining but also *mutually* reinforcing, with every part then seeming absolutely necessary to the unity and cohesion of the whole. *Thirty* suggests analogies with, say, a complexly arcuated architectural interior whose multiple vaults are each at least weakly self-supporting but are made immeasurably stronger as a result of their inclusion within the larger structure. It suggests analogies, too, with the structure of the Hegelian system. As I've argued, both Kandinsky's and Kojève's writings assert that the artist's "concrete" paintings are the product of a particular dialectical-historical development. To the extent that freedom from art's former dependence on nature was won in that development, the paintings might also be regarded as absolute—absolved of all "external" relation. Hence the claim (and the importance of the claim) that those works are "organic," self-supporting wholes—just as is Hegel's philosophical system. In fact, descriptions of that system's structure sound remarkably similar to descriptions we might give of *Thirty*'s composition:

The whole is genuinely whole only in its full, systematic, self-differentiation, and it differentiates itself into parts which, to form a whole, are (and must be) mutually adapted, and internally related as its ordering principle dictates. . . . Accordingly, while the parts are in the whole and constitute its determinate unity, the whole is also immanent in every one of the parts and "informs each part with the nature of the whole."[60]

The idea of a pictorial composition structurally homologous to Hegel's philosophical system had already appeared, albeit in an extremely inchoate form, in *Punkt und Linie zu Fläche*. There, as I argued earlier, Kandinsky had not only described the graphic point in language very close to Hegel's characterizations of classical sculpture; he had also presented the complex "organic unity" of the realized composition as in some sense a return, at a later moment in the dialectic, of the point's undifferentiated cohesion. Extrapolating from these two observations (while bearing in mind Hegel's own frequent recourse to organic metaphors to explain the wholeness or totality of his system), it is possible to sense at least the beginnings of a developing analogy between that system and Kandinsky's art. Insofar as the black-and-white palette and specific shapes of *Thirty* recall the images of *Punkt und Linie*, we might be tempted to see them as recollecting that text's implicit claims for the significance (both artistic and philosophical) of "organic" composition. In any case, *Thirty* advances—if by means that are now wholly visual—a much more articulated version of that argument. It seems to offer its own concrete unity-in-difference as a structural analogue of Hegel's self-sustaining system, and so also as the fulfillment, at a higher level, of classical sculpture's aesthetic promise.[61]

The specifics of the "argument" advanced by *Thirty* are neither found in nor required by "Les Peintures concrètes." Again, according to that essay, all of Kandinsky's paintings from 1910 onward were already fully (and therefore equally) both concrete and absolute. No further changes were called for. That *Thirty* can be construed as having developed beyond any of Kandinsky's earlier compositions suggests, then, a certain departure from the case made by Kojève—even if the strongly Hegelian connotations of that development are largely consistent with (and perhaps unimaginable without) the claims of "Les Peintures concrètes." To further complicate our understanding of the painting's relation to that essay, I'd like to turn once more to Kojève's discussion of the concrete self-sufficiency of Kandinsky's tableaux. To quote again a passage already cited:

Each of Kandinsky's tableaux is a real, complete, and therefore concrete universe, self-contained and self-sufficient: a universe that, just like the nonartistic Universe, the uni-totality of real things, is only in itself, by itself, and for itself. One cannot say that these tableaux "represent" fragments of that nonartistic Universe. One can say at the very most that they *are* fragments of that Universe: Kandinsky's tableaux belong to the Universe in the same way as do trees, animals, rocks, men, States, clouds . . . , as does everything real that belongs to (is in) the Universe while constituting this Universe.[62]

Although it passed unremarked the first time around, we might want to pause now long enough to take stock of that idiosyncratic list of "real things" with which Kandinsky's tableaux are compared. If all the "things" named there belong to the totality of the universe, they nonetheless belong to it in rather different ways. Rocks and clouds, which were discussed in the *Philosophy of Nature* under the rubrics of geology and atmospherics, make up part of what Hegel termed the "terrestrial organism." Trees and animals represent a higher, that is, more complex and more fully developed, level of organic system—as do men (and, one hopes, women), though our simultaneous existence as self-aware, *geistige* beings obviously places us within a category of our own.[63] Most seemingly anomalous of all is the inclusion of *States* among that list of "organic" entities. In fact, twice in "Les Peintures concrètes," Kojève describes Kandinsky's tableaux as being in some way comparable to *États*.[64] In trying to make sense of such comments, we should note that in the spring and fall of 1936—namely, during the two terms bracketing Kojève's work on "Les Peintures concrètes"—discussion in the seminar at the École des hautes études turned to that part of the *Phenomenology* in which Hegel addresses the concept of the modern European state.

It would take us rather too far afield to delve deeply into the issue. Suffice it to say the following: The dialectical struggle between the Master and the Slave, on which Kojève's entire reading of the *Phenomenology* depends, is held by him to reach its end in the creation of a "universal and homogeneous state." The French Revolution, having broken with the ideals of the ancien régime, set the stage for a re-imagining of society based in the reciprocal recognition of all its members. With the arrival of Napoleon these abstract ideals of modern equality and freedom began to be institutionalized. According to both Hegel and Kojève, however, the practical realization of such a modern state depended equally on the theoretical elucidation provided by (Hegelian) philosophy.[65] Much of Kojève's subsequent career can in fact be see as an attempt to fully integrate both halves of this political/philosophical equation.[66] I take it that his mention of *États* in "Les Peintures concrètes" was meant to imply that Kandinsky's tableaux were somehow parallel (historical) achievements, akin to both Hegel's system of absolute knowing and the modern European state in the "organic" relation of their individual parts to one another and the whole.[67]

It's true that "universal and homogeneous," the phrase that Kojève repeatedly uses in the *Introduction* to characterize the modern state, is not a particularly apt description of *Thirty* (or of any of Kandinsky's other compositions, for that matter). Then again, it's not particularly appropriate to Hegel's conception of the state, either. Kojève's generally Marxist convictions seem to be behind its use. I'm even inclined to think that his otherwise fairly inexplicable insistence in "Les Peintures concrètes" that a monochrome—a plane "covered in a uniform color"—would be not only *un tableau* but an "absolutely beautiful" one, is simply an extension of those ideological convictions onto the field of painting.[68] Kojève would subsequently modify his views on the state, substituting the concept of differential *equity* among citizens for any notion of strict equality.[69] Michael Roth has suggested that this reconception of the "Absolute [as] not necessarily a homogenous End or tension-free resting point," but rather a Whole containing contradictions and "passionate counterpoint," was in some sense shaped by Kojève's engagement with his uncle's art.[70] It's an intriguing thought—one roughly the inverse of an argument that might be made for Kandinsky's *Thirty*. That is, the composition of *Thirty* could be seen as comparable in certain respects to that of the ideal state, especially as the latter is described in Hegel's *Philosophy of Right*. As Frederick Beiser has explained, Hegel adheres there to an essentially organic model, which manifests itself in three important features of the state:

First, the whole exists for each of the parts as much as each of the parts exists for the whole; in other words, the individual is as much a means as an end for the state. Second, . . . there must be life in each part of the state, so that each has some degree of autonomy and independence. Third, each part, in maintaining itself and seeking its own self-interest, also promotes the interest of the whole.[71]

Much of this resonates with the descriptions of *Thirty* we've already given. But the similarities don't end there. As noted previously, the whole of the painting's composition is divided into thirty commensurate and largely independent units, each of which serves to organize and hold in balance the competing tensions of its constituent elements. It's these independent units, mediating between the *Kraft* or power of the whole and the variety of particular, often opposed forces pulling the smaller parts in one direction or the other, that give the comparison whatever plausibility it has. In his ideal state, Hegel had assigned a crucial role to independent bodies—civic corporations of one kind or another—which were charged with reconciling the conflicting claims of community and freedom. As Beiser has written,

Hegel believed that the absence of independent groups within the modern state was the common failing of both the absolutist state of the *ancien régime* and the revolutionary state of modern France. Both absolutism and Jacobinism went astray in not providing for sufficient self-government within the state. They reduced the state down to a single centralized power and the masses, abolishing all the intermediary groups between them. This was a source of constant instability.[72]

Whether or not it was a "failing" of Kandinsky's previous tableaux, none of them was subdivided quite the way *Thirty* is into "intermediary groups" organizing and stabilizing the composition. To say it again, the presence of those intermediaries is one of the painting's most distinctive features, and unusual enough before 1936 that it seems to call for explanation. Is it too much of a stretch to imagine Kandinsky reading Kojève's implicit comparison of his tableaux with "States," and then feeling under some obligation to produce a work that could live up to those terms? I don't know. Maybe. But it strikes me as an interesting possibility to play out a bit further before we reach any final conclusion. If *Thirty*'s composition *could* properly be seen as structurally homologous to both Hegel's system of absolute knowing and a modern state founded on the recognition of the universal rights of all its citizens, then it seems to me it would also have to be understood as asserting a certain parallelism between the (*geistige*) spheres of art, philosophy, and, if not religion, at least politics and ethics. The claim would be not that these are distinct moments in the historical unfolding of spirit but, rather, that they are separate, concurrently developing manifestations of *Geist*. One could even say, with Soloviev, that they are different "hypostases" of the Absolute; we might as well call them the Beautiful, the True, and the Good.[73] And their structural similarities would be not a matter of mere coincidence—nor of an attempt to *represent* philosophy, say, in painting—but, on the contrary, a necessary consequence of their shared, essentially dialectical nature. The achievement of a painting like *Thirty* would be simply that it had found a way to make those similarities visible *as similarities*—principally by isolating the structural or formal congruities among the three otherwise different forms of thought in question.

HEGEL HAD ARGUED that art ceded its spiritual role to, first, religion and, finally, philosophy as a consequence of "that deepening of subjective life in which the individual subject separates himself from the whole and the universal in order to be independent in his own inner being."[74] Before then, during the classical period that was the apex of art, no such separation or division had existed:

On the contrary, in Greek ethical life the individual was free in himself, though without cutting himself adrift from the universal interests present in the actual state. . . . There was no question of an independence of the political sphere contrasted with a subjective morality distinct from it; the substance of political life was merged in individuals just as much as they sought this their own freedom only in pursuing the universal aims of the whole.[75]

Hegel seems to be implying here that classical sculptures were unified wholes because ancient Greek society was similarly unified. In fact, though, his position is just the reverse; given the spiritually formative role played by art in antiquity, it would be better to say that Greek society was unified because the images of the gods around which it gathered were themselves undisturbed wholes. As Stephen Melville has written, for Hegel, "the Greek temple was an emanation or further expression of the sculpture that [stood] at and as its center for a people who became one people in being thus centered."[76] According to the *Aesthetics*, romantic—which is to say, *modern*—art could only dream of such unification. Like every other romantic form, painting was condemned "of necessity" to content itself with pluralism and particularities. Terry Pinkard has described its situation this way:

The dissolution of modern art of which Hegel speaks is . . . not the "end of art" in any real sense. It rather testifies to art's basic problem: there can be no form of art that is appropriate to the "spirit of the times" since "spirit" has become too fragmented for any aesthetic presentation to work as presenting the "truth" to us. Each of us has a life to lead, and there are simply too many different ways to lead those lives for any aesthetic exhibition of what that means to count. . . . Anything and everything of human significance becomes a possible topic of art, and art thereby ceases to be *the* vehicle of the truth about spirit. Our problems are more political and social, that is, prosaic; we must figure out how to live together in such a fractured world, and there can be no set of cantos, no "artwork of the future," . . . that can carry forward art's vocation to tell us what it means now to be human.[77]

But one could argue (and in some sense, of course, I have been arguing) that Kandinsky's *Thirty* aims to be just that "artwork of the future"—that it wants both to embody the fragmentation and dispersal of modernity and to give us some sense of how that world, and we in it, might yet be imagined to hang together. (We might even say that it aims to show us the beauty of that imagining.) From the very beginning of his career, Kandinsky had expressed a desire to produce paintings that would "speak" to us despite and about our differences; and he had tied that project quite explicitly to the development of a nonrepresentational pictorial "language."[78] Whether or not we're willing to grant *Thirty* the full significance that I've entertained for it over the last several pages, it seems to me we have to concede at least this much: that the painting presents itself as an achieved unity-in-differ-ence, and that both Kandinsky and Kojève placed great store in such an achievement. As they saw it, the stakes were enormous, and not simply for painting. No doubt there are any number of objections and counterarguments one might make to their assertions. I hope to make some of them myself at the conclusion of this book. Still, it has seemed (and continues to seem) important to me to suspend critique until that point, and to first try to do justice to the complexity of Kojève's and Kandinsky's "argument" as it unfolded from *Über das Geistige* and *Punkt und Linie* to "Les Peintures concrètes" and beyond. Whatever else one might say or feel about the claims those works advance, one has to be impressed, I should think, by the consistency of the argument and the depth of its commitments. Fairness similarly dictates that we postpone our critique until after we've also had a chance to examine how the argument plays itself out within a larger sampling of Kandinsky's *painterly* production. In Part II we'll do just that. My aim is to explore the degree to which the development of Kandinsky's art can be seen as legitimately dialectical, as well as to gauge the nature (dialectical or otherwise) of that art's relation to the various theoretical justifications offered on its behalf.

PART II

PAINTING IN PRACTICE

THE DEVELOPMENT OF KANDINSKY'S OEUVRE

UP TO NOW WE HAVE BEEN PRINCIPALLY CONCERNED with various theoretical arguments about painting, arguments that attempt to account for a particular historical moment, namely, that of the emergence of nonrepresentational art. Discussion has centered on the analysis of texts, with descriptions of individual artworks intervening only on occasion. The present section, Part II, by contrast, will be driven almost entirely by the description and analysis of specific paintings. However clever or compelling the theoretical arguments may be, they amount to very little if they have no real purchase on the art that they purportedly concern. This section of the book is the test of—and, I'd like to think, payoff for—everything preceding it. Clearly if Kandinsky's conception of painting was as Hegelian as (my readings of) his writings and Kojève's suggest, then we ought to be able to see plenty of evidence for it in his artistic practice. Some version of the dialectic should be visible in the composition of individual paintings, and not just in them but also, and even more importantly, in the development of his oeuvre as a whole. The wager on which this chapter is staked is that the numerous changes, both large- and small-scale, that Kandinsky's work underwent over the course of his career can in fact be seen as driven by a dialectical logic   indeed that that logic just *is* what Kandinsky meant by painting's "inner necessity."

The question immediately arises, however: how and where should we begin?[1] Were our time and patience unlimited, we might be tempted to aim at full comprehensiveness, which is to say, at an analysis of every painting Kandinsky ever produced, beginning with his earliest extant work. But that approach is patently untenable, and not only because we have the severely limited time and attention spans that in actuality we do. The other major problem with an approach of that nature is that it assumes the mere givenness of our subject, rather than acknowledging (with Hegel) that, to be free from presupposition, the subject has to unfold and prove itself. We may well discover, for example, that there are paintings by Kandinsky that don't significantly advance the development of his oeuvre or else whose concerns are sufficiently different in kind that we would want to regard them as belonging to an effectively separate body of work. Presumably we would decide to exclude these sorts of paintings from our analysis, and yet—this is the point—they are impossible to identify securely in advance. We can't delimit the objects of our inquiry beforehand, because the terms and criteria for inclusion only become apparent in and through the process of inquiry. A proper Hegelian narrative is self-determining in precisely this way. To imagine that we could proceed otherwise, Hegel suggests, would be akin to Scholasticus' resolution not to venture into the water until after he had learned to swim.[2]

We would be better off simply plunging right in. Still, we need a point of entry, and preferably one that hasn't been chosen entirely at random. There are a number of paintings that would probably prove adequate to the task, but I propose to begin with these three: *Composition IV*, from the winter of 1911 (Figure 16 / Plate 3), *Composition VI*, from March 1913 (Figure 18 / Plate 4), and *Painting with White Border* (Figure 22 / Plate 6), which was done in May of that same year.[3] As a group, they have the advantage of allowing us to chart Kandinsky's progressive abandonment of representational forms. They are also each a significant work, large in scale and evidently regarded by Kandinsky himself as meriting extended consideration. We know this because—and here I come to the real impetus behind my selection—the artist wrote and published his own descriptive analyses of these three paintings, in which he attempted to articulate their major features and something of the process through which they came about.[4] If adopting these essays' terms and criteria can't entirely guarantee that our analyses will be free from presupposition, it can at least help to ensure that the presuppositions are *Kandinsky's*, thereby minimizing any tendency on our part to idiosyncratic or anachronistic projection. Obviously, the appropriateness of even Kandinsky's criteria will have to remain provisional, at least until their objectivity can be ascertained. But they offer us a kind of jump-start, something to get us up and running until the dialectical logic of the works themselves becomes apparent and has a chance to develop its own self-sustaining momentum.

THE EARLIEST OF KANDINSKY'S THREE ESSAYS, concerning *Composition IV*, reads in many ways as less of an essay than a mere outline for an essay or even simply an inventory of the painting's principal attributes.[5] The text is also oddly split into two not-quite-equal halves that are separated from one another by a short row of asterisks. Moreover, the first half is itself made up of two distinct parts, beginning as an enumerated list of (often paired) characteristics, before concluding with a paragraph—the only one in the "essay"—actually written in complete and fully punctuated sentences. As Felix Thürlemann has suggested, these idiosyncratic features of Kandinsky's text stand in mimetic relation to *Com-*

position IV, in that the painting too is highly schematic—Thürlemann refers to its "syntagmatic structure"—and prominently divided into left and right halves by the long, parallel black lines (or "lances") that run from the very top of the canvas to, or almost to, its lower edge.[6] The left side of the painting, like the first half of the essay, also seems to comprise two distinct parts—in this case, left and right sides whose opposition is given emblematic form by the two rearing "horses" in the painting's upper left-hand quadrant.[7] Indeed the entire composition appears organized (again, like the essay) around paired antitheses, the challenge thus facing Kandinsky having been to carefully balance those oppositions while avoiding the absolute symmetries that would have made the painting seem lifeless or inert.[8]

In one of the preparatory drawings (Figure 17), now in the Musée national d'art moderne, Kandinsky sketched out what would become the most important lineaments of the painting's highly calculated equilibrium.[9] The sketch not only indicates the clash of horses and riders; it also singles out for emphasis the diagonal lines that rise outward from the canvas's lower edge, forming a wide "V" that structures the composition as a whole. In his written analysis of the painting, Kandinsky underscored these "countermovements in both directions"—the fact, as he explained, that each "movement to the right is contradicted by smaller forms that move toward the left," and vice versa.[10] The disparities in size and weight suggested in that description are even more evident in the painting than they are in the sketch: the rightmost horse of the finished work rises higher above and so more forcefully dominates its adversary, creating a greater imbalance within their opposition. The "mainly acute movement to the left and upward" produced as a result is in turn checked by the slight asymmetry of the broad "V" below, in that the three "extended lines" of the "reclining figures" on the right-hand side are longer (and more numerous) than the jagged diagonal that serves to counterweight them in the lower left.[11] Once more, the overall impression is of a kind of dynamic equilibrium, of a composition that invokes bilateral symmetry but assiduously avoids the stasis that its strict attainment would have entailed.

Also contributing to the painting's balanced asymmetry is what Thürlemann describes as the almost chiastic arrangement of pictorial elements.[12] Kandinsky himself called attention to this aspect of the work at the very beginning of his analysis, where, under the heading "masses (weights) [*Massen (Gewichtsmassen)*]," he identified four distinct areas of the painting—three of which he directly correlated with separate quadrants of the canvas—and then associated the upper left quadrant with the lower right, while pointing to an inverse similarity between the upper right and lower *central* portions of the composition. Upper left and lower right, he claimed, were dominated by line, whereas the other two regions gave pride of place to color.[13] The displacement of "massed" color from the lower left corner toward

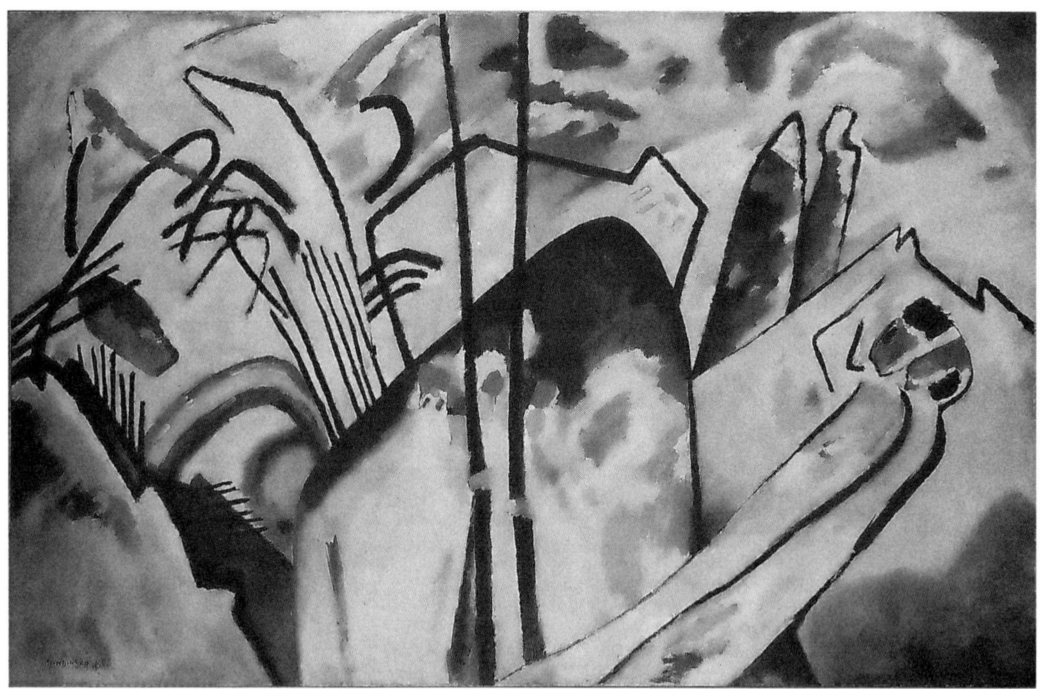

FIGURE 16 Wassily Kandinsky, *Composition IV*, January–February 1911. Oil on canvas, 159.5 × 250.5 cm. Kunstsammlung Nordrhein-Westfalen, Düsseldorf. © Artists Rights Society (ARS), New York.

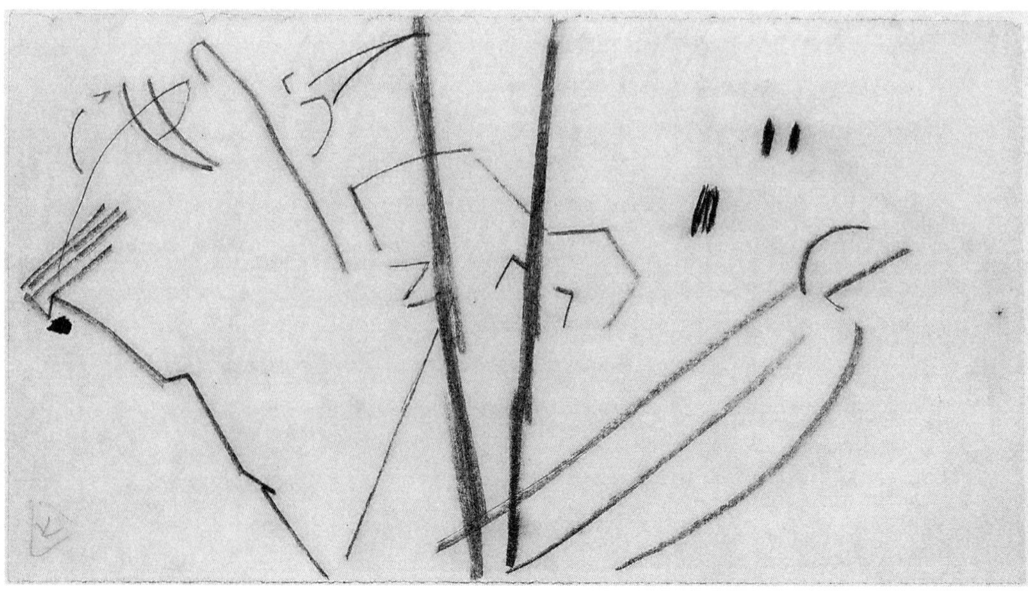

FIGURE 17. Wassily Kandinsky, First sketch for *Composition IV*, 1911. Charcoal, ink, and pencil, 10.2 × 20 cm. Musée national d'art moderne, Centre Georges Pompidou, Paris. CNAC/MNAM/Dist. RMN–Grand Palais/Art Resource, New York. © Artists Rights Society (ARS), New York.

the middle of the canvas again effectively disrupts the overall symmetry (in this instance, a kind of rotational symmetry) that would otherwise have taken hold.[14] The suggestion of such a symmetry remains, however, as does—more prominently still—the antithesis of line and color underlying it. At multiple places within his written analysis of the painting, Kandinsky emphasized this by identifying line and color or, more precisely, the juxtaposition of "angular, sharp movement (battle) and light-cold-sweet colors," as "the principal contrast in the picture."[15]

There is, I think, a certain sense in which we might regard this "principal contrast"—indeed, might regard all of the various contrasts operating within the painting—as continuing or extending the oppositions *among* the "light-cold-sweet colors" themselves. Like *Composition II* before it (see Figure 10 / Plate 1), *Composition IV* employs Kandinsky's dissonant-primary system. Yellow and blue appear not only often side by side but in nearly equal measure, as do the other paired contraries (white/black, red/green, violet/orange) of *Über das Geistige*'s modified color wheel (Figure 9).[16] In *Composition IV*, however, Kandinsky can also be seen working to develop additional, essentially non-chromatic dissonance-generating "systems." Hence the emphasis, in the painting as in the essay, on multiple kinds of "contrasts," from the "countermovements" of opposing diagonals and other compositional forms to the oppositions of "precise and blurred" and (what almost always amounts to the same thing) line and color.[17] Yet the emphasis Kandinsky placed on these new oppositions—and especially the last—had the presumably unintended consequence of weakening the impact of the dissonant primaries themselves. In 1911, the artist still considered it a given that lines would be black, and so felt that an increased presence of white was required "to emphasize the linear element" to the degree that he currently desired.[18] But the greater quantities of white had the effect of muting the intensity of his palette overall. As a result, the opposed primaries of the painting come across as noticeably less jarring than they had in *Composition II*. They may well have anyway, of course, as this is the way the dialectic works: today's dissonance, as Schoenberg asserted, is merely the consonance of tomorrow. In any case, by the time he wrote his analysis of *Composition IV*, in March 1911, Kandinsky was describing as "light, cold and sweet" color combinations that had appeared startlingly, even aggressively, audacious only the year before.

Not surprisingly, in his analysis of *Composition IV* and its "principal contrast," Kandinsky specifically drew the comparison with *Composition II*. At that time he described both paintings as possessing a "bright-sweet-cold tone" that stood in opposition to the "angular movement" conveyed by the paintings' linear and figurative elements. However, he felt that in *Composition IV* that contrast was, "by comparison with *Composition II*, more powerful, but at the same time harder (inwardly), clearer, the advantage of which is that it produces a more precise effect, the disadvantage being that this precision has too great a clarity."[19]

The comment itself patently doesn't suffer from being any too clear. On a first reading, it seems to offer only the tautological claim that greater clarity can lead to increased precision, even if such precision often results in a surfeit of clarity. We're going to need to look at the relations between line and color in the two paintings a bit more closely if we're to tease anything more astute out of the observation. In the meantime, though, we should notice at least this much: Kandinsky plainly regarded *Composition IV* as continuing work on a problematic that he had taken up over a full year earlier, in the painting of *Composition II*.[20]

In *Composition II*, as in the surviving oil sketch (Figure 10 / Plate 1), line served primarily as enclosing contour. It lent definition to the figures and other forms, thereby shoring up the representational aspect of the image. But it also worked to undermine or negate representation, especially the representation of space. The dark, ubiquitous, and almost uniformly thick contours constitute a kind of two-dimensional armature, like the tracery of stained glass windows, emphasizing the painting's existence on a single plane in depth. In *Über das Geistige in der Kunst*, which was published little more than a year after *Composition II* was completed, Kandinsky lauded such attempts "to keep the 'picture' as a painting upon a flat surface" as being important "first steps into the realm of the abstract." Yet he also expressed anxiety over the problem inherent in that sort of flattening, namely, its tendency to identify the painting with the material surface of the canvas.[21] The elements of pictorial illusionism still evident in *Composition II*—the vestiges of perspective and modeling, and the presence of those dark lines in their guise as form-defining contours—preserved enough of a semblance of depth to prevent the tableau's total collapse onto a single, continuous plane.[22]

In *Composition IV*, by contrast, the last remnants of perspective and modeling have been eliminated, with the result that the image looks significantly more two-dimensional than its predecessor. Line, no longer called upon to function as flattening "tracery," has begun to detach itself from color—as a consequence of which it appears to adhere all the more firmly to the plane. (The linear elements' independence from color is especially emphasized in the upper left-hand quadrant, above all in the rendering of the "horses" whose contours remain conspicuously open and placed against a white or neutral ground.)[23] It's not the case that all depth has been eliminated from the painting; but what little remains is entirely a function of apparently overlapping forms. The reclining figures in the lower right-hand quadrant are presented as the closest to us. Behind them are a succession of planes—the first comprising the "lancers" and the "acute form modeled in blue," and then (in order from front to back) the yellow "mountain," "horses," and "castle"—appearing like so many stage flats arrayed in parallel. The multicolored "sky" at the top occupies the furthest reaches, its position behind established by what Kandinsky described as "the running-over of color [*das Über-fließen der Farbe*] beyond the boundaries of form."[24] Here "blurred" patches of yellow and green seep past outlines that, in the earlier work, would have halted their expansion. As a result of both that transgression and their "blurring," the colored patches recede into a perceptible if indefinite depth.[25] It's a relatively isolated phenomenon, not conspicuous within the context of the painting as a whole; but, again, in combination with the overlapping of forms elsewhere, it's enough to keep the tableau from settling flatly onto the surface of the canvas.

In *Composition II*, line and color had appeared, for all their differences, as closely coordinated, line serving exclusively as *out*line, color primarily as a coloring *in*. It's only in *Composition IV*, where the linear elements occasionally appear divorced from color, and where color is sometimes dissociated from form, that the two begin to align themselves in real opposition. I take this to be what Kandinsky had in mind when he declared the "principal contrast" to be sharper and "more powerful" in *Composition IV* than in its predecessor, and therefore able to exercise a "more precise effect." But the work as a whole, he evidently felt, had become in the process overly simplified or diagrammatic; it possessed "too great a clarity." What he seems to have wanted, at least when writing his analysis a month or two after the painting's completion, was something both subtler and more strongly evocative—something, we might say in retrospect, perhaps a bit closer to *Composition VI* (Figure 18 / Plate 4).

CERTAINLY *COMPOSITION VI* is much less diagrammatic, and markedly more nuanced, than *Composition IV*. In large measure we can attribute that difference to line and color no longer constituting the work's principal contrast. In fact, a series of diagonal, colored lines cutting across the upper middle portion of the painting announces the very overcoming or sublation of that opposition. If those lines are yet able to stand out visually from the background against which they are deployed, it is not because they are offset by large quantities of white but rather, now, because the forms behind are less opaque, their edges much less firmly rendered, than are the colored lines themselves.[26] No doubt *Composition VI* benefited significantly in this regard from the discoveries of *Composition V* (Figure 19 / Plate 5). With that painting, Kandinsky was still largely operating under the assumption that line ought to be both black and opposed to color, even though he had all but abandoned the dissonant primaries of his earlier tableaux. Only a few patches of saturated red, blue, and yellow remain, these largely relegated to the upper limits of the composition. Below, the palette is divided fairly evenly between darker earth tones and lighter, pastel shades—the chromatic similarities within each group

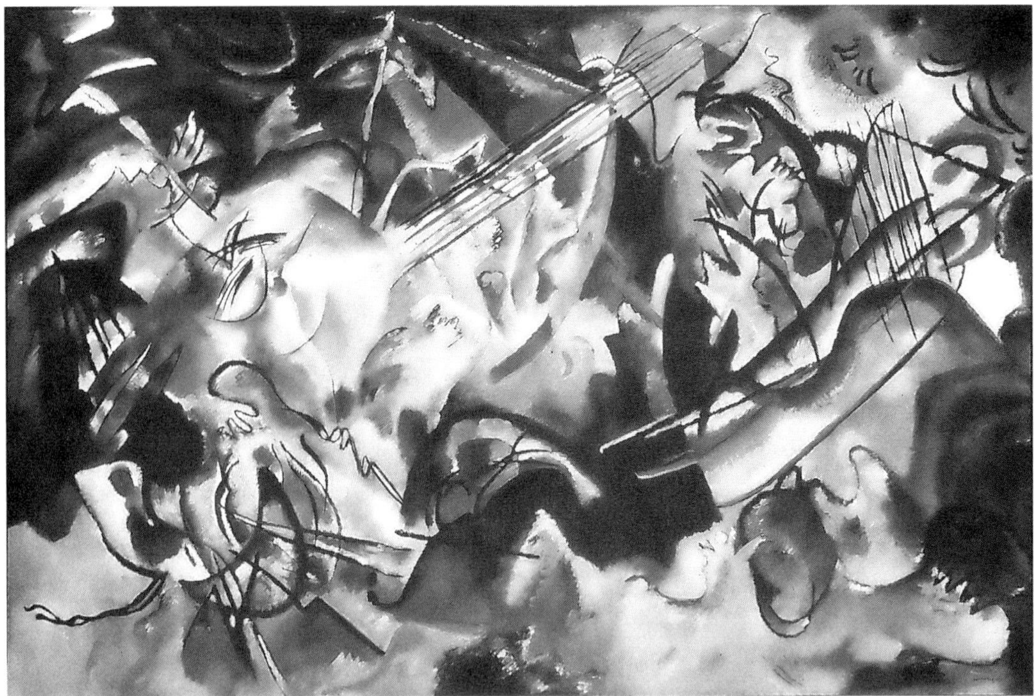

FIGURE 18. Wassily Kandinsky, *Composition VI*, March 1913. Oil on canvas, 195 × 300 cm. Hermitage, Saint Petersburg. Scala/ Art Resource, New York. © Artists Rights Society (ARS), New York.

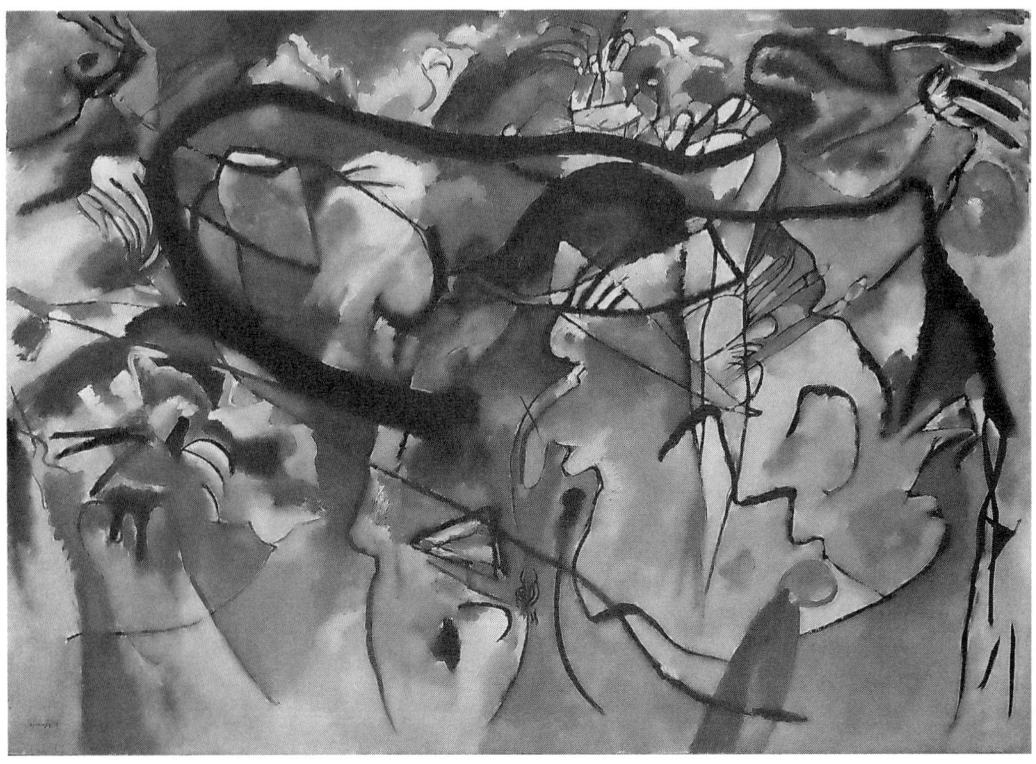

FIGURE 19. Wassily Kandinsky, *Composition V*, November 1911. Oil on canvas, 190 × 275 cm. Private collection. © Artists Rights Society (ARS), New York.

facilitating the "blurring" that Kandinsky evidently now desired. I'm inclined to see this newfound interest in imprecision as following on from "the running-over of color beyond the boundaries of form" that had emerged in the making of *Composition IV*. There Kandinsky had blurred certain patches of color as part of an effort to dissociate it from line—to have the two elements appear to occupy different planes in depth, with color then seeming even further removed from the generally more representational (and therefore more "material") attachments that still characterize the lines within the painting. In *Composition V*, the colored shapes are even more "blurred," and the transitions from one to the next even more indefinite; to achieve these effects, Kandinsky clearly felt he needed colors that were at once less saturated and less dissonant or different from one another than were the opposed primaries of his earlier color system.[27] Difference and dissonance would have to be sacrificed at this level, so that they might return with even greater force in the opposition between (relatively) precise line and blurred color that had now become the principal contrast driving Kandinsky's artistic production.

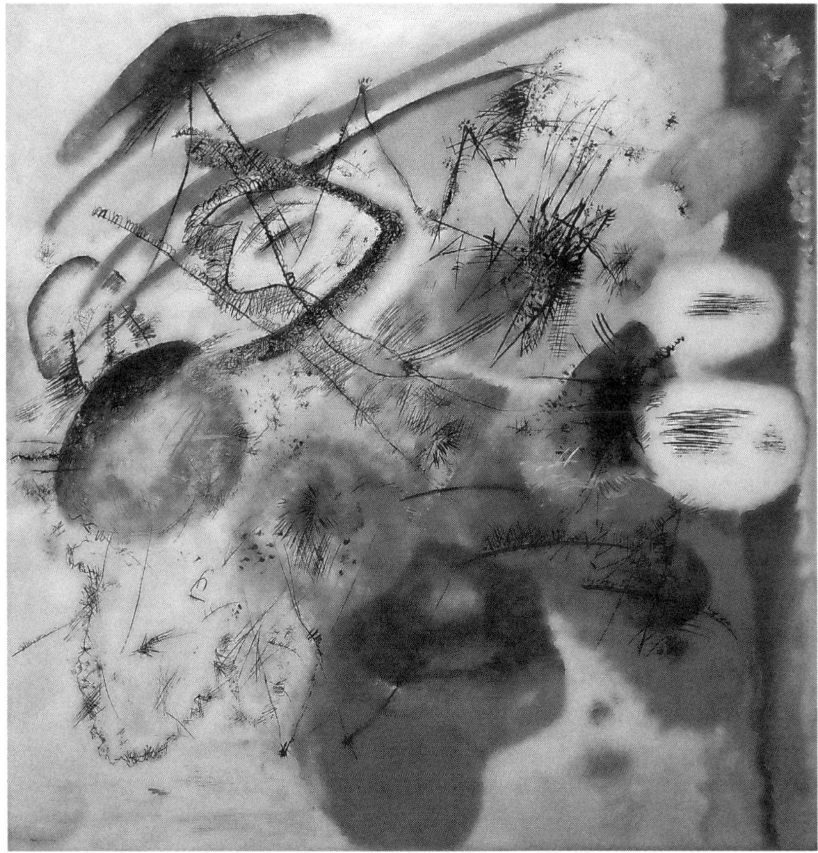

FIGURE 20. Wassily Kandinsky, *Black Lines I*, December 1913. Oil on canvas, 129.4 × 131.1 cm. Solomon R. Guggenheim Museum, New York, Solomon R. Guggenheim Founding Collection 37.241. © Artists Rights Society (ARS), New York.

In his Cologne Lecture, written sometime before the end of January 1914, Kandinsky explicitly addressed the desaturated palette that he had used for *Composition V*.[28] "I deprived my colors of their clarity of tone," he explained, "dampening them on the surface," so that they might "glow forth, as if through frosted glass."[29] Kandinsky's descriptive metaphor suggests that his ultimate intention was to approximate the appearance of the *Hinterglasbilder* he was still occasionally producing, only now without the presence of the literal sheet of glass.[30] As its name suggests, *Hinterglasmalerei* involves painting on the back or reverse side of a glass pane. The technique allows for a variety of subtle spatial effects, owing in part to the fact that the pigments are applied to the glass in distinct layers. Viewed from its front side, those things that were painted first (traditionally, the dark, defining contours of the image) appear to be situated on a plane much nearer to the viewer than do the colors painted subsequently. No doubt Kandinsky was attracted to *Hinterglasmalerei* in part because the multiple planes composing each tableau all seem to exist at some distance from the material support—and because, in being transparent, that support already appears on its way toward immateriality. The artist's effort in *Composition V* to re-create the same effect, now specifically in the absence of the glass, is probably best regarded as an effort to similarly de-realize the surface but in such a way as to emphasize the tableau's status as mere illusion, or *Schein*.

To get a better sense of what Kandinsky was after in both *Composition V* and *Composition VI*, we might look to a more or less contemporaneous glass painting, the *Last Judgment* (*Jüngster Tag*) of 1912 (Figure 7). Here Kandinsky laid down that first layer of black lines in India ink, rather than in paint, so as to guarantee their absolute opacity. For everything else, he used water-based pigments, which allowed him to create a surprising range of effects, some areas seeming all but transparent, others far less permeable to light. The result is devoid of anything we might regard as sculptural illusionism—there's no real sense of volumetric form anywhere in the work—and yet the illusion of (planar) depth persists. Again, Kandinsky's interest in the essentially folk technique of *Hinterglasmalerei* undoubtedly arose from his desire to emphasize the essential flatness of his tableaux while still preserving some semblance of space or depth within them. Glass painting offered a means of "retaining the material surface" of the painting, as he had advocated in *Über das Geistige*, while also "constituting an ideal surface" or, better, *surfaces* on different, slightly more distant planes.[31]

According to his Cologne Lecture, it was not simply *Composition V* that was "painted in this way" (i.e., to mimic the appearance of color seen "through frosted glass"); so too, "for the most part, [was] *Composition VI*."[32] That qualifying "for the most part" was likely intended to register both the significant differences in coloring and the somewhat more complicated spatial effects achieved in the later work. (We will look at those effects in some detail momentarily.) The painting's palette might be described as a combination of those used with *Compositions IV* and *V*. We find a return to the opposed primaries of the earlier painting, yet they have become less saturated overall and interspersed with the earth tones of *Composition V*.[33] The glass-painting-like appearance of that latter work also resurfaces: most of the black lines, despite having been laid down first, seem to float above the other, colored elements.[34] In fact, in his essay on *Composition VI*, Kandinsky claimed that the painting had had its origins in an actual *Hinterglasbild*, a specific work representing the story of the Deluge: "When the glass-painting was finished, there arose in me the desire to treat this theme as the subject of a Composition, and I saw at the time fairly clearly how I should do it."[35] Unfortunately, he reported, "this feeling quickly vanished." Kandinsky carried the "picture around in [his] mind for a year and a half" before he was finally able to execute anything living up to the promise of the work as he had originally imagined it. "This happened," he said, "because I was still obedient to the expression of the Deluge, instead of heeding the expression of the word 'deluge.'"[36] He was over-attentive, that is, to the representational content—to the iconography of the biblical story—when what he wanted was something able to convey the "catastrophic" impact of the event without any specific narrative details.[37] As he made clear subsequently, only after the iconographic imagery had been swept away, effectively submerged in a roiling sea of color, was *Composition VI* completed to his general satisfaction.

Kandinsky detailed in the essay not only this initial inability to reproduce his mental image, but also his progress on the painting once work was finally under way. He articulated three distinct moments. First came the "laying-in" of the "main body of the picture," based on the final preparatory sketch. Although the artist didn't explicitly say so, this part must have entailed above all transferring the basic contours of the composition onto the canvas using pencil and, where appropriate, black paint.[38] His concern at this stage was presumably for the general structure of the composition as a whole. In the second moment, he shifted his focus to the separate parts constituting that whole, and to the "subtle, enjoyable, and yet exhausting task of balancing the individual elements one against the other."[39] Color undoubtedly played a major role at this stage, inasmuch as the majority of the painting's "parts" are differentiated from one another solely on the basis of a perceptible change in hue. Finally came "the third, beautiful and tormenting moment," involving "the tiniest alterations of drawing or color in such a place that the whole painting [was] made to vibrate."[40] It was during this moment, Kandinsky claimed, that the painting became a "living" entity, a "total equilibrium . . . [in which] no single element gains the upper hand." Here the parts were coordinated not only with one another as individual elements but also with a view to the organic or plastic functioning of the whole. It seems that much of what happened at this stage of the painting's production was designed to un-do the distinctness of the separate forms introduced during the preceding (second) moment—to minimize their separation so as to more fully assimilate them to the totality of the composition.

These three moments of the painting's coming-into-being describe a very Hegelian trajectory, one passing from the Universal to the Particular and then, at last, the Individual—from a moment, that is, in which the whole is only imperfectly or provisionally grasped to another characterized by a growing interest in the differentiation of the constituent parts to, finally, a stage offering an integrated understanding of the relation of those parts to one another as well as to the whole. These three moments also have correlates of sorts within the structure of *Composition VI* itself, in the three (relatively) discrete "centers" that Kandinsky identified within the work. Indeed, the presence of *three* centers seems to have been one of the more significant innovations of the year and a half leading up to *Composition VI*.[41] In his 1911 essay on *Composition IV*, Kandinsky had picked out "two centers" to that painting: the "entangled lines" of the rearing horses, and the "acute form [of the "mountain"] modeled in blue." There had been no mention of a third. Presumably we were meant to understand the totality of the composition as itself the sublation, or *Aufhebung*, of its two opposing centers, as well as of the various other contraries which it comprised. By the time he came to paint *Composition VI*, however, Kandinsky plainly felt the need to designate a third center, a specific area within the larger tableau that could be seen as reconciling the contradictions of the composition and so "determin[ing] the inner sound of the whole picture."[42] If, then, he began in his 1913 essay on *Composition VI* by once again enumerating two "centers"—

1. on the left the delicate, rosy, somewhat blurred center, with weak, indefinite lines in the middle;
2. on the right (somewhat higher than the left) the crude, red-blue, rather discordant area, with sharp, rather evil, strong, very precise lines

—he quickly asserted the presence of another: "Between these two centers is a third (nearer to the left), which one only recognizes subsequently as a center, but [which] is, in the end, the principal center."[43]

Again, I think it's not too much to see that third "center"—and certainly not too much to imagine Kandinsky wanting us to see it—as a resolution or sublation of the painting's other two. The essay clearly sets up the first pair as antithetical to one another. The leftmost center is characterized as "delicate" and "blurred," with

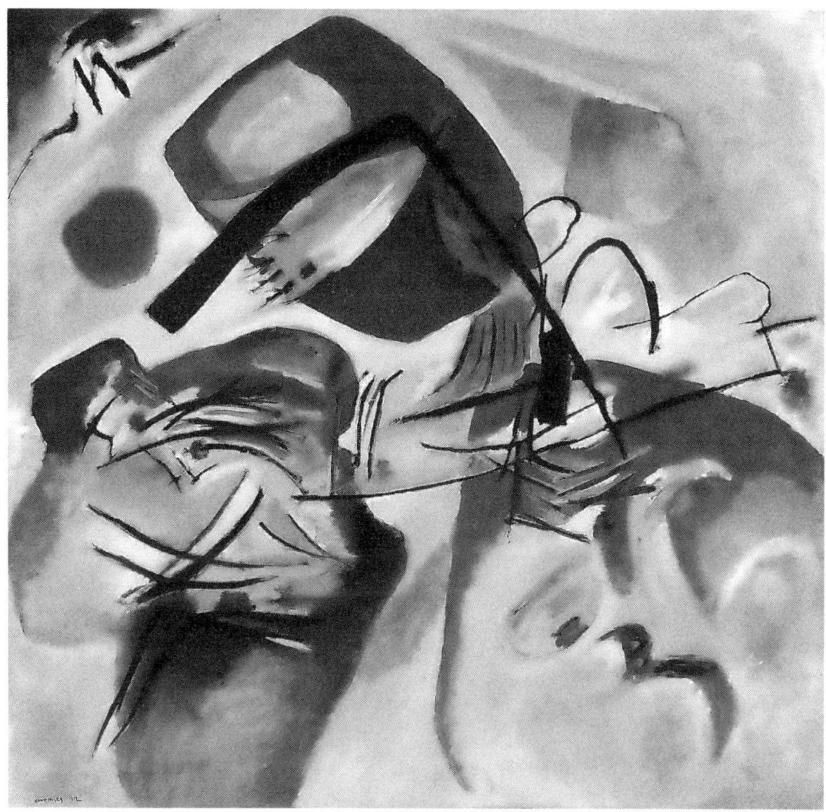

FIGURE 21. Wassily Kandinsky, *With the Black Arc*, autumn 1912. Oil on canvas, 189 × 198 cm. Musée national d'art moderne, Centre Georges Pompidou, Paris. CNAC/MNAM/Dist. RMN–Grand Palais/Art Resource, New York. © Artists Rights Society (ARS), New York.

"weak, indefinite lines," while the rightmost, we are told, is "crude," its linear elements "sharp," "strong," and "very precise." Kandinsky's account also emphasizes that it was in order to "mitigate the dramatic effect of the lines" dominating the right-hand center that the artist "created a whole fugue out of flecks of different shades of pink," which color not only the "rosy, somewhat blurred center" on the left but also much of the third, "principal center" appearing nearer to the middle.[44] Moreover, as we'll see, those most central flecks of pink are both the likely product of the painting's "third moment" and, in some sense, the point of departure for much of the artist's subsequent work. The reasons underlying Kandinsky's interest in them are not terribly difficult to piece together.

Like the other pastel colors of the composition, the scumbled pinks of the first or left-hand "center" are visually recessive—as if occupying a middle ground between the sharper, darker linear elements of the painting and the pockets of brown "shadow" that coalesce especially along its upper edge. Much the same can also be said of the lines in this area; because they are unusually fine and tenuously rendered, they appear distant, as if subjected to a kind of atmospheric perspective (or the intervention of "frosted glass"). The thicker, blacker lines of the right-hand center seem to occupy a plane notably closer to us—this, again, even though they were actually among the first things painted on the canvas. (By the same token, the touches of pink on the right, although added later, appear to be lying beneath or behind that grill of "rather evil" lines.) The general impression is of three or four distinct planes, or perhaps of a partially completed *Hinterglasbild* laid atop a darker, murkier composition. The "precise" linear elements of the right-hand center might be seen as establishing the foremost plane, the various opaque, colored shapes scattered across the composition taking up positions just a bit behind. The "blurred" colors and indefinite lines of the left-hand center indicate a terrain yet another step further into depth. In the area of the third center, however—in the very middle of the composition—we get the illusion of something occupying a region somewhere in between. "Here," Kandinsky wrote, "the pink and white seethe in such a way that they seem to lie neither upon the surface of the canvas nor upon any ideal surface. Rather, they appear as if hovering in the air, as if surrounded by steam."[45]

Space elsewhere in the painting still looks roughly as it does in *Compositions IV* and *V*, which is to say, restricted to a number of discrete planes lined up one behind the other in depth. With this third center, however, Kandinsky seems to have arrived at something genuinely new: "blurred" color that appears divorced from any plane, whether material or ideal. Here, the pink "flecks" constitute a sort of cloud, a passage of variable density, through which we're able to discern bits of yellow, green, and blue on the other side. Instead of a separate plane in space, the pink here conjures atmosphere or space itself—something, that is, within which other, planar elements might plausibly be suspended. In fact, the red, elongated, slightly curving, quasi-rectangular shape at the very center of the composition seems to be buoyed up by that cloud of pink and white. It's like the man at the Russian baths invoked in Kandinsky's essay, who, surrounded by steam, appears "neither close to nor far away."[46] Existing at some remove from both the black lines inscribed on the surface of the canvas and the various colors we can glimpse on its far side, that pink cloud of "steam" appears to reside not at any specifiable distance from us but only, irresolvably, "somewhere" (*irgendwo*).[47] It's "this feeling of 'somewhere' about the principal center," Kandinsky claimed, that "determines the inner sound of the whole picture."

The "atmospheric" effect in this area is not quite like anything seen elsewhere in the composition—or previously in Kandinsky's oeuvre. Once more, what seems to have been at stake for the artist was nothing less than the de-realization of the canvas, which had asserted its physical presence ever more aggressively in the run-up to abstraction. "I toiled over this part," Kandinsky wrote, "until I succeeded in creating what I had at first only dimly desired [but which] subsequently became ever clearer within me."[48] If this account is accurate, the scumbled passages of the painting's third center were not originally planned—or, at any rate, they ended up looking quite different from what Kandinsky had initially intended. They belong, that is, neither to the first "moment" of the picture's making, the "laying-in" of the "main body" of the composition, nor to the second, in which the individual elements were balanced one against the other. Rather, they must have emerged as a largely unanticipated consequence of that third and final moment, when even "the tiniest alterations of drawing or color" could "have a powerful effect on the entire composition." Modifications to the work made during this stage, Kandinsky insisted, were the product of "hidden" yet "indescribably accurate" laws, laws which in general "leave room for the intervention of the trained hand [but] to which that same hand is subservient."[49] The implication here is that the painting's completion turned on a process not wholly, nor even primarily, within the artist's conscious control. Especially at this third stage, Kandinsky would have us know, progress was driven by painting's own logic or "inner necessity."[50]

It was probably also during this third, decisive moment of painting *Composition VI* that Kandinsky discovered something of even greater significance to his subsequent work: the relationality of color. This was the discovery that would finally sound the death knell for his opposed-primary system, in fact for much of his understanding of color as laid out in *Über das Geistige*.[51] In the rudimentary theory sketched there, individual colors had been presented as having innate or natural properties, as being, for example, intrinsically warm or cold. It's specifically on that basis that they were opposed to one another. In the course of painting *Composition VI*, however, Kandinsky was brought face to face with the inadequacy of those assumptions. At some point during the final stage of work on the composition, it appeared necessary to "interrupt" the "tranquility" established by the "fugue of pink" (itself created to counteract the lines' "dramatic" and "excessively importunate voice"), and Kandinsky found himself adding for that purpose "various patches of blue," an "in itself cold" color. Contrary to all expectations, those blue patches yielded "an internally *warm* effect," thereby "heighten[ing] once more the dramatic element" of the painting.[52] "This discovery"—in effect, the discovery of color's fundamental mutability—"was of enormous importance for me," Kandinsky wrote later that year in his Cologne Lecture.

I felt, with an exactitude I had never yet experienced, that the principal tone, the innate, inner character of a color [could] be redefined *ad infinitum* by its different uses. . . . This revelation turned the whole of painting upside-down. . . . The inner, thousandfold, unlimited values of one and the same quality, the possibility of obtaining and applying infinite series simply in combination with one single quality, tore open before me the gates of the realm of absolute art.[53]

Here as elsewhere, "absolute" implies not an ultimate end point—not the last "word" on the subject—but rather something absolved of all external relation. With *Compositions II* and *IV*, color choice and distribution had been regulated by means of a system largely external to the painting.[54] With *Composition VI*, by contrast, the "system" has become internal to the work itself, the artist now understanding that the properties of any one color are dependent upon the specific context in which it makes its appearance. That "context," of course, consists of nothing other than different, individual colors, each one of them subject to redefinition by its surroundings, so that the process of painting suddenly became for Kandinsky infinitely more complex. Every part of the composition would have to remain in play, its status merely provisional, until at some point when the artist judged that the "permanently living, immeasurably sensitive quality of the successful picture" had finally been attained.

Already in *Über das Geistige*, Kandinsky had made it plain that "composition" was for him a matter of juxtaposing contraries, and in such a way that all of the elements—"even those that contradict one another," as he reiterated in his essay on *Composition VI*—would "attain a wholly internal equilibrium."[55] By 1913, however, with the unexpectedly warm appearance of the blue in *Composition VI*, as well as with the increasingly nuanced combinations of his palette, he began to realize that dissonance could be made to inhabit even a single patch of color. In the paintings of this period, he observed in his Cologne Lecture, "I would let cold come to the fore and drive warm into the background. I would treat individual color tones likewise, cooling the warmer tones, warming the cold, so that even one single color was raised to the level of a *composition*."[56]

Whether through "internal" juxtaposition (the layering or mixing of separate, potentially dissonant tones) or via their side-by-side placement, Kandinsky repeatedly discovered that colors could change their appearance, in fact that they almost never looked identical from one occurrence to the next. If he had begun his exploration of color in *Über das Geistige* by intending to define and catalogue the intrinsic properties of each and every hue, now, in 1913, his understanding and interests had shifted. What evidently struck him in the making of *Composition VI* was the way color could shed its natural or innate characteristics, indeed could be transformed into almost the opposite of what it had appeared to be only a moment before. I'm inclined to think Kandinsky saw this negation of color's innate properties, like the dematerialization of the surface of the canvas, as overcoming limitations imposed by nature, and so as being a true achievement of spirit or *Geist*. In that sense, *Composition VI* would have constituted for him nothing less than a demonstration of freedom—a "hymn," as the artist described it in a rather more allegorical mode, "of that new creation that follows upon the destruction of the world."[57]

THE STORY THAT KANDINSKY TELLS about the making of *Painting with White Border (Bild mit Weissem Rand)* (Figure 22 / Plate 6) is similar to his account of *Composition VI*, in that again he describes an initial inability to realize the painting, followed by a sudden insight into how he should proceed. In this case, the white border that runs around the edge of the composition proved to be the solution to his impasse—which is why, Kandinsky explained, he "named the whole picture after it."[58] Despite the border's clear importance, however, Kandinsky says very little about the nature of the problem it was called upon to solve, or which of its features proved definitive in that regard. He remarks only that he treated "this white edge . . . in the same capricious way it had treated me."[59] My sense is that, if we look carefully at the other sections of Kandinsky's essay, and are equally attentive to the corresponding passages of the painting itself, we will begin to see, even

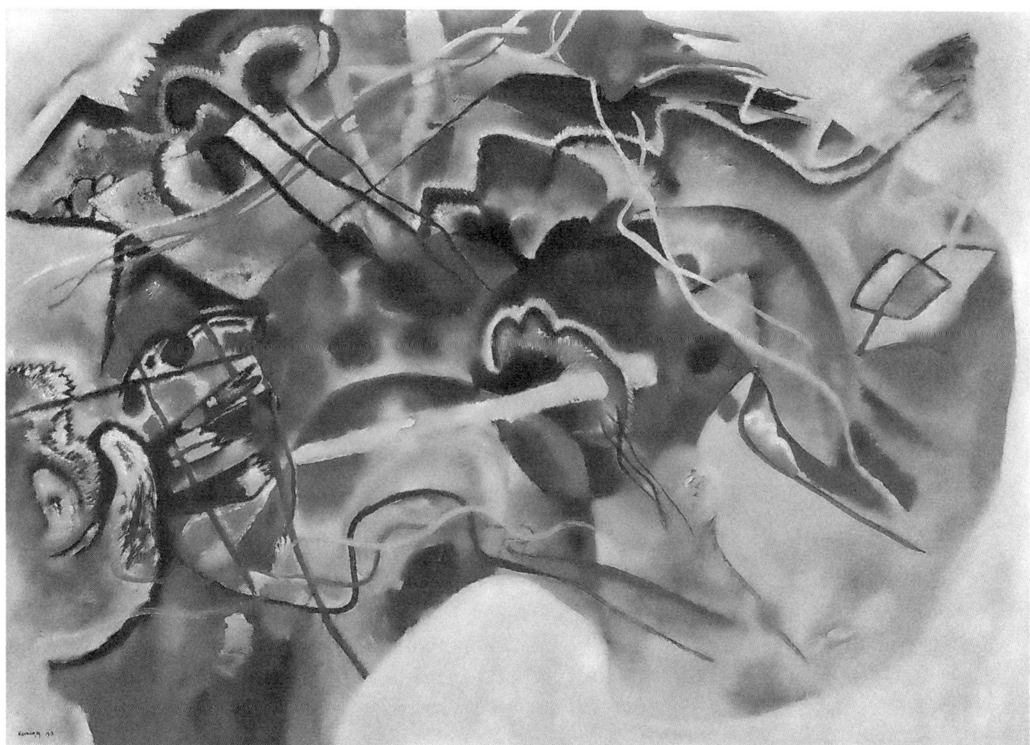

FIGURE 22. Wassily Kandinsky, *Painting with White Border*, May 1913. Oil on canvas, 140.3 × 200.3 cm. Solomon R. Guggenheim Museum, New York, Solomon R. Guggenheim Founding Collection 37.245. © Artists Rights Society (ARS), New York.

in the absence of the artist's explicit commentary, how and why the white border could have served as the epiphany it did.

The essay opens by explaining that the first sketch for *Painting with White Border* was made immediately following the artist's return from a trip to Moscow in December 1912.[60] If in that initial sketch the setting was recognizably a darkened (albeit abstracted) landscape, "already in the second design," Kandinsky claimed, he "succeeded in 'dissolving' the colors and forms of the actions taking place in the lower right-hand corner." "In the upper left remained the troika motif," he added, as well as the "white zigzag forms," the latter suggesting a kind of "obstacle, which is, however, ultimately unable to deter the progress of the troika."[61] These sentences are followed by an apology of sorts, Kandinsky expressing his embarrassment at the overly literal or referential nature of his description, which imparts to the forms a "wooden quality that," he asserts, he "find[s] distasteful." Perhaps as a result of that distaste, beginning with the next paragraph (and continuing thereafter), Kandinsky refers only to "clarity and simplicity in the upper left-hand corner"—which he then goes on to contrast with the "blurred dissolution" and "forms vaguely seen" in the lower right.

Although the upper left- and lower right-hand corners constitute the first opposition that Kandinsky identifies within the painting, neither is named as one of the work's principal "centers." That distinction goes instead to the two poles of a countervailing diagonal, which runs from the lower left side of the composition slightly upward and to the right. Kandinsky points specifically, on the left, to the "combination of standing forms," with their "pure, powerfully sounding touches of color; the red somewhat runny, the blue self-absorbed."[62] In indicating the center to the right of that, his gesture is both broader and a bit more vague. It encompasses primarily the "curved shape" that has, "both toward the outside and on the inside, incandescent (almost white) zigzag forms"—he seems to be indicating the twinned black and orange-brown (horse-and-rider-shaped) lines near the very middle of the composition—but also the "more or less egg-shaped background" of "dull blue tones" in front of which that curving form appears.[63] As several scholars have noted, these two centers resemble, and so likely had their origin in, images of St. George and the dragon, the thick white line connecting them being the vestige of the lance with which St. George ultimately ran the dragon through.[64]

Interestingly, Kandinsky says nothing of a third center to the work. What he does say is that here, in *Painting with White Border*, the centers are "less independent than in, e.g., *Composition VI*, where one could make two pictures out of that one, pictures with their own independent life."[65] As with his comment later in the essay that, in the more recent work, the "two centers are separated, and at the same time linked" by the numerous forms appearing in the space between them, the implication seems to be that the centers have, if not overcome their opposition, at least achieved a certain rapprochement. A third center is no longer necessary because the first two already suggest their eventual or incipient sublation. I'm inclined to draw an analogy with the development we noted earlier, and that Kandinsky himself mentioned in his Cologne Lecture: namely, his shift from juxtaposing colors conceived of as antagonistic to one another toward a mixing or, better, layering of those pigments in such a way that their opposition is effectively brought *inside*, made internal to the particular passage or shape at hand.

A similar analogy could be drawn as well with the numerous, highly textured areas of *Painting with White Border*. "Between the simplicity of the upper part of the picture [i.e., the area of the "troika"] and the two centers," the artist wrote, "my inner voice insisted upon the application of a technique I like to call *Quetschtechnik* [literally, squashing technique]: I squashed the brush against the canvas in such a way that little points and mounds were produced."[66] In its effects, this *Quetschtechnik* is related to the layering and scumbling of pigments at the center of *Composition VI*, as well as the "alternation of rough and smooth, and other tricks in the treatment of the canvas itself" that Kandinsky had developed for that work.[67] As a consequence of such surface variations, the artist hoped, the spectator would "experience a different response again on approaching the canvas more closely."[68] Much the same thing could be said about those passages in *Painting with White Border* where the *Quetschtechnik* was employed. From up close, we are quite aware of the tangible materiality of those "little points and mounds." From a distance, however, their tactile presence withdraws—especially in those instances where the brush being "squashed" was relatively dry. There, a "feeling of 'somewhere'" arises once again: form "blurs" and appears to dissolve into the indefinite, illusory space of the tableau. In these places, the patches of pigment seem to shuttle back and forth in *inverse* relation to our own position. When we're standing close enough to see their *faktura*, they plainly project forward from the canvas.[69] But when we take several steps back, they too recede—into the atmospheric depth of the composition.

In the Bibliothèque Kandinsky in Paris, there exists a drawing, undated, but which almost certainly belongs to this moment in the artist's career (Figure 23).[70] Near the top of the sheet, on the left, is a schematic rendering of an eye seen in profile; it surveys a series of thin, vertical lines arranged in parallel on either side of a darker upright labeled "*Bild*." Representing the plane of the canvas in cross-section, as well as multiple "ideal" or illusionistic planes behind and forward of its surface (both toward and away from the observer, as Kandinsky's caption explains), the drawing testifies to the artist's intense interest at this time in creating an imagined—which is to say, a *geistige*—depth capable of displacing attention from the

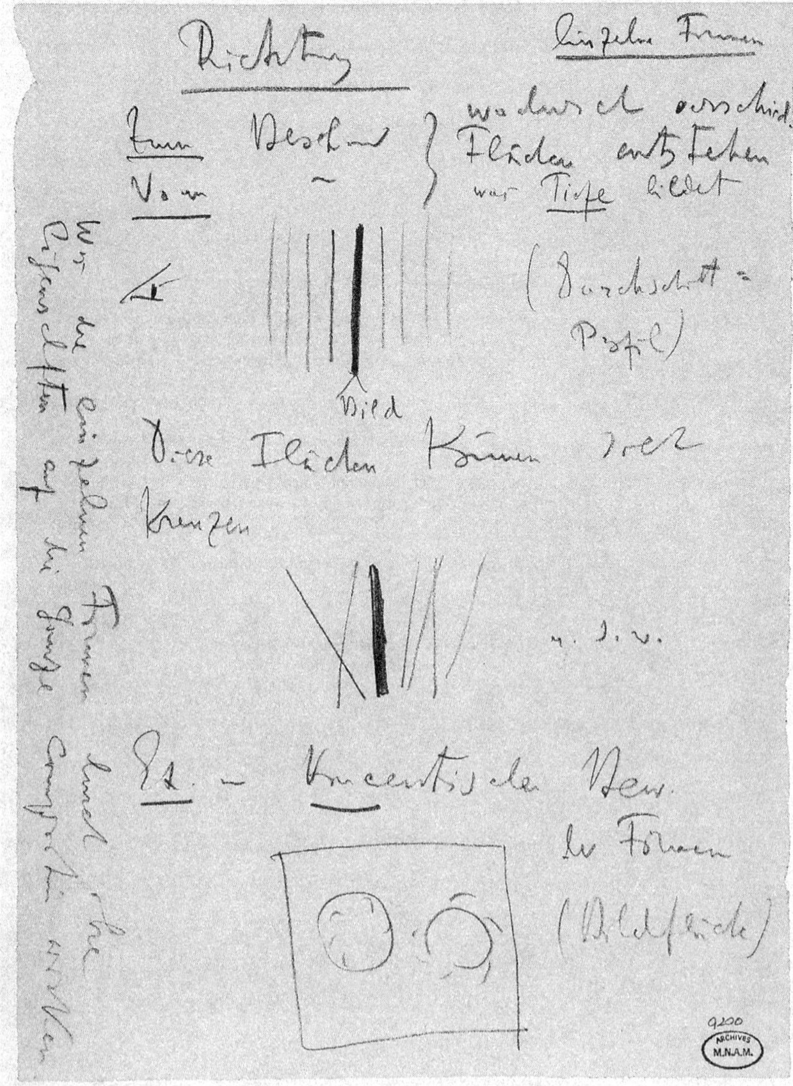

FIGURE 23. Wassily Kandinsky, undated page of notes, before 1914. Bibliothèque Kandinsky, Centre Pompidou, Paris. © Artists Rights Society (ARS), New York.

canvas and its material presence. The significance of the *Quetschtechnik*, as I see it, resides in its ability to take up positions on either side of that physical surface, to project literally forward of the picture plane, even as, in the next moment, its tangible materiality withdraws into the illusionistic space of the tableau. I take it, too, that the persistence of the *Quetschtechnik* in Kandinsky's oeuvre—as we'll see, it recurs in some form or another in almost every painting he made over the course of the next decade—has everything to do with this fundamental spatial ambivalence. In their very structure, the tangibly textured yet "blurred" (and so apparently dissolving) forms created by means of the brush's "squashing" suggest an internal opposition, a here-*and*-there—not unlike what we have already witnessed in Kandinsky's layering of dissonant colors or in his ambition to create a single "center" for *Painting with White Border* that could encapsulate in itself what an earlier, iconographic tradition had regarded as a fundamental, irreconcilable antithesis.

Only at the end of the essay, following his discussion of the quasi-figurative elements—the troika, and the center(s) invoking St. George and the dragon—as well as his explanation of the *Quetschtechnik*, does Kandinsky at last turn to the composition's eponymous white border. As the final piece of the painting to fall into place, it's accorded a comparable position in the unfolding narrative of the artist's analysis. And yet, as already noted, the essay says surprisingly little about the border's actual appearance or function. To quote the relevant paragraph in full:

I treated this white edge itself in the same capricious way it had treated me; in the lower left a chasm, out of which rises a white wave that suddenly subsides, only to flow around the right-hand side of the picture in lazy coils, forming in the upper right a lake (where the black bubbling comes about), disappearing toward the upper left-hand corner, where it makes its last, definitive appearance in the picture in the form of a white zigzag.[71]

The water analogies are a bit misleading. Rather than clarifying things, they tend to trouble our ability to see; we envision a river, say, winding its way through the essentially landscape-like space of the composition. Yet if we look closely at the painting while reading the passage, a rather different picture emerges. The text has the white border rising as a "wave" at the bottom of the composition—a *figure*, then, against the ground of the "chasm" out of which it just emerged. Suddenly, we're told, the border "subsides," flowing around the right-hand side of the picture to form a "lake" in the upper corner. This is the point at which the dual water metaphors of the text are at their most deceptive, in that, although they convey the fluid continuity of the border, they all but prevent us from seeing how its form abruptly shifts from /figure/ to /ground/. We might do better to dispense with the water imagery altogether.[72] Starting over, we would certainly want to emphasize how, along its lower edge, the white border appears to be situated on the threshold of our space, a kind of repoussoir broaching our entry into the composition. During its upward climb, however, its spatial orientation unexpectedly shifts (even while, on the surface, the border still appears to be a seamless, two-dimensional plane). By the time it arrives in the upper right-hand corner, it has completely reversed its position vis-à-vis the other elements of the painting. There, it functions as a cloudy, indistinct background *in front of* or *against which* the large, composite form(s) of the rest of the composition stand out as if in relief.[73]

I imagine what Kandinsky had been looking for, before the white border presented itself as the solution to his problem, was a form that would both fill the empty space of the lower right-hand corner, and yet somehow also continue the "dissolution" that, according to his essay, he regarded as the real achievement of that area of the painting.[74] The white border ingeniously fit the bill. It had the additional advantages of being simple and clear—we have little trouble, for example, tracing the length of its contour, despite its complete spatial reorientation—so that, in a sense, the white border also embodies the opposition between "clarity" and "dissolve" which governs the diagonal descending rightward from the "troika" above. "Capricious" is the term Kandinsky used to describe the border's behavior and, once we become aware of its inconstancy in relation to the other elements of the composition, it's not difficult to see why. At once lucid and equivocal, tangibly present and no less elusively distant, the white border serves as yet another example—indeed the most striking of all—of an *internally* dissonant element within the composition. Little wonder Kandinsky named the whole picture after it. The border's spatial reorientation defies nature (in which, of course, forms cannot be simultaneously solid and atmospheric, close at hand and far away), with the result that we can only recognize it as a *geistige* phenomenon, made possible through illusion and within the space of the tableau.

As Kandinsky tells the story, immediately after the white border presented itself as the answer to his impasse, he rushed to his supplier to order a canvas. But he hesitated over the precise dimensions. Should the length be "160 [cm]? 180? 200?" In the end, he settled on the last of those options, making *Painting with White Border* comparable in scale to his previous (as well as subsequent) Compositions. Coupled with the primary evidence of the three published essays, the painting's dimensions suggest that Kandinsky saw *Painting with White Border* as completing a sequence begun with *Compositions IV* and *VI*. Looking back over the series, we become aware not only of the real differences among the three works, but also of how those differences might be understood as the product of a dialectical development. The "'somewhere' space" of *Composition VI* is, in important respects, a negation of the illusion dominating *Composition IV* (the illusion, namely, that the painting's separate pictorial elements all reside on distinct yet parallel planes in depth). *Painting with White Border* effectively negates that negation: in the white border of its title, the painting reveals an apparently planar element every bit as spatially ambiguous as the "steamy" third center of *Composition VI*. The trajectory among the three works is toward an increasingly complicated illusionism, the evident function of which is to dissolve our awareness of the surface *as surface*, thereby transforming canvas and pigment into what Kojève would have called a realized tableau.

Between the first and last paintings of this series we can also see development toward a more fully unified composition. For Kandinsky in 1911, "composition" was above all a matter of counterbalancing dissonant or antithetical elements, those elements necessarily retaining some measure of independence from one another. (The artist's explicit enumeration and pairing of the work's every feature in his essay on *Composition IV* is evidence enough of that.)[75] By contrast, the components of *Painting with White Border* are much more difficult to disentangle, and they seem to embody dissonance or opposition *within themselves*. To give this development its properly dialectical shape, we might say that movement is from the nearly bilateral symmetry of *Composition IV*, wherein "counterbalancing" was something that happened primarily on the plane, to the more pronounced asymmetry of *Composition VI*, in which tension shifted to an opposition between surface and depth. *Painting with White Border* in turn displays forms—most notably the "two" centers and the ambivalent white edge—that, having folded one or another of those (lateral or "orthogonal") tensions into themselves, consequently create the impression of a tighter, more resolved, and so more fully integrated or unified composition.

EXTENDING THE TERMS OF KANDINSKY'S ANALYSES

The terms laid out over the last several pages are, in my view, the most important of those driving Kandinsky's pictorial production between the beginning of 1911 and May 1913. Having discovered them within the artist's own writings, and then tested them against the paintings themselves, we can, I think, be relatively confident of their overall objectivity. By following their trajectory forward (and making use of the momentum generated in the process), we should be able to proceed at a progressively faster clip through the remainder of Kandinsky's oeuvre. Obviously, in doing so, we're likely to overlook a few things that a slower pace and finer grain would have brought to our attention—though surely we have already missed certain potentially interesting aspects of the work, despite proceeding to this point with the due diligence that we have. I take some comfort in the thought that, if the dialectical perspective opened up by this book does actually seem to show us something important about Kandinsky's paintings, the overlooked features of his art will eventually present themselves to viewers approaching from a similar angle sometime in the future.

Moving forward, then: We need to pay particular attention as we proceed both to how the later paintings continue to suggest (or not) their own de-materialization, and to how, within each work, the various, dissonant elements manage to hold themselves together (if in fact they do) as something recognizably a "composition." We will not, unfortunately, have texts by Kandinsky to guide us in the choice of particular paintings for analysis. Which works become subject for discussion will depend in part on how significant the artist seems to have regarded them, as demonstrated, for example, by the frequency with which he selected them for exhibition. Even more important than evidence of that sort, however, will be our own sense (based on a set of constantly evolving criteria) that the works in question follow on dialectically from those already discussed.

By these measures, *Composition VII* (Figure 24 / Plate 7), from November 1913, is the next obvious candidate for consideration. Its dimensions (200 × 300 cm) are even greater than those of the three paintings we have examined so far. Kandinsky evidently thought the work momentous enough that he had Gabriele Münter photograph it at various stages of completion (see Figures 25–28), the resulting images providing an account of the painting's creation roughly comparable to the written narratives of his earlier essays. Moreover, the painting itself was preceded by over thirty sketches in a variety of mediums, suggesting a level of planning and preparation surpassing that for any previous work.[76]

Composition VII also plausibly continues the dialectical developments we have been tracking over the course of this chapter. Some of its features were drawn directly from the paintings leading up to it: we see both a vestige of the white border from *Painting with White Border* (albeit mirror reversed, so that now it appears to arise near the lower right corner before climbing upward along the left-hand side of the composition) and a "boat" similar to that of *Composition VI*, rendered still more schematically than was its pictographic prototype. Even as we notice these holdovers, however, we are more likely to be struck by the way *Composition VII* departs from its predecessors. Except for the ambiguous, black-outlined "boat" in the lower left corner, the painting is devoid of recognizable figures or objects. Its space is filled instead by a veritable explosion of nonrepresentational form—as if, having now left conventional imagery behind, Kandinsky felt obliged (or perhaps permitted) to deploy an entire repertoire of invented shapes, so many in fact that they appear to spill over into the space *this* side of the receding white "border." Not only are those shapes more numerous and more various than were the abstracted forms of the earlier paintings, they are also more clearly delineated, the "steaminess" and blurring of *Composition VI* and *Painting with White Border* having given way in many places to sharper articulations. The vibrant, highly saturated hues of *Composition VII* play a role here too: if we are no longer dealing with the systematic pairing of opposed primary and secondary colors that we saw in *Compositions II* and *IV*, neither has that practice been entirely forgotten. "Bright, cold, sweet" blues, reds, and yellows, as well as the occasional electric pink or orange, all but overwhelm the darker (and more conventionally harmonious) earth tones that round out the painting's palette. Having first "veiled" the representational imagery

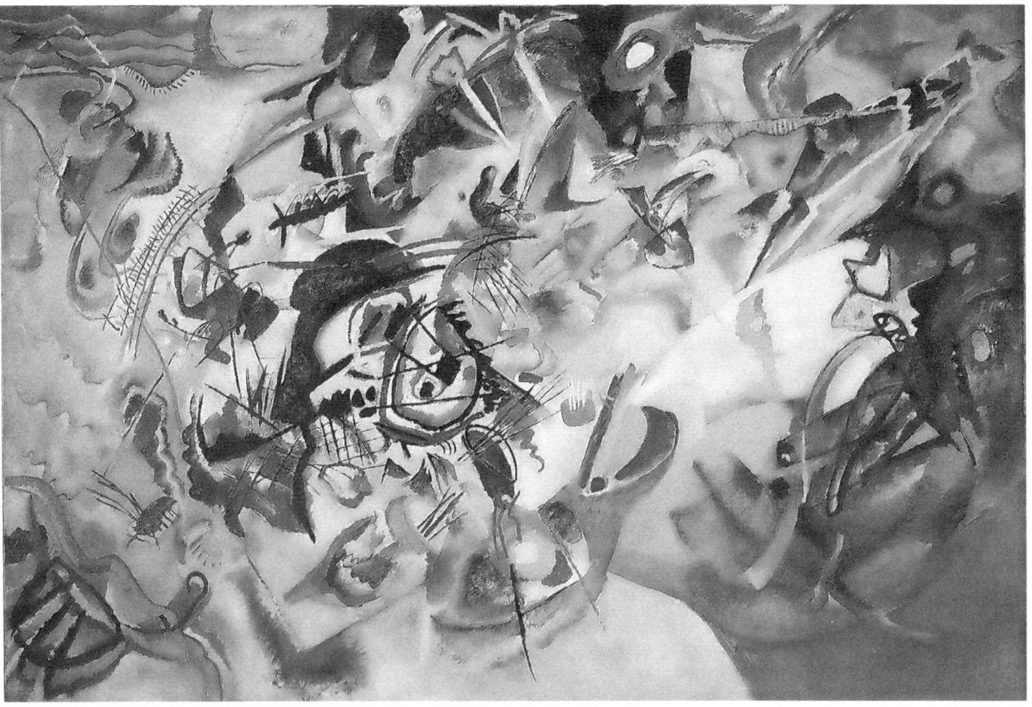

FIGURE 24 Wassily Kandinsky, *Composition VII*, November 1913. Oil on canvas, 200 × 300 cm. Tretyakov Gallery, Moscow. © Artists Rights Society (ARS), New York.

of his earlier paintings and then subjected the later, nonrepresentational forms to an intentional "blurring," Kandinsky seems to have grown anxious that he was heading too far in the direction of the vague or indefinite. With *Composition VII* we witness a notable increase in specificity. Instead of simplified, indistinct or generalized forms, the painting presents us with a collection of emphatic particulars.

Of course, the return of highly saturated colors and precise delineation brought with it the old problem of how to keep everything from settling flatly onto the plane of the canvas. Kandinsky's tactic in *Composition VII* was to emphasize discontinuity at every turn. He constantly varied his treatment of the surface, employing not only the *Quetschtechnik* in certain areas but also an array of other textures throughout: short parallel hatchings appear alongside dry, matte areas that are in turn interrupted by looping, fluid strokes laid down with heavily loaded brushes. Kandinsky simultaneously pursued a strategy of overt spatial disjunction. In a few of the preparatory drawings, which are unfortunately undated but which were presumably made just before (or conceivably just after) work on the canvas had begun, the artist divided the composition into several distinct zones.[77] Inscriptions indicate that a "chasm" was to occupy the lower right-hand corner of the painting, while the top central section was to appear "clear and divided," its

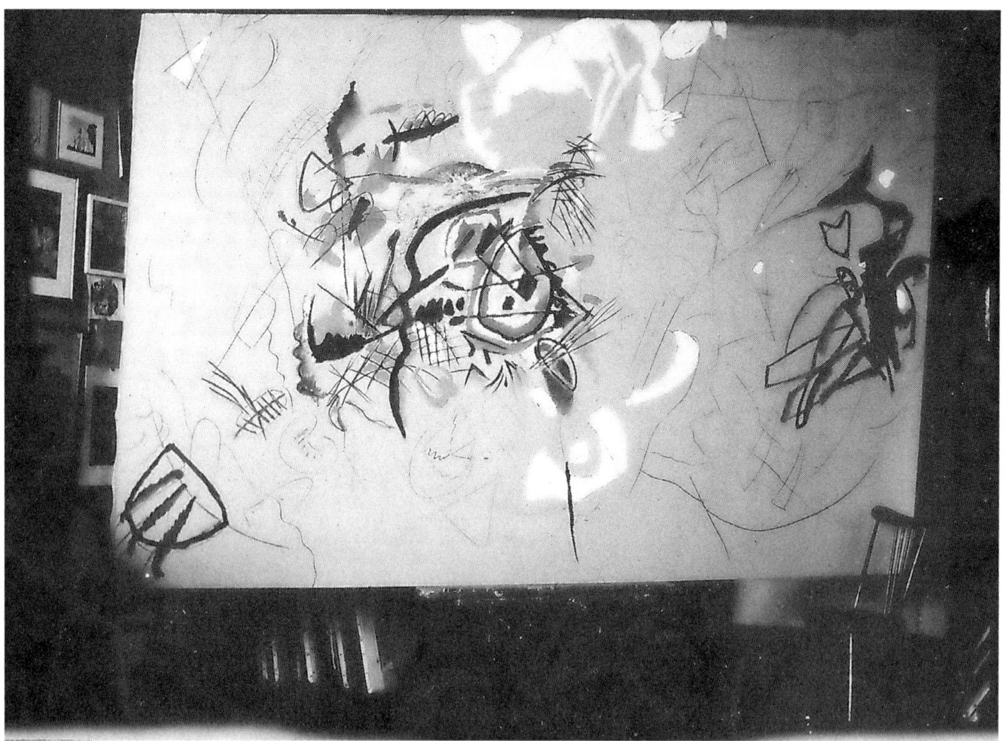

FIGURE 25. Gabriele Münter, Photograph of *Composition VII* in progress, November 25, 1913. Gabriele Münter- und Johannes Eichner-Stiftung, Munich.

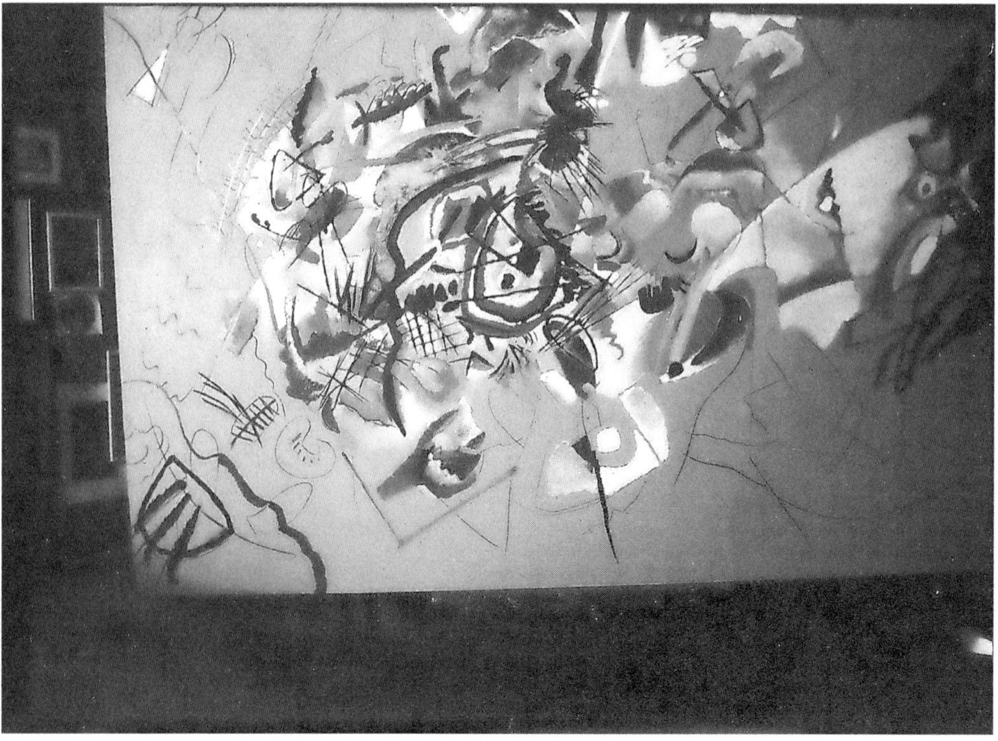

FIGURE 26. Gabriele Münter, Photograph of *Composition VII* in progress, November 26, 1913. Gabriele Münter- und Johannes Eichner-Stiftung, Munich.

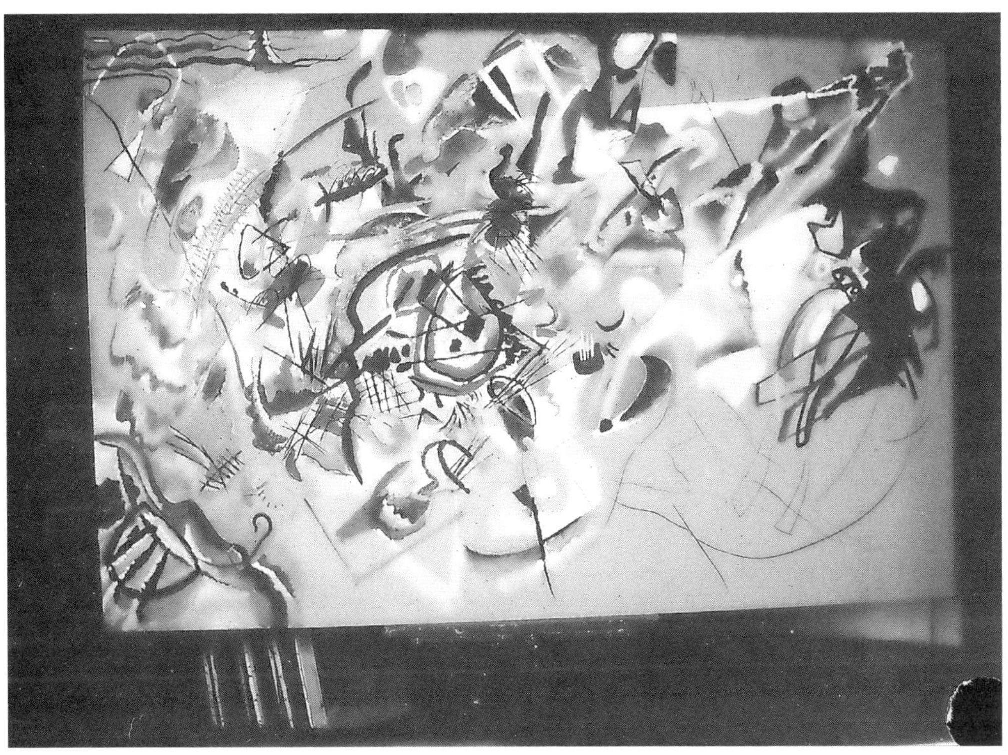

FIGURE 27. Gabriele Münter, Photograph of *Composition VII* in progress, November 27, 1913. Gabriele Münter- und Johannes Eichner-Stiftung, Munich.

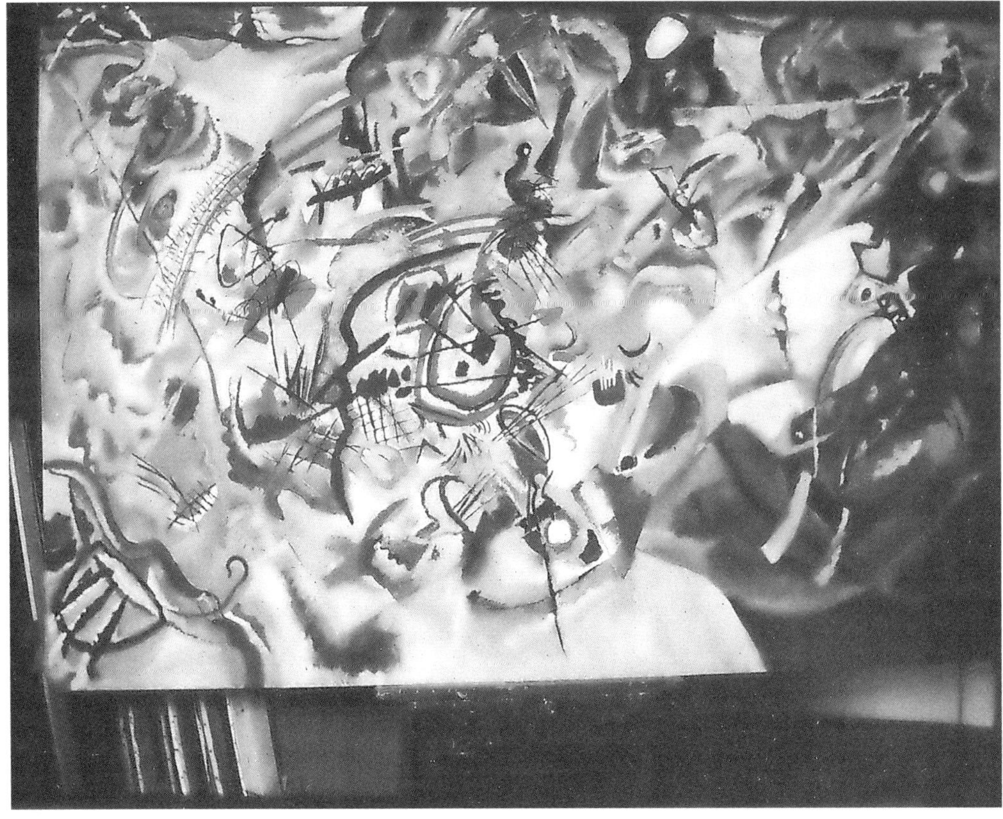

FIGURE 28. Gabriele Münter, Photograph of *Composition VII* in progress, November 28, 1913. Gabriele Münter- und Johannes Eichner-Stiftung, Munich.

"discontinuity" from the adjacent upper left-hand corner explicitly marked.[78] The final painting in fact conforms fairly closely to these specifications. The broad, ocher area in the lower right *does* read as a "chasm," its apparently precipitous drop emphasized by the long vertical strokes along its leftmost edge. The top central area seems flat by comparison, its brightly colored shapes appearing resolutely frontal, insofar as they seem free of foreshortening or anything that might be taken for atmospheric perspective. If we're still unlikely to associate that central section exclusively with the plane of the canvas, it is, I think, primarily because of the abrupt truncation of forms along its rightmost edge. Just to the side of (and slightly below) the prominent, red-and-blue-encircled white spot is a patch of black—a patch that is remarkably tempting to see as having once been of comparable size but that has now been neatly cleft in two with only its left half remaining in our view. Both the "cloud" of green directly above it and (to a lesser extent) the purple touch below end with similar abruptness, the edges of the three forms together constituting an implicit "cut," which runs from the very top of the canvas on a slight diagonal downward toward the bright blue, spindly shape below. The (violet, yellow, red, and pale green) forms to the right of that implicit cut appear similarly truncated, as if they too were somehow passing behind another surface and consequently out of sight. The illusion of overlapping planes is remarkably powerful—except, of course, that we're unable to decide finally which of those two planes, right or left, is forward of the other.[79]

Much the same effect recurs in other areas of the composition. Throughout we glimpse extended lines, sometimes explicitly drawn (as in the long diagonal orange contour on the left side of the painting), but just as frequently only implicitly present (constituted, that is, by an alignment of edges). The pen-ink-and-crayon sketch reproduced here as Figure 29 is essentially a map of the phenomenon. As I understand it, Kandinsky's strategy was two-fold—and, perhaps predictably enough, intrinsically contradictory. On the one hand, he wanted those lines to introduce spatial disjunction. Where several of them come together to suggest larger shapes, the forms "inside" collectively detach themselves from the surrounding elements; we perceive them as peeling off into a separate plane of their own. The attenuated "trapezoid" that occupies the left half of the composition provides the most obvious case in point.[80] We are encouraged to read its sloping sides as perspective orthogonals—in effect, the edges of a form-strewn pathway receding into depth. As a further consequence of that reading, the wavy lines of yellow, orange, and ocher in the upper left-hand corner are shunted into the distance, becoming the undulating contours of some far off horizon. They could not be more different in their orientation from the gaping "chasm" in the lower right—nor more difficult to reconcile spatially with the "clear and divided" area immediately adjacent.

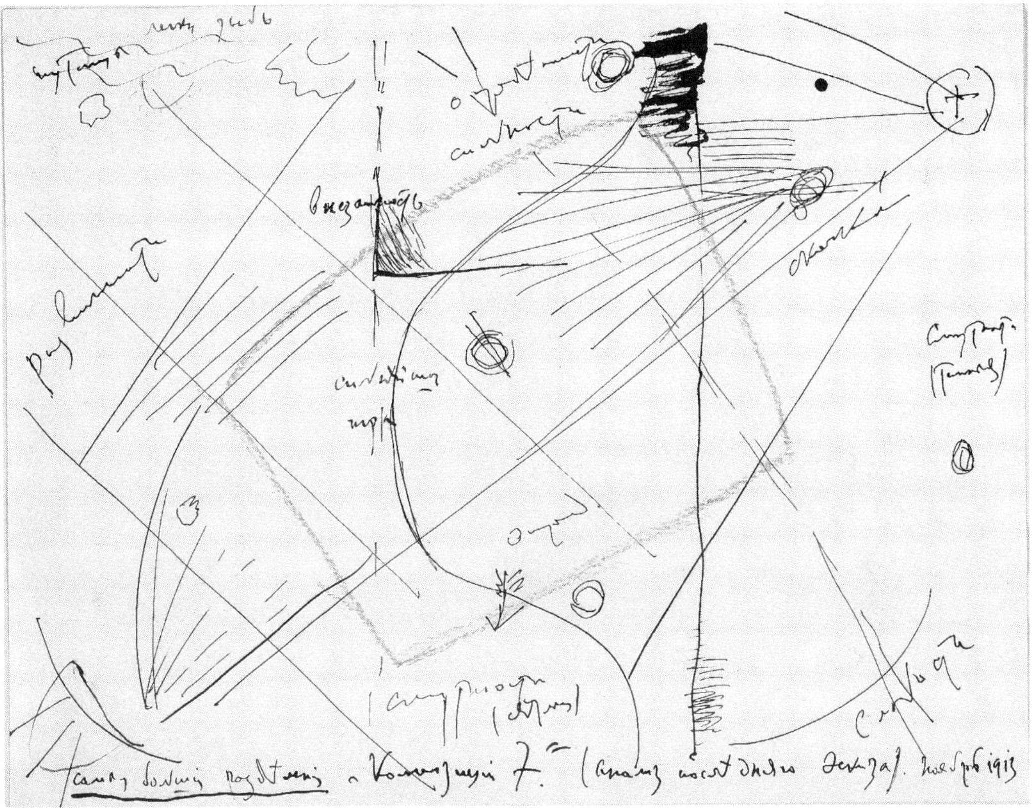

FIGURE 29. Wassily Kandinsky, Sketch for *Composition VII*, 1913. India ink and red chalk on paper, 21 × 27.5 cm. Städtische Galerie im Lenbachhaus, Munich. © Artists Rights Society (ARS), New York.

On the other hand, these large, composite shapes also work in other ways to overcome disjunction and so to establish, if not unity, at least a measure of co-herence within the composition overall. Their ability to do so hinges on the fact that they overlap with one another: our "trapezoid," for example, shares much of its expanse with the off-kilter "rectangle" located near the center of the canvas (see Figure 29), which in turn encroaches substantially on the "clear and divided" swath above. Such overlapping effectively knits together the separate pieces of the composition, however disparate their implied spatial orientations. It helps, too, that our perception of each shape is only ever intermittent. When the contours of that "rectangle" fade from our awareness, as periodically they do, the shape is re-assimilated to the surrounding tumult, its disappearance enabling other shapes—and other, potentially conflicting spatial configurations—to then arise. Any number of scholars have discussed *Composition VII* in terms of cosmological "genesis," and that metaphor accords well enough with the phenomenon at issue here.[81] Because of its structure of interlocking yet perceptually elusive shapes, the composition appears decidedly unsettled. Each slight shift of our attention seems to cause a realignment of pictorial elements, a different set of forms emerging into prominence. As a result the work suggests generative processes actively ongoing and, in that sense, it might be seen as continuous with Münter's photographs of the work in progress. In the painting, as in those pictures, we seem to be presented with a concatenation of still-emerging forms, less a finished composition than something perpetually coming into being.

One of the main lessons Kandinsky appears to have taken from *Composition VII* was that widespread spatial ambiguity could be produced without necessarily having to blur forms or introduce a haze of indistinction. (The works from the early 1920s will turn that realization to particularly good effect.) The artist also found that it was possible to concentrate and localize the figure/ground reversal achieved in *Painting with White Border*, and therefore to scatter such moments throughout the composition. A cluster of forms appearing in one instant to inhabit the foreground could be made to recede visually in the next; all that was required was to align the edges of several of those shapes (so as to produce the illusion of overlapping planes), and then to provide conflicting spatial cues on either side of the resulting line. The strategy enabled Kandinsky to sow ambiguity much more widely than he had before—a practice he carried forward, if by somewhat different means, into the works done shortly after *Composition VII* was completed.

AMBIGUOUS SURFACES

During the first few months of 1914, the artist produced several paintings for which, atypically, he adopted a perfectly square format. We can only speculate as to his motivations, but one impetus may have been a desire to reign in the lateral sprawl that had increasingly become a feature of his major compositions. Perhaps he wanted to impose (if only through compression) a greater sense of unity on the picture as a whole. Then again, maybe the more compact format was intended to compensate for the extraordinary complexity of the new paintings he was planning. Certainly, inch for inch, the results—including *Improvisation Gorge*, *Picture with Red Spot* (Figure 30 / Plate 8), and *Fugue*—are more intricate and more densely worked than any of Kandinsky's earlier canvases.[82] Prompted by the title of *Fugue*, I'm inclined to describe the group as "baroque" in composition. Like some musical offering by Bach, each of the three paintings is exceedingly (one might even say excessively) rich in texture and at least apparently woven of multiple, overlapping layers. Their dominant "sound," to use Kandinsky's expression for the distinctive character of any given work, was produced almost entirely by the *Quetschtechnik*, which all but overshadows any of the paintings' other features. In *Picture with Red Spot*, for example, "squashing" appears throughout the composition, and in fact

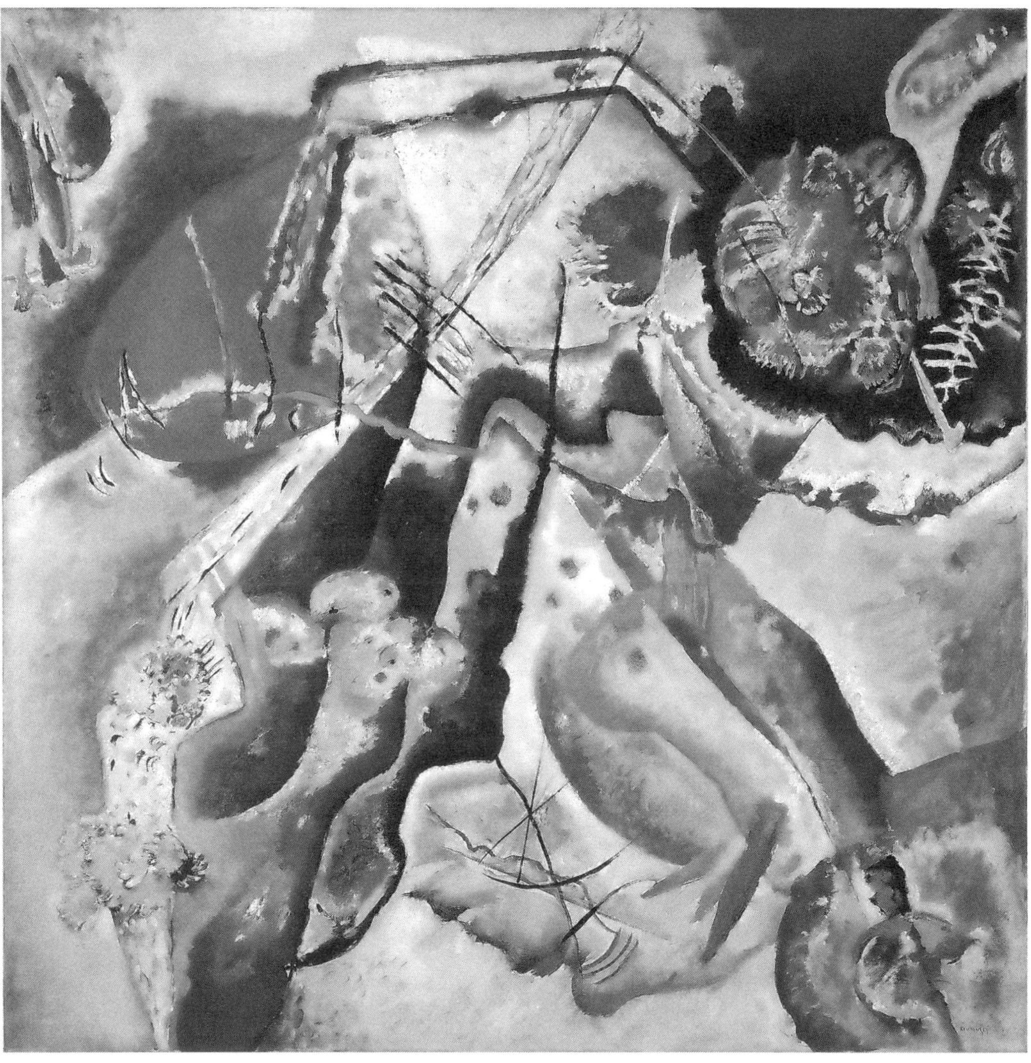

FIGURE 30. Wassily Kandinsky, *Picture with Red Spot*, February 1914. Oil on canvas, 130 × 130 cm. Musée national d'art moderne, Centre Georges Pompidou, Paris. CNAC/MNAM/Dist. RMN–Grand Palais/Art Resource, New York. © Artists Rights Society (ARS), New York.

some form of surface *faktura* or texturing covers every inch—with the notable exception of the large red "spot" after which the tableau is named. (The title draws our attention to that area's exceptional treatment.) Intuitively we might expect that the singularly smooth "spot" would appear to adhere to the physical surface of the canvas, while the other elements, as a result of their texturing, would have a much more ambiguous relation to the picture plane. And sure enough, here, as in Kandinsky's earlier paintings, the areas treated with the *Quetschtechnik* do function in a fully ambivalent manner, literally projecting forward of the surface (as is evident on close inspection) but appearing, from a vantage point only one or two steps more distant, to dissolve into an atmospheric-perspectival haze. Surprisingly, however, the proliferation of these "squashed" areas unsettles the whole, their uncertainty oddly infecting even the eponymous red spot. The painting's allover *faktura* so thoroughly disrupts our sense of planar continuity that the smooth, matte red "oval" itself appears drawn into the illusion. Its location in depth—not only in relation to the other elements of the composition but, equally, in relation to us—appears to fluctuate constantly. Much like the elongated red "rectangle" suspended in the pink "cloud" of *Composition VI* (see Figure 18 / Plate 4), the broad red "spot" of the later tableau seems to inhabit an indefinite space, one that exists not at some specifiable distance from us or from the other elements of the composition but only, irresolvably, *somewhere.*

Spatial ambiguity is also created in *Picture with Red Spot* via means that, in effect, draw on both the reversing white border of *Painting with White Border* and the techniques of *Composition VII.* Here line is the primary operator of uncertainty. Throughout the painting there are multiple instances of the phenomenon in question, but it might be best to begin by focusing on only one: the sharply defined contour of the large blue shape that occupies the upper left side of the composition. Despite its interruption by the long white "zigzag" running from the bottom of the canvas to the very top—and despite the slight green-ward shift of the blue beneath and to the right side of that divide—we are, I think, encouraged to see the shape as a single expansive entity, however obscured its full outline may be by the yellow "glow" along the upper edge of the canvas and on the lower left-hand side. But notice what happens to its contour as it travels upward toward the large red spot: passing *over* the white band that clearly overlapped *it* not so very far below, it suddenly changes into the delimiting edge of another shape— namely, the yellow-white "wave" that rises to meet the painting's upper edge. The dark blue-green coloration that seemed, below, to give three-dimensional heft to the large blue area (so that we read it as a tangible, volumetric form) now shifts in our perception to become shadow, cast by the "wave" above. What we had at first interpreted as "figure" is thereby relegated to the status of recessive "ground."

Similar reversals occur at a number of other places—in fact with the majority of the long contours structuring the composition. Most of these lines ask to be seen as the edge or external limit of particular shapes within the painting; at some point along their trajectory, however, the illusion reverses itself or otherwise breaks down. For example, at the bottom of the painting on the left-hand side, we discern a deep red, almost burgundy-colored shape extending from beneath the large blue form previously discussed. As our eyes move upward, however, tangibility seems to shift to the *other* side of the contour—so that, near the center of the composition, the orange and yellow areas solidify into a single, positive form, while the deep red becomes increasingly less substantial, until eventually it appears simply as the negative ground against which the yellow-orange shape stands out. Further to the right (after its interruption by a patch of blue, which itself hovers at the threshold of consolidation into some larger, continuous shape), the burgundy color reappears, more or less aligned with its previous trajectory but this time as an independent squiggle, no longer articulating the edge of any more extended plane. Throughout the composition the phenomenon is repeated: lines continually shift from serving as contour to becoming detached, "pure lines," often before resuming their earlier role as delimiting edge, if now of some wholly discrete (and spatially separated) shape. Such inconstancy has an unsettling effect. Kandinsky evidently wanted us to feel that, like *Composition VII*, *Picture with Red Spot* consisted less of fixed forms than of forms perpetually coming into and out of being, materializing and dematerializing before our eyes.

NOT LONG AFTER HE COMPLETED THE PAINTING, Kandinsky's life would become equally unsettled. He left Munich following the outbreak of war in early August 1914, traveling first to Switzerland, before arriving in Russia four months later. Except for summers outside the city and a few brief trips abroad, Kandinsky would remain in Moscow until the end of 1921. This period was extraordinarily eventful on both political and personal fronts and, largely as a result of that, during much of it, the artist painted little. From 1918 until 1920 Kandinsky was preoccupied with administrative duties related to the education of artists and the exhibition of art in post-Revolutionary Russia. The years before were even less productive. He made no oil paintings in the latter half of 1914 or at any point during the whole of the following year. Even in 1916, he produced only a single work that can really be regarded as continuous with his earlier concerns.[83]

That work—*Picture on Light Ground* (Figure 31 / Plate 9)—was made during a brief stay in Stockholm early in the year. Despite its relatively small size (100 × 78 cm), Kandinsky clearly regarded the painting as important: it remained in his possession for the rest of his life. No less clearly, the painting signaled a departure from the flamboyance of his 1914 output. Its surface is considerably calmer than that of *Picture with Red Spot*, just as its palette is notably more muted. Earth tones prevail—the likes of which hadn't appeared in Kandinsky's art since *Composition V* (Figure 19 / Plate 5)—this time, with grays and browns providing the dominant tonality. Only a few saturated colors remain, clustered for the most part near the center and upper reaches of the canvas, though paler tints of the same hues are scattered a bit more widely throughout. The "light ground" of the title strongly recalls the white border of *Painting with White Border* (1913), and it's perhaps worth noting that, of the relatively few oil paintings Kandinsky did between 1914 and

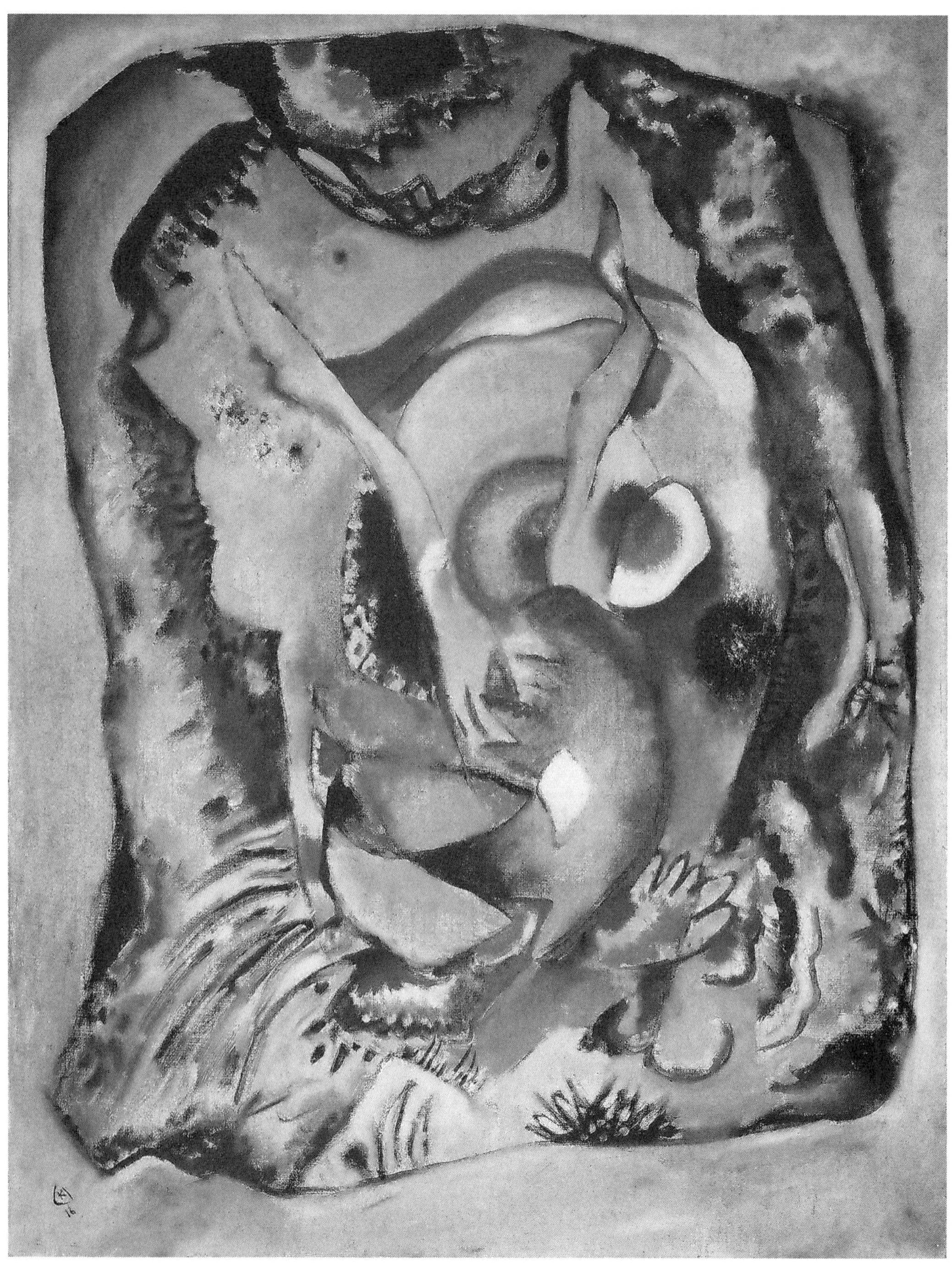

FIGURE 31. Wassily Kandinsky, *Picture on Light Ground*, January or February 1916. Oil on canvas, 100 × 78 cm. Musée national d'art moderne, Centre Georges Pompidou, Paris. Gift of Nina Kandinsky. CNAC/MNAM/Dist. RMN–Grand Palais/ Art Resource, New York. © Artists Rights Society (ARS), New York.

1920, over half a dozen of them include conspicuous borders of one kind or another.[84] In contrast to any of those other works, however, *Picture on Light Ground* is vertical in format, and therefore seems to suggest some relation to our upright bodies. The impression is of a landscape viewed through an open doorway (or, as some have suggested, from inside a cave),[85] that vista additionally flanked by what on first glance appear to be massive trees on either side. Each roughly vertical line of the composition seems to articulate a further passage into depth—the elongated, parallel bands of saturated color in the top half of the painting suggesting a horizon in the distance.

At some point in the viewing process, however, such imaginative projections inevitably come up short. It may be because the bands of saturated blue, green, and red refuse to appear sufficiently recessive; perhaps we notice that the brown, which we had initially taken to be volumetric modeling of the framing "trees," can just as easily be interpreted as shadows cast onto a (plausibly flat) surface by another plane located a short distance in front of it. Whichever the case, our observations trigger a complete reorientation in our perception of the depicted space. We suddenly recognize that space as invertible: its concavity becomes a convexity, the whole then appearing wholly indeterminate.

Once again line and its attendant spatial cues play a pivotal role. Consider, for example, the irregular contour running around the perimeter of the composition. The dark strokes and smudges just above its lower edge (like the bright touch of red that shadows its rightward turn in the upper left) imply that we're looking through a frame into a recessed space on the other side. However, the brown blotch in the painting's upper right-hand corner—which is clearly situated outside the encircling line—insinuates instead a matte surface onto which the central portion of the composition has been (loosely) mounted. The painting's title—both the preposition "on" and its identification of the light area as a *ground* (no less in the German, *Bild auf hellem Grund*)—lends support to such a reading. Just as with the white border of *Painting with White Border*, we're presented with a single planar surface that nonetheless maintains an utterly ambiguous spatial relation to the other elements of the composition (and to us). Again, the physical impossibility of the illusion seems very much to the point. Kandinsky was plainly searching for ever more economical means to create wholesale contradiction, thereby calling into question the factual givenness of the material support.

THE NEXT MAJOR STEP in this process was taken in 1919 with *In Gray (Im Grau)*, the largest and most significant of the paintings that Kandinsky produced in Moscow before 1921 (see Figure 32 / Plate 10).[86] In making it, the artist reverted to his more usual horizontal format, and chose a canvas that, if not so large as those

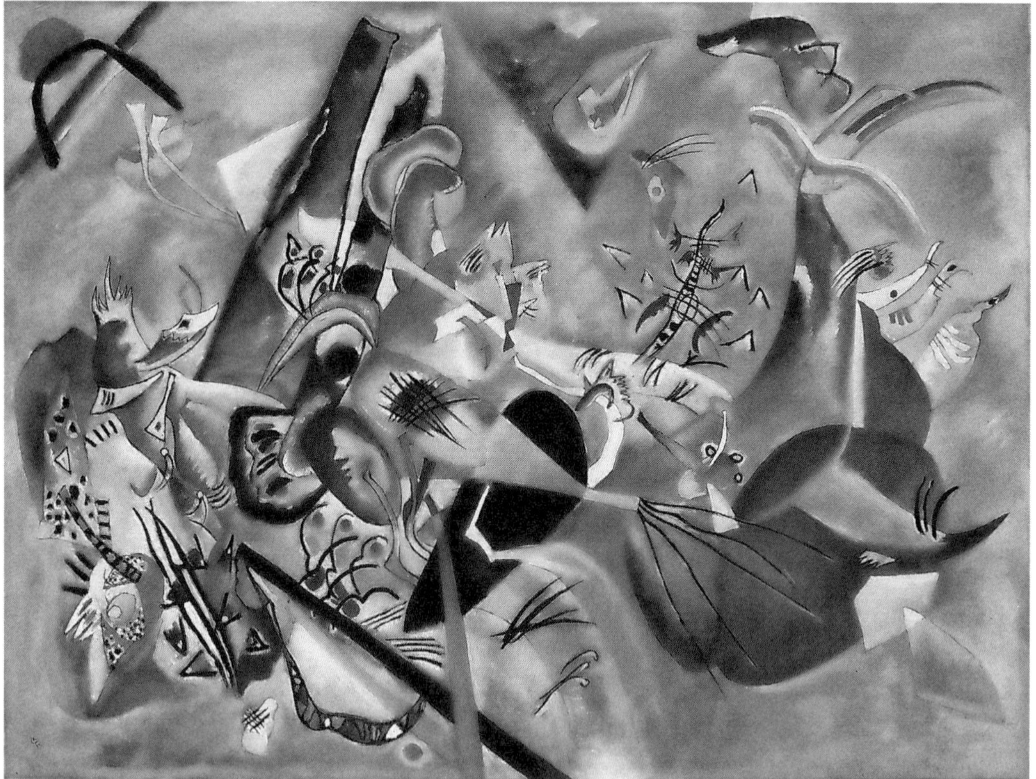

FIGURE 32. Wassily Kandinsky, *In Gray*, 1919. Oil on canvas, 129 × 176 cm. Musée national d'art moderne, Centre Georges Pompidou, Paris. CNAC/MNAM/Dist. RMN–Grand Palais/Art Resource, New York. © Artists Rights Society (ARS), New York.

he used for his earlier Compositions, was at least comparable in size to that of *Painting with White Border*. In fact, *In Gray* seems to invoke that earlier painting specifically, its gray coloration recalling both the white of the border and the neutral, gray-brown tones immediately adjacent. Of course, the 1919 work also evokes, even more forcefully, the light ground of *Picture on Light Ground*. In a sense, we might think of *In Gray*'s gray field as an extension of those paintings' framing ground and border. And yet, unlike either of those earlier elements, the gray field of *In Gray* refuses to acknowledge its literal planarity. Fault lines open up at several places across its expanse, giving rise to the illusion of distinct, if ever-shifting planes. In these places, the painting's gray field seems to recall—and draw more heavily upon—the kinds of ambiguities we saw in *Composition VII* and *Picture with Red Spot*.

The V-shaped patch of chiaroscuro modeling located near the middle of *In Gray*'s upper edge provides a good example of the phenomenon. The choppy, staccato brushwork in this area is reminiscent of any number of passages from paintings by Picasso or Braque done earlier in the decade, as is the attendant illusion of an emerging "facet plane." The effect is particularly pronounced along the left side of the "V," where the graduated modeling suggests a recessed surface—the lighter gray plane at left casting its shadow onto a parallel ground located not far behind. But near the vertex of the "V," and as it rises upward toward the right, the dark gray no longer reads as shadow. There, instead, it constitutes itself as *shape*, a positive form placed atop a lighter, more recessive ground. We find similar ambiguity surrounding the long serpentine line that winds its way from the upper right-hand corner toward the lower central portion of the composition. Along most of its length, that line is accompanied on its right side by a yellowish tint. The yellow is much brighter, however, at the lower end of the line, changing to a considerably browner shade above. This chromatic shift produces a contradictory pair of illusions: below, we perceive the yellow as "figure" against a (darkened) gray ground, whereas, above, it seems to play "ground" itself to a large, overlapping (lighter) gray plane.[87] It's worth noting, too, the ocher-colored line running through the large red "spot" below and to the right; its chromatic similarity encourages us to see it as continuous with the yellow-tinted area just discussed. Together, the two passages suggest the edges of a semitransparent plane set at an angle to, and intersected by, the opaque red oval in the lower right-hand corner. The presence of that second yellow-ocher line serves to detach both larger forms from the surface of the canvas, onto which, Kandinsky must have feared, they would otherwise have all too easily seemed to settle.

We should also note that dark black line makes a reappearance with *In Gray*. Despite the significance of line in general to Kandinsky's practice over the preceding several years, those lines were not the thick, insistent graphic elements that resurface in this painting. (Either they were colored or much more finely rendered, signaling an edge rather than an independent pictorial element.) Here, by contrast, we're reminded of the black markings in the left half of *Composition VII*, except that, in that work, lines of different colors were simultaneously present. *In Gray* partially reinstates the old opposition between (black) line and color.[88] Realizing this, we might easily assume that the opaque black elements of the painting were intended to function—in good *Hinterglasmalerei* fashion—to establish an ideal plane behind which the rest of the composition could then illusionistically assemble. In fact, though, Kandinsky appears to have been at considerable pains to force at least some of those assertive blacks into a semblance of depth. This is especially the case with the larger or more extended elements. For example, the long black diagonal stripe that rises from the bottom edge of the painting is crossed by an orange-red band whose tapered end pointedly suggests recession into depth. (If we focus on the orange band, it becomes all but impossible to read the black line any longer as a stripe resting on, or even running parallel to, the picture plane.) The large black "teardrop" above also seems shunted into depth—and rotated away from the plane of the canvas—through its contact with that colored band. Approaching the teardrop's upper edge, the band becomes increasingly dark, abruptly reverting to a pale orange after crossing to the other side. Pictorial convention has trained us to interpret changes of this nature in naturalistic terms: we read the band as semitransparent, its darkening color indicating increasing proximity to the black shape's uprighted edge. As a collateral effect, the literal flatness of the gray field is also negated; in the immediate vicinity at least it seems transformed from two-dimensional ground into atmospheric continuum, both the band and teardrop appearing suspended *in* gray rather than sitting flatly on its surface.

No less importantly, however, the illusion is not sustained. At its far end, our orange-red band changes back to a darker red, a development not easily reconciled with any naturalistic explanation.[89] Kandinsky may have found pictorial illusionism useful here and there as a means of de-literalizing the canvas, in some sense overcoming its factual planarity. But there would have been little point in turning away from representation of the natural world were the machinery developed for its mimetic depiction going to be left entirely intact. What Kandinsky seems to have wanted—indeed to have been actively pursuing—was a wholly new set of conventions specific to painting and constituted out of its recent, dialectical development. Neither based in nor directly appealing to perception of the natural world, such conventions would demonstrate that painting was (or ought to be) a thoroughly *self*-legislated practice, its governing norms arising from nothing other than its own ongoing history. Obviously, in 1919, the medium was not yet at such a point in its development. Painting would still have to draw on the techniques of an outmoded pictorial illusionism, but it could also contradict them at every turn. Kandinsky seems to have felt that this simply was how progress would be made—through a continual process of dissonance and negation.

THE TENSION IN *IN GRAY* between a depth evoked through pictorial illusionism and a no less insistent planarity is in some sense played out again in the contrast between *In Gray* as a whole and *Red Spot II* (Figure 33 / Plate 11), a work done two years later. If the earlier composition is underwritten by both chiaroscuro modeling and changes in hue that are equally suggestive of obliquity and recession, the shapes constituting *Red Spot II* present themselves to us as resolutely frontal, their surfaces running parallel to the picture plane. This is true even of those shapes, such as the large yellow "swoosh" on the left-hand side, that are tapered at one end. Any temptation we might have to see them as receding into depth is effectively neutralized by the presence of overlapping or intersecting shapes that insist instead on their parallelism with the surface. Similarly, except in the case of the titular red "spot," whatever changes in saturation or value we find within the central section

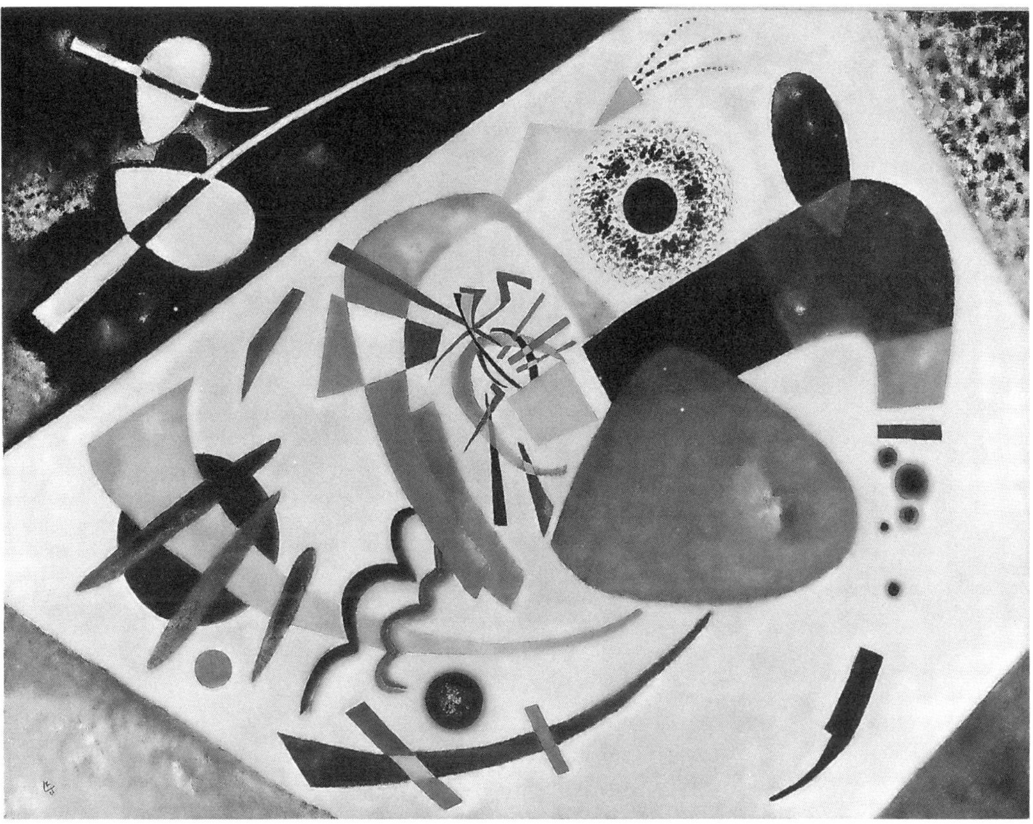

FIGURE 33. Wassily Kandinsky, *Red Spot II*, 1921. Oil on canvas, 131 × 181 cm. Städtische Galerie im Lenbachhaus, Munich. © Artists Rights Society (ARS), New York.

of the painting read as simply that—changes in saturation or value—rather than as part of any sculpturally illusionistic system. (It should be noted, too, that even with the red spot, the volumetric modeling is conspicuously compromised by the presence of a dark patch just where we would expect the sheen to be its brightest.) The overall effect is reminiscent of Kazimir Malevich's so-called aerial suprematist compositions (see Figure 34), where the geometric shapes, simply by virtue of their overlapping and off-axis rotation, appear to float above the underlying white field.[90]

Previously, Kandinsky had avoided such monochromatic fields, presumably out of fear that they would seem unambiguously two-dimensional and therefore wholly aligned with the literal plane of the canvas. Ever since *Composition V* (Figure 19 / Plate 5), he had in fact worked hard to eliminate any sense of a continuous surface, his first move being to dissolve it into a haze of indistinction. The sfumato grounds of *Composition VI* and *Painting with White Border* (Figures 18 and 22; Plates 4 and 6) are the fruits of those efforts. With *Composition VII* (Figure 24 / Plate 7) and subsequent paintings, Kandinsky reversed course, covering the surface

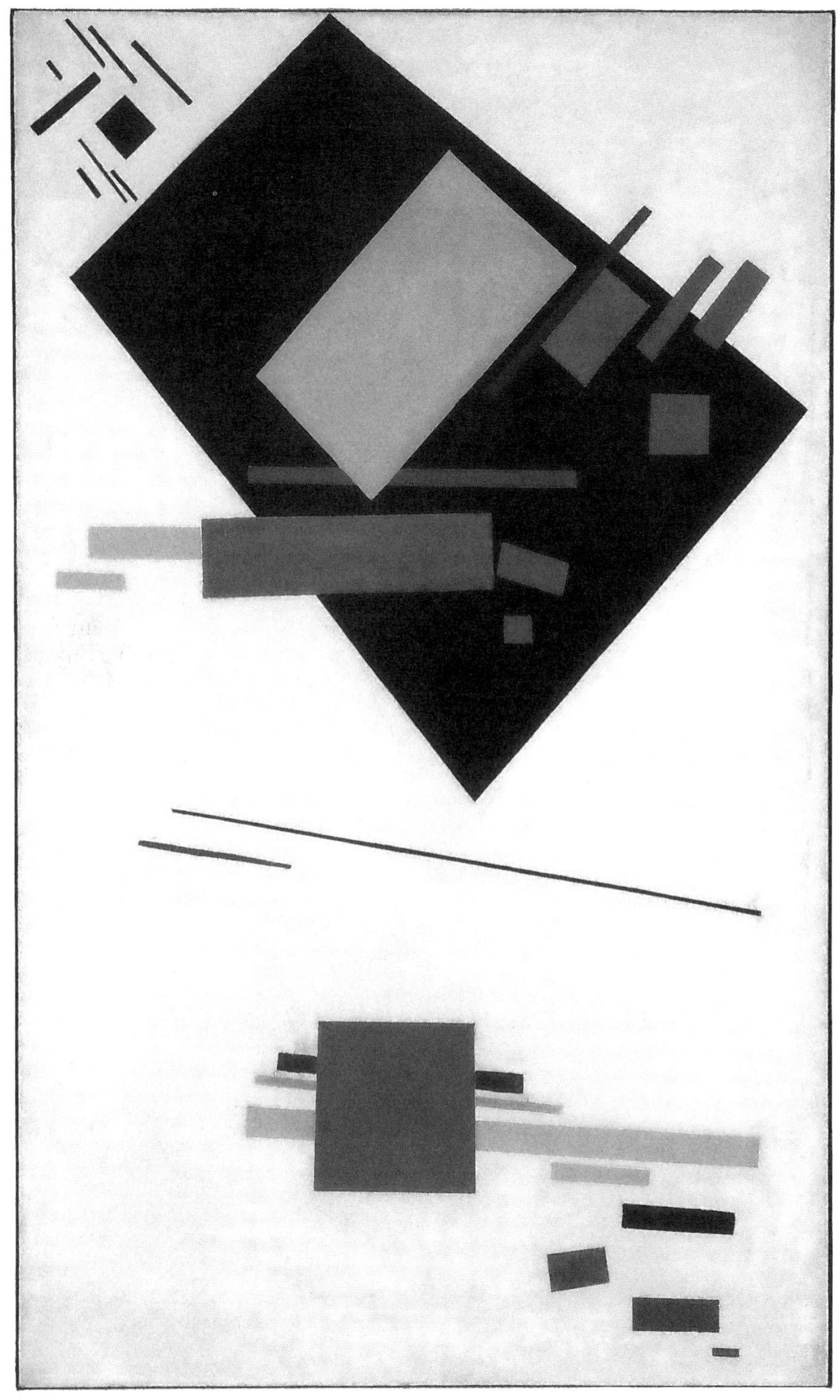

FIGURE 34. Kazimir Malevich, *Suprematist Painting (Black Trapezium and Red Square)*, 1915. Oil on canvas, 10.5 × 62 cm. Collection Stedelijk Museum, Amsterdam.

of the tableau with ever more clearly articulated and manifestly planar elements but introducing among those elements ambiguity regarding their spatial relationships with one another. *Picture on Light Ground* (Figure 31 / Plate 9)—and, above all, the surrounding light "ground" itself—might be seen as the culmination of that particular line of experiment.[91] *In Gray*'s attempt to, in effect, spread that ground across the entire composition was accompanied by a relatively high degree of pictorial illusionism, specifically, a quasi-sculptural modeling designed to open up "facet planes" within the otherwise undifferentiated field, thereby discouraging any easy association of that field with the physical surface of the canvas.

In contrast, with *Red Spot II*, Kandinsky eliminated chiaroscuro modeling from the composition's central field, presenting us with an apparently continuous white expanse.[92] Again, this area of the painting generally recalls suprematism in its more intricate or elaborated mode. Presumably Kandinsky intended to acknowledge Malevich's own, parallel strategies for de-literalization, above all, his ability to effectively liberate the compositional elements from the laws of gravity so as to apparently transform the material painting into an idealized, aesthetically achieved tableau. Yet, despite *Red Spot II*'s central tribute to suprematism, Kandinsky was clearly still not entirely willing to allow a single, continuous monochromatic field to provide the basis for his own compositions. However buoyant the other pictorial elements might appear against such a ground, he evidently regarded that ground itself as all too easily (mis)taken for the canvas, the tableau's illusionism made to seem entirely dependent (as in fact it was) on its physical, material substrate.

The solution Kandinsky arrived at with *Red Spot II* was to provide the composition with four framing (and distinctly mismatched) corners.[93] The central white ground doesn't read consistently as "ground"—doesn't even read as wholly planar—because we feel as though we're looking through a kind of aperture into a space behind.[94] The differences among the four distinct components of the frame further deepen the complexity, since each seems to take up a different position vis-à-vis the central section. The purple of the lower left corner can be perceived as either lying underneath (but fairly close to) the white field—that field casting a small shadow upon it—or, alternatively, as a closer, more tangible presence (the darker touches in that instance suggesting the downward slope of its own beveled edge). The brown in the lower right corner includes no really comparable spatial markers, and so appears either flush with the central white field or perhaps laid directly overtop of it (in either case, concretizing that central section as a two-dimensional plane). The upper right corner, which Kandinsky treated with his *Quetschtechnik*, is a great deal more ambiguous, thanks to both its literal tactility and the deliberate blurring of the edge that joins it to the central field. Viewed from up close, we're conscious that it resides above or on top of that central area, whereas from a distance it seems to lose its solidity altogether, implying the collateral breakup or dissolve of the adjacent monochromatic white plane. The black area in the upper left of the composition suggests the deepest space of all; in describing it, scholars have frequently resorted to astronomical imagery.[95] Together, the composition's four mismatched corners manage to dislocate the central white section of *Red Spot II* and render it wholly indeterminate: now it appears as surface (oscillating between near and far), now as infinite abyss.

Our perceptual experience of the composition is, as a result, remarkably similar to what we faced with *Picture on Light Ground*. Here, too, the elements of the central section appear to shuttle back and forth, sometimes seeming to project forward of the surface, sometimes retreating behind the "frame" into an illusory depth on the other side. In the case of *Red Spot II*, however, the shuttling is produced almost entirely without the aid of chiaroscuro modeling, the imaginary space of the tableau having shed all but the last vestiges of traditional pictorial illusionism.

APPARENT TRANSPARENCY

In *White Center* (Figure 35 / Plate 12), a work done later that same year, the grayish ground of *In Gray* returns, lighter this time, and without the sculptural modeling of the earlier composition.[96] Here value gradations suggest not the changing inflections or ruptures in the surface that they had earlier but, on the contrary, ambient space, a shadow-filled atmosphere that virtually dissolves our awareness of the painting's surface as a solid, tangible plane. (In that sense, we might see the "field" of *White Center* as sublating the differences between the tactile gray of *In Gray* and the central "abyss" of *Red Spot II*.) The illusion of depth is secured through multiple means, among them the six diagonal black stripes that cut across the lower left corner of the composition. Clearly derived from the framing edges of *Red Spot II* (as well as—at a further remove—the white border of *Painting with White Border*), they share some of their predecessors' spatial ambiguity. Foremost they function, collectively, as a repoussoir, interposing themselves between the other elements of the composition and space *this* side of the pictorial surface (i.e., the space in which we stand). Although each stripe is opaque and unmodulated and its width remains roughly consistent over its entire length, the unevenness of the group's spacing creates an impression of recession: each stripe reads like a transversal in a linear perspective construction, the space between them diminishing as they approach the implied vanishing point in the composition's lower left-hand corner. Through that variable spacing, we are encouraged to see the stripes, much as we're encouraged to see the majority of the compositional elements, as occupying different planes in depth, each of them nonetheless running parallel with both the picture plane and one another.

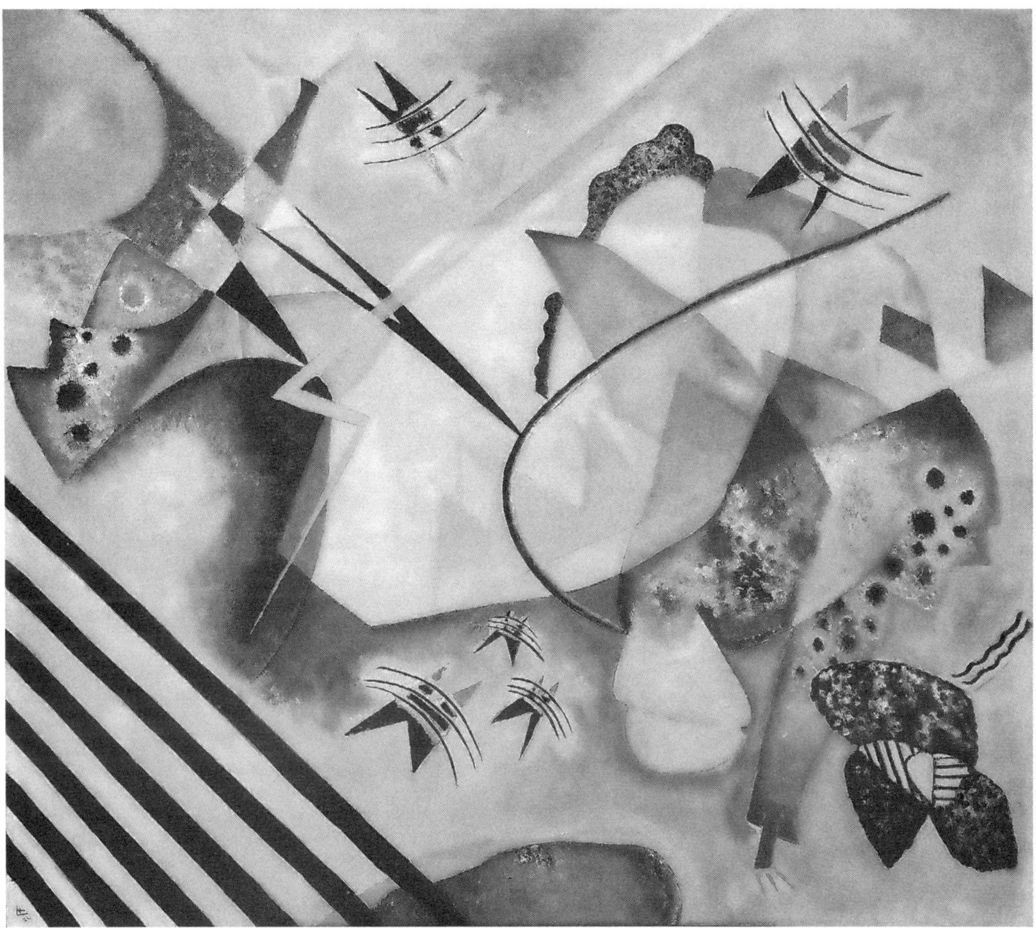

FIGURE 35. Wassily Kandinsky, *White Center*, 1921. Oil on canvas, 118.7 × 136.5 cm. Solomon R. Guggenheim Museum, New York, Hilla Rebay Collection 71.1936.R98. © Artists Rights Society (ARS), New York.

The most powerful illusion of depth within *White Center* is created not by any of the peripheral elements, however, but by the ghostly white center itself. Indeed the very fact that we accept that central shape as "white" (when a significant majority of the area within its borders is actually painted some other color) testifies to the strength of the illusion. The impression is of a hovering, transparent, all but intangible form—a milky film *through which* other, more brightly colored shapes are visible. (So convincing is the conceit that we feel certain we're seeing their true shades where those shapes extend beyond the center's external limits.)

Of course, one doesn't have to look very long or carefully before numerous inconsistencies and contradictions emerge within the illusion. To isolate but one example: the yellow "lightning bolt" that stretches down from the top of the canvas seems to pass underneath the white center's uppermost edge, yet it also somehow manages—after having become semitransparent itself—to appear above the narrow black "V" further along its course. (The bolt then slips once more beneath the white center before emerging clearly overtop of everything again at its lower, zigzagged end.) These, and the painting's other, analogous inconsistencies, aren't enough to dispel the illusionism; indeed they themselves depend on a certain measure of it. Yet, taken all together, they do undermine or negate any sense we might have had of that illusionism serving to re-create a set of relationships possible in the world outside the frame. In that regard, they forcefully assert *White Center*'s status as mere appearance, or *Schein*, as well as its achievement of a freedom from nature's determinacy far greater than that of any previous (even nonrepresentational) painting.

The transparency developed in *White Center* might be seen as having been precipitated by (or even as being a precipitate of) the pink "cloud" of *Composition VI* (Figure 18 / Plate 4). Overlapped by several pictorial elements and overlapping others in turn, *White Center*'s central, see-through plane seems to exist in the kind of vague, "somewhere" space—neither on the surface nor relegated to the ground—that Kandinsky worked so hard to create in and for *Composition VI*. But whereas the vaporous "cloud" of that painting appeared to inhabit a plausible three-dimensional space (hence Kandinsky's reference in his essay to the steam-filled Russian baths), the transparent center of *White Center* flatly declares its own two-dimensionality, even as it insists on its illusory status. (Its flatness appears detached at once from any tangible plane and the normal conditions of physical reality.) In that sense, the white center stands as a figure for the painting as a whole, demanding that we see it precisely not as a painting—not as pigment on canvas—but, rather, as an instance of a fully realized tableau.

In a significant majority of the works Kandinsky made following *White Center* (from 1921, then, until his death in 1944), transparent planes figure as prominent features of the composition. Their recurrence suggests that the artist saw them as resolving certain problems inherent in the art of painting. I tend to think they laid to rest—or at least greatly allayed—the fear he first expressed in *Über das Geistige* that the flatness required to put an end to painting's representational dimension would be misconstrued as a commitment to the literal materiality of the medium. In the apparently transparent plane, Kandinsky discovered a form that was unambiguously two-dimensional (and therefore proper to the art of painting) but no less evidently distinct from the tangible, opaque surface of the canvas. Transparency also enabled a degree of clarity not possible with the earlier compositions, which generally relied on techniques of "blurring" to dissolve the surface's physical presence. Henceforth the elements of each tableau could be neatly distinguished from one another without worry that they would appear consubstantial with the material plane of the painting.

On White II (Figure 36 / Plate 13), from the late winter–early spring of 1923, provides a striking case in point.[97] By this time—nearly two years after his invention of the illusionistically transparent plane—Kandinsky was sufficiently adept with the device that he could deploy it throughout the composition. Almost every shape is affected by it in one way or another. In contrast to the changes of value produced by the eponymous center of *White Center*, the transparent planes of

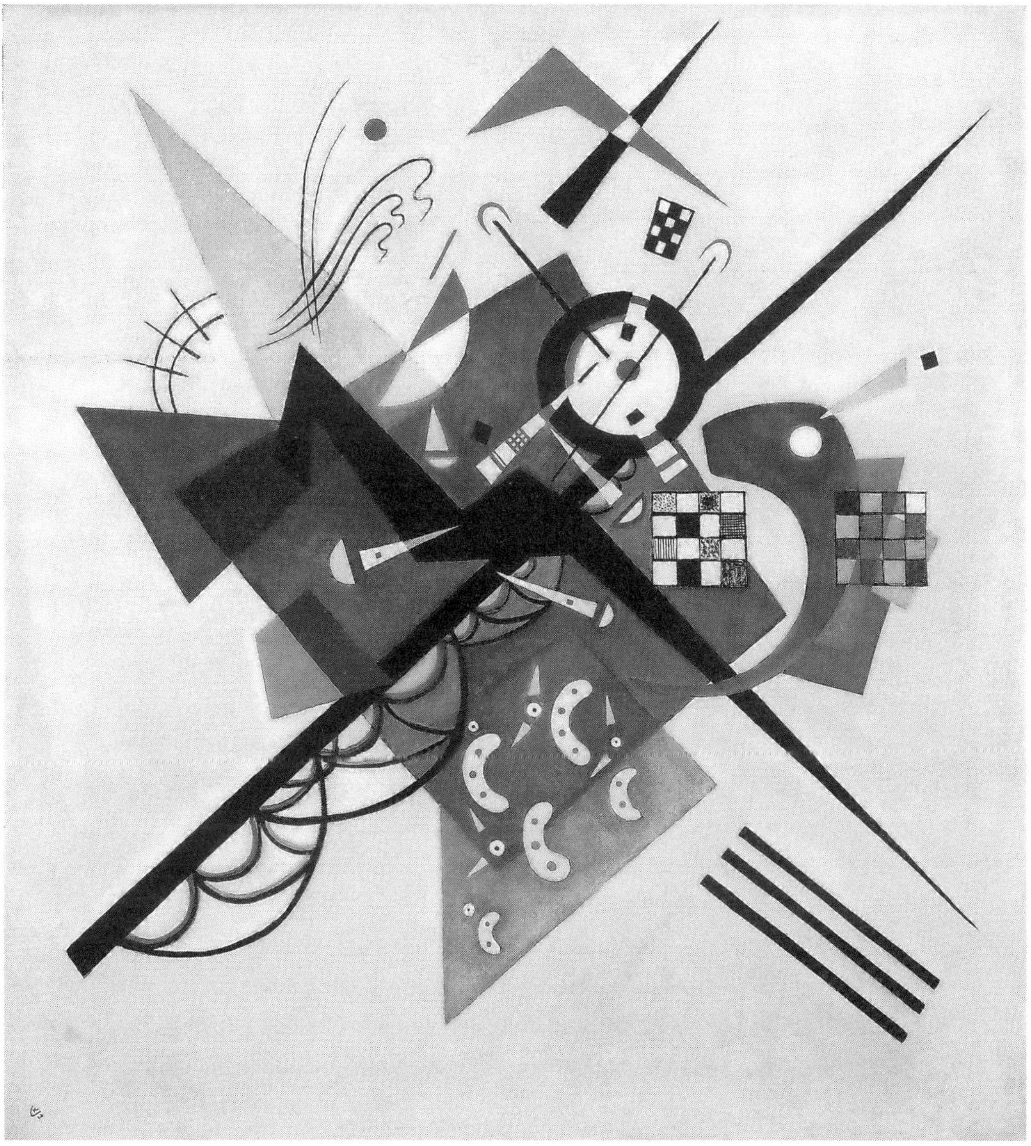

FIGURE 36. Wassily Kandinsky, *On White II*, between February and April 1923. Oil on canvas, 105 × 98 cm. Musée national d'art moderne, Centre Georges Pompidou, Paris. CNAC/MNAM/Dist. RMN–Grand Palais/Art Resource, New York. © Artists Rights Society (ARS), New York.

On White II generate—or, rather, their illusion of transparency is generated by—abrupt changes of hue. Where one shape apparently overlaps another, a new color is engendered; where three are involved (as is the case with the small area shared by both the red and yellow triangles and the central olive-green quadrilateral), even subtler chromatic changes come into play.[98] Kandinsky clearly relished the various spatial possibilities that transparent color opened up. By adjusting the proportions of the parent hues, he could control which plane appeared in front of which (and at what distance) or, alternatively, suggest differences in the shapes' relative transparency or opacity.[99] Evidently the resulting illusions were enough to convince him to produce at last the wholly monochromatic ground with which he had been flirting for some time. Transparency fostered the impression that each colored plane was situated at a different distance in depth, that illusion in turn serving to detach even the white ground from the literal surface of the canvas—and with far more efficacy, Kandinsky must have felt, than even Malevich's suprematism had been able to achieve (see Figure 34).[100]

Importantly, all of this was accomplished without the aid of either cast shadows or chiaroscuro modeling. Sculptural illusionism plays absolutely no role within the composition. Whatever depth *On White II* seems to possess is generated out of manifestly planar elements—as is only appropriate (we can almost hear Kojève saying) to any *vrais tableau*. Apparently in keeping with their wholly planar existence, the various components of the composition have also now become regularly geometric, the circles and rectangles that first emerged in *Red Spot II* and other works of that era having at last displaced the irregular, eccentric or frequently amorphous shapes of Kandinsky's earlier compositions.[101]

We should probably also note that *On White II* is both slightly vertical in orientation—the dimensions of the canvas are 105 × 98 cm—and comparatively symmetrical. Kandinsky may have opted for such a compact format, and then chosen to cluster forms around its central area, in order to maximize the opportunities for overlapping and thereby to showcase his newly invented transparency.[102] Be that as it may, neither the compactness of *On White II* nor its privileging of the center was carried over into the much larger *Composition VIII* (Figure 37 / Plate 14), completed less than three months later. On the contrary, with that work the elements are widely—and irregularly—dispersed across the painting's considerable expanse. Each element registers as visually distinct from the others, even where they intersect or overlap. Partly as a result, they all also appear to be free-floating, as if they were suspended in a vaporous (and therefore potentially non-static) medium. That impression is further aided by the fact that, in place of the utterly monocolored ground of *On White II*, we find one ever so subtly tinted, yet virtually devoid of any evidence of the artist's hand. Its gradual chromatic shifts so

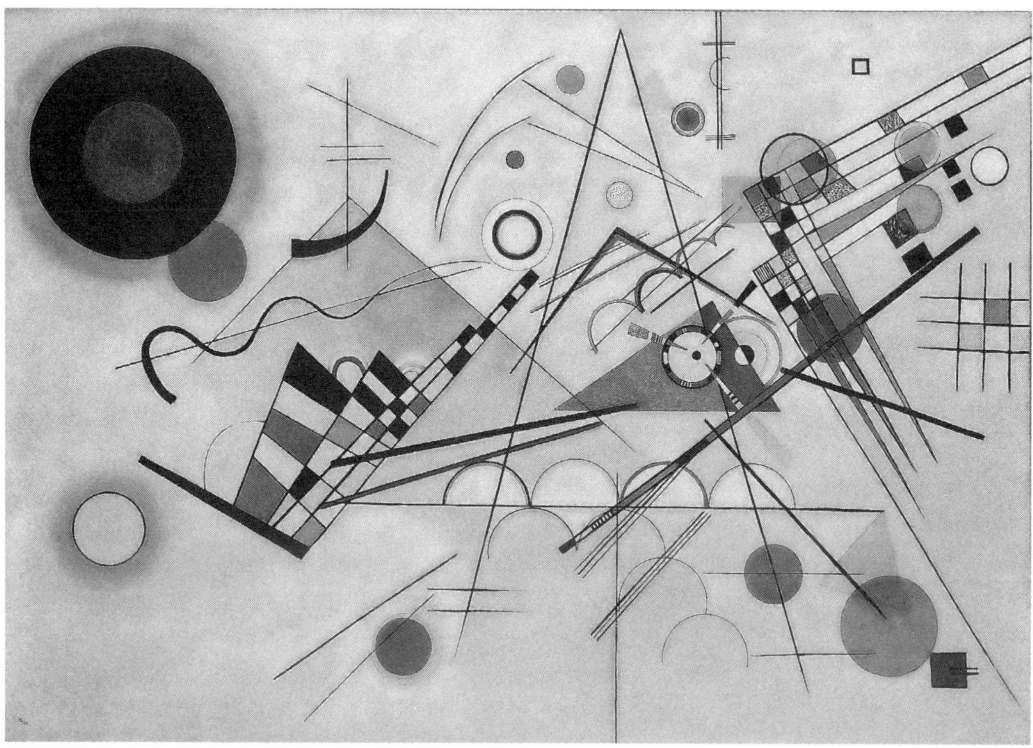

FIGURE 37. Wassily Kandinsky, *Composition VIII*, July 1923. Oil on canvas, 140 × 201 cm. Solomon R. Guggenheim Museum, New York, Solomon R. Guggenheim Founding Collection 37.262. © Artists Rights Society (ARS), New York.

effectively de-solidify the surface that the earlier composition seems flatly literal by comparison.[103]

Similarly, if the elements of *On White II* are more clearly articulated than anything in the paintings that preceded them, they are yet nowhere nearly so precisely drawn as their counterparts in *Composition VIII*. There, we're presented with an unparalleled degree of technical rigor: finely ruled lines comingle with circles at whose centers compass points are plainly visible. Alongside these perfected geometries, *On White II* appears almost casual—full of freehand drawing and all sorts of inexactitudes, both graphic and chromatic.[104] In combination with the uneven, asymmetrical distribution of elements in *Composition VIII* and the generally generous spacing (especially on the painting's left-hand side), this precision of execution testifies to an increasing tendency toward particularization in Kandinsky's oeuvre: an emphasis on the individual element over and above even its integration into some larger whole. Clearly we've come a long way from the widespread indistinction of *Composition VI* or *Painting with White Border*. Although it's common to attribute these developments—particularly the increasing clarity and geometrization of the forms—to the "external" influence of the artist's Bauhaus colleagues, they are just as plausibly (and perhaps more interestingly) seen as outgrowths of the dialectical opposition between "precise" and "blurred" that first arose in Kandinsky's paintings of 1911, if not before. The transparencies and subtle tinting found in *Composition VIII* can similarly be viewed as products of that dialectic: they mark the return, at a higher level, of the "blurred" color that, in separating itself from line, introduced a measure of depth into the otherwise highly planar *Composition IV* (Figure 16 / Plate 3).[105]

MATERIALITY AND IMMATERIALITY

Following *Composition VIII*, Kandinsky's production would be driven to a large extent by the related dialectic of materiality and immateriality, that dialectic playing itself out both within individual tableaux and from one painting to the next.[106] Although most of his compositions from 1923 have little or no visible *faktura*, in many of those painted the year after, the pigment, at least in certain areas, has a manifestly tangible presence. These textured surfaces are plausibly seen as outgrowths of the *Quetschtechnik* that Kandinsky first developed for *Painting with White Border* (Figure 22 / Plate 6) and that lent the "baroque" compositions of the following year (see Figure 30 / Plate 8) their distinctively pointillist character. For that reason, it may be worth taking a brief accounting of the *Quetschtechnik*'s own somewhat spotty history before proceeding on to our discussion of the works from 1924 and after.

Having made its first appearance in 1913, and later come into its own with *Fugue* and *Picture with Red Spot*, the *Quetschtechnik* then gradually began to recede in prominence; it plays only a very minor role (in the lower left-hand corner) of 1919's *In Gray* (Figure 32 / Plate 10), for example. Conspicuously resurfacing in several paintings from 1921 (including *Red Spot II* and *White Center*), it appeared on and off over the next year or so before all but disappearing again during the first half of 1923. *In the Black Square* (*Im Schwarzen Viereck*), painted in June of that year, just one month before the completion of *Composition VIII*, marks the technique's final reemergence.[107] A variety of textured surfaces would appear with increasing frequency thereafter, reaching a local high point in the deliberately retrospective painterliness of 1924's *Backward Glance* (*Rückblick*).[108] In subsequent works—including *In Blue* (Figure 38 / Plate 15) from January 1925—we witness Kandinsky's attempts to integrate these renascent textures with his recently developed interests in transparency and geometric form.[109]

In many important respects, *In Blue* seems to reverse the gains of *Composition VIII*. Rather than the delicate lines and pastel hues of the earlier painting, we find areas of textured impasto—most prominently within the large red circle just above and to the right of center—and a ground that, although still essentially mono-

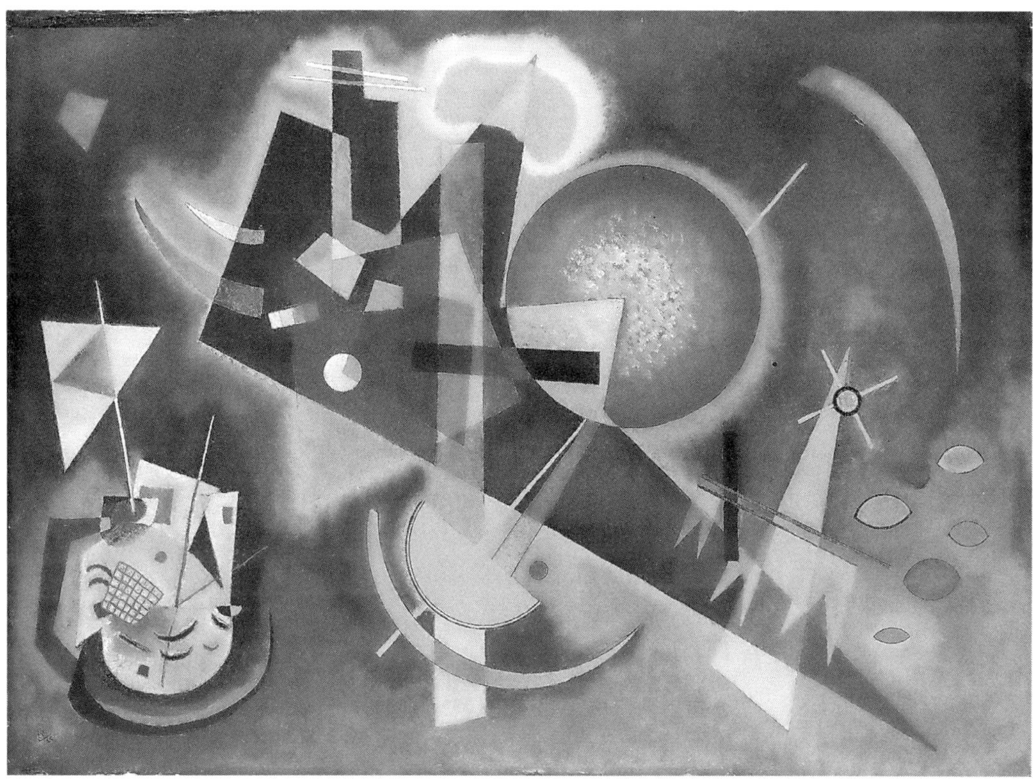

FIGURE 38. Wassily Kandinsky, *In Blue*, January 1925. Oil on cardboard, 80 × 110 cm. Kunstsammlung Nordrhein-Westfalen, Düsseldorf. © Artists Rights Society (ARS), New York.

chromatic, appears much heavier and more somber than anything since *In Gray*. Where the spacing within *Composition VIII* lent the elements an airy buoyancy, *In Blue* presents us instead with a dense accumulation of forms, especially along the diagonal stretching from the painting's upper left- to lower right-hand corners. (It's as if Kandinsky suddenly grew dissatisfied with the earlier work's scattering of particulars, and vowed a greater cohesiveness in subsequent compositions.) The cumulative effect of these differences is to make *In Blue* seem much more visibly material than any of its immediate predecessors. And yet, implausibly, a semblance of weightlessness attaches to even the heaviest of its forms. Variations of value, saturation, and hue make the "ground" appear atmospheric, or perhaps aqueous—in any case, permeable rather than solid. As with earlier works, the title reinforces that impression: the elements of the tableau float *in* blue, rather than array themselves on or against a backdrop it comprises. The clustering of shapes near the center of the composition becomes the occasion for numerous instances of overlapping transparencies, each of which was clearly designed to further de-realize the physical presence of the painting. Most striking of all are the several cases where the illusion is not of a transparent *plane* coloring another shape or shapes seen through its surface, but rather of two or more convergent *areas of light*, the color of their intersection the apparent product of an additive mixing.[110] The most conspicuous example of the phenomenon occurs within the vertical "yellow-orange" bar just to the left of the composition's central axis. Where it intersects with the red and blue counterposed quadrilaterals, the result is a notable brightening of their initial colors, the pigments approximating—however improbably—the effects of spectral light.

I am inclined to think that, even with the earlier instances of illusionistically transparent planes, Kandinsky specifically avoided a simple, literal combination of the parent hues.[111] Near the center of *Composition VIII*, for example, where the green triangle seems to pass behind the large, upright, pink-tinted wedge, the "resulting" light brown color was clearly not produced through an actual mixing of the green and pink pigments. We were meant, I think, to recognize the wholly fictional status of the illusion, even as we experience its full effect. For similar reasons, Josef Albers would later insist that his students use pasted papers rather than paints in their various experiments with color. "What counts here—first and last—," Albers instructed, "is not so-called knowledge of so-called facts, but vision—seeing," which he went on to associate with both imagination and a larger *Weltanschauung*.[112] Only cut-out opaque papers would adequately emphasize the role of intuition and imagination in color "mixing" and "transparency." Kandinsky, by using pigments to create the illusion of *additive* mixtures (of projected rather than reflected light), was plainly aiming at a similar degree of visible self-contradiction. The phenomenon of color, as he presents it with *In Blue*, is preposterous—patently less physical or chemical than *geistige*. Both its transparencies and additive mixtures are factual impossibilities that nonetheless manage to make their appearance within the composition, thereby effectively transforming the work from painting to tableau.[113]

Kandinsky seems to have been toying, albeit half-heartedly, with the illusion of additive mixing for even the large red, heavily textured circle, the most tangibly material component of the entire composition. Where the circle overlaps the irregular, central blue-black shape, it negates that shape's defining darkness, substituting in its place a much more luminous gray. The effect is (perhaps deliberately) too schematic—more diagram than illusion, its result a merely cut-out form—and yet an idea seems to have been planted in the process. My sense is that Kandinsky first began to realize here, at just this moment, that the dialectic of materiality and immateriality developing in his work would soon arrive at a point where it would become necessary to accentuate the literal, physical properties of at least some portions of the composition—that it was, paradoxically, only through such accentuation that further progress in the direction of de-materialization could be made.

That idea returns in a more fully realized form the following year, in the work known as *Several Circles* (*Einige Kreise*), now in the collection of the Guggenheim Museum, New York (Figure 39 / Plate 16). The work's velvety black ground both reprises and transforms the modulated field of *In Blue*, even as its compass-drawn circles and their pastel coloring recall the lighter, lilting geometries of *Composition VIII*. In their new context, those colors evince an unprecedented luminosity. In fact, both the magentas and the blues—the bright blue of the largest disk no less than the lighter cyans of the small circles scattered throughout—seem to

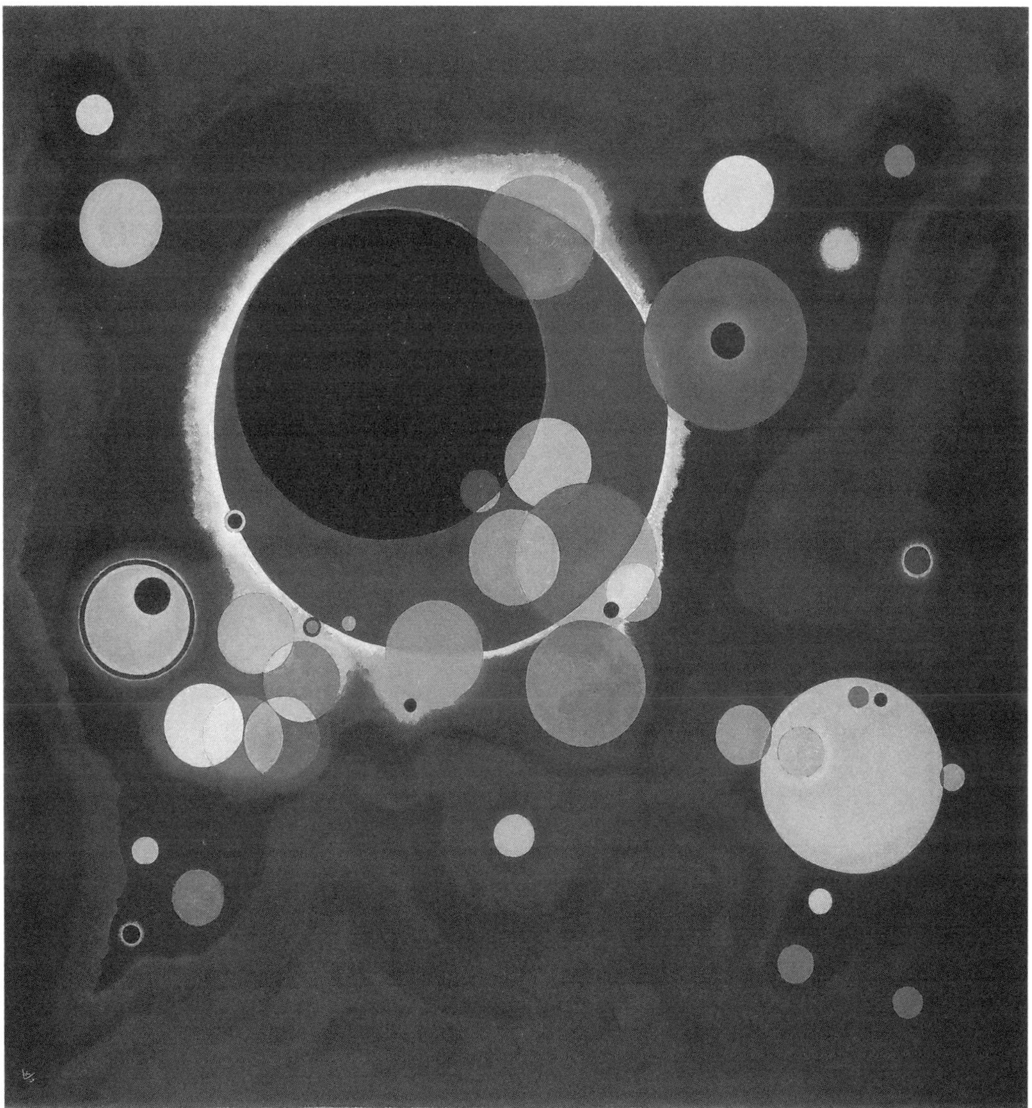

FIGURE 39. Wassily Kandinsky, *Several Circles*, January–February 1926. Oil on canvas, 140.3 × 140.7 cm. Solomon R. Guggenheim Museum, New York, Solomon R. Guggenheim Founding Collection 41.283. © Artists Rights Society (ARS), New York.

have been chosen specifically to invoke *additive* color mixtures. (It's worth recalling here that diagrams of additive mixing almost always entail intersecting circles placed against a black ground, the black indicating the absence of light outside the color spectrum; see Figure 40 and Plate 17.) Although a few of the circles within *Several Circles*—for example, the largest of the orange ones near the center of the composition—affect the illusion of subtractive transparency (the area of intersection being darker than either of the parent hues), the majority of the disks instead hint at additive mixtures, as if they were composed of light rather than of the pigments that they actually are.[114]

In the case of the large, unmodulated black disk above and to the left of the center of *Several Circles*, we seem to be dealing again mostly with subtractive effects—though the results are far more confounding than anything we've seen so far. Kandinsky carefully varnished the surface of the disk, so that it appears substantially different from the other, surrounding elements of the composition.[115] The varnish both calls our attention to the circle's surface, giving it a tactile presence absent elsewhere, and periodically obscures our visual apprehension of it; from certain angles, the glossy disk virtually disappears in the gleam of (real) reflected light. Even if one avoids the glare, however, the evident opacity of the circle seems in doubt. What we're confronted with, in relation to both the bright violet disk along the circle's upper edge and, even more, the smaller blue one located a quarter-turn below, is the circle's improbable transparency. We can only make sense of the smaller disks' chromatic changes if we assume that we're somehow see-

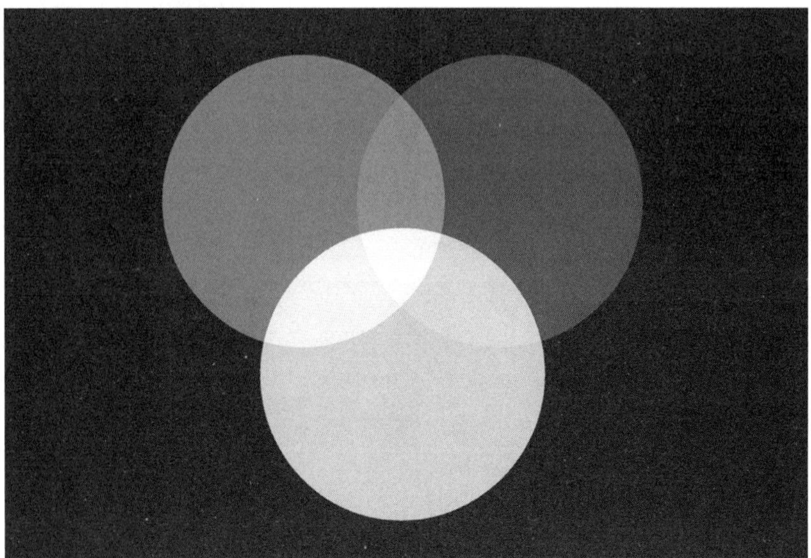

FIGURE 40. Diagram of projected light / additive color mixing, © 2013 Shutterstock, Inc.

ing each of them *through* the larger circle's glossy, jet-black surface.[116] The illusion isn't perfect, of course—given its natural impossibility, how could it be?—and yet, once we've see it, it's surprisingly difficult to dismiss. Despite being both counter-intuitive and counterfactual, the perception of transparency persists.

Several Circles's title and subject matter clearly link it to *Circles within a Circle* (*Kreise im Kreis*) from 1923 (Figure 41); and both compositions bring to mind the "circle of circles" (*Kreis von Kreisen*) that Hegel regularly invoked as a figure for the integrated, "plastic" structure of his speculative philosophical system.[117] Kandinsky

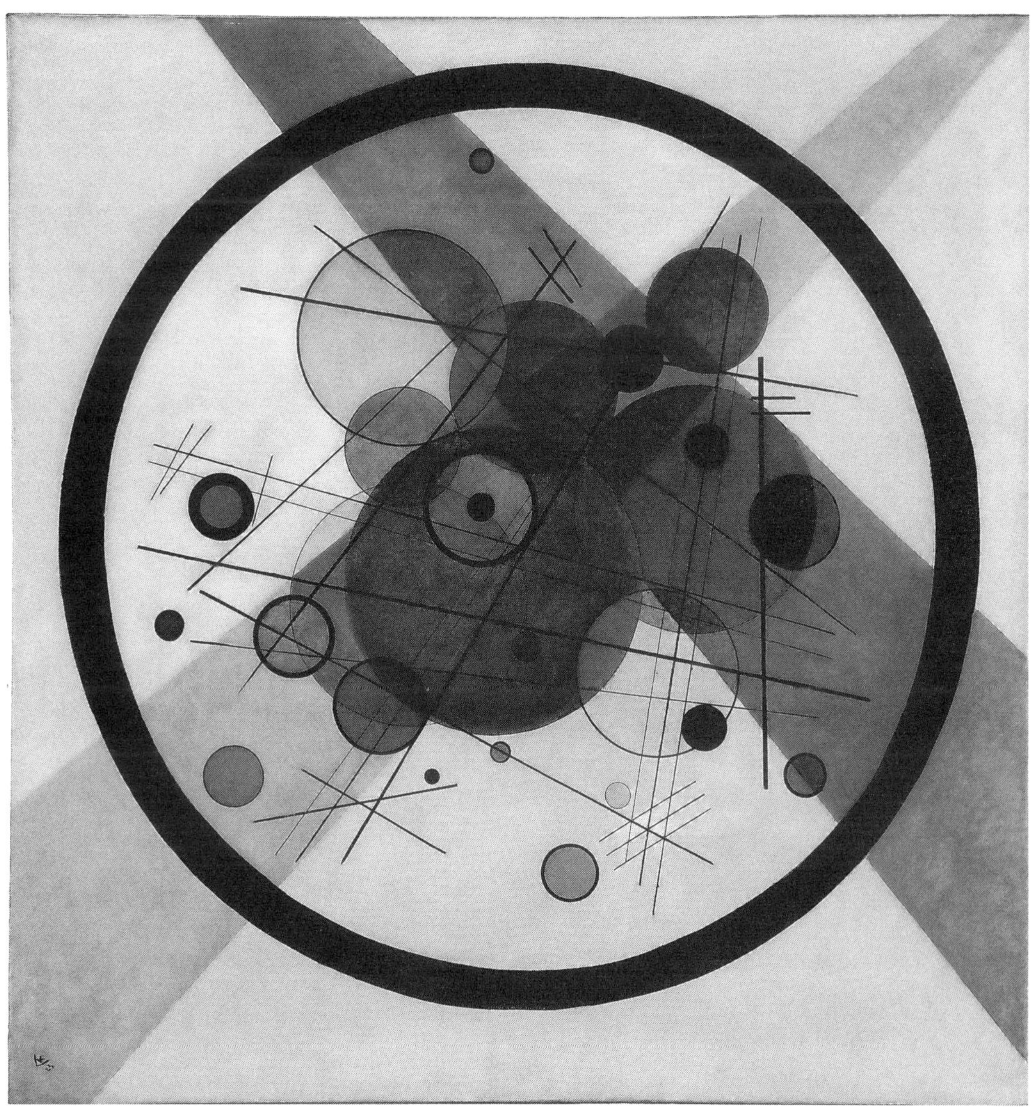

FIGURE 41. Wassily Kandinsky, *Circles within a Circle*, July 1923. Oil on canvas, 98 × 95 cm. Philadelphia Museum of Art, Louise and Walter Arensberg Collection. © Artists Rights Society (ARS), New York.

himself would argue, in 1930, that, of all the geometric shapes, the circle was the "synthesis of the greatest oppositions," combining "the concentric and the excentric in a single form."[118] Tellingly, it was *Several Circles*—or, rather, his encounter with the work at a 1929 exhibition in Dresden—that motivated the 27-year-old Alexandre Kojève to renew contact with his artist uncle. As their correspondence attests, the two had been out of touch for many years, and Kojève, by his own admission, was largely unaware of the changes that Kandinsky's oeuvre had undergone in the interim. Expecting to see something more akin to the earlier paintings with which he was familiar, Kojève was brought up short by the more recent work on display in Dresden. Writing specifically of *Several Circles*, he confessed to his uncle of having been dismayed by the asymmetry of the composition and what he initially mistook for the arbitrary arrangement of its forms: "the center is absent," he observed, the work's external limits "completely fortuitous."[119] It was only after having stood, perplexed, before it for some time that Kojève realized the different elements of the tableau had a significance "tying them all together."[120] (It seems likely that the idea for "Les Peintures concrètes" began to germinate at just that moment.) He came to see, as he explained in his letter to Kandinsky, that each of the circles was "as infinite as the world whose aesthetic aspects they reflect[ed]." "Since they are infinite," he added, "they cannot have a 'center,' or rather—this is the same thing—each point of the tableau becomes a 'center.' . . . They are already aspects of the totality."[121]

Perhaps even more directly than Hegel's "circle of circles," Kojève's description of Kandinsky's composition invokes the infinite circle of Nicholas of Cusa—the circle whose center is everywhere and circumference nowhere, and that is, as a result, absolved of all external relation.[122] Recalling the parallel Kandinsky himself drew (at least implicitly) in *Punkt und Linie zu Fläche* between the point "in repose" and the centeredness of classical sculpture, we may be tempted to follow Kojève's lead, and so to see *Several Circles*, much as Hegel saw his philosophical system, as the repetition at a higher level of classical sculpture's achievement: the fact and thought of center made absolute.[123] I'm at least inclined to believe that such thoughts were not far from Kandinsky's own understanding of his composition. Certainly I take it as a given that, in these years, Kandinsky was trying to achieve the kind of self-sustaining unity-in-difference that Hegel regarded as the defining characteristic of absolute knowledge—and which was for both men visually encapsulated in the circle's rounded geometric form.

Circles in fact figure exceptionally prominently, often exclusively, in a great many of Kandinsky's compositions of this period. Among the key works, in addition to *Several Circles*, are the suggestively titled *In Itself* (*In Sich*) and *Conclusion* (*Schluss*), both also, like *Several Circles*, from 1926.[124] In retrospect, it's evident that that year marked a major turning point in Kandinsky's oeuvre. Apparently attracted by the completeness of the circle's form, the artist returned to it again and again; it's not a stretch, I think, to imagine him weighing the possibility that the dialectic that had driven his production over the last fifteen years might finally be drawing to a close. Rather than declaring the End of Art History, however, and settling comfortably into repetition of what he had already achieved, Kandinsky pressed on, returning to those achievements only as so many platforms from which to strike out anew. As we'll see, his production from the late twenties on is every bit as varied, if not more, than the work of the preceding decade and a half. I would go so far as to say that what's most remarkable about Kandinsky's oeuvre, both late and early (and what sets it most apart from the claims that Kojève's "Les Peintures concrètes" would make on its behalf), is its constant transformation—what we might call its "plasticity" or, again, its absolute commitment to developmental change.[125]

Consider, for example, *On Points* (Figure 42 / Plate 18), a work from 1928. Manifestly related to *Several Circles* via the numerous circles of its own composition, the work also invokes the light yellow ground, acute angles and delicate line of *Composition VIII*. In *On Points*, however, those features are combined with a pronounced painterly *faktura* altogether foreign to either of the earlier paintings. We would have to look to 1924's *Backward Glance*—or, better, 1911's *Composition IV* (Figure 16 / Plate 3)—to find a surface truly comparable. Here Kandinsky employs that painterliness to lend the rendered geometric elements a tangible presence, even as he tries to dissolve their materiality at the level of the tableau. A specific color attaches to each of the geometric shapes, and yet it refuses to coalesce into a solid plane. Partly as a result, the kind of illusionistic (subtractive) color mixing familiar from works past is notably more muted here. Kandinsky seems to have wanted the elements to appear at once more insistently material (hence their evident facture) *and* more thoroughly see-through than even the transparent disks of *Several Circles*. The spatial implications are equally contradictory. We find ourselves peering into a dense thicket of indeterminacy, in which it's impossible to ascertain which element is in front of which, despite an abundance of spatial cues. Shapes constantly seem to change places with one another in depth, enacting a compositional instability far greater, even, than that suggested by the imagery of all those triangles precariously balanced on their points.

And what of that imagery? To my mind at least, it's a bit too diagrammatic, too blunt in its insistence that we regard the composition as a balance of countervailing forces. The work leans too heavily on an iconography of unsteadiness. Yet the underlying impulse—to upset or unsettle the tidy harmonies of *Several Circles*, and so to restart the dialectical movement of his art—perhaps justifies (and does

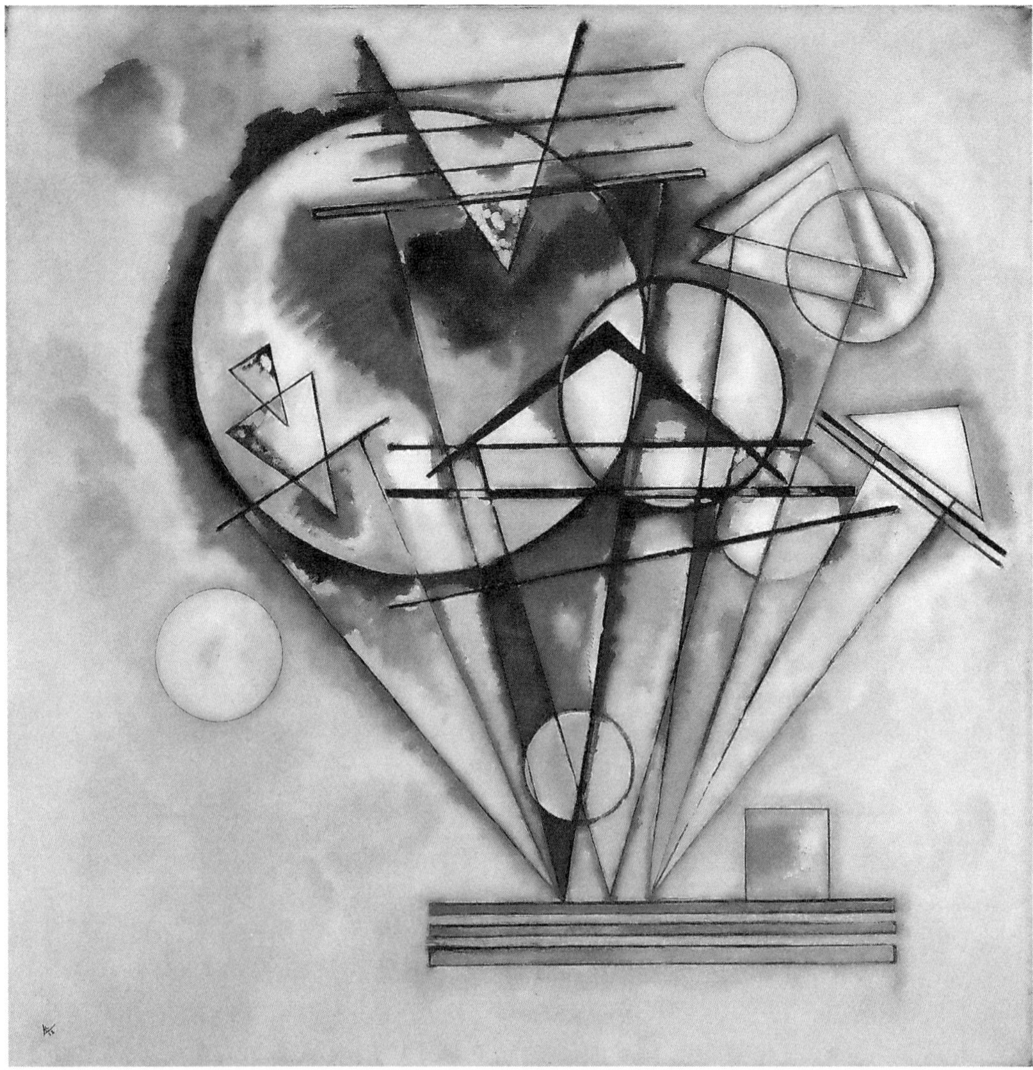

FIGURE 42. Wassily Kandinsky, *On Points*, 1928. Oil on canvas, 140 × 140 cm. Musée national d'art moderne, Centre Georges Pompidou, Paris. CNAC/MNAM/Dist. RMN–Grand Palais/Art Resource, New York. © Artists Rights Society (ARS), New York.

even more to explain) Kandinsky's recourse to such obvious measures.[126] It must be said, too, that the triangles do their job. Where the geometric shapes of *Several Circles* had been differentiated from one another only by variation in size and color, those of *On Points* are plainly more heterogeneous—even as they're also drawn into tighter clusters, multiple elements coming together to form larger, more complicated compounds.

In fact *On Points* can be seen as launching a new period of pluralism in Kandinsky's oeuvre. His early works, those done in Munich, also seemed to be progressing toward an ever-greater diversity of forms (no less than of *faktura*) yet those forms' external contours were never completely evident. Both *Composition VII* (Figure 24 / Plate 7) and *Picture with Red Spot* (Figure 30 / Plate 8), for example, present us with a kind of "primordial soup" out of which shapes begin to emerge, only to be re-assimilated. In the works of the early twenties, by contrast, we find a progressive clarification of the shapes' external limits but, at the same time, a strong movement toward regularization: the shapes themselves are becoming ever more geometric, with the circle eventually emerging as the dominant pictorial form. (One might even argue that it's only the homogeneity of *Several Circles*'s elements that holds that composition together.) Beginning with *On Points*, however, Kandinsky seems to have become progressively more concerned with diversifying his formal repertoire. At least initially, he did so simply by combining the basic geometric shapes of his recent work into a variety of more complicated aggregates.

Levels (*Etagen*) (Figure 43 / Plate 19), a work from 1929, offers a further example of the practice. The painting as a whole is relatively small—its dimensions are 56.6 × 40.6 cm (roughly, 21 × 16 inches)—the individual geometric forms bordering, then, on the minute. As with *On Points*, circles and triangles predominate, but now they're brought into even closer conjunction, forming larger, collective entities. In addition, many of the basic geometric shapes are themselves subdivided, with each section painted a different color. That internal articulation complements the subdivision or compartmentalization of the composition at large. Running down the vertical axis of the painting is a skeletal armature—an apparent cross between étagère and phylogenetic tree—which neatly brackets off the geometric entities into twelve distinct zones or "levels." It functions both to impose a certain symmetry on the composition and to provide the various components, whatever their differences, with a common frame of reference, thereby lending them a degree of commensurability. In this current phase of work, which I referred to earlier as a period of pluralism within Kandinsky's oeuvre, diversification is accompanied by a pronounced effort not only to integrate those individual heterogeneous elements into the composition as a whole, but also to make evident their interrelatedness. This is the central purpose of the diagrammatic "tree": it helps to articulate the relation of part-to-part and part-to-whole. In that sense, it seems intended to make visible what we could call the *jointure* of the tableau—or, more simply, the means by which it holds itself together (*se maintien* / *sich erhalten*).

A useful contrast might be drawn here between *Levels* and *Composition VIII* (Figure 37 / Plate 14), done six years earlier. Previously I claimed that *Composition VIII* belonged to a moment of increasing particularlization in Kandinsky's oeuvre, its elements both clearly distinguished from one another and emphasized in that distinction over and above their integration into the structure of the whole.

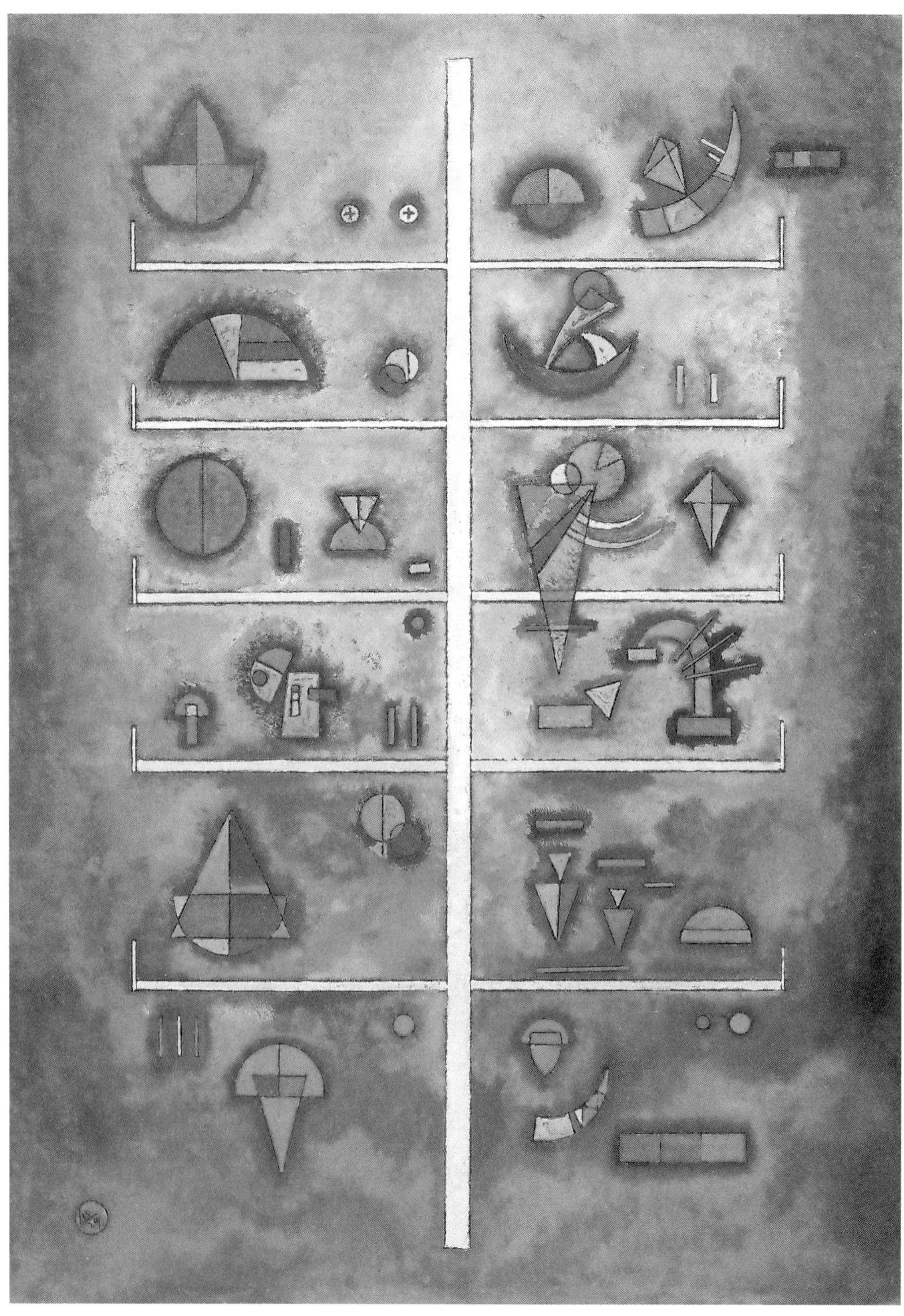

FIGURE 43. Wassily Kandinsky, *Levels*, March 1929. Oil on Masonite, mounted on wood, 56.6 × 40.6 cm. Solomon R. Guggenheim Museum, New York, Solomon R. Guggenheim Founding Collection 46.1049 © Artists Rights Society (ARS), New York.

In fact, with *Composition VIII* it isn't evident that the whole even has a structure, much less that it's sustained by the integration of its parts.[127] If *Levels* preserves that era's interest in the precise delineation of forms, it moves not only in the direction of greater diversity, but also, perhaps of necessity, toward an increasing emphasis on the individual parts' belonging to the composition they constitute. In this sense as well, we might see *Levels*, and the work of the late twenties generally, as looking back to the densely interwoven compositions of 1913 and 1914. Where those tableaux appeared largely indivisible, however—their "sound" comparatively inchoate or inarticulate—Kandinsky's later works, from *Levels* onward, are oriented toward ever more exact articulation.

Before turning to subsequent (and more developed) examples of the phenomenon, a word or two should be said in regard to the palpable materiality of *Levels*. In comparison with the broad, distinct strokes marking *On Points*, the brushwork here is tighter, more compacted, the pigments notably scumbled. Despite the apparent density of the background color, much of it was clearly applied with a dry brush that was repeatedly dabbed against the surface. In combination with the blue-green tonalities, the effect is generally vaporous or aqueous, as if *Levels* were reprising the ground of *In Blue*, only now with even greater variety and nuance. Moreover, in most areas of the composition the darker tones were laid down first, and they remain visible in the immediate vicinity of each of the geometric forms: they appear as a kind of penumbral shadow surrounding but also oddly advancing or promoting those forms in their difference from the ground.[128] Crucial to the effect is that Kandinsky used Masonite rather than canvas, the smoother, harder, darker surface imbuing the colors with a surprising depth. Indeed, in the several years following his production of *On Points*, the artist took up an increasingly diverse range of materials, including tempera, gouache, and watercolor sprayed from an atomizer; he also frequently worked on cardboard, as he had more or less continuously since his arrival at the Bauhaus, and on panels of one kind or another. Presumably at stake in all of this restless experimentation was a desire to develop a technique that would appear at once materially assertive and, ideally, susceptible to de-materialization.

In 1934, not long after his relocation to Paris, Kandinsky hit upon the idea of adhering sand to the surface of his compositions (see Figure 44 / Plate 20; and Figure 45).[129] It's possible that he had seen some of the cubist paintings by Picasso or Braque in which sand had been selectively added to the pigments; he could also have easily encountered one of André Masson's sand-and-gesso pictures from the 1920s.[130] The sanded areas of Kandinsky's compositions appear fundamentally different, however, from what we find in any of those "external" precedents. (Whatever his immediate inspiration, the actual appearance of the sand in Kandinsky's work seems to owe more to his own earlier *Quetschtechnik*.) Kandinsky used an extremely coarse grade of sand, some of its particles as large as pebbles, and, in contrast to either Picasso or Braque, affixed it to the surface in a densely compacted layer. It has as a result a strikingly material presence more closely recalling the texture of Masson's pictures than that of any cubist work. Unlike Masson, however, Kandinsky subsequently painted overtop the sand— and with a lightness and precision utterly foreign to the French artist.[131] It's that overpainting, too, that makes all the difference. In the case of both *Blue World* (Figure 44) and *Accompanied Contrast* (Figure 45), works done some ten months apart, the sand is subjected to an illusionism specifically designed to negate its tangible materiality. Employing again the subtractive color mixtures and apparent

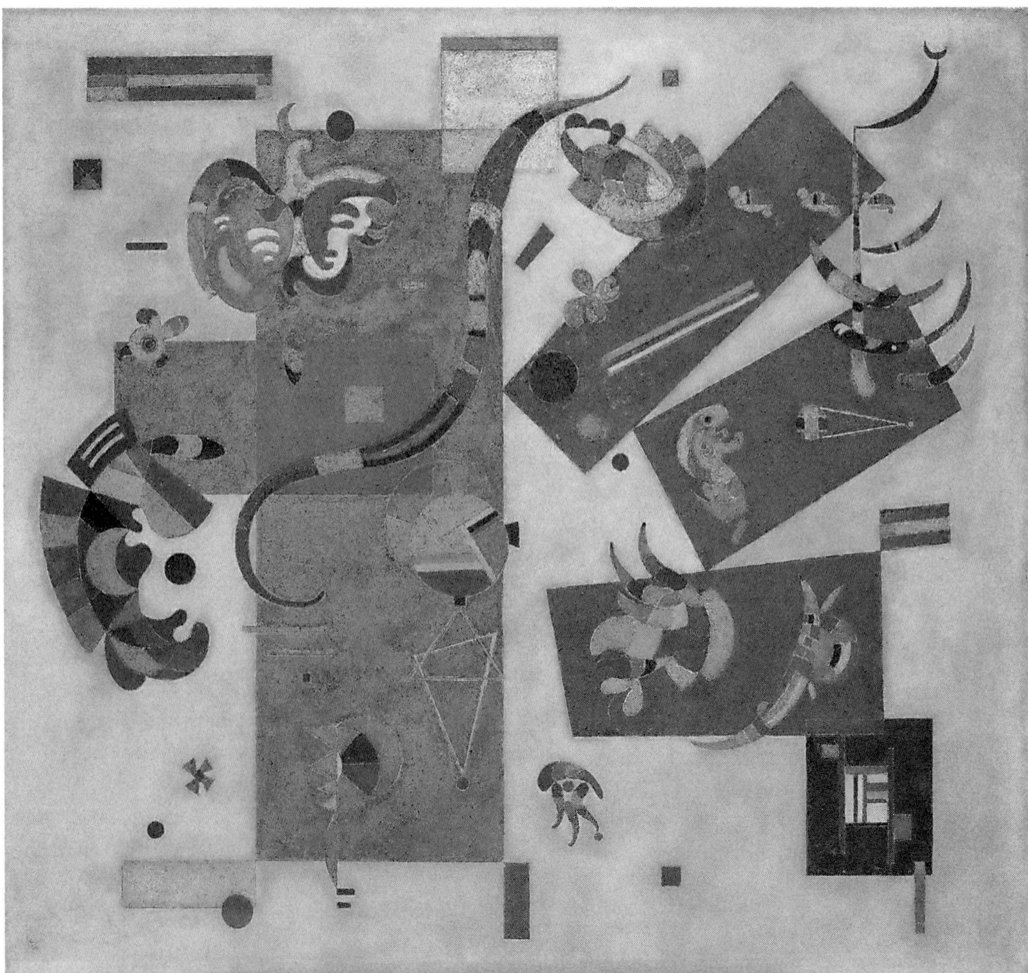

FIGURE 44. Wassily Kandinsky, *Blue World*, May 1934. Oil with sand on canvas, 110.6 × 120.2 cm. Solomon R. Guggenheim Museum, New York, Solomon R. Guggenheim Founding Collection 45.969. © Artists Rights Society (ARS), New York.

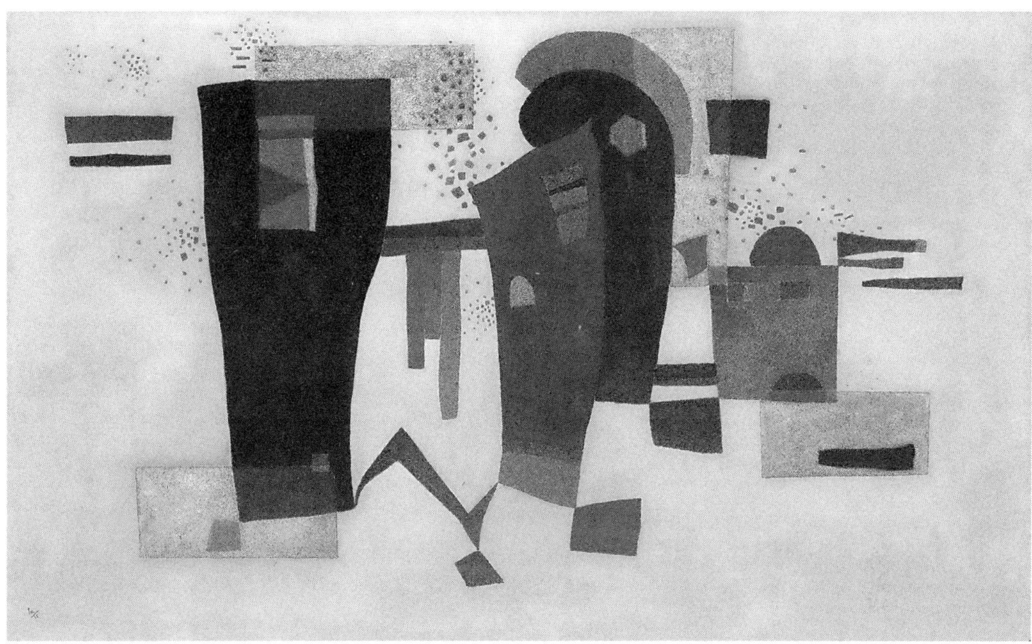

FIGURE 45. Wassily Kandinsky, *Accompanied Contrast*, March 1935. Oil with sand on canvas, 97.1 × 162.1 cm. Solomon R. Guggenheim Museum, New York, Solomon R. Guggenheim Founding Collection 37.338. © Artists Rights Society (ARS), New York.

transparencies he had developed years before, Kandinsky effectively transformed the paintings' thickly encrusted shapes into floating, diaphanous planes. The sand functions in these works much as does the glossy varnish of *Several Circles*. Yet its materiality is more manifestly natural, its negation-by-color registering explicitly as an overcoming of nature's determinacy, and therefore as a freedom won specifically by (and to the benefit of) spirit.

Other important developments are also registered in *Blue World*. Perhaps the subtlest is the elimination not of modeling—that had already happened long before—but of any *modulation* from the composition's colored ground. At least since *Several Circles*, most of the "figural" elements of Kandinsky's paintings had presented themselves as wholly planar; the backgrounds, however, were another matter. Although many tended toward the monochromatic, there was always some variation in their color, some change of hue that suggested they were other than a continuous or solid plane.[132] In *Blue World*, by contrast, whatever unevenness remains in the pale turquoise ground seems incidental—a byproduct of the work's (hand-)making rather than a conspicuous feature intended for our focused contemplation. In Kandinsky's subsequent work, as we will see, undifferentiated planes of color become the norm, whether for "figure" or for ground, and regardless of how that ground might itself be subdivided.

Blue World is also one of the first tableaux to be inhabited by biomorphic shapes. In her 1985 essay, "Kandinsky and Science," Vivian Endicott Barnett called our attention to the various "embryological and larval" forms populating Kandinsky's Paris-period work.[133] Among the things she hoped to explain was "the remarkable incidence in his painting [beginning in 1934] of images of amoebas, embryos," and other rudimentary life forms, and how we, as viewers of the work, were meant to understand the presence of this "new iconography."[134] En route to answering those questions, Barnett amassed a great deal of physical evidence, from coffee stains to bookmarks bearing dates, all of it indicating that during precisely these years (no less than during the writing of *Punkt und Linie zu Fläche*) Kandinsky had been examining the scientific illustrations in the encyclopedia he owned. The evidence is convincing. What seems to me less clear—indeed the part of Barnett's argument that I specifically want to question—is whether "iconography" is the proper term in this instance, and whether regarding the artist as having "introduced" biological imagery into his paintings (presumably from some source "outside") accurately captures Kandinsky's own sense of the work he was then making. The free-form curvilinearity of the biomorphic shapes may be new, but their complexity has a precedent in—and so might be seen as having been prepared for or prefigured by—the intricate, composite geometries of the paintings, such as *Levels*, that Kandinsky was producing just a short time before. By the same token, the organic or even organismal appearance of *Blue World*'s compositional forms (and of many entire compositions that he would produce soon thereafter) can be seen as an extension of Kandinsky's growing concern to integrate the various elements of his work, to articulate the relations among the individual parts or members, as well as their place within the larger whole.[135] Hadn't the artist already, in *Punkt und Linie zu Fläche*, compared the successful composition to a "fully developed organism"? Might it not be better, then, to see the biomorphic shapes of Kandinsky's Paris-period work as operating in a similarly comparative or analogical mode, evoking associations with organic life, but certainly not reintroducing iconographic representation into an oeuvre whose entire significance was predicated on its overcoming?

Parallel analogies occur repeatedly in Hegel's writing. Hegel's discussions of organic life play an important role within his philosophy in that they help him to explain (and us to comprehend) how a system might be driven by inner necessity or purposiveness, its individual parts or members fully integrated because they have developed together over time.[136] For Hegel, the whole of reality is structured into different "levels," inorganic phenomena—precisely because they don't partake of such purposiveness—occupying the lowest tier. Things at this level can be understood (imperfectly) only by *external* means: through empirical observation rather than dialectical or speculative thought.[137] Biological organisms, however, belong to a different, higher level. "The living thing is articulated purposefully," Hegel insists; "all its members serve only as a means to the one end of self-preservation," an end that he glosses elsewhere as the way "in which life realizes and maintains itself [*sich erhalt*]."[138] We are able to comprehend the living thing *internally*—systemically—because of the organism's own internal articulation. Even so, Hegel emphasizes, only *geistige* phenomena occupy the highest level; wholly free of "externality," they are also wholly intelligible to our historical understanding.

Painting, for Kandinsky, is plainly a *geistige* phenomenon of this order. Having shed its earlier involvement with the representation of natural forms—having become in that sense "abstract"—it was now, in 1934, in the process of becoming ever more "concrete," which is to say, both more complex and more explicit about the means by which it held itself together. It's not merely coincidental that biomorphic forms emerge within Kandinsky's practice at approximately the same time that organizing structures (of the sort we see in *Levels*) also do. Here again I have to insist on the difference between biomorphic forms and forms designed to represent or depict specific biological entities. I feel certain that Kandinsky would have balked at the notion that in this period his work had returned—or, rather, regressed—to representation of the natural world. All evidence suggests instead that, for him, it was a matter of painting having become increasingly self-conscious of its own "organic" or systemic nature, and progressively more articulate in that awareness. As he wrote in *Punkt und Linie zu Fläche*:

Abstract art, despite its emancipation [from determination by nature], is subject here also to "natural laws" [i.e., to "internal necessity" or purposiveness], and is obliged to proceed in the same way that nature did previously, when it started in a modest way with protoplasm and cells, progressing very gradually to increasingly complex organisms.[139]

The internally differentiated, biomorphic entities of *Blue World* point toward the way that the composition itself is an "organic" totality, a system maintaining itself through both the diversification of its component members and those members' coordinated interaction within the larger "organism." Insofar as they can be seen to have developed out of the composite geometric forms of *Levels* and other works of that moment, they might also be seen as pointing toward the systemic nature of Kandinsky's oeuvre as a whole, and so to the complex interrelations among the individual compositions that are its own component members.

Before turning from *Blue World* to discuss Kandinsky's subsequent work, I want to say just a word or two about the role of color within the composition. The palette of *Blue World* is surprisingly (conventionally) harmonious, with many shapes painted in what are clearly only tints of the other hues employed, all of them relatively close in saturation.[140] Gone is the dramatic chromatic dissonance of earlier tableaux. Even black, which had played such a prominent role in the work of the 1920s, has been eliminated, presumably in order to keep contrast to a minimum. Kandinsky may have grown anxious that, with the emergence of the biomorphic forms, and therefore the heightened heterogeneity of the composition, the work would fail to register as an integrated totality. He may well have reasoned that colors similar in saturation and value would make clear that the various elements of *Blue World* did in fact belong together in and as a coherent, "organic" whole.

DIVERSITY AND INTEGRATION

Whatever concerns about chromatic dissonance Kandinsky had been harboring in 1934, he clearly set them aside two years later for the making of *Composition IX* (Figure 46 / Plate 21). The color combinations in that work—delicate pastels placed alongside black and various highly saturated hues—are exceptionally jarring, perhaps more so than in any other composition by the artist. Even in comparison with the opposed primaries of his early paintings, the contrasts here register as highly dissonant, the extreme disparities in saturation and value clashing far more than equally weighted primaries ever could.

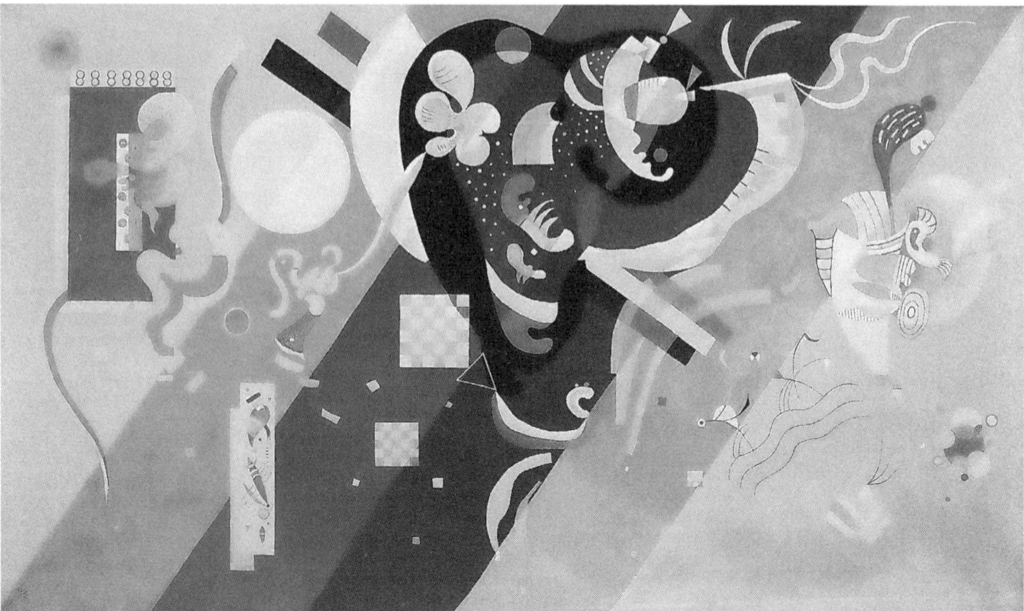

FIGURE 46. Wassily Kandinsky, *Composition IX*, February 1936. Oil on canvas, 113.5 × 195 cm. Musée national d'art moderne, Centre Georges Pompidou, Paris. CNAC/MNAM/Dist. RMN–Grand Palais/Art Resource, New York. © Artists Rights Society (ARS), New York.

Exacerbating the overall sense of disjunction in the work is the relation (or non-relation) of the background to the other compositional elements.[141] The diagonal subdivisions of the ground both impart a strong sense of movement and foreclose any possibility of real integration. None of the other elements align themselves within the limits of the diagonal "stripes"; in fact, their trajectory seems wholly other. Concentrated near the top of the composition, they appear to be drifting upward—potentially out of view. The artist Frank Stella has given one of the best accounts of this painting that I know:

Kandinsky did something in *Composition IX* that we might consider obvious and un-memorable, perhaps even undesirable: he put a series of disparate geometric and or-ganic figures into motion, floating in front of . . . colored planes. These figures are a miracle of balance, movement, and placement. Yet they do not particularly appeal to us, and as a result there is a tremendous temptation to see the painting without them, to see the painting as a wonderful dispersement of planar color. . . . The figures have a kind of directionless, weightless motion associated with freedom from gravity. This unfettered, almost purposeless motion is a perfect foil and support for the motion imparted to color, whose tense, controlled dispersion makes up the background. The motion guiding these figures is random and independent, at odds but also somehow interwoven with the diagonal thrust of the truncated rainbow backdrop. As the color and figuration both move, we see them released into the abstract space of a white, imaginary pictorial wall.[142]

This upward drift of the figures threatens, as Stella's description suggests, to un-do the composition, which seems to hover, as a result, on the very edge of incoherence.

The lineage of *Composition IX*'s diagonal stripes can be traced back to the organizing scaffold of *Levels* (Figure 43 / Plate 19), the line of development passing directly through *Blue World* (Figure 44 / Plate 20). In *Blue World*, *Levels*'s upright, central bracket became a series of free-floating rectangles, those on the right-hand side displaced from any strictly horizontal or vertical orientation, contributing especially to an impression of release. Even in *Levels*, one of the composite geo-metric forms seemed to be transiting between two tiers; another, in the upper right, appeared in the process of drifting outside the bracket altogether. With *Blue World*, however, the balance between freedom and constraint achieved in *Levels* clearly shifts in favor of the former. The work's geometric forms still provide some sense of underlying structure, but they have undergone (or, rather, seem in that moment to be undergoing) a radical reorientation. We can easily imagine the diagonal stripes of *Composition IX* as the outcome—an imagination facilitated, in no small part, by the recurrence of *Blue World*'s pale turquoise ground along the later painting's right-hand side and lower corner.

As if recoiling from the immanent dissolution of *Composition IX* (as well as the chaotic heterogeneity of the later and even larger *Dominant Curve*),[143] *Thirty* (Figure 15) reimposes a strict sense of order and gravity. Plainly it was time to shore up the potentially wayward drift of those earlier tableaux. However dynamic the composition of *Thirty*'s individual "squares," they are each placed within a structure that enables us to clearly gauge the relation of every one to all the others, and so also the position they hold within the larger whole. Even the chromatic dissonance of *Composition IX* has been reduced to a simple, black-white opposition. Encountering the work this time around—seeing it, that is, in its place within the ongoing development of Kandinsky's oeuvre—we are better able to assess its difference from the paintings that preceded it. I repeat my earlier claim: the composition of *Thirty* is as surprising as anything within Kandinsky's oeuvre. That's not to say that there are no precedents. The oil-and-sand *Striped* (1934), with its background of alternating black and white bands, and the pale green-and-blue "checkerboard" of *Delicate Accents* (1935), clearly helped to shape its overall structure.[144] But neither of those works possesses the strong sense of commensuration that governs *Thirty*. Its composition seems designed specifically to highlight both the distinct individuality of every "square" and their collective interdependence—to show us, then, the self-sustaining nature of the whole. As much or more than with any other work by Kandinsky, with *Thirty* we are able to see—and are clearly meant to see—just how it is that the tableau "maintains itself" (to borrow Kojève's Hegelian phrasing), how it holds itself together by means of the counterbalanced tensions among its various component members.

Again, the composition of *Thirty* is significantly different from those of the paintings that preceded (or indeed followed) it. But that difference is more one of degree than of kind. In all the works of this period, *Thirty* included, we find the same set of tensions active—tensions between heterogeneity and integration, movement and stability, the geometric and the organic or biomorphic. We might even say that these are the tensions that constitute Kandinsky's oeuvre at this moment, the set of oppositions that both drive its development and allow it to cohere or maintain itself as an integrated oeuvre.

Unsurprisingly, then, the same oppositions animate *Composition X* (Figure 47 / Plate 22), which was completed almost exactly two years after *Thirty*. In this case, however, the balance has shifted back in favor of heterogeneity and movement (the opposition between geometric and biomorphic form having been resolved—"sublated," even—in the irregular, composite, and quasi-cartoonish shapes of the composition). Retracing the developments just charted, we might say that the trajectory leads from the radical asymmetry and disjunction of *Composition IX* to the much more regulated organization of *Thirty* to this, whose structure, in com-

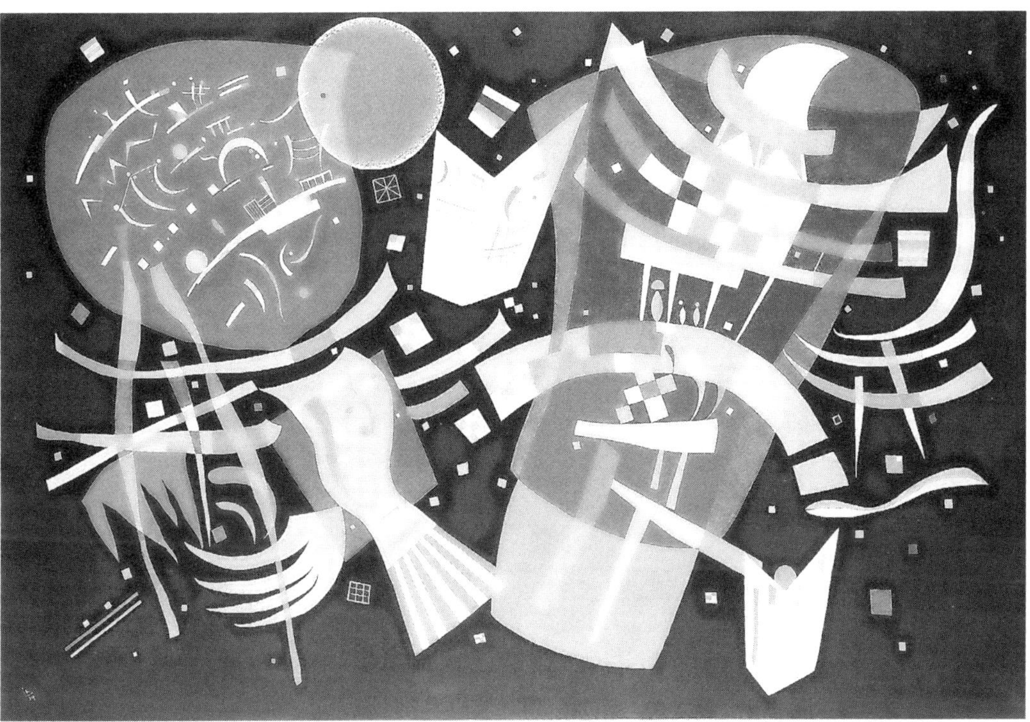

FIGURE 47. Wassily Kandinsky, *Composition X*, December 1938–January 1939. Oil on canvas, 130 × 195 cm. Kunstsammlung Nordrhein-Westfallen, Düsseldorf. © Artists Rights Society (ARS), New York.

parison with its predecessor's, seems close to random: a veritable explosion and scattering of forms. With sustained looking, however, we are able to discern order within the apparent chaos; we see, for example, that the discrete, individual "corporations" of *Thirty* have been maintained, but without the earlier work's rigid, regulating framework. We again find compositions within the larger composition, though the differences among the various entities are far greater here than the controlled heterogeneity of *Thirty* had allowed. In addition, with *Composition X*, everything seems much more fluid. Not only do the larger composite forms incline toward (or otherwise respond to) one another, they also overlap in places, with the result that a single element often appears to participate in two distinct clusters or "communities." Transparency, which had no place at all in *Thirty*, returns in *Composition X*, serving—much as in a Venn diagram—to articulate the features held in common. (We see this most clearly on the right-hand side, where the large green and pink shapes overlap, resulting in a deep brown-mauve; the arcs and other composite forms cutting through the area likewise respond with a change of hue.) The small squares and checkerboards floating between the larger constellations play a role here, too, in that they suggest an ongoing process of transformation: forms coming together or breaking away to become part of some new and different grouping. In that sense, *Composition X* appears much more plastic than did even *Composition IX*, the earlier work's dynamism and disjunction having been reconfigured so as to model or enact reconfiguration itself.[145]

With the aptly titled *Various Parts* (Figure 48 / Plate 23), we return once again to a more overtly ordered structure. As with *Thirty*, the geometric subdivision of the painting's ground effectively organizes the composition into discrete units, enabling them to be measured one against the next. Now, however, those units are conspicuously different in both size and shape—and no longer simply colored black or white in alternation. The palette in general recalls the dissonance of *Composition IX*, although the specific colors of the ground, at least of the rectangles at the center and to the right, look back to the more harmonious color scheme of *Blue World*. The orange-brown strip on the left-hand side is an altogether different matter. In a sense, the relative evenness and cohesion of the colors elsewhere accentuates not only that edge's difference from the others but also, oddly, the dissonance of the work at large.[146] Certainly it results in a markedly asymmetrical

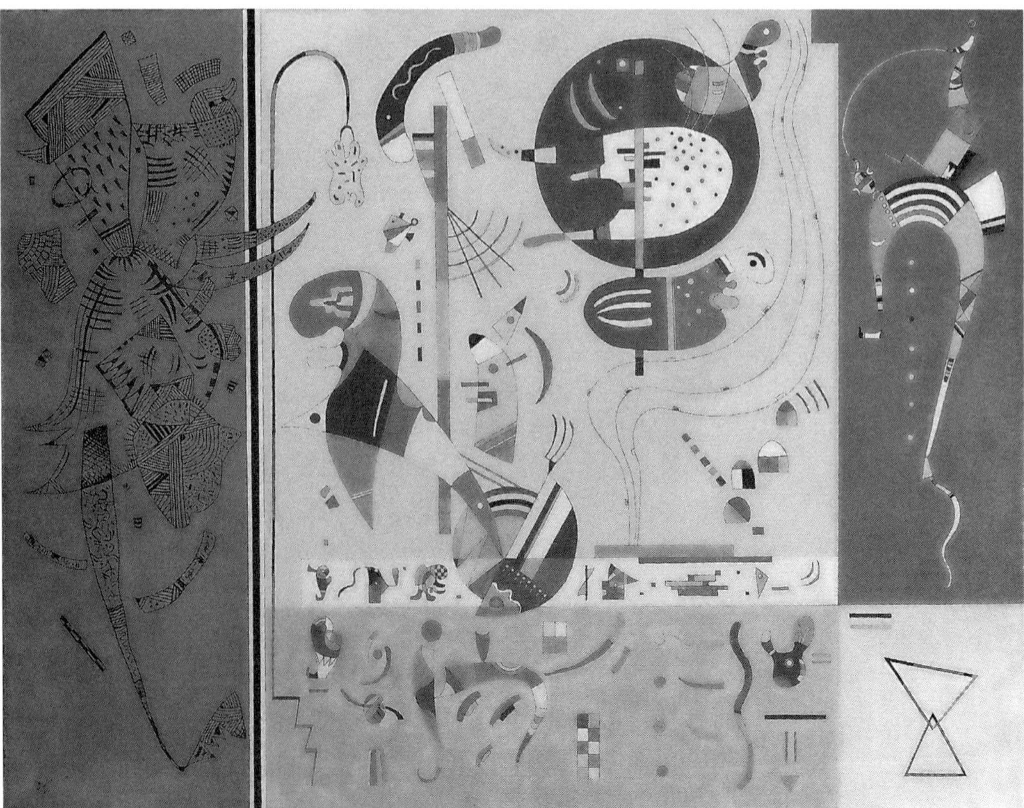

FIGURE 48. Wassily Kandinsky, *Various Parts*, February 1940. Oil on canvas, 89 × 116 cm. Gabriele Münter- und Johannes Eichner-Stiftung, Munich. © Artists Rights Society (ARS), New York.

composition, its leftmost portion threatening to break away at any moment. The emphatic white-black-white stripe that interposes itself between the left-hand side and the rest of the painting only heightens the sense of insurmountable difference. And yet, that off-colored edge manages—if only just—to adhere to the rest of the composition. By virtue of formal similarities between some of its parts and elements located elsewhere, and, above all, as a result of the two small "arms" that reach out to join it with the pale turquoise field at right, it refuses total separation. There is, to my mind, something almost poignant in the demonstration. As I understand it, the question posed by *Various Parts* is of this order: How diverse or dissonant can the various parts or members of a composition be and still maintain themselves (*se maintiennent*) in and as an integrated composition? The painting seems intent on pushing against the very limits of the Beautiful. I myself can't quite decide if the work succeeds; to judge from his subsequent compositions, even Kandinsky may have felt he'd overstepped the limit. In any case, I regard *Various Parts* as a courageous painting, far bolder in its imagination of unity-in-difference than the comparatively homogeneous *Thirty*, produced just three years earlier.

Reciprocal Accord (Figure 49 / Plate 24), from the beginning of 1942, is the last large painting Kandinsky made before his death in 1944. It seems only fitting, then, that we conclude our survey of the artist's oeuvre with a brief discussion of its composition. In doing so, however, I don't want to suggest that there's anything particularly conclusive about *Reciprocal Accord* itself. Nothing indicates that Kandinsky regarded it in any sense as final: it doesn't appear to have been offered as a summa of his work to date or anything like a declaration of the End of Painting. In fact, its ostensible aims are modest in every respect. The composition is at once less heterogeneous than *Various Parts* (both in its palette and in its repertoire of forms) and less overtly structured. Where the earlier tableau seemed intent on thinking the "whole" in all of its extraordinary diversity, *Reciprocal Accord* appears to focus in on a single moment or instance of opposition. It's not, I think, merely coincidental that its ground is divided into three not-quite-equal parts: the work wears its dialectical commitments on its sleeve.[147] We are presented with two large composite forms, one predominantly gray, the other mostly black and red, each seeming to turn or open toward the other across the pale turquoise field they hold common. The smaller forms scattered in between and to either side suggest, much as we saw with the analogous entities of *Composition X*, ongoing metamorphosis and reconfiguration.

In many ways, the near-symmetry of *Reciprocal Accord* recalls nothing so much as the structure of *Composition IV* (Figure 16 / Plate 3), with its explicit "countermovements in both directions." That similarity suggests in turn that a comparison of the two works, done some thirty years apart, might be a fitting way to round

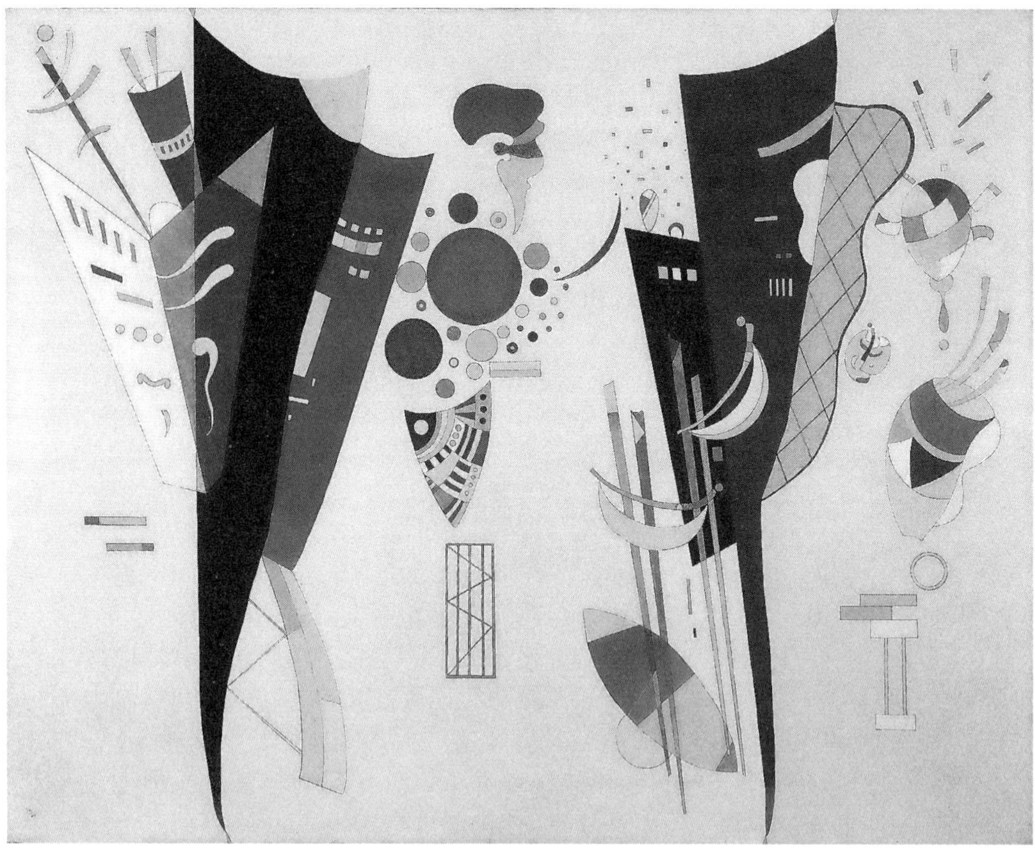

FIGURE 49. Wassily Kandinsky, *Reciprocal Accord*, January–February 1942. Oil on canvas, 114 × 146 cm. Musée national d'art moderne, Centre Georges Pompidou, Paris. CNAC/MNAM/Dist. RMN–Grand Palais/Art Resource, New York. © Artists Rights Society (ARS), New York.

out our discussion. We may want to remind ourselves, too, of Kandinsky's written analysis of *Composition IV*, and in particular of the antitheses he saw structuring the work—antitheses between line and color, "precise" and "blurred," "angular, sharp movement (battle) and light-cold-sweet colors," this last pair serving as the "principal contrast in the picture." Three decades' worth of work stands between the two compositions, the initial terms having been transformed in the interim almost beyond recognition. Earlier in this chapter we saw how the related oppositions between line and color and "precise" and "blurred" were first resolved or sublated in colored lines and the practice Kandinsky referred to as his "*Quetschtechnik*." Almost all of the artist's subsequent major innovations—the planar surface that shifts over the course of its expanse from being "figure" to becoming "ground"; the apparently transparent colored plane; and the pigments that mimic the effects of additive mixing—can be regarded as so many further developments from out of those primary oppositions. The way the individual elements of *Reciprocal Accord* seem to float within fields of color that read simultaneously as surface and as space is but another extension of those same generative ideas.

The appearance of opposition itself also changed significantly in Kandinsky's work between 1911 and 1942. In *Composition IV* it was dramatized as an all-out struggle, a pitched battle to the death—witness the picture's marshaled lancers and rearing horses. In *Reciprocal Accord*, by contrast, the forms (now divested of all natural likeness) appear mutually responsive. The principal entities of the composition are complicated aggregates, related to one another as much by commonality as by difference. By the same token, although the composition's ground is neatly divided into differently colored thirds, those colors are similar enough in saturation that fairly subtle observation is required to discern where one ends and the next begins. We've come a long way, too, from *Composition VI* (Figure 18 / Plate 4), for example, in which the blurring of color and form was primarily responsible for the elements' apparent indissociability. With *Reciprocal Accord*, and Kandinsky's late work generally, we find ourselves engaged in increasingly subtle discriminations. The careful articulation of the work's component members and their nuanced interactions speak to a kind of unity far different from that merely gestured toward by *Composition VI*. Again, what these late works seem to have been aiming for was an explicit unity-in-difference, the individual tableaux presenting themselves as complex, self-sustaining "systems," at once integral to and reflective of the structure of Kandinsky's oeuvre as a whole. For Kojève at least (and, I think, Kandinsky as well), that oeuvre and those tableaux—precisely to the extent that their dialectical oppositions made them self-sustaining—were true achievements of spirit, indeed nothing less than concrete embodiments of the Beautiful.

CONCLUSION

IN HIS POSTHUMOUSLY PUBLISHED *AESTHETIC THEORY*, the German philoso-pher Theodor Adorno castigated Kandinsky for having compromised the "concept of spirit." "In his justified revolt against sensualism," Adorno wrote, "Kandinsky abstractly isolated the contrary of this principle and reified it," rendering it overly "exalted" and altogether too ideal.[1] *Aesthetic Theory* sought to redress the balance:

That through which artworks, by becoming appearance, are more than they are: this is their spirit. The determination of artworks by spirit is akin to their determination as phenomenon, as something that appears, and not as blind appearance. What appears in artworks and is neither to be separated from their appearance nor to be held simply identical with it—the nonfactual in their facticity—is their spirit. It makes artworks, things among things, something other than thing. . . . Spirit is not simply *spiritus*, the breath that animates the work as phenomenon; spirit is as much . . . the force of [the work's] objectification; spirit participates in this force no less than in the phenomenality that is contrary to it.[2]

Adorno's point seems to be that spirit is only able to appear through (and as) the negation of "facticity." The artwork needs to demonstrate that its factual determinants—including the very materials out of which it's made—are not in fact determining or, rather, that they only *under*determine the final appearance of the work. For that demonstration to be made, however, the determinants must also be clearly manifested in the art, since it's there that their negation has to be brought about.[3] Again, according to Adorno, Kandinsky was all too ready to imagine spirit as merely an immaterial "animating breath," rather than something won through protracted struggle and dialectical negation. It becomes clear in reading through the several pages of his extended critique, however, that Adorno's view of Kandinsky was shaped almost wholly by the artist's writings and, more, that *Über das Geistige* was the text foremost—perhaps even exclu-sively—on Adorno's mind. *Aesthetic Theory* is hardly unique in that regard. In fact, it seems to me that the canonical understanding of "Kandinsky" associates him almost wholly with the Munich period, paying scant attention to work done either in Moscow or at the Bauhaus, and all but entirely ignoring anything produced in Paris.[4] This kind of reification, too, has its costs. It not only precludes any awareness that a number of Kandinsky's later works (among them *Several Circles* [Figure 39 / Plate 16], with its varnished black disk, or *Blue World* [Figure 44 / Plate 20], whose sand-encrusted planes are rendered similarly "transparent") actually accord quite well with the negative-dialectical logic championed by Adorno; it also blinds us to the incessant process of transformation that Kandinsky's oeuvre underwent over the course of the last three decades of his life.

Symptomatic of this latter, larger problem is the tendency to regard Kandinsky as simply—and finally—an expressionist. During his years in Munich, to be sure, he demonstrated various expressionist proclivities in both his paintings and his writings. We could point, for example, to the apparent (if only apparent) spontaneity of his brushwork or numerous things he said about the fundamental connection between feelings and the properties of color. No doubt his repeated references to "inner necessity" have further contributed to the popular (mis)understanding of his art. That phrase has typically been taken to refer to the artist's own subjective will or desire, as if the "necessity" in question were his, rather than the imperative of a logic internal to painting. Kandinsky borrowed the phrase more or less directly from Hegel, however, for whom it designated a drive not toward personal expression but, on the contrary, toward the utmost objectivity. As I have argued, its appearance in Kandinsky's writings was plainly intended to signal movement in the same direction, which is to say, in the direction of a progressive elimination of the subjective, the idiosyncratic, the merely one-sided (*Einseitig*). "Internal necessity" ought to be heard in opposition to "external" determinism, on the one hand, and arbitrariness (that is, non-necessity), on the other. Kandinsky's entire oeuvre is oriented toward demonstrating that painting could be an activity, like philosophy, that is (or has now become) wholly self-legislating, its governing norms having been determined by no authority other than itself, outside of its own history. His oeuvre, in its totality, simply *is* that demonstration.

The tendency to overlook that fact and to focus exclusively on Kandinsky's Munich period clearly shaped the characterization of the artist's work in Stephen Houlgate's relatively recent essay on Hegel and the art of painting, surely one of the best and most thoughtful accounts of that subject that we currently possess.[5] For Houlgate, Kandinsky represents one of the two major ways that modern "abstract" painting has failed, and failed specifically as painting. Kandinsky is presented in the essay as having abandoned representation of the natural world so as to allow the viewer to concentrate "wholly on the inner feelings that are aroused by color and form as such."[6] In Houlgate's view, Clement Greenberg represents the other, virtually antithetical position, its adherents claiming that modern painting should concern itself exclusively with the material qualities of the medium, specifically "the texture of the pigment and the flatness of the canvas."[7] Both alternatives, Houlgate argues, are contradictory to the very nature of painting:

To reject illusion, as Kandinsky does, in the name of freeing painting from external nature, is thus to push painting too much in the direction of music; and to reject illusionism, as Greenberg does, in the name of emancipating the materiality of painting itself, is to push painting too much in the direction of sculpture (sculpture being characterized, not as Greenberg thinks, by modeling and relief, but by free-standing material presence).[8]

As I tried to show in Part II, despite disavowing representation, Kandinsky in no sense "rejected illusion." On the contrary, it was absolutely essential to his practice, from early in his career until the very end. And while it may be true that during the Munich period, and especially as he was writing *Über das Geistige in der Kunst*, he championed an alignment of painting with music, it's also the case that, by the early twenties, his rhetoric and his ambition, no less than his painting, had significantly changed.[9] It seems likely that Kandinsky himself became aware of the problems inherent in identifying painting so thoroughly with music. His response, however, was not to turn toward sculpture—at least not toward the materiality that Houlgate sees as sculpture's defining characteristic. Kandinsky held fast to his conviction that the composition needed to distinguish itself from "the texture of the pigment and the flatness of the canvas" were it to be successful as a composition (were it to become a realized tableau). His later works in particular—including *Several Circles* and *Blue World*—are in some sense about, precisely, the negation of "free-standing material presence." Yet those works also avoid the kind of subjective expressivity that both Hegel and Houlgate consider characteristic of music.

The tendency to associate Kandinsky exclusively with the paintings and writings from his early years in Munich is, therefore, particularly one-sided, resulting in an understanding that is a complete abstraction from the reality of his oeuvre. The artist himself would likely have compared that tendency to extracting a single element from one of his painted compositions and then imagining that it could adequately stand in for the composition as a whole. In this context it seems appropriate to quote once more from Kandinsky's essay "Painting as Pure Art": "In isolation, these individual parts are lifeless, like a chopped off finger. The life of the finger, its effectiveness, is determined by its ordered juxtaposition with other parts of the body."[10] We might invoke here, too, that passage in the Preface to the *Phenomenology of Spirit* where Hegel criticizes the field of anatomy for being merely an aggregate of information and not a "true science," because it treats the parts of the body as if they were inanimate rather than belonging to a larger, living whole. In place of the "anatomizing" impulse of reflective understanding, Hegel's philosophical project would be driven, he announced, by a speculative reason able to grasp things not merely as substance but also as *subject*, by which he meant in relation to the dialectical unfolding of their concepts.[11]

In "Painting as a Pure Art," Kandinsky asserted that the work of art—or, more specifically, the beautiful work of art—was "an ordered combination of . . . the internal and the external." "It is this combination," he insisted, "that confers upon the work its unity" and allows it to "become a subject."[12] I think we have to hear this passage as essentially an appeal for speculative reason rather than reflective understanding: we are being asked to approach painting (and indeed even the individual painting) not as though it were an inert thing, a mere substance. Kandinsky would have us grasp it instead as a dynamic entity or activity—to see it not as form, but as formation. This is ultimately why the individual work is inseparable from the larger corpus, and why we're left with a false impression of Kandinsky's oeuvre if we focus simply on the early, Munich-period paintings. Speculative reason demands that we try to comprehend them in their conceptual unfolding, which is to say, in the context of the artist's lifelong practice (as well as within the ongoing history of modern and contemporary art).[13]

Again, speculative philosophy—or what has sometimes been referred to simply as the Hegelian "system"—aimed to be radically self-supporting, having no foundation in anything outside itself. As Kojève and many others have recognized, however, in the absence of external anchoring, such a self-supporting structure could only attain stability on completion. Alexandre Koyré, from whom Kojève inherited the Hegel seminar at the École des hautes études, phrased matters this way: "The philosophy of history—and in that respect the philosophy of Hegel as a whole, the System, so to speak—can only be a possibility if history has come to an end."[14] For Kojève and Koyré alike, the problem was that progress, the *sens* of history, would be indistinguishable from mere change were not some securing end-point ultimately established.[15] In Kojève's account, absolute knowing serves as just this terminus, marking the end of history, after which the dialectical process of negation must necessarily grind to a halt. Any number of scholars have challenged such a view of absolute knowing, arguing that it marks instead only a self-conscious awareness of that dialectical process as in fact being the motor of historical change. Certainly I find their "open-ended" interpretation more congenial—and more relevant to thinking in the present—than Kojève's Hegel of the End of History. Regardless, though, of how one might adjudicate matters with respect to Hegel, it's clear Kandinsky never imagined his art as having reached some final resting point. Even the compositions left unfinished upon his death signal their departure from the "finished" works that preceded them.

It is above all in light of the incessant transformation evident throughout his oeuvre that I find myself in open disagreement with the only other account I know of explicitly linking Kandinsky to Hegel: Jean-Joseph Goux's discussion of the two in his book *Symbolic Economies*.[16] To be sure, Goux gets much right about Kandinsky's relation to Hegel. Although he doesn't cite Kojève, I have to think he had read Kojève's essay on the artist and taken its argument thoroughly to heart.[17] Goux claims that Kandinsky's nonrepresentational compositions rendered "obsolete Hegel's dialectical classification, which applie[d] only to a historically particular form of painting"—but also that they (and Kandinsky's accompanying texts) did so "in a way that could hardly [have been] more Hegelian."[18] On that level, Goux's understanding and mine are wholly in accord. The conflict begins to arise in that, for him, Hegel is not the philosopher of continual, dialectical change, but the architect of a finite system, in which everything may have its place but is nonetheless theoretically exchangeable or interchangeable with everything else. (He seems to have in mind something like the "truly homogeneous humanity" that Kojève saw "realized as State at the end of History.")[19] It's this understanding that allows Goux to claim that both "manifestations"—both Kandinsky's "abstract art" and Hegel's "perfected idealism"—"anticipate a subsequent and far more developed moment of the bourgeois-capitalist mode of symbolizing, in a sense close to its 'supreme phase.'"[20]

Leaving aside whatever counterargument one might be tempted to mount for Hegel, Goux's claims fall flat in the face of Kandinsky's practice. We (still) get Kandinsky wrong if we perceive his "Hegelianism," yet fail to take account of the persistent transformation at work within his work. Kandinsky would have us see that each of his compositions was generated out of a dialectical engagement with the past. They are each, in that sense, grounded in a particular history—that history being, in fact, what constitutes the "system"—even as they also seek to transform it from within. To my mind, Kandinsky's lifelong commitment to change is perhaps the single most impressive aspect of his oeuvre. Rarely has a practice been so thoroughly self-critical, so exemplarily plastic. Like Goux, Kojève failed to recognize— or, in any case, failed to acknowledge—this aspect of his uncle's work. (Perhaps it was simply too difficult to square with his other Hegelian commitments.) As for us, however, having recognized it, we are obliged not only to acknowledge it, but also to try to make sense of it within the larger scheme of things.

Stephen Melville has argued that, in the *Aesthetics*, "art's ending is thought's coming to be at peace with its own material conditions"[21]—which is also to say that it was only through art that speculative thought came to take the (dialectical) shape that it eventually did. This is why Hegel presents his system as the return, at a higher level, of the self-subsisting shape of classical sculpture. Given that—and given, specifically, Hegel's investment in the form of the dialectic—Kandinsky might well have argued that, in his tableaux, and *only* in his tableaux, such "form" becomes concretely visible. Both individually and collectively, his compositions might be taken as manifestations of plasticity, their appearance being an achievement, then, within not simply the history of the Beautiful but also the history of thought.[22] For him, painting was not merely a necessary prelude to absolute knowledge but itself an instance of speculative thinking. Obviously, one would be hard pressed to present Kandinsky as a radical materialist (indeed as a materialist of any sort); and yet, his entire practice seems to have been oriented specifically in opposition to Hegel's altogether too premature dismissal of the sensuous. The significance of Kandinsky's art lies here. If it is, ultimately, the form of Hegel's thought that strikes us as especially compelling, then surely painting—even painting as plainly "formalist" as Kandinsky's—still has something left to show us.

WHAT DIFFERENCE MIGHT IT HAVE MADE to the past century or so of art and art history if we had had a different conception of abstraction—seen its origin not in some "mystical" or highly subjective personal experience, but rather in an attempt to enter into a debate about the social and intellectual climate of the modern world and the place of art within it? We can only speculate. Still, it seems safe to say that we would have had a richer, more nuanced understanding of modernism—something to balance against and interestingly complicate the more materialist (yet often overly reductive) accounts that have dominated discussion in the past. We aren't likely to feel that Kandinsky got things right either. But we may be inclined to think that, in grappling with the unresolved—and no doubt irresolvable—tensions between matter and thought, the sensuous and spirit, he was at least engaging with issues that still count for us today, that remain central to our sense of the world we inhabit.

APPENDIX

ALEXANDRE KOJÈVE,
"THE CONCRETE PAINTINGS OF KANDINSKY"

I have tried to stay as close as possible to Kojève's original prose, even retaining his often odd (some might even say excessive) punctuation. Where he capitalized a letter, I have capitalized it; where he employed italics, I have followed suit. If he used a particular word or phrasing consistently—*le Beau*, for example—I have tended to do likewise, even when it produces rather strained locutions on the order of "one and the same Beautiful."

Where the word in question has clear Hegelian connotations, I have generally used the standard English translation of that term (e.g., "concrete" for *concret* or "absolute" for *absolut*). The one exception is the verb *maintenir* (or *se maintenir*)—*erhalten* and *sich erhalten* in German—which I have most often rendered, following translations of both Hegel and Kojève's *Introduction à la lecture de Hegel*, simply as "to maintain" and "to maintain itself." Occasionally I have translated it otherwise—as "to be preserved," "sustained," or "upheld," depending on the context. The term refers to something that is held—or, better, holds itself—together by means of its immanent constitution. As Kojève employs it, it carries connotations of "composition" (or, closer still, of the German *Zusammenhang*), yet it also suggests the kind of articulated relation of part to whole characteristic of organic (and other self-sustaining) systems. As the term appears in "Les Peintures concrètes de Kandinsky," it is closely associated with both the tableau (as distinct from the painting [*la peinture*]—an all-important distinction I have also purposefully preserved in the translation) and the Beautiful: tableaux exist essentially to uphold or maintain the Beautiful, and any tableau able to maintain itself (i.e., to hold itself together in this way, by itself) is absolutely beautiful.

THE CONCRETE PAINTINGS OF KANDINSKY

ART

Undoubtedly there is a relationship between art and beauty.

However, they are clearly not the same thing. Even setting aside the "pretty"—(everywhere—and in art the "ugly" and the "pretty" can be beautiful or not-beautiful) there is the Beautiful in Art: a piece of music, a painting, a building, poetry ... and the Beautiful in that which is not Art: a plant, a human body, a birdsong, a machine, etc.[2]

The Beautiful that is specified in being incarnated in the tree is the beauty of the tree, of trees, of this tree; in a locomotive it is the beauty of the locomotive; in a painting [*tableau*] it is the beauty of the painting. But in all these specifications, two types are confronted: the Beautiful in Art or of Art and the Beautiful in non-Art or of non-Art. The two Beautifuls are the same Beautiful. However the Beautiful-in-Art is not the Beautiful-in-non-Art. How and why?

One and the same Beautiful is incarnated in the real tree and the painted tree.[3] But the incarnation of the Beautiful in the real tree—that is to say, the beauty of this tree, the Beautiful in the tree or of the tree—differs from the Beautiful in the painted tree. The real tree is "in the first place" a tree; it is only following—"in the second place"—that it is beautiful, that it is an incarnation of the Beautiful. The real tree is "in the first place" thing, plant, giver of shade to the stroller, furnisher of wood to the carpenter, etc., etc. And it is only "subsequently" beautiful: for the "aesthete" who contemplates it, for the painter who paints it. The real tree is beautiful "in addition," "also," and it remains a tree even if it is not beautiful or ceases to be beautiful. Things are completely different with the painted tree, the painting "Tree." It is not a thing; it is not a plant. It shelters no one and serves no one. It *is* not and is of no usefulness. And in *being* not, it is not a beautiful tree; it is the Beautiful as tree. Or better still: it is not beautiful "also" and "in addition": it is only beautiful—or nothing at all. The painting [*tableau*] "Tree" is beautiful and beautiful only or it is not a tableau, but merely some colors on a surface.[4]

The painter who paints a beautiful tree does not paint the tree, but the beauty of the tree, the Beautiful in the tree or as tree: he neglects everything in the tree except its beauty, that is to say the Beautiful in it, and if he is not able to represent the Beautiful of the tree, he is not able to *paint* the tree, to make a *tableau*: he only dirties (colors) a surface.

Art is thus the art of extracting the Beautiful from its concrete incarnation, from this "other thing," which is—"also"—beautiful, and of preserving it [*et de le maintenir*] in its purity. In order to preserve it, art also *incarnates* the Beautiful, in a painting [*tableau*] for example. But the tableau is beautiful "first and foremost" and it is only "also" and "subsequently" that it is canvas, colors, etc.... If it is not beautiful, it is *nothing*: good for nothing, good for being destroyed; the real tree is a *tree* which is "also" beautiful and which can *be* without being *beautiful*; the painted tree is the *Beautiful* that is tree or—if you prefer—the tree that is only beautiful and nothing else, that is *nothing* outside of its beauty. The beautiful in the real tree is the ornament of that tree; the beautiful in the painted tree is its very being, the painted tree being *nothing* [*néant*] without its beauty, outside of its beauty.

Thus: the Beautiful-in-non-Art is the beauty of a *being*, the Beautiful in being; the Beautiful-in-Art is the *being* of beauty itself, the Beautiful existing as such, the Beautiful being "in and for itself."[5] Art is the art of preserving [*de maintenir*] this Beautiful "in and for itself" by incarnating it in a being—painting, statue, music, poetry, etc.—which *is* only insofar as it is *beautiful*, the incarnation of the *Beautiful*. Specifically, Art is the art of "extracting" the Beautiful from the being (real, useful, etc.) that is "also" beautiful and incarnating it: the Beautiful in a being that is *only* beautiful, without then adding to the "extracted" and "incarnated" Beautiful something that, in being real, useful, or otherwise, would not be beautiful. For one cannot say that the painter, for example, "adds" to the Beautiful the oil and the canvas of his painting [*tableau*]: the oil and the canvas are not the tableau, and the tableau is only the "incarnation" of the Beautiful and nothing else. What is this Beautiful that Art "extracts" from the beautiful thing by "incarnating" it in its pure state, in making of it a Beautiful-thing? It is a "value"—without any doubt. And—also without any doubt—a "useless" and "unreal" value. Useless, because it serves no purpose and is not made to serve. "Unreal" because it "does" nothing; it would not weigh down the pan of a scale, would not alter the needle of a galvanometer, would not stop a projectile ...; it would do nothing to avoid a blow, but the blow would be able to do nothing to it.

Being a value, the Beautiful is. It is without serving another thing, without being served by another thing, without being able to create or destroy anything other than itself, without being able to be created or destroyed by something other than itself. If, then, this value is a *value*, it is simply because it is what it is, *in* itself only, for itself only, and *by* itself only.

Thus: the Beautiful is a value simply because it *is*. And everything that has a value *solely* on account of the simple fact of its being is beautiful, is the Beautiful, is the Beautiful that *is*, the incarnation of the Beautiful. One makes something Beautiful—in and through Art—solely in order to make something Beautiful, that is, solely because of the simple fact that the *being* of the Beautiful has a *value*. And everything that one makes for the sole reason of its *being*, is made of the *Beautiful*, and made for *Art*.

This is the reason one makes a painting [*tableau*], for example. One makes it *solely* so that it might *be*. And that is why it is necessary to make it beautiful. If [it is] not, it has no reason *for being*. And, having no reason to be, it is not: it is not a *tableau*, but a dirtied surface, which is there only to be destroyed (or in the future, unnoticed, to be consigned to artistic oblivion).

The Beautiful is being that has a value on account of the simple fact of its being, in itself, for itself, by itself. In order to be beautiful, being must then be able to be, that is, to be sustained [*se maintenir*], in-for-and-by-itself. In being sustained thus, it is beautiful, and it is only in being sustained thus that it is beautiful. The real tree is sustained by itself, by its imminent constitution, by the relationship of its parts; but it is sustained also by the ground that supports it, by the salts, water, and rays of the sun that nourish it, that is, by things *other* than itself; it is sustained in itself in its branches, its trunk, its roots, etc., but it is sustained also in the universe, which is something *other* than itself; it is sustained for itself, but it is so sustained for the birds that it shelters, for the man that it serves, that is, for things *other* than itself. That is why it is beautiful only "also" and "secondarily"—it is beautiful only insofar as it is sustained in-by-and-for-*itself*; insofar as it is sustained in-for-and-by-something *other* than itself, it is not beautiful; but this is precisely why it can be sustained even without being beautiful, independently of its being-beautiful. The painted tree, by contrast, is sustained only by its being-beautiful: the tableau "Tree" must thus be sustained solely in-by-and-for-*itself*; the tableau is sustained only in the tableau, not outside of its "frame," and it is not in the universe of real things (there, it exists not as a tableau, but only as canvas, oil, etc.); the tableau is sustained only for the tableau, because it is there—as a tableau—only for those who can transpose themselves in *it*, see it "like an artist," that is to say, live—for as long as the artistic contemplation lasts—in it, for it, and by it. The tableau is sustained as a tableau only by itself, by the equilibrium of its parts, by the immanent laws of its interior life, nourished by nothing, save itself.

In summation: the Beautiful is that which is sustained solely in-by-and-for-itself, and all that is sustained in this way is beautiful. Art is the art of creating beings that are sustained in this way, and that are sustained only in this way. Specifically, Art can be [described as] the art of extracting from a being everything in it capable of being sustained in-by-and-for-itself, and of making from it something that is sustained solely in-by-and-for-itself.

PAINTING

We have spoken of Art while making use of the example of painting. Let us now speak of painting while making use of what we have said about Art.

Each of the senses has its art. Painting is the Art of the sense of sight. One sees space and surface. The Art of the sight of space or of a form enclosed by Space is sculpture. The art of the sight of space or of a form enclosed in Space is architecture.

(This is why one sees only the space closed by the surface of the statue, whereas one can also see the space enclosed within the surface of a building: one does not enter a statue.) The Art of the sight of the surface is painting.

The statue is a space closed by the surface. The tableau is *only* surface. That is why the tableau is essentially *flat*. Not the canvas (which can be concave or convex, etc.), but the tableau as tableau.

Generally, the tableau "represents" a space, that is, a statue (living or not) or a building (artificial or natural). In it, then, there is "perspective," depth. But the *maintenance* [*maintien*] of the tableau, which is to say the *beauty* of the tableau, which is to say the tableau as *tableau* or work of art, does not depend on this "depth" that it "represents." The law of its maintenance is realized in two dimensions only: it is in the plane [*plan*] and only in the plane that the balance affecting its maintenance or, rather, that *is* its maintenance—which is to say its beauty, its artistic value—is brought about: the balance of forms and colors.

The beauty of the tableau is thus the beauty of the single surface, that is, of what remains of the beauty of a body if one suppresses its extension in depth. If nothing remains, the body cannot be *painted*, even while it could be sculpted, for example. The Art of painting is, therefore, the art of making a surface that has a reason for being in-by-and-for-itself, which has a value solely because it *is* and [which] can be sustained [*se maintenir*] without needing the existence of something external to it. Clearly it is only the *tableau* that can exist wholly on such a pure, flat surface, for the canvas necessarily has depth.[6] Note that a white plane, or a black one, or one covered in a uniform color, exists as a plane without depth only insofar as it is considered as a tableau. Without doubt, it can be so considered: a uniformly black sheet *is* a tableau, and only man can make a uniform black sheet, nature having made nothing uniform. A museum consisting exclusively of sheets covered in different uniform colors would be, without a doubt, a museum of *paintings* [*peintures*]: and each of these paintings would be beautiful—and even *absolutely beautiful*—independent of whether or not it was "pretty," which is to say, "pleasing" to some and "displeasing" to others.

But uniform coloration does not exhaust the Art of painting. One again has tableaux if one divides the uniform surface with strokes of another uniform color, these strokes serving only to divide the surface: such tableaux are called *drawings*. And one also has tableaux if one inserts into a uniform surface other uniform surfaces of different colors (which can be of any dimensions whatsoever and can completely cover the original surface): these tableaux are called *paintings*. One can also make *colored drawings*, if one accentuates the division of the uniform surface by assigning different colors to the different parts of the divided surface (i.e., of the drawing). Finally, one can make a *drawn painting* if the inserted surfaces are surfaces of a single color, different only in the intensity of that color.[7]

These four types exhaust the possibilities of painting. But the possibilities of these four types are practically infinite.

Still, there will be—in all of these types—*tableaux*, which is to say works of Art or instances of pure incarnated Beauty only if the manufactured flat surface manages to be sustained [*se maintenir*] in-by-and-for-itself, thus having a *value* by the simple fact of its *being*.[8] The man who makes a beautiful flat surface is a painter who has made a tableau: the one who has not succeeded in doing that has only managed to dirty a bit of paper or some other thing.

In order to explain the beauty of the surface of a body, that is to say, of its visual aspect, which, being closed to the body in *three* dimensions, is independent of its extension in depth—in other words, in order to explain a *tableau*—we will use an example borrowed from the domain of the nonartistic Beautiful.[9]

A woman's breast can be *beautiful* (even without being "pretty" or "pleasing"). In this case, we attribute a value to the simple fact of its *being*, independent of its belonging completely to the body and to the universe, independent also of its "utility," of the fact that it can, for example, appease the hunger of an infant or the sexual desire of a man. But the Beautiful incarnated in this breast—taken as the *visual* Beautiful—can be revealed in its three aspects of the architectural, the sculptural, and the pictorial Beautiful.

The architectural aspect, that is, the beautiful of the space contained by the surface, cannot—it is true—be *seen* in the proper sense of the term (one cannot *enter* to see the interior). But touch here can play the role of sight: the hand can transmit to us the Beautiful of the space limited by its skin. (The Beautiful in question here—and which the hand transmits to us—is not that of touch, but something completely different; it is the Beautiful of the geometric *form* of *solid* [*plein*] space become beautiful because it is a breast.) As for sight itself, it reveals to us above all the sculptural Beautiful, that is, the form contained in the surrounding space, form in the everyday sense of the term, which—although three-dimensional—does not evoke the *interior*, covered and forever hidden by the surface. In short, vision will make us see the Beautiful of the surface itself, that is to say, the beautiful of the *skin* of the breast or, more exactly, of its visual aspect. The Beautiful is incarnated in the skin, which follows the form of the breast. But *this* Beautiful is absolutely independent of that form, which is why it can be preserved as such [*être maintenu tel quel*] in being incarnated in a *flat* surface. And it is only this *flat* visual surface of the skin that is a *pictorial* value.

The painter who paints the Beautiful of the breast extracts what exists in-by-and-for-itself [*extrait le maintien en-par-et-pour-soi*] from the composing *planes* of the visual aspect, and from them *alone*. His painting can certainly also "reproduce" the *form* of the breast, but—in doing so—it will have no *pictorial* value. The painting can reproduce the sculpture and architecture of the breast, and this reproduction *cannot* harm its pictorial value. But if the painting does nothing but reproduce the sculpture and the architecture, it will not be a *tableau*: it will be a "photograph," that is, a reproduction without proper artistic value, of a "sculpture" (colored or not) or of an architecture reproducing (artistically or not) the sculptural and the architectural *Beautiful* of the breast: the pictorial Beautiful will remain un-"reproduced." And in this case it would be better to employ a sculptor (who can, if he wants, color his statue) without making a tableau at all. (This is why a painter will relinquish to the sculptor the model with breasts of impeccable form but skin that does not embody the Beautiful.)

In sum: the Art of painting is the art of creating—or of extracting from the real—two-dimensional visual aspects that are sustained [*se maintiennent*] in-by-and-for-themselves and that, as a result, *are* solely because they have a *value*, and have a *value* solely because they *are*.

ABSTRACT AND SUBJECTIVE PAINTINGS

We just said: "create or extract." In other words, we have distinguished two fundamental types of the Art of painting. Let's attempt to distinguish between them by beginning with the latter, with the art of *extracting* the pictorial Beautiful from the *non*artistic real.

This is the Art of painting in the standard sense of the term, such as it was practiced everywhere and always, since the beginning until the appearance of the first painting that was not a "representation" of the nonartistic real, of a thing, a plant, an animal, a human being, etc. And it is practiced still alongside the Art of "nonrepresentational" painting, of which we will speak later.

We will define "representational" painting by saying that it is an *abstract* and *subjective* painting. Here is why.

This painting is *abstract* above all in the sense that the Beautiful it embodies is "extracted," which is to say "abstracted," from the nonartistic real.

The Beautiful embodied by the tableau "representing" a beautiful tree is in-by-and-for-itself. But this Beautiful was not *created* as such by the painter. He himself "extracted" or "abstracted" it from the beautiful tree: before being in the tableau it was in the real tree. Because of its origin, then, the Beautiful of the "representational" painting is an *abstract* Beautiful. Thus, for example, the Beautiful of the tableau "Tree" was abstracted from the real tree, or rather this Beautiful was already real before being realized in and by the tableau; in this way, as far as its origin is concerned, the Beautiful of the tableau is "less" real than the Beautiful of the tree, which is to say more abstract than it. The attitude of the painter who "paints" the tree is analogous to that of the botanist who describes it in his book: the pictorial and verbal "representations" are less real—that is to say, more abstract—than is the tree [being] represented.

It follows that, being "abstract" in and through its origin, the Beautiful of the "representational" painting is also "abstract" in its very being.

In order to see this, let's take the example of the real tree and the painted tree. Rough [to the touch], the real tree is "primarily" a tree and beautiful only "after that" and "also," whereas the painted tree is "primarily" *beautiful,* and it is *nothing* "after that." The Beautiful incarnated in the real tree is thus essentially attached to the *reality* of the tree, whereas the beautiful of the painted tree is essentially *detached.* The Beautiful-of-the-real-tree, while being—insofar as beautiful—in-by-and-for-itself, is not *only* in-by-and-for-itself, but still in-by-and-for the *tree*, which is *not* in-by-and-for-itself, whereas the Beautiful-of-the-painted-tree is in-by-and-for-itself only: the second is therefore—in its very being—less real, that is, more abstract, than the first.

In fact, the real tree is large, it has a thickness, it is heavy and rough, its branches can be moved under the pressure of the wind, it has a smell peculiar to it, its leaves can make sounds, and so on, almost to infinity. There is none of that in the painted tree: the painted tree is only the flat visual *aspect* of the real tree, and even if—drawn in perspective—it renders the visual *aspect* of the latter's real depth, it does not itself have real depth in reality. Now, the Beautiful-of-the-real-tree is not only in the Beautiful of the flat visual aspect of this tree but also the Beautiful of the entire concrete, real tree: the Beautiful of the tree is also the Beautiful of its depth, of its sounds, of its smell, of its rough trunk, etc. Just like the tree itself, the Beautiful-of-the-tree is a Beautiful in three dimensions: tall, wide, and deep. The Beautiful-of-the-painted-tree, by contrast, is only the Beautiful of the *flat* surface of the tableau. Besides, the tree does not exist in a vacuum: it is on earth, under a sky, etc., etc.—in short, it is part of the *Universe*, and it cannot be isolated from this universe, from the concrete world of real things. Accordingly, the Beautiful-of-the-real-tree is also a non-isolated Beautiful, not withdrawn into itself, but a Beautiful inserted into the Beautiful of the Universe and, above all, into the Beautiful of the "landscape" of which it is a part. The Beautiful-of-the-painted-tree, by contrast, is inserted only into the part of the flat visual aspect of the surrounding landscape that is "represented" in the tableau, within the limits of its "frame."

Thus, the Beautiful-of-the-painted-tree is much *poorer* than the Beautiful-of-the-real-tree: everything there is suppressed, one has made an *abstraction* of everything, except the flat visual aspect, and there again only a fragment is preserved [*on n'en maintient qu'un fragment*].

In order to avoid all possible misunderstandings, let us say here and now that the *limited, flat* surface of the tableau *can* incarnate a Beautiful that is concrete, complete, withdrawn into itself, [and] self-sufficient. [But] the Beautiful incarnated in the flat, limited surface of the tableau "Tree" is an *abstract* Beautiful, that is to say, one incomplete and unreal, *solely* because the Beautiful of the tableau is a Beautiful-of-the-tree, because this Beautiful is the Beautiful of a tableau that "represents" a tree. In wanting to paint the Beautiful of a *tree*, one is inevitably led to suppress certain interesting elements of that Beautiful, to "extract" from them, that is, to "abstract" from them the visual aspect alone, to reduce this aspect to a planar state, which is to say, to make an abstraction of depth and—in general—of everything that is not offered to sight directed from a fixed [vantage] point, and to cut into that flat aspect an area limited by the straight or curved lines of the "frame," i.e., to make again a—final—*abstraction*. And if the concrete Beautiful of the real tree is *real*, sufficient unto itself, the abstract Beautiful of the painted tree is not; in order to be *real*, it needs all of its constituent elements; yet only some of them have been retained.

Obviously, it is the same in all "representational" paintings, that is, in every tableau that incarnates a Beautiful already existing outside of the tableau [and] before the tableau, without the tableau—in a real, nonartistic object. As soon as the pictorial Beautiful must "represent" a Beautiful that is not only and uniquely pictorial, the pictorial Beautiful is poorer and less real than the Beautiful "represented": said otherwise, it is an *abstract* Beautiful.

The Art of "representational" painting is in the art of *abstracting* the pictorial component of the full Beautiful incarnated in the nonartistic real, and of presenting [*de mantenir*] that abstract Beautiful in—or as—the tableau. The "representational" painting is a painting of the abstract Beautiful: it is an *essentially abstract* painting.

Now, being *abstract*, this painting is necessarily *subjective*.

It is that—above all—in and because of its origin. For, if this painting "extracts" something from something, it is necessary that someone—a subject—

made this extraction; if this painting carries out an "abstraction," it is necessary that this abstraction is carried out in and by a "subject." The concrete Beautiful of nonartistic reality passes through this "subject"—the painter—before being incarnated, as the abstract Beautiful, in the tableau. The Beautiful of the tableau is thus a Beautiful transmitted by the subject—a Beautiful subjectivized in and by this transmission, it is a *subjective* Beautiful.[10]

Let's take again the example of the tree. The painter paints it just as he *sees* it from the location where he finds himself: it is he who makes the choice of aspect, he who chooses what he wants to abstract from the total Beautiful of the tree in order to paint it. But the intervention of the subject is not exhausted in the choice of visual perspective. Having made that choice, the painter, unable ever to "represent" the totality of the Beautiful, will again have to make an abstraction of certain constitutive elements of this aspect of it, and it is again *he* who must do it. In short, the painter of the "representational" painting can paint only the Beautiful of the *impression* that the thing to be "represented" produces in *him*: "representational" painting is always more or less "impressionist," that is to say, subjectivist, subjective.

But that still is not all. The tree is not exclusively in-by-and-for-itself: it is also for another thing, notably for man, thus also for the painter insofar as he is a man: it "pleases" or displeases him, arouses in him—in a general manner—various feelings, is "useful" to him or not, etc., and so on. All of this applies to any nonartistic object whatsoever, and it applies to a nude body, a deity, an historic event, etc., even more than it does to the tree. The Beautiful of the nonartistic object is also the Beautiful of all that the object is used for, of everything that it evokes in other things. In other words, the painter always has an "attitude" toward the object to be painted, and the revelation of the Beautiful in the object is also affected in and on account of these "attitudes." Certainly the painter can make an "abstraction" of these attitudes, that is to say, of the aspects of the complete Beautiful revealed by them. But, first of all, if he does that, he simply takes—in making it—a particular attitude, that of "disinterest"—which is also *his*; and, secondly, it is very rare that he makes that abstraction completely. He generally maintains one or several of his "attitudes," and paints, in addition to the Beautiful of the object, the Beautiful of the *attitude* that he takes toward the painted object; he *expresses* the Beautiful in this personal attitude, so that his tableau is always more or less "expressionist," and thus—again—subjective.

Everything that can be said of the *origin* of the Beautiful of the representational painting must be said as well of its very *being*: having an *origin* that is subjective or subjectivist ("impressionist" or "expressionist"), it *is* subjectivist or subjective ("impressionist" or "expressionist").

In effect, the Beautiful of the painting "Tree" must be the Beautiful-of-the-tree. Now, the Beautiful of the painting is not the Beautiful of the tree but only a "fragment" of this Beautiful. (For example: a pencil drawing neglects the color of the tree, etc.) It is therefore a Beautiful *other* than the Beautiful of the tree. If it is nevertheless a Beautiful-of-the-*tree*, it is yet necessary to add to it the elements that it *lacks*, those that the painter abstracted, which are not in the painting. Obviously, it is only a *subject* who can add them, and he can add them only himself, out of the *impression* that the painting made on him. In short—it is the spectator who must add them, and in order to be able to do that he must be familiar with real trees and recognize that it is a real tree that is "represented" by the tableau. The "representational" painting must therefore always be subjectively completed by the spectator in order really to be what it is supposed be: a painting that "represents" the Beautiful of a real nonartistic object. The being of the Beautiful-of-the-"representational"-painting is not, then, complete in itself: in order to be complete, which is to say, to *be* completely, it needs a contribution from the spectator, from a subject. The being of the Beautiful-of-the-"representational"-painting necessarily implies, therefore, a subjective constituent: it is *subjective* or subjectivist, and it is so because it is *abstract*.

Let's clarify, in order to avoid possible misunderstanding. In what was just said, we had in mind a subjective contribution that was purely pictorial. In fact, the contribution provided to the "representational" painting by the "subject" of the spectator is much richer than that. In the first place, while contemplating the Beautiful of a "representational" painting, one generally adds the sculptural and architectural elements of the complete Beautiful of the object "represented," that is, of the elements that not only are not in the contemplated painting, but which have nothing to do with painting in general. In addition to that, however, one involuntarily adds even some essentially nonartistic elements, which are in the object "represented," but necessarily absent from the artistic representation of the object: one need think only of the erotic or even sexual element that one sometimes "adds" to a "nude." But even apart from these nonpictorial—indeed nonartistic—elements, the subjective contribution is necessary to the very *being* of the purely pictorial Beautiful of the "representational" painting: in order for the Beautiful of the painting to be able to "represent" the pictorial Beautiful of a real nonartistic object, it is necessary to add to it some purely pictorial elements that are in the object, but that are necessarily lacking in the painting.

Once again, then, representational painting is essentially abstract and subjective.

Nevertheless, one can distinguish *four types of "representational" painting*, each being more or less subjective and abstract than the others: "symbolic" paintings, "realist" paintings, "impressionist" paintings, and "expressionist" paintings.[11]

Expressionist paintings embody the pictorial Beautiful of the subjective "attitude" that produces in the painter the nonartistic object that he wants to "represent." So, for example, in painting a tree, the painter paints not the pictorial Beautiful of the tree, but the pictorial Beautiful of the "attitude" that he himself takes vis-à-vis that tree. The expressionist painting is thus the most subjective of all possible paintings: it "represents" not the object but the subjective attitude provoked by the object. But this painting is also the least abstract of all: the painter "represents" the *totality* of the Beautiful of the "*attitude*" (precisely because it is his attitude), and there is abstraction only insofar as the attitude is conditioned by the Beautiful of a nonartistic object, this latter Beautiful being impossible—as we have already seen—to "represent" totally.

Impressionist paintings embody the Beautiful of the visual *impression* that the beautiful in the object makes on the painter. There is therefore less subjectivism than in the expressionist painting: if—in this case again—the painter paints less the object than himself, he is now absorbed by the object, whereas before it was the object that was absorbed by him. On the other hand, there is more abstraction in this painting: the painter's impression being produced by the object and by it alone, the Beautiful of the impression must be submitted to almost the same process of abstraction as was the object.

The *realist* painting embodies the Beautiful of the nonartistic object seen by the artist. Here, therefore, there is less subjectivity. It is not the Beautiful of the momentary impression that is painted, but the Beautiful of the object, such as it is revealed to the artist's in-depth ocular study (the painting reproducing even the "unimpressive" elements, etc.). However, the subjective element always remains present, as it is always the aspect seen by the painter that is painted and nothing else. Of course, with the diminution of subjectivism, the degree of abstraction increases.

Finally, the *symbolic* painting: this is, for example, the painting called "primitive." Here, the Beautiful of the painting is not embodied in an accurate (or "realist") representation of the nonartistic object embodying the Beautiful to be painted: this object is "represented" symbolically or schematically. This signifies a new and final reduction of subjectivism: the schema refers neither to the personal "attitude" of the painter nor to the visual impression that the object produces in him, nor again to the visual aspect that the object presents to all those who see it, but to the object itself, independent of how it appears in concrete vision. (For example, no one sees a face [like those] "represented" in an Egyptian painting, where the eye is represented frontally and the nose in profile.)

The "schematic" painting "represents" the Beautiful of the seen *object*, and not the Beautiful of the *sight* of the object. The subjective element is thus reduced to its minimum. But it is still present since it is the *seen* object that is "represented," the scheme or symbol always being a combination of visual elements. And it goes without saying that the minimum of *subjectivism* is seconded by a maximum of *abstraction*: the Beautiful of the symbolically "represented" object "represents" only a very small portion of the Beautiful of the real object "represented."

These four types exhaust the possibilities of "representational" painting. But, of course, these types are exact only in theory. In fact, there are symbolic, realist, impressionist, and expressionist elements in *every* "representational" painting: it is only a matter of more or less. One speaks of a "realist" painting if the three other elements are much less pronounced there than the realist element; and so on. It is also possible that two or three elements will be almost equally pronounced, giving the appearance of a new type of painting, without it being one in reality.

We cannot get distracted here by these questions of detail. We will say a few words only about the painting called "modern" or "Parisian," of which Picasso is the most typical and most important representative.

This is a painting in which the realist and impressionist elements are almost totally absent, and where the two others are about equally developed: it is an expressionist symbolism or a symbolic expressionism. That combination is carried out in such a way that this painting is at once the most *abstract* and the most *subjective* of all possible representational paintings: the *abstraction* of the objective symbol serves to "represent" the *subjectivism* of the painter's personal attitude. Consequently, at every step this painting runs the risk of completely annihilating itself in the void of absolute abstraction and pure subjectivism, both of which fall outside the realm of painting and even of art in general. The *genesis* of such a tableau demands as a result an enormous effort ("genius") on the part of the painter, and its *maintenance* is possible only thanks to an effort just as considerable ("congeniality") on the part of the spectator. It is hardly surprising, as a result, that even a painter of Picasso's caliber succeeds in making a tableau only about once in every hundred times that he puts colors to canvas. And even less surprising is the fact that the vast majority of his admirers are absolutely incapable of distinguishing—within his oeuvre—the tableaux from the [merely] gaudy canvases.

But, once again, it is in the "representational" painting of our day that subjectivism and abstraction are pushed to their maximum, they are not—and cannot be—absent from any "representational" painting: every tableau that incarnates a Beautiful already incarnated first in a real, nonartistic object is necessarily and essentially an *abstract* and *subjective* tableau.

CONCRETE AND OBJECTIVE PAINTINGS
(THE ART OF KANDINSKY)[12]

For centuries, humanity knew how to produce only "representational"—that is, *subjective* and *abstract*—paintings. And it was only in the twentieth century in Europe that the first *objective* and *concrete* tableau was painted, that is, the first "nonrepresentational" tableau. The Art of "nonrepresentational" painting is the art of embodying in and by a drawing, a colored drawing, a drawn painting, or a painting proper, a pictorial Beautiful that is not, has never, and never will be embodied anywhere else: in no real object other than the painting itself, which is to say, in no real, nonartistic object. This art can be called the art of Kandinsky, as Kandinsky was the first to paint (beginning in 1910) objective and concrete paintings.

Concrete first and foremost. Here is why:

Let's take as an example a drawing, in which Kandinsky incarnates a Beautiful involving a combination of a triangle with a circle. This Beautiful was not "extracted" or "abstracted" from a real, nonartistic object, which would be—"also"—beautiful, but—"primarily"—something else again. The Beautiful of the tableau "Circle-Triangle" exists nowhere outside of that tableau. Just as the tableau "represents" nothing external to it, its Beautiful is also purely immanent, it is the Beautiful of the tableau that exists only in the tableau. This Beautiful was *created* by the artist, just as was the circle-triangle that embodies it. The circle-triangle does not exist in the real, nonartistic world; it does not exist before, outside of, or apart from the tableau; it was created in and by—or as—the tableau. And it is only in and for this creation of the circle-triangle that the Beautiful incarnating it was created. That Beautiful too did not exist before the tableau, and it does not exist outside of it, independent of it.

Now, if the Beautiful was not *extracted* or *abstracted* but created whole cloth, it is—in its very *being*—not *abstract* but *concrete*. Being created whole cloth, that is entirely, it is as whole: nothing is missing from it, nothing was removed from it, since this Beautiful—nonexistent outside of the tableau—cannot be richer and more real than it is in the tableau or as the tableau. The Beautiful is thus in the tableau in the full plenitude of its being, which is to say, it is there in all its concretion; the Beautiful of the tableau is a real and concrete Beautiful, the tableau is a real and concrete Beautiful; the real tableau is concrete.

In the case of the tree and the tableau "Tree," it is the tree that is real and concrete, whereas its "representation" in the painting, or the painting that "represents" it, is unreal and abstract. It is the same for the Beautiful of the tree and of the tableau. In the case of the circle-triangle, by contrast, there is only one circle-triangle, which is precisely the circle-triangle of the tableau or the tableau "Circle-Triangle" itself. The Beautiful of the tableau "Circle-Triangle" is therefore just as real and concrete as the Beautiful of the real and concrete tree: the tableau "Circle-Triangle"—and its Beautiful—are at the level of reality and concretion of the real tree, and not at the level of reality of the tableau "Tree," which only "represents" the tree and its Beautiful, being the abstraction of the tree and of the Beautiful of the tree.[13]

In a certain sense, the tableau "Circle-Triangle" is even more real and complete, which is to say, more concrete, than the real tree. In fact the tree is not uniquely in itself, for and by itself: it is on the earth, under the sky, alongside other things, etc.; in short—it is in[,] by and for the Universe, the entire real world, and to extract it from this world is to transform it into an abstraction (just as, for example, the painter who "represents" it isolated on a white sheet or in a tableau that is inevitably *limited* does not include the *whole* Universe). By contrast, the circle-triangle is nothing except in itself, and it is nowhere save in itself, that is to say, in the tableau "Circle-Triangle"; it is not *in* the Universe; it *is* a Universe, complete and unto itself; it is itself its own universe, and it is only through this universe, which it is, and for this universe, which is its own being. Said otherwise, the tableau "Circle-Triangle" does not "represent" a *fragment* of the Universe, but an entire universe. Or, more precisely, since this tableau "represents" nothing but only *is*, it *is* itself a complete universe. In that sense, it then is—and its Beautiful with it—more real and more complete, which is to say, more concrete, than the tree and the Beautiful that it embodies.

Each of Kandinsky's tableaux is a real, complete, and therefore concrete universe, self-contained and self-sufficient: a universe that, just like the nonartistic Universe, the uni-totality of real things, is only in itself, by itself, and for itself. One cannot say that these tableaux "represent" fragments of that nonartistic Universe. One can say at the very most that they *are* fragments of that Universe: Kandinsky's tableaux belong to the Universe in the same way as do trees, animals, rocks, men, States, clouds …, as does everything real that belongs to (is in) the Universe while constituting this Universe. But where the *Beautiful* of Kandinsky's tableaux is concerned, it is more accurate to say that it is independent of the Beautiful of the Universe and of the Beautiful of the things that belong to this Universe: the Beautiful of each tableau by Kandinsky is the Beautiful of a complete universe, and these artistic Beautifuls come to stand alongside—in a sense—the unique and artistic Beautiful of the real Universe.

Each tableau by Kandinsky is thus a real and complete, that is, concrete universe, just as is the Beautiful of that tableau. And that is why Kandinsky's "nonrepresentational" painting can be called "total" or "uni-total" painting: [it is] the art of creating Universes whose being comes down to [*se réduit*] their Beautiful. This "total" painting stands in contrast, then, to "representational" painting, that is, to "symbolic," "realist," "impressionist," and "expressionist" paintings. But, just like the other paintings, this painting can be made in [any of] the four pictorial types of drawing, colored drawing, drawn painting, and painting proper.

Being essentially concrete and not abstract, "nonrepresentational" or "total" painting is necessarily *objective* and not subjective. It remains only for us to show that this is the case.

For one thing, "total" painting is not subjective in its origin. An abstraction can be performed only if a "subject" performs it: for abstraction signifies choice, and choice signifies a personal, which is to say, a subjective, attitude: the tree—in its totality—(and without me) exists; but the particular aspect of the tree "represented" in the tableau is in me and exists only if I do. Now, the "total" tableau is not an abstraction: the circle-triangle is in it in its totality; it exists then without me, just as does the real tree. And if the circle-triangle is born, it is born like the tree is born from the seed; it is born without me; it is an objective birth; it is the birth of an object.

Admittedly, the tableau is "born" of the painter: Kandinsky's tableau "Circle-Triangle" would not exist without Kandinsky; Kandinsky is its "father." But this has nothing to do with "subjectivism" and the birth of a "representational" tableau. The "birth" of the tableau "Tree" is in some sense double: there is first the "birth" of the *abstraction* "Tree" and then the "birth" of the *tableau* "Tree," which incarnates that abstraction.[14] In the case of the tableau "Circle-Triangle," there is, by contrast, only this latter "birth," the first having no place, as the tableau is not abstract. Now, obviously, it is only the first "birth" that is subjective. No subjective element intervenes in the "birth" of the "total" tableau.

In fact, "to be born" from someone does not mean "to be born from a subject or subjectively," and that which is "born" from another is not for that reason subjective. Is the tree "subjective" in being born from the seed produced by another tree? Is the act of fathering a child a "subjective" act? Is it necessary to say that the Universe is "subjective," that it is the result of a "subjective" act, if one admits that it was created by God? Of course not. It is the same with a "total" tableau, a tableau by Kandinsky.

Kandinsky is the "father" of his tableau "Circle-Triangle." But that painting is just as independent of him, just as objective—in its origin and in its being—as a son is objective and independent of his father. Kandinsky creates his tableaux—and the Beautiful in them—as a living being begets another, or rather—since he is "father" and "mother" at once—as Nature engenders beings, or better still—since he creates out of nothing—as God creates the Universe: in each of his tableaux he creates a concrete and objective universe, which is created *ex-nihilo*, since it did not exist before and was not extracted from anything, and which is complete in itself and unique, since it does not exist apart from itself.

Consequently, one should say not "Kandinsky's tableau" [*tableau de Kandinsky*] but "a tableau *by* [*par*] Kandinsky." And it would be better still to do away with the "Kandinsky" completely and to say simply "tableau." For if every "representational" tableau is a thing seen by ..., in such a way that it is relevant to know *by whom* the thing is seen, that is, *whom* the tableau is *by*, the "total" tableau is the thing itself, and it is just as irrelevant to know who saw or sees that thing as it is to know if a real tree is seen by someone and by whom it is seen, if it is seen. If—for those who do not know Kandinsky personally—he is nothing without "his" tableaux, those tableaux are *everything* that they are *without* Kandinsky. His art is the art of the creation of the Beautiful, in the strong and proper sense of the term, and this creation, like all true creation, is independent of the creator, of the *creating* subject. Now, being independent of the subjectivity of their creator, Kandinsky's tableaux are absolutely independent of everything that this subjectivity implies. In particular, these tableaux are as little "intellectual" as possible; if it is nonetheless necessary to use one's "intelligence" in order to "represent" a tree, one can engender a circle-triangle like Nature—which certainly does not think in engendering a being.[15]

Thus, in regard to their origin or genesis, the concrete tableaux of Kandinsky are objective. And they remain objective in their being.

Needing no subjective contribution during its "birth," the "total" tableau has no need for it during its "life" either: it *is*, or is maintained [*se maintient*], every bit as objectively as it is born, that is, it does not depend on the subjective contribution of the spectator, and that is why it can *be*, it has a reason *to be*, even if it is contemplated by no one. The Beautiful-of-the-painted-tree is not what it is supposed to be—a Beautiful-of-the-*tree*—as long as the spectator does not complete—subjectively—the abstraction of the painted-Beautiful, thereby bringing it closer to the real Beautiful: the tableau "Tree" thus needs the spectator in order to be what it is supposed to be, namely, a tableau that "represents" a tree (and this spectator must "know" that it is a tree, must have previously seen real trees, etc.). The Beautiful-of-the-circle-and-triangle, by contrast, *is* what it is supposed to be in and by itself, and it does not need anyone in order to be what it is. It is what it is without the contribution provided by the "subject" of the spectator, and that is why the spectator does not need to be a "subject" while contemplating it: he can "forget himself" in the act, and the tableau will be for him what it is without him. Thus, he does not need to "know" that it is a circle or a triangle, he does not need to have seen them previously, etc. In short, the spectator plays the very same role in regard to a Kandinsky tableau that someone who sees a real object plays in regard to it.

Generally speaking, the "total" tableau, in not being the "representation" of an object, *is* itself an object. Kandinsky's tableaux are not paintings of objects but painted *objects*: they are objects in the same way that trees, mountains, chairs, States ... are "objects"; only they are pictorial objects, "objective" paintings. The "total" tableau *is* as objects *are*, that is, it *is* in an *absolute* and nonrelative way; it *is* independently of its *relations* with anything else; it *is*, like the Universe *is*. And that is why the "total" tableau is also an "absolute" tableau.[16]

In sum: in contrast to "representational" painting, which—in all of its four avatars of "symbolism," "realism," "impressionism," and "expressionism"—is abstract and subjective, Kandinsky's "nonrepresentational" or "total and absolute" paintings are concrete and objective: objective—because they neither imply nor demand any subjective contribution from either the painter or the person contemplating them; concrete—because they are not abstractions of anything existing outside of them, but are instead complete and real Universes existing in-by-and-for-themselves in the same way that the real, nonartistic Universe does.

ADDENDA

1. One might well ask me why—in speaking of "nonrepresentational" or "total and absolute," which is to say, of concrete and objective painting—I speak only of Kandinsky.

It is quite simply because, having seen very few intentionally "nonrepresentational" tableaux, it is only in the work of Kandinsky that I have found things which—in my opinion—are *tableaux*, which is to say, works of art.

I say: "in my opinion" because—at least so far—it is impossible to demonstrate rigorously the artistic value of a tableau. Can one prove that Rembrandt is "greater" than a Meissonier, for example, or that Monsieur X is not an artist? The purely subjective element is inevitable here, and that is why I allowed myself to mention Kandinsky, who is the only "nonrepresentational" artist that I know, without trying to familiarize myself with the others, all the others.

But in spite of the presence of a subjective element in artistic appreciation, certain judgments bearing on Art nonetheless have an objective and absolute value. Thus, for example, it is incontestable that Kandinsky is an artist: to deny it is simply to show a total incapacity to distinguish a painting [*tableau*] from a colored surface. Now, the simple fact of the existence of Kandinsky's tableaux is enough to provide a basis for my argument concerning the essence of the painting that I call "absolute and total" and which I said is—in contrast to all the others—concrete and objective.

I discovered the "idea" of this painting while contemplating Kandinsky's tableaux, and it is thus completely natural that I lay out that idea while using his tableaux as examples and evidence.

Conversely, one could ask me why, in writing on Kandinsky, I write an article three-quarters of which has—on first glance—nothing to do with him.

It is because I believe one cannot say what must be said about Kandinsky without saying that his painting is not a painting akin to others, like one genre among several, but rather that it is opposed to all of those genres taken as a group.

Now, in order to be able to say—in section 4—that Kandinsky's painting is opposed, as "nonrepresentational" or "total and absolute," i.e. concrete and objective, to all painting that is "representational," "symbolic," "realist," "impressionist," or "expressionist," which is to say, subjective and abstract, I had to say what I said in the first three sections of my article, where—obviously—it was not a question of Kandinsky himself.

2. One might wonder how it happens that certain people declare themselves hostile not just to Kandinsky's painting—which is not an interesting problem—but also to "nonrepresentational" painting in general, to, as it were, the "idea" of that painting.

At first glance, it is incomprehensible. There is no longer anyone today who would seriously deny the right of the painting I call "realist" to exist, and who, for example, would argue that all painting must necessarily be "impressionist," say. Generally speaking, we are willing to recognize the equal right of existence of all four types of "representational" painting that I distinguished. And we protest only very rarely against the combination of those types: even against the combination that I mentioned under the name of "symbolic expressionism." In short, we recognize the right of any genre whatsoever of "representational" painting to exist, and we are undoubtedly right to do so.

Why then do we want to deny the right to exist to "nonrepresentational" painting, when common sense would demand that we recognize it in the same way that we do "representational" painting (which—incidentally—the partisans of "nonrepresentational" painting recognize as having an artistic value in no way "inferior" to theirs)?

There are, I think, two reasons:

First, there are the throngs of those who more or less completely lack any sense of painting, that is to say, who, in contemplating a tableau, see only the object "represented" by it, and who, as a result, can experience only the "sensations" and "feelings" that that object provokes in them, and [so who experience] the tableau only to the extent that it "represents" (one need only think of the success of certain "Nudes"). It is obvious that a "nonrepresentational" tableau does not exist for them, and it is normal that they "deny" nonrepresentational painting. But it is obvious that, in denying it, these people deny painting itself: they do not know that there is something called "painting," and when they find themselves in the presence of something which is only "painting," they see *nothing*, and therefore say that it is nothing, that it is "nothing at all."

Then there are the people who think that they can distinguish a tableau from a colored surface (certain art critics, for example). Now, even for them, this distinction is always difficult, it always demands an effort (one need think only of the errors made by even the most competent critics!). In the realm of "nonrepresentational" painting the task is even more arduous than in the realm of "representational" painting. Here [in the case of representational painting], the purely technical perfection or imperfection (the attained degree of "resemblance," etc.)—easily observed—generally permits—although not always—the recognition of artistic perfection, or its absence: there [in the case of nonrepresentational painting] this aid is completely lacking. Thus out of intellectual laziness and an unacknowledged but felt fear of being deceived, many critics and "amateurs" refuse to even attempt the difficult task of appreciating the artistic value of a given "nonrepresentational" tableau; instead they prefer the easier route, to deny the value of "nonrepresentational" painting as such.

It is obvious that neither of these two motives can provide supporting evidence for that negation [i.e., the denial of nonrepresentational painting]. And one might well say that that [evidence] cannot be provided, [the negation] being essentially absurd.

It is, therefore, generally only absurdities that one airs when speaking or writing against "nonrepresentational" painting. Is it not, for example, an absurdity to say that it is "easier" to paint a "nonrepresentational" tableau than a "representational" one, or that the former are easier to "imitate," and that all-purpose recipes for their production are easily given, or other things of this sort.

3. Certain people, who do not contest the artistic value of "nonrepresentational" tableaux, nevertheless want to see in them only works of *decorative* Art.

I cannot analyze here the essence of "decorative" Art. I will say only that, in my opinion, the entire domain of art can be divided into autonomous Art and decorative Art, and that, in all probability, there is no sense in attributing more artistic value to one of these Arts than to the other.

But what seems certain to me is that Kandinsky's "nonrepresentational" painting has nothing to do with decorative Art. There is a decorative Art of sight, as there is a decorative Art of hearing (music), etc. And there is a decorative painting, as there is decorative sculpture and architecture. And decorative painting can just as well be "representational" painting (in all of its genres) as "nonrepresentational." But Kandinsky's painting is not decorative.

"Decorative" painting, in contrast to "autonomous" painting, is called on to *add* a Beautiful to something that exists outside of painting [and] that is nonpictorial. Thus, one adds a Beautiful to a vase that one "decorates" by coloring it or embellishing it with a design, etc., the vase itself being able to incarnate a Beautiful that is its own, or not. The "decorative" Beautiful is, then, a Beautiful that is sustained [*se maintient*] not by itself alone, but which needs other things in order to be what it is supposed to be, that is, in order to be *a Beautiful*: the pictorial Beautiful of the painting that decorates a vase does not exist in that vase. (On these grounds, the "decorative" Beautiful approaches the "natural" nonartistic Beautiful: the Beautiful of a tree also needs the tree to be what it is—the Beautiful-of-a-tree.)

In contrast, the Beautiful of the "autonomous" painting, in order to be what it is, needs nothing, except the painting itself: the Beautiful of the *painted* tree does not need the tree to be what it is supposed to be, but only the tableau "Tree" ... And that is precisely why the "autonomous" tableau is not "decorative."[17]

Now, it is evident that Kandinsky's paintings are as little "decorative" as possible; they are just as "autonomous" as the tableaux by whatever other artist-painter one agrees to describe as non-decorative.

One could say, certainly, that Kandinsky's tableaux are called on to "decorate" an "interior." But that can be said of any tableau whatsoever. And in fact it is necessary to say that a tableau by Kandinsky, perhaps more than any other, is called on much more to *be* "decorated" by an interior (by the "interior" of a museum gallery, for example) than *to* decorate an interior, that of a "boudoir," for example, which seems to be formed as if by magic, around such "valued" tableaux.

4. To close, I would like to present a diagram that can facilitate comprehension of my article, by making more visible the place that I assign to Kandinsky's art, or, if you prefer, to nonrepresentational painting, within the broad domain of art in general:[18]

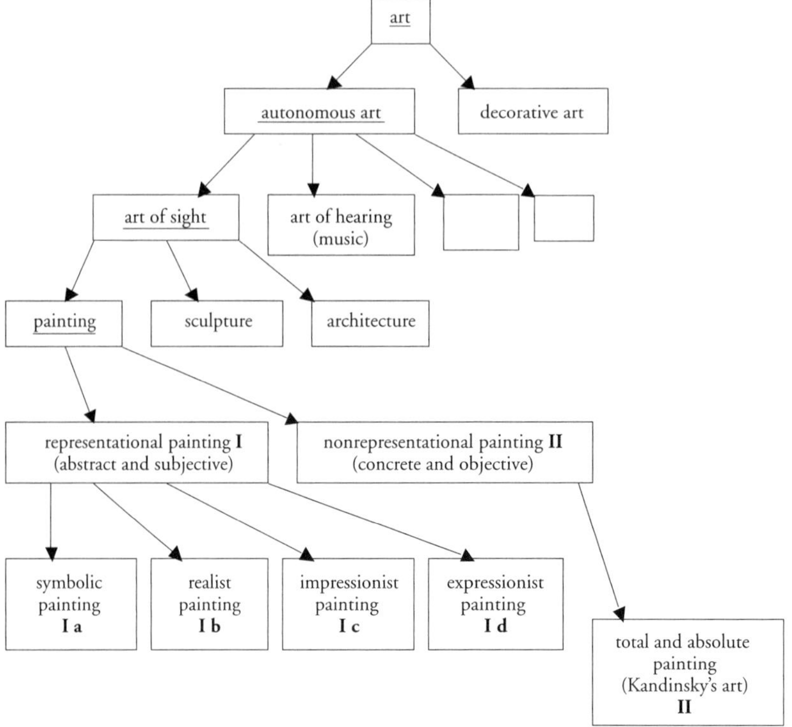

The diagram clearly shows that Kandinsky's painting is not, in my opinion, a fifth genre [or type] of painting in general, but a second, the first [i.e., representational painting] implying four species or subdivisions.

Vanves 23–25 VII 1936

NOTES

INDEX

ABBREVIATIONS USED IN THE NOTES

Aesthetics   *Hegel's Aesthetics: Lectures on Fine Art*, 2 vols. Trans. T. M. Knox. Oxford: Oxford University Press, 1975.

KCW   *Kandinsky: Complete Writings on Art*. Ed. Kenneth C. Lindsay and Peter Vergo. Boston: G.K. Hall, 1982.

KGS   *Kandinsky, Gesammelte Schriften 1889–1916: Farbensprache, Kompositionslehre und andere Unveröffentliche Texte*. Ed. Helmut Friedel. Munich: Prestel, 2007.

OSA   Wassily Kandinsky, *On the Spiritual in Art* (*Über das Geistige in der Kunst*). Pp. 114–220 in *KCW*.

PCK   Alexandre Kojève, "Les Peintures concrètes de Kandinsky." The pagination refers to the English-language translation of the essay included in the Appendix, which was done from the handwritten manuscript preserved in the Bibliothèque Kandinsky, Paris.

Phenomenology of Spirit   *Hegel's Phenomenology of Spirit*. Trans. A. V. Miller. Oxford: Oxford University Press, 1977.

Philosophy of Nature   *Hegel's Philosophy of Nature: Part Two of the "Encyclopaedia of Philosophical Sciences" (1830)*. Trans. A. V. Miller. Oxford: Clarendon, 1970.

PLP   Wassily Kandinsky, *Point and Line to Plane* (*Punkt und Linie zu Fläche*). Pp. 524–700 in *KCW*.

R&B   Hans K. Roethel and Jean K. Benjamin, *Kandinsky, Catalog Raisonné of the Oil Paintings* (Ithaca, NY: Cornell University Press, 1982–1984).

NOTES

INTRODUCTION

Throughout the book, the emphasis in quotations is in the original unless otherwise noted.

1. Wassily Kandinsky, *Über das Geistige in der Kunst* (Munich: R. Piper Verlag) appeared in December 1911, though it bore the publication date of 1912; the first draft seems to have been written in 1909 or 1910. The Russian text, "O dukhovnom v iskusstve," was presented as a lecture on Kandinsky's behalf by Nikolai Kulbin at the All-Russian Congress of Artists in Saint Petersburg on December 29 and 31, 1911—that is, roughly at the same time that *Über das Geistige in der Kunst* first appeared in print. The talk was published three years later in the initial volume of the transactions of the congress, *Trudy vserossiiskago sé'zda khudozhnikov* (Petrograd: Golike and Vilborg, 1914). There has been considerable debate over the relation of the Russian text (and talk) to the German manuscript, but it seems most likely that it was written sometime before 1911, and so in some sense served as a draft for *Über das Geistige*. On these matters, see *KCW*, esp. 873.

2. See, for example, Sixten Ringbom, "Art in 'The Epoch of the Great Spiritual': Occult Elements in the Early Theory of Abstract Painting," *Journal of the Warburg and Courtauld Institutes* 29 (1966), and *The Sounding Cosmos* (Åbo: Åbo Akademi, 1970), as well as Rose-Carol Washton Long, "Occultism, Anarchism, and Abstraction: Kandinsky's Art of the Future," *Art Journal* 46, no. 1 (1987), 38–45. It is undeniably true that in *Über das Geistige* Kandinsky mentions both Madame Blavatsky and Rudolf Steiner, and discusses Theosophy at some length (*OSA*, 143–145)—but his position is plainly that of an outsider, even a slightly skeptical outsider, rather than that of an initiate. Moreover, his theosophical interests seem to have been of remarkably short duration, as he never mentions them in any of his writings after 1911. I largely agree, then, with Lindsay and Vergo's assessment that the section of *Über das Geistige* in which Kandinsky "quotes from Madame Balvatsky's *Key to Theosophy* is nothing other than an extended review of contemporary intellectual and artistic trends, in the course of which [he] refers to figures as diverse as Boecklin and Skriabin, Karl Marx and Edgar Allen Poe" (*KCW*, 117). As I hope to show, there are other "sources"—both more proximate and ultimately more interesting—for Kandinsky's concern with *Geist*.

3. Many of the letters have been translated into French and published by Christian Derouet and Nina Ivanoff in a special issue (hors-série/archives) of *Les Cahiers du Musée national d'art moderne, Vassily Kandinsky: Correspondances avec Zervos et Kojève* (Paris: Centre Georges Pompidou, 1992).

4. Notes and texts of Kojève's lectures were subsequently assembled by another one of the participants, Raymond Queneau, and published as Alexandre Kojève, *Introduction à la lecture de Hegel* (Paris: Gallimard, 1947). For more on the seminar and Kojève generally, see Dominique Auffret, *Alexandre Kojève: La philosophie, l'état, la fin de l'histoire* (Paris: Grasset, 1990), and Michael S. Roth, *Knowing and History: Appropriations of Hegel in Twentieth-Century France* (Ithaca, NY: Cornell University Press, 1988), 83ff.

5. Michael Roth first published Kojève's essay in *La Revue de métaphysique et de morale* 90, no. 2 (1985), 149–171; it appeared again in the special Kandinsky-Kojève-Zervos issue of *Les Cahiers du Musée national d'art moderne* (as in n3, above), 177–193, and has since been released in book form by La Lettre volée (Brussels, 2002). The shorter version of the essay, "Pourquoi concret," appeared in *XXe Siècle*, no. 27 (December 1966). Manuscripts of both texts are preserved in the Bibliothèque Kandinsky at the Centre Pompidou in Paris.

6. As it is, very little has been written on the connection between Hegel's *Aesthetics* and Kandinsky's art theory. Within the English-language art historical literature, it is limited to a few pages of Christopher Short's *The Art Theory of Wassily Kandinsky, 1909–1928* (Bern: Peter Lang, 2010), roughly the same number again in Mark Cheetham's *The Rhetoric of Purity: Essentialist Theory and the Advent of Abstract Painting* (Cambridge: Cambridge University Press, 1991), and an unpublished doctoral dissertation: Jeremy Caslin, "Kandinsky's Theory of Art: Hegel, the Beginnings of Abstraction, and Art History" (University of Virginia, 1998). The philosophical literature is somewhat richer, but tends to take up the rise of abstraction generally, without focusing on Kandinsky's (or anyone's) work in particular. See, for example, Robert Pippin, "What Was Abstract Art? (From the Point of View of Hegel)," in *The Persistence of Subjectivity: On the Kantian Aftermath* (Cambridge: Cambridge University Press, 2005), 279–306; and Lucian Krukowski, "Hegel, 'Progress,' and the Avant-Garde," *Journal of Aesthetics and Art Criticism* 44, no. 3 (Spring 1986), 279–290. The German-language art-historical scholarship is better, but it too dramatically underestimates Kandinsky's relation to Hegel. For example, Matthias Haldemann, in his otherwise excellent study, *Kandinskys Abstraktion: Die Entstehung und Transformation seines Bildkonzepts* (Munich: Wilhelm Fink Verlag, 2002), confines his remarks to the following (from p. 32): "'Geistige Kunst' begründet die Autonomie der Kunst und bringt angeblich gerade den 'Geist' am unmittelbarsten zur 'Offenbarung,' den Kandinsky als Prinzip allen Lebens, als Seelisches denkt. Wie für die idealistische Philosophie, vor allem Schelling und Hegel, bliebe die Kunst damit an einen *metaphysischen* Begriff gebunden ["Geistige (spiritual) art" justifies the autonomy of art and purportedly moves the very "spirit"—which Kandinsky considers to be the principle of all life, the intellect per se—most immediately to "revelation." As in Idealist philosophy, especially that of Schelling and Hegel, art thereby remains bound to a metaphysical concept]." Haldemann pushes the analogy no further, even though one section of his book is titled "Dialektik als übergeordnetes Bildprinzip" (Dialectic as Overarching Pictorial Principle). Similarly, Reinhard Zimmermann, in his *Kunsttheorie von Wassily Kandinsky* (Berlin: Gebr. Mann Verlag, 2002), never mentions Hegel, though his descriptions of Kandinsky's development sound remarkably dialectical: "Das Evolutionsdenken Kandinskys fußt auf der begrifflich-konzeptuellen Grundlage einer dualistischen Weltsicht. Dieser grundlegende Dualismus, der die beiden Pole der Evolution definiert, ist der Dualismus von Materie und Geist. Materie ist der Ausgangspunkt, Geist der Zielpunkt [Kandinsky's evolutionary thought is rooted in the intellectual-conceptual

foundation of a dualistic worldview. This underlying dualism, which defines the two opposing poles of the evolution, is the dichotomy of matter and spirit: Matter is the starting point, spirit the goal]" (p. 148).

The one exception to this general silence is the lengthy section on "Hegel et Kandinsky" in Jean-Joseph Goux's *Les Iconoclastes* (Paris: Seuil, 1978), 78ff.; an English translation is included in Goux, *Symbolic Economies: After Marx and Freud,* trans. Jennifer Curtis Gage (Ithaca, NY: Cornell University Press, 1990), 178ff. Although Goux doesn't cite it, I suspect he was deeply familiar with Kojève's essay; at any rate, his argument is wholly consistent with the one laid out there. I will discuss Goux's text directly in the Conclusion.

I might add that, although the art-historical literature on Hegel and Kandinsky is thin, the connection between Hegel and Mondrian has been more fully studied. See, for example, Yve-Alain Bois, "The Iconoclast," in Angelica Rudenstine, ed., *Piet Mondrian: Life and Art* (Boston: Little, Brown, 1994); and Harry Cooper, "Mondrian, Hegel, Boogie," *October* 84 (Spring 1998), 118–142.

7. I should say at the outset that, in constructing this book as a three-way exchange, I am obviously limiting my focus, necessarily disregarding other voices and concerns that also helped to shape Kandinsky's painting and theory. One can't write about everything, alas. Both Russian symbolism and Russian religious philosophy (including that of Vladimir Soloviev and his followers) likely contributed to Kandinsky's understanding of art and history. Initially Theosophy may have played some role as well. In putting those things to one side and instead directing attention exclusively to the Hegelian thread of Kandinsky's thought, I will doubtless be accused by some of overstating my case. So be it. Certainly the image we have at present—of Kandinsky the mystic, Kandinsky the Theosophist—is an even more egregious overstatement, which has all but obscured the broader significance of his work.

In any case, no one can seriously doubt that Hegel was well known in the Russia of Kandinsky's youth. Writing of the situation in the mid-nineteenth century, Ivan Kireevsky marveled that "there is hardly a young man who cannot talk about Hegel; there is hardly a book or magazine article where one cannot pick up a trace of German influence; ten-year-old boys speak of concrete objectivity" (*Polnoe sobranie sochinenii* [Moscow: Moscow University Press, 1911], vol. 2: 133; cited by Edith W. Clowes, *Fiction's Overcoat: Russian Literary Culture and the Question of Philosophy* [Ithaca, NY: Cornell University Press, 2004], 42). Russian intellectuals during the second half of the century—including Soloviev and the Symbolists—were no less affected by Hegel, even if what they knew of his work was in many cases gleaned from popular introductions to German philosophy or a highly selective reading of the original texts. Obviously, Germany, where Kandinsky had been living for the better part of fifteen years when he wrote *Über das Geistige*, was even more thoroughly steeped in Hegelian thought.

FIRST MOMENT

1. Recent scholarship suggests that the existing version of the *Aesthetics* ought to be understood as in no small measure the product of H. G. Hotho, who attended Hegel's lectures on the fine arts and oversaw the posthumous publication of the notes in 1835. Plainly Hotho reworked much of Hegel's material. In fact, he acknowledges as much in his introduction to that first edition, when he says that his task has been to restore "structure to the whole" by supplying missing "dialectical transitions" and "additional artistic `

examples." Be this as it may, Hotho's edition of the text was the one known to Kandinsky as Hegel's *Aesthetics*. Although present-day readers may very well want to question how much that edition accurately reflects Hegel's thinking on the arts, it nonetheless gives us a wholly reliable image of what Kandinsky knew (or believed he knew) of the lectures. For this reason, whatever our other doubts, I will continue to refer to the Hotho edition (as translated by Knox—see the Abbreviations Used in the Notes) as Hegel's *Aesthetics*. Regarding Hotho's "contributions," see Jason Gaiger, "Catching Up with History: Hegel and Abstract Painting," in Katerina Deligiorgi, ed., *Hegel: New Directions* (Montreal: McGill-Queen's University Press, 2006), 159–176, and "Hegel's Contested Legacy: Rethinking the Relation between Art History and Philosophy," *Art Bulletin* XCIII (June 2011), 178–194, as well as the works by Annemarie Gethmann-Siefert and Helmut Schneider to which Gaiger refers, especially Gethmann-Siefert's "Ästhetik oder Philosophie der Kunst: Die Nachschriften und Zeugnisse zu Hegels Berliner Vorlesungen," 92–110, and Schneider's "Eine Nachschrift der Vorlesung Hegels über Ästhetik im Wintersemester 1920/21," 89–92, both in *Hegel-Studien* 26 (1991).

2. *Aesthetics*, I, 603–604.

3. *OSA*, 127. Unless otherwise noted, all quotations from *Über das Geistige in der Kunst* will be taken from the *OSA* translation, which is from the second (1912) edition of Kandinsky's text. In this particular case, the translation was slightly modified.

4. Frederick Beiser, *Hegel* (New York: Routledge, 2005), 171.

5. As Robert Pippin says, "art is regularly treated [by Hegel] as the attempt by spirit to externalize its self-understanding in a sensible form, and thereby to appropriate such externality as its own, to be at home therein, and to express more successfully such a self-understanding." See Robert Pippin, "What Was Abstract Art? (From the Point of View of Hegel)," in *The Persistence of Subjectivity: On the Kantian Aftermath* (Cambridge: Cambridge University Press, 2005), 288.

6. *Aesthetics*, I, 49: "Art . . . while remaining within the sensuous sphere, liberates man . . . from the power of sensuousness. . . . [It] lifts him with gentle hands out of and above imprisonment in nature." See also Robert Pippin's comments on this passage in Pippin, "What Was Abstract Art? (From the Point of View of Hegel)," 290: "In fact, fine art, and especially its history, Hegel claims, should be understood as a *liberation from nature*, . . . the achievement of a mode of self-understanding and self-determination no longer set, or limited by nature as such, as well as a humanizing transformation of the natural into a human world."

7. See *Aesthetics*, I, 304–306. Stephen Bungay usefully summarizes that section: "The symbol is distinguished from the sign, in that a sign has no intrinsic relation to the meaning it designates. A sign is an arbitrary signifier, related to a signified meaning by convention. A symbol, however, does bear some non-arbitrary relation to its meaning (its content), but the relation is indeterminate. For example, a lion is a symbol of strength because a lion actually possesses strength, so that it, as a signifier, bears some relationship to what it signifies. But the relationship is indeterminate because a lion is many other things besides strong, and many other things besides lions have strength. Although it is not arbitrary that a lion should signify strength, there is no necessity that it signify strength rather than, say, regality or hunting prowess, and no necessity that strength be signified by a lion rather than, say, a bear or an ox. The relationship between the form (signifier) of a symbol and its content (signi-

fied) is indeterminate, because it is not apparent exactly what the content is from the form, for they do not exhaust each other's determinacy. Symbolic art will therefore be enigmatic, for its meaning is indeterminate, the form and content in only partial unity." See Bungay, *Beauty and Truth: A Study of Hegel's Aesthetics* (Oxford: Oxford University Press, 1984), 57.

8. For an excellent discussion of Hegel's understanding of symbolic architecture, see Stephen Melville, "Plasticity: The Hegelian Writing of Art," in Stephen Melville and Margaret Iversen, eds., *Writing Art History* (Chicago: University of Chicago Press, 2010), 151–173, esp. 164ff.

9. *Aesthetics*, II, 806. On these matters see also Stephen Houlgate, "Presidential Address: Hegel and the Art of Painting," in William Maker, ed., *Hegel and Aesthetics* (Albany: State University of New York Press, 2000), esp. 62–71.

10. On this point see Beiser, *Hegel*, 302, as well as Stephen Melville, "Des marques (ce qui reste de Hegel) ou Daniel Buren en tant que peintre," *Le Part de l'oeil*, 17–18 (Dossier: Peinture pratique théorique), 2001–2002, 187.

SECOND MOMENT, PART 1

1. Actually, Kandinsky does include a fairly extended discussion of Maeterlinck's work (see *OSA*, 146–147), though its conclusions are never applied to poetry at large, with the result that the Belgian playwright seems more the exception than the norm. (It's perhaps worth noting here that, in 1911, as Kandinsky was preparing the publication of *Über das Geistige*, Maeterlinck was awarded the Nobel Prize in Literature; his mention in the text would have given Kandinsky's treatise a kind of up-to-the-minute currency.) There are also passages in *Über das Geistige* in which the spiritual insufficiency of poetry in comparison with either painting or music is implied; more on these below.

2. *OSA*, 131.

3. See Michael Inwood, *A Hegel Dictionary* (Cambridge, MA: Blackwell, 1992), 283–285. Inwood suggests that "to kick upstairs" might be the most accurate rendering, but feels that "it is too colloquial to win general approval."

4. We might compare Kandinsky's assessment of the present (i.e., early twentieth-century) state of affairs with what Hegel had to say in the *Phenomenology of Spirit* about his own day. Here, for example, is a passage from the preface to the *Phenomenology*, §8:

> Formerly . . . the eye of the Spirit had to be forcibly turned and held fast to the things of this world. . . . Now we seem to need just the opposite: sense is so fast rooted in earthly things that it requires just as much force to raise it. The Spirit shows itself so impoverished that, like a wanderer in a desert craving for a mere mouthful of water, it seems to crave for its refreshment only the bare feeling of the divine in general. By the little which now satisfies Spirit, we can measure the extent of its loss.

Hegel then adds in section 11:

> It is not difficult to see that ours is a birth-time and a period of transition to a new era. Spirit has broken with the world it has hitherto inhabited and imagined, and is of a mind to submerge it in the past. [*Phenomenology of Spirit*, 5–6]

5. *Aesthetics*, I, 605.

6. *OSA*, 135 (translation slightly modified). Hegel had claimed that, when represented in painting, a natural object becomes *vergeistigt* (imbued with spirit) and so acquires a distinct sort of meaning, namely, what that object *is* in and for a human community.

Kandinsky's argument here seems to be that painting of the recent past had reached such a spiritual low point that it was unable to communicate even that; thus the objects remained "the same, unaltered."

7. *OSA*, 128 (translation slightly modified). In the original version of *Über das Geistige*, the reproduction of the Ravenna mosaic appeared immediately following the text's references to "primitive" art, thereby suggesting that the mosaic was an example of the kind of "primitive" work Kandinsky had in mind. Lindsay and Vergo's claim that the book's reproductions "were originally placed more or less at random, bearing no evident relation to the surrounding text," thus seems to me wholly mistaken in this instance—as does their (unexplained) decision to move the Ravenna photograph into the following chapter. See *KCW*, 118 and 136.

8. See especially Rose-Carol Washton Long, *Kandinsky: The Development of an Abstract Style* (Oxford: Clarendon, 1980).

9. *OSA*, 128.

10. "Kuda idet 'novoe' iskusstvo?," *Odesskie novosti* (Odessa, 1911), translated as "Whither the 'New' Art?" in *KCW*, 100.

11. "Whither the 'New' Art?," *KCW*, 102 (translation slightly modified). The German translation of the text reads: "So wie der neue Zweig die Forsetzung desselben Baumes ist. Und das Blatt die Forsetzung des Zweiges" (*KGS*, 425).

12. In *Über das Geistige* itself, Kandinsky employs a similar metaphor of organic growth in his discussion of ornament and its (as yet unrealized) potential as a vehicle for spirit: "At the juncture we have reached today, any attempt to create such a style of ornamentation by force would be like trying to open a scarcely formed bud into a full-blown flower with one's fingers" (*OSA*, 199).

13. Much has been written about Kandinsky's use of the phrase *innere Notwendigkeit*. Unfortunately, a bit too much effort has been spent on trying to find a "source" for the phrase, rather than understanding it in the context of Kandinsky's argument. For a summary of the literature on the subject, see Jeremy Caslin, "Kandinsky's Theory of Art: Hegel, the Beginnings of Abstraction, and Art History," Ph.D. diss. (University of Virginia, 1998), 151ff. Again, in *Über das Geistige*, *innere Notwendigkeit* is used to emphasize the "organic" nature of art's development—to insist, in other words, that change is not simply the product of external causes but rather the result of a particular history that has its own internal logic. When it is understood in this way, the apparent contradiction between "necessity" and "freedom," which some have seen as a flaw of Kandinsky's essay, largely disappears. Kandinsky's claim is that, like the spiritual with which it is aligned, art—of its own necessity—develops an increasing freedom or autonomy from mere (nonhuman, ahistorical) nature. For a discussion emphasizing the apparent opposition of "necessity" and "freedom" in Kandinsky's theory, see Mark Cheetham, *The Rhetoric of Purity: Essentialist Theory and the Advent of Abstract Painting* (Cambridge: Cambridge University Press, 1991), 73–74.

14. *Phenomenology of Spirit*, 2.

15. *OSA*, 208 (translation slightly modified).

16. *OSA*, 136–137 (translation modified).

17. In "Development of Art Forms" ("Entwicklung der Kunstformen"), an essay likely written a year or two after *Über das Geistige in der Kunst* but published only recently, Kandinsky revisited and refined this historical account. He explained that the "conscious

use of painterly means" championed by the proponents of *l'art pour l'art* was at the same time a movement away from the natural world and its depiction, and that it carried with it revolutionary implications: "The total separation of art from nature, which begins here, the radical emancipation and restless liberation of the first from the second, the emergence of absolute art, all this forms the *third period* of development, which at the same time begins the second epoch of art history or, to be more exact, the first period of the second epoch [Die von hier beginnende Trennung der Kunst von der Natur, die radikale Emanzipierung und restlose Befreiung der ersten von der zweiten, die Enstehung der absoluten Kunst, bildet die *dritte Periode* der Entwicklung, die zur selben Zeit die zweite Epoche in der Kunstgeschichte beginnt, oder genauer gesagt die erste Periode der zweiten Epoche]." The accompanying chart (an English version of which appears below), leaves little doubt as to the dialectical nature of these changes, in that it clearly presents the first and second periods as antithetically opposed, and the third as constituting both the sublation of those earlier moments and the starting point for all future developments. "Entwicklung der Kunstformen" appears in *KGS*, 476–479.

	I. Epoch		II. Epoch
I. Period	II. Per[iod]	III. Per[iod] =	I. Per[iod]
Pure Nature	Removal of		Pure Art
Object[ive]	Nature		Paint[erly]
Means	g[raphic]		Means
	paint[erly]		
	means		
	Augmentation [?] of means		
unconscious	conscious		scientific
mechanical	instinctual		(theory)
involuntary	arbitrary		
Representational Art	Dec[orative]- Art		Absolute Art

18. Even this description is more or less directly engaged with Hegel, who, in the *Aesthetics*, had claimed that landscape painting's raison d'être was not the imitation of a natural scene but rather the imbuing of that scene with *Stimmung*, that is, with human feeling and therefore a *geistige* dimension. See *Aesthetics*, II, 831–832.

19. *OSA*, 129 (translation modified).

20. *OSA*, 153 (translation modified).

21. It should be noted, however, that the word actually employed by Hegel was *beweisen* (to prove or manifest), rather than Kandinsky's *prüfen*. I suspect the substitution was an effect of the artist having encountered the *Aesthetics* first in Russian, and then having made his own translation back into German without verifying it against Hegel's original text. In any case, *prüfen* clearly functions (a bit idiosyncratically) as a synonym for *beweisen* in Kandinsky's writing. In fact, its rather nonstandard usage makes translation difficult if one misses the Hegelian allusion. Thus Lindsay and Vergo render the phrase in question—"Bewußt oder unbewußt wenden sich allmählich die Künstler hauptsächlich zu ihrem Material, prüfen dasselbe" (Kandinsky, *Über das Geistige in der Kunst* [Munich: R. Piper Verlag, 1912], 33)—as "Consciously or unconsciously, artists

turn gradually toward an emphasis on their materials" (*OSA*, 153), as if Kandinsky were advocating a kind of high modernist attention to the planarity of the canvas and the tactility of paint. In fact he is at considerable pains throughout *Über das Geistige* to dissociate himself from such a materialist view; everything turns on the audience seeing nonrepresentational form as decidedly *immaterial*, and so adequate to the interiority of human self-consciousness in its present state of development.

22. *Aesthetics*, I, 11. Certainly if one is looking for a "source" for the term *innere Notwendigkeit* frequently employed by Kandinsky, this would be as good a place as any.

23. For an art-historical meditation on Hegel's requirement that a discipline prove its object, see Stephen Melville, "Object and Objectivity in Damisch," *Oxford Art Journal* 28, no. 2 (2005), 183–189.

24. *OSA*, 154.

25. *Aesthetics*, I, 88.

26. *OSA*, 189–191. "There will always be something extra that cannot be exhausted by words," he adds, "and yet that is not merely an elaborate accident of the particular tone, but its very essence."

27. *OSA*, 138.

28. Kandinsky's position here is close to that of the young Schelling. I have no idea whether he might have read Schelling's *System of Transcendental Idealism*, for example, but it may be worth remarking that the most important Russian philosopher of the nineteenth century, Vladimir Soloviev, was deeply influenced by Schelling's work. On this point, see Alexandre Kojève, "La métaphysique religieuse de Vladimir Soloviev," *Revue d'histoire et de philosophie religieuses*, vols. 14 (1934), 534–554, and 15 (1935), 110–152.

29. *Aesthetics*, II, 891. Hegel appears to be reverting to the more standard use of the word "abstract" here.

30. *Aesthetics*, II, 848.

31. *Aesthetics*, I, 599–600.

32. *OSA*, 160.

33. Kandinsky also frequently compares particular colors to specific musical instruments (e.g., "light blue resembles the flute, dark blue the cello, darker still the wonderful sounds of the double bass," *OSA*, 182). For a discussion of the idea of *audition colorée*, or "the synaesthetic phenomenon of color-hearing," and Kandinsky's place within its history, see John Gage, *Color and Culture: Practice and Meaning from Antiquity to Abstraction* (Berkeley: University of California Press, 1993), 236–241.

34. Hegel excused himself from a fuller discussion of music on the grounds that he was "little versed in this sphere" (*Aesthetics*, II, 893). That point has been underscored, and its implications analyzed, by, among others, Stephen Bungay, *Beauty and Truth: A Study of Hegel's Aesthetics* (Oxford: Oxford University Press, 1984), 136ff.; and Andrew Bowie, *Aesthetics and Subjectivity: From Kant to Nietzsche* (Manchester, UK: Manchester University Press, 1990), esp. 159–160.

35. *Aesthetics*, II, 893n1.

36. For the reference to Beethoven, see *OSA*, 133–134.

37. Hegel's "Concept" is closely related to the object of "science" as discussed earlier. Andrew Bowie, in his book, *Aesthetics and Subjectivity* (p. 154) gives a useful explication of the term: "The 'Concept' includes the whole process of which it is the Concept: the process

and the Concept are identical in the specific sense of being unable to be what they are without each other. The Concept 'tree' therefore does not refer to the transient empirical object I have in front of me, nor is it my thinking of a tree when I cannot see one. Instead, the Concept includes all stages of the tree that have preceded what I might now see (as well as what will succeed these stages), *and* their reflection in my and others' thinking. . . . The Concept in Hegel's sense obviously cannot be thought by an individual all at once, but if the Concept is to be 'of' the object it must take us beyond the contingency and temporally determined nature of the particular. Hence . . . his rejection of the immediate as a locus of truth, and his requirement that thinking be 'speculative,' in the sense of refusing to take finite propositions about reality as definitively true. The ultimate result is that the highest Concepts must be . . . able to include all concrete particulars within themselves."

38. Hegel, *Ästhetik*, II, 296. I have used the translation of this passage given by Bowie in *Aesthetics and Subjectivity*, 155. My general understanding of Hegel's account of music is heavily indebted to Bowie's text.

39. Bowie, *Aesthetics and Subjectivity*, 155.

40. *Ästhetik*, II, 297; again I use Bowie's translation, *Aesthetics and Subjectivity*, 155.

41. See Theodor Adorno, *Beethoven, Philosophie der Musik* (Frankfurt: Suhrkamp, 1993). The analogy has also been expressed the other way around by Bowie, for example, in his *Aesthetics and Subjectivity* (156): "In the same way as all the notes of the chromatic scale may appear in a symphony at some point, and at the end will become part of the path to the re-establishing of the tonic key, the divisions involved in conceptual thinking are reintegrated into the teleology of the Idea, a sort of ultimate harmonic resolution."

42. Arnold Schoenberg, *Theory of Harmony*, trans. Roy E. Carter (Berkeley: University of California Press, 1978), 20–21: "In the overtone series, which is one of the most remarkable properties of the tone, there appear after some stronger-sounding overtones a number of weaker-sounding ones. Without a doubt the former are more familiar to the ear, while the latter, hardly perceptible, are rather strange. In other words: the overtones closer to the fundamental seem to contribute more or more perceptibly to the total phenomenon of the tone—tone accepted as euphonious, suitable for art—while the more distant seem to contribute less or less perceptibly. But it is quite certain that they all do contribute more or less. . . . Hence, the distinction between them is only a matter of degree, not of kind. They are no more opposites than two and ten are opposites, as the frequency numbers indeed show; and the expressions 'consonance' and 'dissonance,' which signify an antithesis, are false. It all simply depends on the growing ability of the analyzing ear to familiarize itself with the remote overtones, thereby expanding the concept of what is euphonious, suitable for art."

43. Ibid., 423–424. On Schoenberg's own general Hegelianism, see Michael Cherlin, *Schoenberg's Musical Imagination* (Cambridge: Cambridge University Press, 2007), esp. chap. 2, 44–67.

44. In the first edition of *Über das Geistige*, Kandinsky included a footnote that referred the reader to an excerpt from the *Harmonielehre*, "Über Oktaven- und Quintenparallelen" (On Parallel Octaves and Fifths) which was published, before Schoenberg's book appeared, in the journal *Die Musik* X, no. 2 (Berlin, 1910), 104. Lindsay and Vergo report (*KCW*, 876n32) that, "between the publication of the first and second German editions of *On the Spiritual*, Kandinsky had received a copy of the newly published *Theory of Harmony* as a

gift from the composer." With Franz Marc, Gabriele Münter, and several others, Kandinsky had attended a concert of Schoenberg's music on January 2, 1911. Two weeks later, after making several sketches and a painting, *Impression III (Concert)*, inspired by that evening's program, Kandinsky wrote to Schoenberg, thereby initiating a remarkable correspondence and, eventually, friendship. See *Arnold Schoenberg–Wassily Kandinsky: Letters, Pictures and Documents*, ed. Jelena Hahl-Koch, trans. John C. Crawford (London: Faber and Faber, 1984); and Esther da Costa Meyer and Fred Wasserman, eds., *Schoenberg, Kandinsky, and the Blue Rider*, catalogue of an exhibition of the same title, held at the Jewish Museum, New York, from October 2003 to February 2004 (London: Scala Publishers, 2004).

45. In certain passages of the *Harmonielehre* Schoenberg argued not so much that modern composition had moved away from natural harmonies as that the present vantage point allowed one to see that what had previously been taken for natural laws were not, in fact, quite that. He says, for example, on p. 28: "It is easy for us now to say that 'the church modes were unnatural, but our scales conform to nature.' That they conformed to nature was undoubtedly also believed of the church modes in their day." In other places, he takes a firmly relativist position—arguing, for instance, that "we could just as well have found a different scale, as did . . . the Arabs, the Chinese and Japanese"—even as, in the next breath, he speaks of the natural basis of the overtone scale. In other places yet again, his language suggests (in a way not so different from Kandinsky's) that recent developments reflect a shift in authority from "external nature" toward "inner nature" or *Geist*. Thus, the opening sentences of his chapter on "Consonance and Dissonance" declare: "Art in its most primitive sense is a simple imitation of nature. But it quickly becomes imitation of nature in the wider sense of this idea, that is, not merely imitation of outer but also of inner nature" (Schoenberg, *Theory of Harmony*, 18).

46. *OSA*, 149.

47. *OSA*, 149 (translation slightly modified).

48. The word "necessary" here perhaps requires some clarification. At least in Schoenberg's case, the claim is not that music *had to* develop in the way that it did; his assertion that the West might easily have discovered a different scale (as did the Arabs and Chinese) is evidence enough of that. Rather, the argument is simply that, in looking back from our present vantage point, we are clearly able to see the (dialectical) path that led us to the place where we now stand. The shape and structure of that path have a certain explanatory power; they enable us, in other words, to understand why we "necessarily" hold the particular values that we do.

49. *KCW*, 125; see also 876n32. In *Über das Geistige* itself, in the chapter on "Theory," Kandinsky indicated why the time was not yet quite ripe for the formulation of a *Harmonielehre der Malerei*: "Music . . . has its own grammar, which, like all living things, changes during great periods, yet is of continual help and value as a kind dictionary." He then immediately added: "Our painting today is, however, in a different state: its emancipation from direct dependence on 'nature' is in its very earliest stages" (*KCW*, 197; translation slightly modified).

50. Quoted by Magdalena Dabrowski, "Kandinsky and Schoenberg: Abstraction as a Visual Metaphor of Emancipated Dissonance," in da Costa Meyer and Wasserman, eds., *Schoenberg, Kandinsky, and the Blue Rider*, 83.

51. "Whither the 'New' Art?," in *KCW*, 102.

52. Ibid., 193 (emphasis added).

53. Schoenberg, *Theory of Harmony*, 11. For Kandinsky's claim about consonance and dissonance, see *OSA*, 217; the comment about beauty and ugliness appears in a footnote on p. 177.

54. Kandinsky won't fully articulate the underlying rationale for his claims about the temporal or developmental nature of the individual composition until 1926, in his *Punkt und Linie zu Fläche*. It probably makes sense, then, to save our own fuller discussion of the issue until we turn to an analysis of that text (in Part 2 of the "Second Moment," 33ff.). For now, it may be enough simply to quote from the book:

The apparently clear and justified division:

painting—space (plane)

music—time

has on closer (even if, until now, cursory) examination suddenly been called into question— and to the best of my knowledge, in the first instance by painters. [*PLP*, 550]

55. *OSA*, 193 (translation slightly modified).

56. To my knowledge, only John Gage and Clark Poling have previously drawn any connection between Kandinsky's color theory and Hering's opponent-process scheme; see Gage, *Color and Culture*, 207; and Poling, *Kandinsky's Teaching at the Bauhaus* (New York: Rizzoli International Publications, 1986), 67. By contrast, Alberto Worth, in "Kandinsky and the Science of Art," *British Journal of Aesthetics* 19, no. 4 (1979), 361–365, claimed (although not on the basis of any cited evidence) that Kandinsky was wholly unacquainted with Hering's work. In regard to these matters, we should also note that there are parallels between Kandinsky's color theory and Hegel's descriptions, such as the following, from the *Aesthetics*: "Pure red is the effective regal and concrete color in which blue and yellow, contraries again themselves, are fused together. Green can also be regarded as such a unification, not however as a concrete unity but as purely expunged difference, as saturated and calm neutrality. These [four] colors are the purest, simplest, and original fundamental colors" (II, 842).

57. For a thorough account of the debate and its stakes, see R. Steven Turner, *In the Eye's Mind: Vision and the Helmholtz-Hering Controversy* (Princeton, NJ: Princeton University Press, 1994). Kandinsky may have been attracted to Hering's opponent-process theory in part by its own strongly oppositional nature—that is, that it overtly challenged the Young-Helmholtz model, which remained the dominant model of color vision well into the twentieth century. (Real advances, Kandinsky was convinced, were ever only made through radical contradiction.) I find it curious, though, that there are no explicit references to Hering or the opponent-process theory in *Über das Geistige*. Even more remarkable, the one footnote that does seem to allude to Hering's controversy with Helmholtz suggests certain sympathies with Helmholtz's position. In the foreword to his 1872 treatise, *Zur Lehre vom Lichtsinne* (On the Theory of the Light Sense), Hering had attacked Helmholtz for being less concerned with physiology than with spirit (*Geist*). "The spiritualist," Hering wrote, "will always be inclined to restrict the realm of the innate, in order to win a fuller and freer scope for the human spirit, and to be able to portray the spirit as being as independent as possible from its organic basis." Therefore, Hering concluded, "spiritualists are empiricist by preference" (3; quoted in Turner, *In the Eye's Mind*, 123). In the footnote to *Über das Geistige*, Kandinsky pointedly declared that all of his assertions about color were "the results of empirical-spiritual experience and [were] not based upon any positive science" (*OSA*,

179). Given that those "results" supported (and almost certainly were in part derived from) the opponent-process theory, Kandinsky may have intended the footnote to suggest that his position represented a sublation of the two competing views. In light of that speculation, it seems especially interesting to note that the scientific debate has in fact reached a kind of dialectical resolution in the present; once understood as mutually exclusive, the opponent-process and Young-Helmholtz theories are now *both* used to help explain how our system of color vision works. (On this point, see Turner, *In the Eye's Mind*, esp. 265ff.)

58. The priority Kandinsky accorded to yellow and blue—and his alignment of them with warmth and coldness, respectively—seems to derive from Goethe's 1810 *Theory of Colors*, which similarly argued for the primacy of yellow and blue as tonal opposites. In fact, the table of polarities that Goethe included with his text, which aligned yellow with "light" and "warmth" as well as with "proximity," and which contrasted each of these with the "darkness," "coldness," and "distance" characteristic of blue, closely accords with Kandinsky's own descriptions. Kandinsky, too, saw warm colors—foremost among them yellow—as moving "in the direction of the spectator, striving toward him," and so as being the polar opposite to blue, which appeared to move "away from him" (*OSA*, 179). It was partly for these reasons that Kandinsky also regarded blue as the most spiritually evocative color; he saw it as internally oriented (its force, he said, was "concentric" or centripetal), so that, like spirit in the modern world, it always seemed in the process of withdrawing from exteriority into itself. For Goethe's chart, see Ruprecht Matthaei, ed., *Goethe's Color Theory* (New York: Van Nostrand Reinhold, 1971), 51.

59. An interesting footnote to this discussion: Goethe's color wheel reduced by one (to six) the number of discrete colors that Newton had articulated in his. As John Gage and others have observed, Newton's seven-part wheel was based on analogy with the seven notes of the diatonic scale in music. See Gage, *Color and Culture*, 232.

60. *OSA*, 163 (translation slightly modified).

61. For a summery of the literature on the painting, see Magdalena Dabrowski, *Kandinsky: Compositions* (New York: Museum of Modern Art, 1995), 25–29.

62. See Long, *Kandinsky*, 179–180n67.

63. Letter from Signac to Charles Angrand (January 14, 1906), trans. in Alfred H. Barr Jr., *Matisse: His Art and His Public* (New York: Museum of Modern Art, 1951), 82.

64. Tavernier, "Le Salon des Indépendants," *Le Grande Revue* 38 (April 1, 1906), 105, quoted in Alastair Wright, *Matisse and the Subject of Modernism* (Princeton, NJ: Princeton University Press, 2004), 97.

65. It should also be pointed out that what at first glance or in reproductions of the painting look like black lines are often instead (or additionally) rendered with very dark blues or greens. Even these conform to Kandinsky's system, however, in that they are counterweighted by certain "white" areas of the painting into which small amounts of yellow or red pigment were added. In all of these instances, then, Kandinsky preserved dissonance, even while mixing colors—giving us, that is, a combination or hybrid of two separate oppositional pairs (i.e., those labeled on his chart by the Roman numerals II and III). One might want to observe as well that, visible underneath some of the paint in the Guggenheim sketch are Kandinsky's penciled notations to himself: "gelb" in the lower left-hand corner, for example, or "w" (presumably for *weiss*) in the long, whitish diagonal shape above. This evidence suggests that color distribution within the painting began in an

extremely systematic fashion—each shape being assigned in advance to but a single color specified by the chart, presumably so as to ensure the overall balance of contraries. Only subsequently, in the process of actually painting on the canvas, did Kandinsky complicate matters by mixing in different hues.

66. Quoted in Esther da Costa Meyer, "Arnold Schönberg and Wassily Kandinsky—Emancipations," cited in da Costa Meyer and Wasserman, eds., *Schoenberg, Kandinsky, and The Blue Rider*, 39.

SECOND MOMENT, PART 2

1. In fact, I would argue, all of Kandinsky's writings on art are informed by his understanding of Hegel's *Aesthetics* and its dialectical development. I will limit myself here, however, to a discussion of only those texts that best convey the depth of the artist's engagement with Hegel and the principal points of contention between them.

2. *KCW*, 378. At this point, in 1913, Kandinsky was still reluctant to assert that nonrepresentational painting had superseded painting done from nature. A few sentences after the passage just quoted, he claimed only that he had "come to conceive of nonobjective painting not as a negation of all previous art, but as an uncommonly vital, primordial division of the one old trunk into two main branches of development, [both] indispensable to the creation of the crown of the green tree." As we will see, Kojève's essay "Les Peintures concrètes" largely discourages any such belief in "two main branches of development," implying that, by 1913 (or 1910 even), representational painting had become a thing of the past.

3. The first occurrence is in the catalogue of an exhibition at Gummesons in 1922. Kandinsky repeated the sentence, with minor variations, at least three times subsequently, including in a 1928 treatise on art pedagogy that he produced after the Bauhaus had moved to Dessau and he had begun teaching analytic drawing as part of the school's foundation course. For all four instances of the claim (i.e., that the world had moved from a period of "either-or" to "and"), see *KCW*, 485, 509, 716, and 723.

4. "Und, Einiges über synthetische Kunst" (1927) and "Gestern-Heute-Morgen" (1925), in Paul Westeim, ed., *Künstlerbekenntnisse* (Berlin, 1925); these articles are translated and reproduced in *KCW*, 708–717 and 508–509, respectively. Kandinsky also wrote a catalogue essay in 1935 with the very dialectical title "Thèse-antithèse-synthèse" (Thesis-Antithesis-Synthesis). This, however, was the name given to the exhibition itself, probably by the painter Hans Erni, who organized the show for the Kunstmuseum Lucerne. For Kandinsky's essay, see *KCW*, 772–773.

5. *Punkt und Linie zu Fläche: Beitrag zur Analyse der malerischen Elemente*, eds. Walter Gropius and László Moholy-Nagy (Munich: Albert Langen, 1926). There exist two English translations: the first, by Howard Dearstyne and Hilla Rebay, was published in 1947, under the title *Point and Line to Plane*, by the Solomon R. Guggenheim Foundation for the Museum of Non-Objective Painting, New York, and then republished by Dover (New York, 1979); the second, much better one is by Lindsay and Vergo, *PLP*. Unless otherwise specified, references here will be to the Lindsay and Vergo translation.

6. *PLP*, 530.

7. *PLP*, 533.

8. *PLP*, 537.

9. *OSA*, 176.

10. See *PLP*, 533:

Painting in particular, which in the course of the last few decades actually has made a marvelously strenuous leap forward, has only recently been emancipated from "practical" meaning and from its adaptability to many of its former applications. Now it has attained a level that inevitably demands a precise, purely scientific examination of pictorial means for pictorial purposes. Further steps in this direction cannot be attained without such an examination—neither for the artist nor for the public.

11. Hegel's reference to color as the "element of painting" comes from H. G. Hotho's transcription of the 1823 lecture series, and is cited by Bernadette Collenberg, "Hegels Konzeption des Kolorits in den Berliner Vorlesungen über die Philosophie der Kunst," in Anne-Marie Gethmann-Siefert, ed., *Phänomen Versus System* (Bonn: Bouvier, 1992), 125. In an unexpected echo of that comment, Kandinsky claims (twice) in *Punkt und Linie* that "the point is the *proto-element of painting* [*das Urelement der Malerei*]"—thereby suggesting that it's not quite sufficient for painting, but nonetheless necessary to it. See *PLP*, 536 and 547.

12. *KCW*, 349–350. "Malerei als reine Kunst" first appeared in *Der Sturm* 4, no. 178/179 (September 1913), 98–99; the English translation appears in *KCW*, 349–354. The original German of the paragraph quoted reads: "Damit der Inhalt, der erst 'abstrakt' lebt, zu einem Werk wird, muß das zweite Element—das äußere—der Verkörperung dienen. Deshalb sucht der Inhalt nach einem Ausdrucksmittel, nach einer 'materiellen' Form" (98).

13. See "The Basic Elements of Form," in *KCW*, 499–501. The original essay, "Die Grundelemente der Form," was published in the anthology *Staatliches Bauhaus Weimar, 1919–1923* (Weimar and Munich: Bauhausbücher, 1923) and served in many ways as precursor to *Punkt und Linie zu Fläche*. In the essay, Kandinsky writes:

The question of form in general must be divided into two parts:

1. Form in the narrower sense—surface and volume

2. Form in the broader sense—color and its relationship with form in the narrower sense [*KCW*, 500]

14. It should be said that Hegel too considered color superior to drawing. As Stephen Houlgate explains, "this is because Hegel believes that the purpose of painting as art is not simply the creation of beautiful form, but the creation of a beautiful and credible illusion of natural objects through which human spirituality can become manifest, and because he believes that color is the means through which that illusion is fully generated." See Houlgate, "Presidential Address: Hegel and the Art of Painting," in William Maker, ed., *Hegel and Aesthetics* (Albany: State University of New York Press, 2000), 61–82, esp. 66.

15. Here we may be reminded of the argument Kandinsky had once made regarding the empty formalism of *l'art pour l'art*, and how it had provided the "seedling," as he'd said, for painting's further advance (see p. 16 of the present text). In *Punkt und Linie zu Fläche*, Kandinsky makes several such claims regarding his current *theoretical* concerns and their origin in an earlier materialism. He says (*PLP*, 670–671), for example: "The viewpoint of common materialism, which of course had to extend to the phenomena of art, produced as a natural-organic consequence an exaggerated appreciation of the material surface, with all its complications. It is to this prejudice that art owes its healthy, indispensable interest in . . . technical expertise and, particularly, in a thorough examination of 'material' generally." The scare quotes around "material" in that last line are presumably meant to indicate that,

at the present moment in art's development—i.e., on the current level of the dialectical unfolding of its Concept—painting's "materiality" has become qualified, having already attained a certain degree of spiritualization.

16. To repeat, the four pairs of opposing terms enumerated in "Yesterday-Today-Tomorrow" are (in their implied developmental order):

"the materialistic movement"–"the spiritual movement"

"the intuitive method of construction"–"the theoretical method"

"the analytical movement"–"the synthetic movement"

"in practice—a partly new, partly reborn synthetic, 'monumental' art"—"in theory—

a partly reborn, partly newborn science of art" [*KCW*, 508–509]

The second term of each pair is closely aligned with the first on the next "level," so that there is a close association between, for example, the "spiritual movement" and "intuitive methods of construction," just as there is between the "synthetic movement" and "'monumental' art" in "practice." Conversely, the "materialistic movement" is linked to "theoretical methods of construction," and this pair in turn to both "analysis" and a "science of art." Like Kandinsky's inversion of the line/color hierarchy, his associations of "theory" with science (especially the material or natural sciences), and "practice" with spirit, strike us today as counterintuitive. They are, however, absolutely central to Kandinsky's understanding of art's role in the world.

17. In May 1920, following the Russian Revolution, Kandinsky was invited by Anatole Lunacharsky, the People's Commissar of Enlightenment, to become the founding director of the INKhUK (the Institute of Artistic Culture) in Moscow. In that role and as part of INKhUK's inaugural program, Kandinsky announced that the institution's main objective would be the elaboration of a science of art (*nauka ob iskusstve*). Approximately a year after having been deposed as director of the INKhUK by its younger, contructivist members, Kandinsky accepted an invitation from Walter Gropius to visit the Weimar Bauhaus. Kandinsky was asked to join the Bauhaus faculty the following spring (1922), initially as master of the Wall-Painting Workshop and instructor for one of the Theory of Form classes required as part of the Preliminary Course.

18. *Philosophy of Nature*, §247.

19. The full quotation being referenced here is from Hegel's *Enzyklopädie*, §246, *Zusatz*, 18: "This unity of intelligence and intuition, of the spirit's being-within-itself and its comportment to externality, must however not be the beginning but the goal, not something immediate but rather a unity that is produced." It is quoted in Terry Pinkard, "Speculative *Naturphilosophie* and the Development of the Empirical Sciences: Hegel's Perspective," in Gary Gutting, ed., *Continental Philosophy of Science* (Oxford: Blackwell, 2005), 25. Kandinsky's goal was likewise to develop a systematic "philosophy" that integrated art's "inner" spiritual *and* "outer" material dimensions—and so enabled art itself to achieve, and to be seen as achieving, their absolute integration.

20. The *Philosophy of Nature* is perhaps Hegel's most understudied and least understood work. Interpretations of it vary widely, as do estimations of its value (philosophical or otherwise). Critics tend to see it as advancing a wholly a priori metaphysics, with the order and structure it purportedly "deduces" from nature having in fact simply been imposed from Hegel's *Logic*. (The philosophers among this group tend to regard it as a dispensable part of his larger philosophic project.) Even among defenders of the book,

there is wide disagreement. For example, Alison Stone, in her recent *Petrified Intelligence: Nature in Hegel's Philosophy* (Albany: State University of New York Press, 2005), reads the text as asserting that nature originates in a creative act on the part of "absolute idea," with reason thus preceding the natural world that instantiates it. At the other extreme are those who argue that the *Philosophy of Nature* was never intended as a metaphysical account of how natural processes occur; in their view the text aims instead at an "account of what kind of view of nature as a whole (as 'infinite,' as 'Idea') we are implicitly committed to when we try to make sense of ourselves as the kind of rational creatures that do empirical physics in the first place and try to understand how the nature studied by physics is also the nature in which we are free, rational agents." For this latter view, see Terry Pinkard, *Hegel: A Biography* (Cambridge: Cambridge University Press, 2000), 570, from which the above quotation comes, as well as Pinkard's "Speculative *Naturphilosophie* and the Development of the Empirical Sciences." For the purposes of the present chapter, I have relied principally on those metaphysical interpretations that emphasize the centrality to Hegel's entire system of the ideas of organic development and organic unity developed in the *Philosophy of Nature*. See Frederick Beiser, "Hegel and *Naturphilosophie*," in *Studies in History and Philosophy of Science* 34 (2003), 135–147; and Stephen Houlgate, *An Introduction to Hegel: Freedom, Truth and History* (Oxford: Blackwell, 2005), esp. 106–121, "Reason in Nature."

One of the strongest critics of the *Philosophy of Nature* was Alexandre Kojève, who spent a good number of his student years studying physics precisely as a means of testing the legitimacy of Hegel's claims. Kojève was clearly of the opinion that the *Philosophy of Nature* was meant as a metaphysical and even *anthropomorphic* account of natural development, which he came to view as inadequate for making sense of the accomplishments of modern science. Kojève lays out his argument most fully in "The Dialectic of the Real and the Phenomenological Method in Hegel," the principal text of seminar lectures 6–9 during the 1934–1935 academic year, especially in the extended footnote that runs from the bottom of p. 212 of the *Introduction to the Reading of Hegel* to p. 215 (pp. 483–485 in the original French edition: Alexandre Kojève, *Introduction à la lecture de Hegel* [Paris: Gallimard, 1947]). The crux of the matter, in his view, is this:

> The final foundation of Nature is identical given static Being (*Sein*), [and] one finds in it nothing comparable to the negating Action (*Tun*) which is the basis of specifically human or historical existence. . . . Therefore it seems necessary to distinguish, within the dialectical ontology of revealed Being or Spirit (dominated by Totality), a nondialectical ontology . . . of Nature (dominated by Identity), and a dialectical ontology . . . of Man or History (dominated by Negativity). [Alexandre Kojève, *Introduction to the Reading of Hegel: Lectures on the "Phenomenology of Spirit,"* assembled by Raymond Queneau, ed. Allan Bloom, trans. James H. Nichols Jr. (Ithaca, NY: Cornell University Press, 1980), 213n15]

Fortunately, although we'll encounter some of these issues again in the next section when we turn to consider Kojève's discussion of art and nature in "Les Peintures concrètes," we should be able to avoid wading too deeply into the larger debate.

21. *Philosophy of Nature*, 4. Immediately following the sentence just cited, Hegel adds: "A consideration of Nature according to this [external] relationship yields the standpoint of finite teleology. In this, we find the correct presupposition that Nature does not itself contain the absolute, final end." Hegel's claim here is that a thing's purpose or Concept

or, again, its *telos* is inherent in it, and not simply formed by an external mind or *nous*; this is what he means by a thing's inner "purposiveness" (*innere Zweckmässigkeit*). External *purposes*, by contrast, involve an agent who uses something for one purpose or another, but who could just as well have used something else, since that purpose was merely *externally* imposed. Our practical and scientific dealings with nature are generally of this order. But a philosophy of nature aims to examine scientific findings in light of their internal purposiveness—or, as Hegel also might say, in view of their relationship to the self-determining development of the Concept. Here we might invoke that passage from the *Aesthetics* cited earlier: "Philosophy has to consider an object [in this case, natural science], not merely according to . . . external ordering, classification, etc.; it has to unfold and prove the object, according to the necessity of its own inner nature" (*Aesthetics*, I, 11). This is what Hegel means by "absolute knowledge": it is a form of knowledge absolved of all external relation. What it is knowledge "of" does not somehow lie outside of it.

22. *PLP*, 532.

23. *PLP*, 535. Here we also ought to note that, although much of *Punkt und Linie* proceeds as if there were no cultural or historical differences impinging on its project, there are several places within the text where those differences are explicitly acknowledged. In fact, under the heading "Culture and the question of form" (*PLP*, 658), Kandinsky says that he has chosen "examples exclusively from [his] own times," the better to "illuminate the organic, often inevitable links between the question of pure form in art and [other] cultural . . . forms." Elsewhere in the text it becomes clear that Kandinsky imagines social and cultural differences in art eventually being overcome; still, he acknowledges their existence in the present. And he is careful to emphasize that any science of art must retain a fully historical dimension. The "dictionary" of elements he is in the process of writing will be, he says, just like the dictionary of a living language, which is "not a petrified thing, since changes occur constantly: words are submerged, die; words emerge, newborn; 'foreign' words are brought home from across the frontiers" (*PLP*, 62).

24. *Philosophy of Nature*, §256, 31. "Motion," Hegel states in the *Zusatz* to §261, "is the transition of time into space and of space into time" (*Philosophy of Nature*, 44).

25. *PLP*, 536.

26. *PLP*, 572.

27. *PLP*, 637.

28. In the scenario I'm outlining here, Kandinsky looked to the *Philosophy of Nature* in the hope of discovering affinities between the natural entities discussed by Hegel and the formal elements that were to be the subject of *Punkt und Linie zu Fläche*. Insofar as he regarded pictorial "form" as (still) substantially material, despite having already become at least partially *vergeistigt*, he saw it as a return, albeit on a higher level, of nature's mere materiality. In *Punkt und Linie*, he puts it this way:

> The compositional laws of nature give artists the possibility not of external imitation, which they not infrequently see as the main purpose of natural laws, but of juxtaposing these laws with those of art. In this point, which is of decisive importance for abstract art, we now discover again the law of opposition and of juxtaposition. This law gives rise to two principles—the principle of parallelism and the principle of contrast—in the same way as has been shown in the case of the combination of lines. The thus divided and independently existing laws of these two great realms—art and nature—will lead ultimately to an under-

standing of the general law of world-composition, and reveal the independent operation of each within a higher synthetic order—External + Internal. [*PLP*, 625–626]

29. For example, Hegel, in his discussion of celestial motion, describes the central body in any planetary system as having "its center absolutely within itself" (*Philosophy of Nature*, §269, *Zusatz* [77]). Perhaps obviously enough, Hegel's specific comments regarding the *point* have little bearing on Kandinsky's, in that Hegel was concerned with the geometric point rather than the graphic one. Kandinsky nonetheless begins his essay by mentioning the geometric point—he terms it "an invisible entity" (*PLP*, 538)—before moving on to discuss the visible graphic mark. The descriptions of the (graphic) point as "in repose, absorbed in itself" and subject to a "tension [that] is ultimately always concentric" come from *PLP*, 570 and 546, respectively.

30. *PLP*, 592. Hegel discusses this phenomenon in the *Philosophy of Nature*, §334.

31. *PLP*, 611. After explaining that all lines are the external manifestation of internal forces, Kandinsky goes on to discuss the various colors, sounds, and temperatures evoked by different lines and angles; light, color, sound, and heat are all discussed as well by Hegel in the Physics chapter of the *Philosophy of Nature*.

32. Hegel arrived at this conclusion in part because recent findings in chemistry suggested that bodies consisted of electrical and magnetic forces, something for which mechanistic theories had no explanation. Hegel's understanding of Force is also, if somewhat more abstractly, elaborated in his *Logic*, §136ff. On all of this, see Frederick Beiser, *Hegel* (New York: Routledge, 2005), 82–86.

33. See the discussion on p. 25 above.

34. *PLP*, 611. It is also in the chapter on line that Kandinsky makes his most direct references to nature. For comparative purposes, he includes diagrams of crystal structures, the linear formation of lightning—and we should note that both crystallography and electricity were included in Hegel's chapter on Physics—as well other images drawn from botany and biology. "One should refrain from drawing false conclusions from such instances," Kandinsky says, adding that "the difference between art and nature lies not in their underlying laws, but in the material that is subject to these laws" (*PLP*, 630). We will return to this question of the relation between art and nature in the "Third Moment," concerning Kojève's essay "Les Peintures concrètes."

35. *Aesthetics*, I, 121. The same idea—which Hegel derives from Aristotle—is repeated in the *Encyclopedia Logic*, §216; see *Hegel's Logic*, trans. William Wallace (Oxford: Clarendon, 1975), 280.

36. *KCW*, 350.

37. *PLP*, 639.

38. The physical layout of the appendix and the ordering of its pages are important, principally because a general developmental progression is evident within it. For example, the first five plates involve "points" (or circles) exclusively, and we witness a gradual increase in complexity thereafter, the last black-and-white image—which diagrams the linear structure of the painting *Little Dream in Red* (1925)—being the most elaborate. The appendix as a whole then culminates with a full-color reproduction of *Little Dream in Red* itself. Presumably we are meant to see that, in the painting—the lone work manifesting "*all* the characteristics of a developed organism" (emphasis added)—the opposition between form (in its narrower sense) and color has been sublated. It should also be said that, even among

the black-and-white images, there is the suggestion of explicitly dialectical development. In both plates 5 and 6, for instance, two separate images are presented, the one on the right being the exact inverse of the left (white forms substituting for black and vice versa). Moreover, plate 6 is clearly intended as a linear complication of plate 5's "punctual" arrangement. Captions accompanying the images explicitly mark that transition: the first five plates bear the designation "Point," while the twenty following are labeled "Line." Significantly, however, there is no similar reference to "Plane"—an omission perhaps explained by the fact that the plates of the appendix are all independent, self-sustaining planar compositions (again, with *Little Dream in Red* being the most fully elaborated example of them all). Indeed the appendix might be regarded as the one place where the ambition announced in the book's title—from point and line *to plane*—is concretely realized. In that sense, the appendix can be seen as actualizing the claims of the text, following not only literally after but also dialectically from the latter's more abstract, theoretical analyses.

39. *PLP*, 552 (translation slightly modified). The phrase "internally purposive" is one that, as we have seen (n21), has specific Hegelian connotations—as, of course, does the word "Concept" (*Begriff*). Here the point seems to be that composition is not something imposed on the painting or its material elements by the artist (and so in accordance with his "purposes") but rather is or ought to be generated out of the materials themselves. In theory, this sounds very close to the ambition of the Russian constructivists, but of course, for Kandinsky, the "materials" in question were always *vergeistigt*, already wholly in the service of spirit.

40. *PLP*, 617.

41. The pages of the first German edition of *Punk und Linie zu Fläche* (see n5, above) were less vertical than is the original drawing, with the result that, in the book, the forms of the composition have a different relation to the (wider) surrounding space. For reasons that aren't entirely clear to me, the lower margin was also enlarged, nearly doubling the distance between the black "point" and the bottom of the sheet of paper. Moreover, because the printer centered the image on the unbound page, the entire composition effectively shifted leftward when the book was bound, its extreme edge having been lost to the fold. In the original edition, then, the crossing of the composition's main diagonals seems to occur just left of center (and considerably further above). As it's difficult to know how much say Kandinsky had in the image's placement on the page, I have chosen to concentrate on those aspects—such as the relative emptiness of the composition's lower half—that are common to both the original drawing and its published reproduction. According to the text, the upper portion of the picture plane (like the left-hand side) carries connotations of "lightness, emancipation and, ultimately, of freedom"; see *PLP*, 639 and 642–643. On the "tensions that stream forth in [a] diagonal direction" from the center of the picture plane, see *PLP*, 650–651.

42. See *PLP*, 650–652.

43. See *PLP*, 615.

44. On the "external limits" of lines, see *PLP*, 610.

45. In *Punkt und Linie*, Kandinsky describes straight and curved lines such as these as "the original pair of [linear] opposites" (*PLP*, 598). Their juxtaposition in the upper right-hand quadrant of plate 20's composition is undoubtedly meant to show how, even without losing their identity as opposites, they can be employed in concert to a single end.

46. Kandinsky explains that the bottom of the picture plane has an intrinsic weight roughly twice that of the upper portion, so that, even if there is a preponderance of forms above, the composition can still attain equilibrium (*PLP*, 640–641). Nonetheless, in the case of plate 20, he clearly feels that the additional weight and gravity of the "point" is required for the work's overall balance. Note, too, that in the German edition of *Punkt und Linie*, the caption for plate 20 appears on the facing page, rather than below the composition (as in *PLP*, where it effectively becomes part of the work and so unsettles the original balance).

47. See *PLP*, 549, where Kandinsky says that the point's "lack of any impulse to move either upon or from the surface" makes it "indispensable in composition," as well as 670–671, where he discusses means to achieving the surface's "optical annihilation." The success of the illusion in this case—which I'm convinced Kandinsky intended—depends to a large extent on the degree of white space surrounding the composition. In the Lindsay and Vergo edition of Kandinsky's collected writings, the illustrations have been cropped significantly, with the result that all of the component pieces of plate 20 (and not just the "point" placed near the bottom edge) appear rather firmly rooted to the page.

48. *PLP*, 671.

49. Kandinsky refers to the "in sich geschlossenen, ruhenden Punktes [the point in repose, absorbed in itself]" and "der höchsten in sich geschlossenen Ruhe des Punktes [the ultimately self-contained repose of the point]"; he also describes the point as "ein in sich gekehrtes Wesen voller Möglichkeiten [an introverted entity pregnant with possibilities]" (*KCW*, 570, 572, 555). See *Punkt und Linie zu Fläche* (Bern: Benteli Verlag, 5th ed., 1964), 56, 57, and 39, respectively. Compare this phrasing with Hegel's, when he speaks of classical sculpture "in its eternal self-repose [in dem ewigen Beruhen in sich]" or points to its "most austere repose [diese strengste Ruhe]" (G. W. F. Hegel, *Ästhetik*, 2 vols., ed. F. Bassenge [Frankfurt am Main: Europäische Verlagsanstalt, 1966], I, 486). Hegel also describes the individual standing or reclining figure as "immersed in itself, something pregnant with possibilities [ein in sich versunkenes Dastehen oder Liegen . . . ; dies in sich Trächtige . . .]" (ibid., II, 123).

50. On the relationship between classical sculpture and Hegel's system, see Stephen Melville, "Plasticity: The Hegelian Writing of Art," in Margaret Iverson and Stephen Melville, *Writing Art History: Disciplinary Departures* (Chicago: University of Chicago Press, 2010), 151–173.

51. On the organicism of Hegel's system, again see Beiser, *Hegel*, esp. 80: "The absolute develops in the same manner as all living things: it begins from inchoate unity; it differentiates itself into separate functions; and it returns into itself by re-integrating these functions into a single whole."

52. This would help to explain Kojève's otherwise rather out-of-place assertion in "Les Peintures concrètes" that drawing—i.e., the stuff of *Punkt und Linie zu Fläche*—is an integral part of painting, and that in fact the two exist on a single continuum, which also includes "drawn paintings" and "colored drawings." See *PCK*, 155, as well as *PLP*, 634, where Kandinsky himself explicitly addresses the role of line in painting as well as his critical disdain for those "theoreticians [who] judge the use of line in graphics favorably but condemn its use in painting as contrary to its nature, hence unallowable."

THIRD MOMENT

1. Alexandre Kojève, "La métaphysique religieuse de Vladimir Soloviev," *Revue d'histoire et de philosophie religieuses*, vols. 14 (1934), 534–554, and 15 (1935), 110–152.

2. In correspondence with his uncle, Kojève periodically mentioned Kandinsky's theoretical writings—though mostly by way of asserting his preference for the paintings. See Dominique Auffret, *Alexandre Kojève: La philosophie, l'état, la fin de l'histoire* (Paris: Grasset, 1990), 273; and, among the Kandinsky-Kojève correspondence, especially the letter by Kojève dated September 20, 1931.

3. *Aesthetics*, I, 104.

4. *Aesthetics*, I, 11. For the full quotation, see "Second Moment, Part 1," 19.

5. The *Critique of Judgment* concerns itself first and foremost with the nature of the Beautiful. Kant argues there that our judgment of an object as beautiful is wholly subjective (based in our pleasurable experience of that object), even as we feel that the judgment itself ought to receive universal assent and so have an objective status.

6. *Aesthetics*, I, 2.

7. Kojève, "La métaphysique religieuse de Vladimir Soloviev."

8. See Kojève, "La métaphysique religieuse de Vladimir Soloviev," esp. 551ff.

9. As Kojève's review makes clear, Soloviev's philosophy was above all a religious philosophy, a kind of Orthodox metaphysics that nonetheless drew heavily on German idealism—on Hegel but also, crucially, on Schelling. Soloviev followed Schelling in "intuiting" an all-encompassing unity, an Absolute, which he identified not with nature (as Schelling had) but instead with God or the Divine. On the one hand, Soloviev argued, the Absolute was perfect and therefore had to be understood as eternal, atemporal: always already complete and fully self-contained. On the other hand, Soloviev also emphasized that the Absolute was something to be realized by humanity in history, specifically through the creation, fall, and redemption of mankind in a universal reunification with God. Perhaps obviously enough, it was this emphasis on the human and the historical—what might be termed Soloviev's anthropological interpretation of Christian dogma (rather than the dogma itself)—that was of greatest interest to Kojève, and that in turn shaped his own reading of Hegel's *Phenomenology*. For a much fuller discussion of Kojève's work on and interest in Soloviev, see Michael S. Roth, *Knowing and History. Appropriations of Hegel in Twentieth-Century France* (Ithaca, NY: Cornell University Press, 1988), esp. chap. 4, 83–124; and Auffret, *Alexandre Kojève*, esp. 221ff.

10. Vladimir Soloviev, "The Meaning of Art," in S. L. Frank, ed., *A Solovyov Anthology*, trans. Natalie Duddington (London: SCM Press, 1950), 140. The original essay, "Obshchii smysl iskusstva," was written in 1890.

11. Ibid., 149.

12. Ibid., 139.

13. Ibid.

14. In the more metaphysical or idealist interpretations of Hegel, the relation of art to nature is similar. Frederick Beiser, for example, makes just this case: "Hegel conceives the artist as one part of the organic whole of nature and history, a whole that is inseparable from each of its parts and that reveals itself entirely in each of them. Furthermore, the artist, as a vehicle of human self-awareness, is one of the highest forms of organization and development of all the powers within the organic whole. This means that the activity of

the artist is simply one of the highest manifestations and developments of all the organic powers at work in nature and history, so that what he creates is what nature and history create through him" (Frederick Beiser, *Hegel* [New York: Routledge, 2005], 297). For an illuminating discussion of the different "Hegels" currently in circulation and the consequences of those differences for understanding his theory of art, see Jason Gaiger, "Hegel's Contested Legacy: Rethinking the Relation between Art History and Philosophy," *Art Bulletin* 18, no. 2 (June 2011), 178–194.

15. *Aesthetics*, I, 106. For an explication of the Concept in Hegel's thought, see "Second Moment (Part 1)," n37.

16. *Aesthetics*, I, 106. Later (p. 111) Hegel elaborates on the Idea of the Beautiful:
Now we said that beauty is Idea, so beauty and truth are in one way the same. Beauty, namely, must be true in itself. But, looked at more closely, the true is nevertheless distinct from the beautiful. That is to say, what is *true* is the Idea, and the Idea as it is in accordance with its inherent character and universal principle, and as it is grasped as such in thought. In that case what is *there* for thinking is not the Idea's sensuous and external existence, but only the *universal Idea* in this existence. But the Idea should realize itself externally and win a specific and present existence as the objectivity of nature and spirit. The true as such *exists* also. Now when the truth in this its external existence is present to consciousness immediately, and when the Concept remains immediately in unity with its external appearance, the Idea is not only true but beautiful. Therefore the beautiful is characterized as the pure appearance of the Idea to sense.

As I read this passage, and as I think Kojève (and indeed Kandinsky) read it too, for Hegel, that which is beautiful is structurally homologous with the Concept. It possesses, in other words, the same unity-in-diversity, its various individual parts or members being thoroughly integrated, whatever their differences, into the larger whole.

17. *Aesthetics*, I, 119.

18. I am paraphrasing a passage (p. 193) from Edward Halper's closely argued (and highly "systematic") essay, "The Logic of Art: Beauty and Nature," in William Maker, ed., *Hegel and Aesthetics* (Albany: State University of New York Press, 2000), 187–202. According to Halper, "Hegel identifies the Idea of beauty with a complex of the Absolute Idea, the culminating category of the *Logic*, and an additional component," which Halper identifies (on the basis of its place within the system) as "life": the Absolute Idea, he asserts, "is manifest as a living thing in art." Given this identification, the following observations by Michael Inwood are relevant here: "Despite its inferiority to spirit, life is for Hegel a potent metaphor for the active unification of diversity and diversification of unity involved in spirit and its forms. Dialectical logic is alive, in contrast to the dead logic of the understanding." See Inwood, *A Hegel Dictionary* (London: Blackwell, 1992), 177.

19. *PCK*, 151. There is an interesting mistranscription of the first sentence of this passage both in the version of the essay published by Michael Roth and, as a result of that, in the small paperback edition released by La Lettre volée. In each, the sentence reads: "Un seul et même Beau s'incarne dans l'arbre réel et dans l'esprit peint." Kojève's handwriting could hardly be more legible: the penultimate word in the sentence is clearly *l'arbre* rather than *l'esprit.* The only explanation would seem to be that Roth—recognizing the generally Hegelian nature of Kojève's argument, and anticipating (somewhat incorrectly) the distinction that Kojève would soon draw between the Beautiful-in-Art and the Beautiful-outside-

of-Art—projected "spirit" onto the painted tree. Ironically, the mistranscription calls our attention to the surprising absence of any reference to "spirit" in Kojève's text, and so also to the complicated (if unarticulated) relation between the Beautiful and *Geist* implied by his argument.

20. *PCK*, 152.

21. *PCK*, 153.

22. *Aesthetics*, I, 38; quoted (with the translation slightly modified) by John Sallis in "Carnation and the Eccentricity of Painting," in Stephen Houlgate, ed., *Hegel and the Arts* (Evanston, IL: Northwestern University Press, 2007), 94.

23. *Aesthetics*, I, 38. For a discussion of Hegel's use of *Erscheinung* and related terms (*Schein, herausscheinen*, etc.), see Inwood, *A Hegel Dictionary*, 38–40; and, more directly relevant to the *Aesthetics*, Sallis, "Carnation and the Eccentricity of Painting," 90ff. Soloviev, for his part, had effectively transposed the "shining" quality of art onto the Beautiful at large, defining the latter as "the transfiguration of matter through the incarnation in it of another, super-material principle" (see Soloviev, "Beauty in Nature," in *A Solovyov Anthology*, 129). Thus, for example, he explains the beauty of a diamond, almost chemically indistinguishable from a lump of coal, as the product of the diamond's receptivity to, and refraction of, (God's) light: "The play of light, retained and transformed by [the stone's material] body, completely conceals its crudely material appearance. . . . A ray of light falling upon a lump of coal is absorbed by its substance, and the blackness of coal is the natural symbol of the fact that in this case the power of light has not conquered the dark forces of nature" (128–129).

24. *Aesthetics*, I, 36–37.

25. *Aesthetics*, I, 38.

26. Hegel's discussion of these things intriguingly echoes a number of comments made by Federico Zuccaro in his 1607 *Idea of Painters, Sculptors and Architects*. Consider, for example, the following thought experiment, assigned by Zuccaro to his readers: "If you place a large mirror of very fine crystal in a room full of exquisite paintings and magnificent sculptures, it is obvious that when I look at it, this mirror will not only be at the end of my gaze but will also be an object which in its turn will, clearly and distinctly, present me with all the paintings and sculptures. And yet these paintings and sculptures are not physically present in it. They only appear in the mirror in their *spiritual* form" (Zuccaro, 154 [emphasis added]; quoted in Victor Stoichita, *L'Instauration du tableau: métapeinture à l'aube des temps modernes* [Paris: Méridiens Klincksieck, 1993], 114). "Reflection" becomes thereafter an important word for Zuccaro, which he closely identifies with "philosophizing" and the very "idea of art." "Reflection" (*Widerschein*) is similarly an important term for Hegel, in some sense summarizing his entire conception of art—i.e., as enabling us to regard what we see specifically not as a material presence but, rather, as a manifestation of what is immaterial and inward, a shining forth of human spirit. Whether Hegel actually read Zuccaro's text, however, is beyond my knowledge (and, frankly, also a bit outside the range of our present concerns).

27. *Aesthetics*, II, 805 (emphasis added). Jason Gaiger has glossed the argument this way: "Like a work of sculpture or architecture, a painting is also a physical object, consisting in pigment on a ground; but in so far as it creates a new imaginative space that exists only for the viewer it is discontinuous with the physical world. Hegel maintains that the transition from the objective substantiality of [classical] sculpture to the creation of sem-

blance on a plane allows 'responsive subjectivity to be set free.' What we see in a painting is produced by the mind and is the result of the artist's own, free activity." See Jason Gaiger, "Catching Up with History: Hegel and Abstract Painting," in Katerina Deligiorgi, ed., *Hegel: New Directions* (Montreal: McGill-Queen's University Press, 2006), 160.

28. *PCK*, 154.

29. *PCK*, 154. Obviously, it's important not to pass over Kojève's distinction between the canvas and the tableau without catching the full weight of their difference. Otherwise, "Les Peintures concrètes" might be taken as offering at this point some variation (*avant la lettre*, of course) on Clement Greenberg's "Modernist Painting," in which the medium is said to have found its essence in "the ineluctable flatness of the canvas."

30. *OSA*, 194. Kandinsky goes on to recommend "constitut[ing] the picture upon an ideal plane," an idea that he would take up and further elaborate (as we've already partly seen) in *Punkt und Linie zu Fläche*; see his comments under the heading "Dematerialized surface," *PLP*, 670ff. Similarly, in his 1935 essay for *Cahiers d'art*, "Toile vide, etc.," Kandinsky wrote: "The 'action' in the picture must not take place on the physical surface of the canvas, but 'somewhere' in 'illusory' space" (*KCW*, 783).

It seems reasonable to speculate that Kandinsky's early experiments with *Hinterglasmalerei* (see Part II), which began around 1908, were motivated precisely by a desire to keep his own "flattened" yet still representational images from fusing with the picture plane's material surface. By painting on glass (or, more specifically, on its reverse side), he could effectively locate the image at an uncertain distance *behind* the plane presented to the viewer. Later, when he had given up that technique as too unwieldy and taken the definitive steps toward nonrepresentation, Kandinsky devised other means to achieve comparable effects, including what the artist Frank Stella has termed "the principle of weightless composition." See Stella, *Working Space* (Cambridge, MA: Harvard University Press, 1986), 116ff.

31. *PCK*, 152.

32. *PCK*, 157–158.

33. Hegel, *Wissenschaft der Logik*, III, §50; quoted and translated by Philip T. Grier, "Abstract and Concrete in Hegel's Logic," in George di Giovanni, ed., *Essays on Hegel's Logic* (Albany: State University of New York Press, 1990), 66. On Hegel's definition of these terms and their role in his philosophy, see not only Grier's essay but also the response to it in that same volume: Errol E. Harris, "A Reply to Philip Grier," 77–84. Kojève himself explicates the terms in his posthumously published book, *Le Concept, le temps et le discours: Introduction au système du savoir* (Paris: Gallimard, 1990), 111ff. Significantly, in that discussion, Kojève adduces as examples both trees and vantage points in ways that suggest his understanding of "abstract" and "concrete" was substantially worked out in the essay on Kandinsky.

34. *PCK*, 162. Kandinsky wrote in the margin of the original manuscript at this point: "Pure realism is abstract!"

35. *PCK*, 161.

36. *PCK*, 161.

37. Alexandre Kojève, "Pourquoi concret," *XXe Siècle*, no. 27 (December 1966), 65n1.

38. *PCK*, 162. Kojève unfortunately failed to specify which paintings, or even which period of Picasso's oeuvre, he had in mind when characterizing the artist's work. My own sense is that any of the cubist paintings would be exceedingly difficult to assimilate to

the category of symbolic expressionism (or expressionist symbolism)—principally because, while they are highly "abstract," they are not expressive of a particular subjectivity. Many of the paintings from the 1930s, however, better fit the bill. Clearly *Guernica*, not having been painted until 1937, couldn't possibly have been in Kojève's sights; and yet we might well feel that that painting's ambition was precisely to convert the private (and highly subjective) "expressionist symbolism" of the preceding years into something that could serve as a shared, public expression of horror.

39. *PCK*, 162.

40. In many ways this characterization of Picasso's art is not so very different from that offered by Georges Bataille in his essay in homage to the artist, "Soleil pourri." Of course, for Bataille, unproductive expenditure was something to be desired, and specifically because of the way it thwarted sublation and the Hegelian system it sustained. See Bataille, "Soleil pourri," *Documents* 30 (1930), 173–174, as well as my own discussion of that essay and its relation to Picasso's work, in *Myth and Metamorphosis: Picasso's Classical Prints of the 1930s* (Cambridge, MA: MIT Press, 2000), esp. chap. 4, "On Myth and Picasso's Minotaurs."

41. *PCK*, 165–166.

42. *PCK*, 163.

43. See *PCK*, 166, where Kojève writes: "The 'total' tableau *is* as objects *are*, that is, it *is* in an *absolute* and nonrelative way; it *is* independently of its *relations* with anything else; it *is*, like the Universe *is*. And that is why the 'total' tableau is also an 'absolute' tableau."

44. Preface, *Phenomenology of Spirit*, 81–82.

45. Although scholars have long argued about whether Hegel really imagined the dialectical process of history ever coming to an end—and whether that imagination is integral to an appreciation of his thought—Kojève was adamant on both counts. In the *Introduction to the Reading of Hegel* he asserts: "This dialectic of Action and Knowledge is essentially temporal. Or, better still, it *is* Time—that is, a nonidentical Becoming—in which there is truly and really a *progress*. . . . [And] if this dialectical Becoming *is* Time, it is because it has a beginning and an end. Hence there is a goal (*Ziel*) which can no longer be surpassed" (Alexandre Kojève, *Introduction to the Reading of Hegel: Lectures on the "Phenomenology of Spirit,"* assembled by Raymond Queneau, ed. Allan Bloom, trans. James H. Nichols Jr. [Ithaca, NY: Cornell University Press, 1980], 164). For a good general introduction to the debate, see Joe McCarney, *Hegel on History* (London: Routledge, 2000), chap. 11, 169ff.

46. *PCK*, 164.

47. *KCW*, 379. I confess to cheating a bit here. To keep the textual correspondence as close as possible, I omitted one problematic phrase. Kandinsky actually described these recent "absolute," "objective" works as coming "into existence 'of their own accord,' *as the product of natural laws*, as independent beings." (The emphasis now is my own.) I think we have to regard this as an attempt on Kandinsky's part to underscore the "internal necessity" of the process that generated those paintings—a "necessity" having the *force* of a natural law. But, obviously, the Hegelian aspect of his argument demands we see those works as definitively moving away from nature's normative authority. The inconsistency here is, in my view, but one of several in Kandinsky's earlier writings that "Les Peintures concrètes" was intended to correct.

48. *OSA*, 173ff.

49. *OSA*, 175.

50. Kojève, "Pourquoi concret," 63. Kandinsky's handwritten annotations to "Les Peintures concrètes" generally bear out Kojève's claim, in that they consistently restate or underscore points made in the text, rather than suggesting any real difference or dissent.

51. See especially the essays, "L'Art Concret" (1938) and "The Value of Concrete Work" (1939), both of which were published, like Kojève's "Pourquoi concret," in *XXe Siècle*. Both also appear in *KCW*, 813–817 and 820–828, respectively.

52. Specifically, Kojève says: "The Art of 'nonrepresentational' painting is the art of embodying in and by a drawing, a colored drawing, a drawn painting, or a painting proper, a pictorial Beautiful that isn't, has never, and never will be embodied anywhere else: in no real object other than the painting itself, which is to say, in no real, nonartistic object. This art can be called the art of Kandinsky, as Kandinsky was the first to paint (beginning in 1910) objective and concrete paintings" (*PCK*, 163). Here Kojève obviously sets the date for Kandinsky's turn to nonrepresentational painting very early—probably closer to that moment's *theorization* than to its actual occurrence.

53. Presumably, too, this is because those works, with their clean lines and geometric forms, look far less "subjective" than the paintings that had preceded them—even though, again, Kojève's argument asserts that all of the nonrepresentational tableaux are equally "concrete" and "objective."

54. The obvious parallel here is with Kojève's claim that history had reached its conclusion with the French Revolution. His point, as Michael Roth has explained, "is not that all people are now happy or that complete freedom exists throughout the world. It is rather that the idea of universal equality in a homogeneous state is introduced during the epoch of the French Revolution, and all subsequent battles of import are fought for this same goal." See Roth, *Knowing and History*, 117. Similarly, Kojève seems to feel that painting achieved its freedom in 1910, when Kandinsky first introduced the idea of nonrepresentation; everything subsequent has been a matter of implementation or mere technical refinement rather than the stuff of history.

55. Again, see Kandinsky's essay "Entwicklung der Kunstformen" (ca. 1912–1913), where he speaks of the "emergence of absolute art" in the early twentieth century as marking the first period of art's second epoch, suggesting a new phase in art's historical development but by no means the end of the line. "Entwicklung der Kunstformen" appears in *KGS*, 476–479. Similarly, although Kojève argued the impossibility of distinguishing progress from mere change until history had reached its conclusion, Kandinsky seems to have felt that aesthetic judgments, at least, could be rendered in the meantime. For more on Kojève's End of History thesis, see not only Roth, *Knowing and History*, 83–146, and Auffret, *Alexandre Kojève*, 241–271, but also James H. Nichols Jr., *Alexandre Kojève: Wisdom at the End of History* (Plymouth, UK: Rowman and Littlefield, 2007).

56. By "modernist" practices, I mean those driven by the twin engines of essentialism and historical progression: thus (dialectical) development toward the revelation of painting's (purported) essence. Both Kandinsky and Mondrian were committed to this model; yet the trajectories that their works trace seem to me quite different in tempo and cadence. The sense of trial-and-error experimentation that marked Mondrian's practice prior to 1924 slows considerably thereafter—as if at that point the artist felt he had finally arrived at his goal. Not until the 1930s does a strong sense of development reenter the picture with Mondrian. On these issues, see Yve-Alain Bois, "The De Stijl Idea," in his *Painting as Model* (Cambridge,

MA: MIT Press, 1990), 101–121; and "The Iconclast, " in Bois et al., *Piet Mondrian, 1872–1944* (Milan: Leonardo Arte, 1994). Also relevant here is Harry Cooper and Ron Spronk, *Mondrian: The Transatlantic Paintings* (Cambridge, MA: Harvard University Museums, 2001).

57. Because Kandinsky used veiled imagery so often in his run-up to nonrepresentation—precisely as a means to ease the transition for his audience—one might even argue that those first "concrete" paintings are less (visually) different from their predecessors, and therefore less surprising, than is *Thirty*.

58. I know of only two other paintings by Kandinsky, the 1930 *White on Black* (handlist 530, R&B 976) and *Black Forms on White* (1934), now in the Musée Zervos in Vézaley (handlist 600, R&B 1037), that use this same highly limited "color" scheme. I might add that, in the case of *Thirty*, the white has a distinctly bluish tint, and that the ground—still visible at various places across the surface—is a warm, faintly orangish-yellow. As we've seen, yellow and blue were antagonistic colors in Kandinsky's universe, and it may well be that blue was added to the white pigment specifically as a means of (dialectically) toning down the warmth of the prepared canvas underneath. In any case, the effect is to make the composition seem "colder" than it would otherwise and, consequently, as that much more "objective."

59. Specifically, the top two rows of the grid are taller than the bottom two (with the uppermost being the tallest of all), while the three columns on the left are wider than their counterparts on the right; consequently the (3×3) units in the lower right-hand corner are smaller than any of the others on the picture plane. In *Punkt und Linie*, Kandinsky had asserted that the lower right quadrant of any canvas was the "heaviest"; presumably the compression of forms in that area of *Thirty* is a reflection of this condition.

60. Harris, "A Reply to Philip Grier," 80.

61. Given its dynamic complexity (as well as the echoes we've already noted between the point of *Punkt und Linie* and classical sculpture), I'm tempted here, in discussing the composition of *Thirty*, to invoke Hegel's description of his philosophical system as "a Bacchanalian revel" that "is just as much transparent and simple repose" (*Phenomenology of Spirit*, 27).

62. *PCK*, 164.

63. Kojève in fact insisted that human being was not defined by its place within nature but, on the contrary, through its *negation* of the natural order. Rather than being simply what it is "by nature," humanity is self-determining and so historical—at least until it is no longer.

64. The second occasion is on p. 166, where we read:
Kandinsky's tableaux are not paintings of objects but painted *objects*: they are objects in the same way that trees, mountains, chairs, States ... are "objects"; only they are pictorial objects, "objective" paintings. The "total" tableau *is* as objects *are*, that is, it *is* in an *absolute* and nonrelative way; it *is* independently of its *relations* with anything else; it *is*, like the Universe *is*. And that is why the "total" tableau is also an "absolute" tableau.

65. Kojève phrases it this way: "Napoléon agit, mais ne se comprend pas; c'est Hegel qui le comprend ('révélation' = Napoléon + Hegel) [Napoleon acts, but doesn't comprehend; it is Hegel who comprehends it ("revelation" = Napoleon + Hegel]" (*Introduction à la lecture de Hegel* [Paris: Gallimard, 1947], 147). His point seems to be that, in 1807, historical development had produced both Napoleon's empire and, as a direct result of reflection on that achievement, Hegel's *Phenomenology of Spirit*. As Kojève tells it, Hegel

believed history had come to an end factually with Napoleon's victory at Jena and theoretically with his own philosophy—specifically with his description in the *Phenomenology* of *Geist*'s self-realization through the historical process. On these matters, see Errol E. Harris, "Marxist Interpretations of Hegel's *Phenomenology of Spirit*," in *The Spirit of Hegel* (Atlantic Highlands, NJ: Humanities Press, 1993), esp. 58–59.

66. After the Second World War Kojève worked in the French Ministry of Economic Affairs, where he served as one of the leading architects of the European Economic Community and the General Agreement on Tariffs and Trade. For more on Kojève's political career, see Auffret, *Alexandre Kojève*, and Nichols, *Alexandre Kojève*.

67. Kandinsky and Kojève were certainly not the first to conceive of painterly composition on analogy with the ideal political state. One predecessor, Roger de Piles, wrote in his 1708 *Cours de Peinture par Principe* (Principles of Painting): "The last point depending on disposition is *the whole together* [*le tout-ensemble*], which is the result of the parts that compose the piece; but the whole, arising from the combination of several objects, must not be like a number made up of several unities, independent and equal among themselves, but like one political whole [*un tout politique*], where the great have need of the lower people [*des petits*], and these have need of the great [*les grands*]. . . . We may define *the whole together* to be, *Such a general subordination of objects one to another, as makes them all concur to constitute but one*." My thanks to Éric Michaud for pointing me in the direction of de Piles's analogy. In the course of tracking down the passage, I discovered that all of the extant English-language editions of the *Cours*—dating back to 1743—mistranslate the phrase "un tout politique" as "one *poetic* whole," thereby rendering the entire paragraph not only apolitical but also largely nonsensical. See, for example, the 1743 English edition published by J. Osborn: the passage in question appears on p. 65. In de Piles's original (Paris: Jacques Estienne, 1708), it appears on p. 99.

68. For Kojève's discussion of the monochrome, see *PCK*, 154.

69. See Kojève, *Esquisse d'une phénoménologie du droit: exposé provisoire* (Paris: Éditions Gallimard, 1981 [originally written 1943]), translated into English as *Outline of a Phenomenology of Right*, ed. and trans. Bryan-Paul Frost and Robert Howse (Lanham, MD: Rowman and Littlefield, 2000).

70. See Roth, *Knowing and History*, 92–93.

71. Beiser, *Hegel*, 240. He adds, "Hegel read a more specific political meaning into each of these general features. The first feature means that there should be no dispute between liberalism and communitarianism regarding the purpose of the state. Since the whole exists for the parts, the liberal is right that the state should promote the rights and interests of everyone as an individual; but since the parts also exist for the whole, the communitarian is correct that the individual should devote himself to affairs of the state since doing so is ultimately in his self-interest. The second feature means that the state must respect the rights of individuals as individuals, and that there should be some autonomous groups within the state, independent of central administration and control, which represent economic interests and engage in local government. The third feature means that there should be no conflict between self-interest and the public good. The great strength of the modern state over that of antiquity, Hegel argued, is that the individual is tied to the state not through virtue but self-interest. The individual can recognize that his own private

interest depends upon his participation in public life, and that he does not have to sacrifice himself for the public good."

72. Ibid., 241.

73. Michael Roth noted when he first published "Les Peintures concrètes" that, during the seminar of 1936, Kojève had specifically mentioned "the ideology of the True, the Beautiful, and the Good," but that he had done so in a condescending voice. Associating that ideology with the "passive individualism" of the scholar, the artist, and the philosopher (in that order), he said that it was the "religion" of those who sought satisfaction *immediately*. Such "individualists" believed that they could attain the Beautiful, for example, without having to put forth "the effort of the negative or negating *action* necessary for the real transformation of the given natural and social World." It would seem, then, that it wasn't the *values* of the True, the Beautiful, and the Good that Kojève was ridiculing. It was the mistaken assumption that they were directly and permanently available rather than dialectical-historical achievements, the product, that is, of work. In "Les Peintures concrètes," Roth writes, Kojève "develops *another* ideology of the Beautiful. He attempts to avoid the bad faith of the intellectual artist who seeks to change the world through the expedient of ideas rather than through action, by completely dissociating the world of art from the world-in-becoming." See Roth's prefatory remarks to Kojève's "Les Peintures concrètes" in *La Revue de métaphysique et de morale* 90, no. 2 (1985), 149–150, as well as Kojève, *Introduction à la lecture de Hegel*, 109–110. In Soloviev's religious philosophy, each "hypostasis" of the trinity of the True, the Beautiful, and the Good was regarded as both an eternally existing entity and something that had to be (re-)won by mankind in history. It was only the latter half of this dualism that interested Kojève; on this point, see Roth, *Knowing and History*, esp. 86ff.

74. *Aesthetics*, I, 437.

75. *Aesthetics*, I, 437.

76. Stephen Melville, "Plasticity: The Hegelian Writing of Art," in Stephen Melville and Margaret Iversen, eds., *Writing Art History* (Chicago: University of Chicago Press, 2010), 166.

77. Terry Pinkard, "Symbolic, Classical, and Romantic Art," in Stephen Houlgate, ed., *Hegel and the Arts* (Evanston, IL: Northwestern University Press, 2007), 22–23.

78. In a posthumously published manuscript titled "Definition of Color" ("Definieren der Farbe") from 1904, Kandinsky wrote: "If destiny shall grant me enough time, I shall discover a new language that will endure forever and continually enrich itself. And it will not be called Esperanto. Its name will be *Malerei* [painting]—an old word that has been misused. It should have been called *Abmalerei* [copying]; up until now it has consisted of imitating" (8). The manuscript is in the Gabriele Münter Stiftung, Munich. The passage quoted is cited by Hans Roethel and Jean Benjamin, *Kandinsky* (New York: Hudson Hills Press, 1979), 13; the full essay appears in the original German in *KGS*, 249–253.

THE DEVELOPMENT OF KANDINSKY'S OEUVRE

1. For a discussion of Hegel on the problem of beginnings, see Daniel Watts, "The Paradox of Beginning: Hegel, Kierkegaard and Philosophical Inquiry," *Inquiry* 50, no. 1, (2007), 5–33. Kandinsky himself pointed to some of these same difficulties when he complained in *Über das Geistige* that "construction upon a purely spiritual basis . . . is a lengthy process, which begins relatively blindly and at random" (*OSA*, 197).

2. *Hegel's Logic: Being Part One of the Encyclopaedia of the Philosophical Sciences*, trans. William Wallace (Oxford: Oxford University Press, 1975), §41.

3. Ten times over the course of his career Kandinsky chose to title a painting *Composition*, followed by a number designating its place within the sequence. As he explained in *Über das Geistige* (*KCW*, 218), Compositions often appeared to be spontaneous, but each was preceded by multiple, highly detailed studies. All ten are (or were—numbers I–III were destroyed during World War II) also exceptionally large works, Kandinsky clearly intending them to be masterpieces, occasions on which to take stock of recent advances and to explore possible avenues for the future. In the following pages, where I use "Compositions" with a capital "C," I am referring to this select group of tableaux.

4. The three descriptions were published, along with the artist's "Rückblicke" (Reminiscences) and sixty full-page reproductions of his paintings, in the monograph *Kandinsky, 1901–1913* (Berlin: Verlag "Der Sturm," 1913). Of the texts, "Rückblicke" is by far the longest and best known, but the three shorter, descriptive essays are no less interesting. They are also unique; never before had Kandinsky published (nor would he ever again) individual analyses of his own pictorial compositions. All three have been reproduced and discussed at length in Felix Thürlemann, *Kandinsky über Kandinsky: Der Künstler als Interpret eigener Werke* (Bern: Benteli Verlag, 1986). English translations of the three texts are in *KCW*, 355ff.

As Lindsay and Vergo note (*KCW*, 356), Kandinsky did write other descriptions of individual paintings, but none of these were published during his lifetime. Several from 1911—"Zum Bild *Moskau*," describing the genesis of the now-lost *Impression 2*; "*St. Georg*, Februar 1911"; and "*Arabisches III (Zweikampf)*," on the painting that would come to be called *Araber III (mit Krug)*—were found among the artist's papers after his death. They have recently been published in *KGS*, 441–447. A fragment of another (from 1913), concerning the painting *Small Pleasures*, was first published by Angelica Rudenstine in *The Guggenheim Museum Collection: Paintings, 1880–1945* (New York: Solomon R. Guggenheim Museum, 1976), 268–269; the complete text appears in *KGS*, 497–498. Yet another, discussing *Stabilité Animée* (1937–1938), was written at the request of Max Bill, who had intended to publish it in 1938 in the Zurich periodical *Werk*; the text was not used, however, and Bill only published it seventeen years later in a book he edited, *Essays über Kunst und Künstler* (Bern: Bümpliz, 1955). That text, too, is discussed and reproduced in Thürlemann, *Kandinsky über Kandinsky*, 165–178 and 228.

5. In what amounts to a subtitle for the text (which simply takes *Composition IV* as its title), Kandinsky characterized the essay as a "subsequent" or "after-the-fact" (*nachträgliches*) definition of the painting. Presumably he meant thereby to underscore that the text was written more than a month after the painting was completed so that, even for Kandinsky, it reflected a retrospective account of a no-longer-quite-contemporary work—a work, that is, whose developmental significance *and* limitations were already beginning to become apparent. See Kandinsky, "Komposition 4," *Kandinsky, 1901–1913*, 33.

6. See Thürlemann, *Kandinsky über Kandinsky*, 90ff.

7. In his essay (*KCW*, 384), Kandinsky specifically identified the "entangled lines" of these horses as one of the painting's "two centers." He located the other in the "acute form modeled in blue" (i.e., the "mountain") further to the right. Clearly at this point he conceived of a "center" as the place where two opposing diagonals meet—and contrived that that should happen at approximately the middle of the canvas, and halfway between there and the leftmost edge.

8. That the painting is governed by paired oppositions of various sorts has made it ripe for structuralist analysis. See both Thürlemann, *Kandinsky über Kandinsky*, and Jean-Marie Floch, "Kandinsky: sémiotique d'un discours plastique non figuratifs," *Communications* 34 (1981), 135–157; the latter was reprinted with slight modification in J.-M. Floch, *Petites mythologies de l'oeil et de l'esprit: pour une sémiotique plastique* (Paris: Hadès, 1985), 39–77.

9. Kandinsky was evidently so pleased with this basic arrangement that he reproduced it in pen and ink as plate 11 in the appendix to *Punkt und Linie zu Fläche*. There it appears facing the caption "Linear Structure of *Composition 4*—vertical-diagonal ascent" [Linienaufbau der "Komposition 4"—vertikal-diagonaler Aufstieg] (*Punkt und Linie zu Fläche: Beitrag zur Analyse der malerischen Elemente*, eds. Walter Gropius and László Moholy-Nagy [Munich: Albert Langen, 1926]).

10. *KCW*, "Composition 4," 384.

11. We should note, too, that the generally triangular shape of the opposing-horse group is counterbalanced by the (smaller) triangle of the yellow mountain on the right. It is also repeated in both the rainbow immediately below the horses and the large, central blue mound, and appears yet again, inverted, in the broad "V" of the painting's lower half. Kandinsky seems to have had composition of this sort—perhaps even *Composition IV* specifically—in mind when he wrote in *Über das Geistige* that the "harmonies" of modern paintings might be constructed out of *opposing* elements (whether linear or chromatic), and that such "hidden constructions" could often "consist of forms apparently scattered at random upon the canvas" (*OSA*, 209).

12. Thürlemann, *Kandinsky über Kandinsky*, 105–107.

13. In the original German essay (Kandinsky, "Komposition 4," 33), brackets appeared in the first section, grouping the four main parts of the picture as follows:

1. Weights (masses):

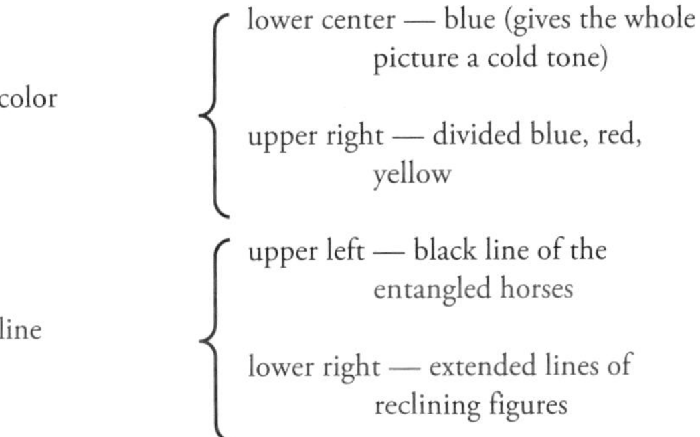

In the Lindsay and Vergo translation of the text (*KCW*, "Composition 4," 383), the association of the first pair with color (*Farbe*) and the second with line (*Linie*) has been omitted.

14. It also obviously shifts the balance of color to the right-hand side of the painting, leaving the clashing black-on-white lines of the left to dominate that side.

15. *KCW*, 383–384.

16. On the dissonant-primary system, see the discussion in the "Second Moment," 26ff.

17. Kandinsky refers first to "oppositions between precise and blurred [Gegensätze des Präzisen zum Verschwommenen]" and then, on the following page, to the "contrast

between blurred and contoured forms (i.e., line as itself . . . but also as contour, which itself has in addition the effect of pure line) [Gegensatz der verschwommenen Formen zu den konturierten (also Line als Line . . . und als Kontur, wo sie auch als Linie mitklingt)]." See *KCW*, 383–384, and Kandinsky, "Komposition 4," 33–34.

18. Kandinsky discusses his use of white as a foil for the black lines of his compositions in his Cologne Lecture; see *KCW*, 397–398.

19. *KCW*, "Composition 4," 384. The original German (Kandinsky, "Komposition 4," 34) reads:

> Dieses Hell-Süss-Kalte zum Spitz-Bewegten (Krieg) is der Hauptgegensatz im Bilde. Hier ist, scheint mir, dieser Gegensatz (in Vergleich mit Komposition 2) noch stärker, aber dafür auch härter (innerlich), deutlicher, was als Vorteil des präzisere Wirken hat und als Nachteil eine zu große Deutlichkeit dieser Präzisität.

20. In fact there are many similarities between the two works. In addition to the near-sameness of the palette, we find in both an opposition between left and right halves; rearing horses that face off against one another; and figures reclining in the lower right-hand quadrant of the painting. Indeed, Felix Thürlemann has argued on the basis of these similarities that *Composition IV* ought to be regarded as a fairly direct transformation of the earlier work (see Thürlemann, *Kandinsky über Kandinsky*, 93). Given that Kandinsky's own comments can be read as gesturing in that direction, I'm inclined to follow Thürlemann's lead. But my understanding of the relationship between the two paintings is a bit different from his, a bit more dialectical. And, again, it takes for its starting point that "principal contrast" Kandinsky identified within each picture, the opposition of "angular movement ('battle')"—articulated above all through *line*—and the ("bright-cold-sweet") colors with which those lines are juxtaposed.

21. The pertinent parts of the passage from *Über das Geistige* in question (*KCW*, 194–195) read:

> As far as drawing and painting are concerned, the turn away from the representational—and one of the first steps into the realm of the abstract—was the exclusion of the third dimension, i.e., the attempt to keep the "picture" as a painting upon a flat surface. Modeling was abandoned. In this way, the real object was moved nearer to the abstract, a move that indicated a certain progress. As an immediate consequence, however, one's possibilities became pinned down to the real surface of the canvas, so that painting took on new, purely material overtones. This pinning down was at the same time a limitation of possibilities. An attempt was made to constitute the picture upon an ideal plane, which thus had to be in front of the material surface of the canvas. In this way, composition with flat triangles became composition with triangles that had turned plastic, three-dimensional, i.e., pyramids (so-called "Cubism"). . . . [However,] one should not forget that there are other means of both retaining the material surface and constituting an ideal surface, not only of fixing the latter as a flat plane, but also of exploiting it as a three-dimensional space. The very thinness or thickness of a line, the positioning of the form upon the surface, and the superimposition of one form upon another provide sufficient examples of the linear extension of space. Similar possibilities are offered by the correct use of color, which can recede or advance, strive forward or backward, and turn the picture into a being hovering in mid-air, which signifies the same as the pictorial extension of space.
>
> The unification of these two kinds of extension in harmonious or disharmonious combinations is one of the richest and most powerful elements of linear-pictorial composition.

It might be said that the line-bound forms of *Composition II* still largely belong to that first moment, when artists were directing their energies toward negating the last remnants of pictorial illusionism by emphasizing "the 'picture' as a painting upon a flat surface." Although the overall impression of *Composition IV* is even flatter, Kandinsky had already begun experimenting there with those "other means"—varying a bit the thickness of the lines, superimposing one form upon another, and trying to open up spatial dimensions through "the correct use of color."

22. In his (undelivered) Cologne Lecture, Kandinsky claimed that with *Composition II* "one can see the free use of color without regard for the demands of perspective" (*KCW*, 395). The claim is only relatively valid, however (that is, is only valid in relation to his previous works), as the comparison with *Composition IV* reveals. When the two paintings are viewed in tandem, it's apparent that the central white form of *Composition II* still reads as foreshortened, its edges functioning like perspective orthogonals to suggest recession into depth.

23. Toward the end of his analysis of the painting, Kandinsky drew a distinction between "line as itself" or "pure line" and line "as contour," lending definition to "contoured forms" (*KCW*, 384). Whereas the linear elements of *Composition II* had served almost exclusively "as contour," with the separation of line and color in *Composition IV*, we begin to see the emergence of each "as itself."

24. *KCW*, "Composition 4," 384. Kandinsky asserted the importance of this "running-over" on two separate occasions within the essay (the other appears on 383). If he also emphasized the "predominance of color over form" in *Composition IV*, it was presumably on account of just these places where line seems unable to contain color and thereby make it over into colored form.

25. Again, the contrast Kandinsky articulated in his text between "precise and blurred" is foremost a reiteration of the principal contrast between line and color. Whatever "blurring" there is, is a blurring of color; the lines, for their part, are consistent in the "precision" of their rendering.

26. If it's right to see the earlier paintings' contrast of line and color as being sublated in the colored lines of *Composition VI*, we might want to say that "precision" emerges here as the truth of that opposition—and so also align the sharp-edged shapes of the painting (e.g., the elongated red "rectangle" and yellow "quotation marks" at its center) with that sequence of diagonal, colored lines. Both could then be regarded as standing in opposition to the increasing number of "blurred" or indefinite elements—the patches of color but also the faint or tenuous lines that are found, for example, in the middle of the left-hand side of the composition.

27. Although *Composition V* marks the end of Kandinsky's strict adherence to the opposed-primary palette, that palette will have a final efflorescence at the end of 1913. In December of that year, with *Black Lines I* (Figure 20), and to a lesser extent *Light Picture*, paintings that are now both in the Guggenheim Museum, New York, the artist returned one last time not only to the Hering primaries of his earlier paintings but also to those paintings' opposition of line and color. (In fact, Kandinsky's description of the principal antagonism of *Compositions II* and *IV*—the pairing of "bright-cold-sweet colors" and "angular, sharp movement [battle]"—seems wholly relevant once again. The artist's unpublished note, "Bild ist Kombination der Farbe und Linie . . . ," which is undated but was probably written before 1914, is relevant here too; see *KGS*, 555.) In *Black Lines I*, the eponymous

hatchings appear like so many scratches on the very surface of the canvas; by the force of the contrast, the saturated colors seem displaced into an ambiguous depth behind. In most areas of the painting, line and color operate relatively independently of one another. In a few places, however—with the yellow "U" in the lower left-hand corner, the blue form overwritten by a kind of starburst near the middle of the right-hand side and, perhaps most strikingly, the pink chevron in the upper left-hand quadrant—there is a much closer correspondence between the two. In the last case, for example, the lines knit themselves to the general form of the chevron, with the result that the colored shape itself is apparently pulled closer to the surface of the composition. Ultimately Kandinsky seems to have decided, however, that the (still essentially) binary opposition of line and color could not produce the degree of spatial complexity he wanted, and so he abandoned it once again in favor of other pictorial devices.

28. The Kreis für Kunst Köln staged an exhibition of Kandinsky's work in early 1914, and invited the artist to deliver a lecture about his work at the opening. Although Kandinsky decided not to make the trip to Cologne, he sent a typescript of the talk that he had written—though it was in fact not read at the opening. Indeed, the typescript has disappeared, but Kandinsky's handwritten manuscript is preserved among his papers.

29. *KCW*, "Cologne Lecture," 398–399.

30. On Kandinsky's *Hinterglasmalerei*, see the exhibition catalogue, *Kandinsky: Painting on Glass* (New York: Solomon R. Guggenheim Museum, 1966), including the short essay by Hans Konrad Roethel.

31. *OSA*, 195.

32. *KCW*, "Cologne Lecture," 398–399.

33. In fact, only blue and red appear at all in saturated form. There are just a few touches here and there of pure yellow, and no saturated green whatsoever. Where green—or blue-green or yellow-green—appears, it has always been mixed with white or gray to produce some much more subdued shade or tint.

34. Up until at least 1920, Kandinsky continued to paint the black lines of his compositions first, out of an interest in just this effect. Although they literally reside on a plane beneath that of the other colors (whose edges frequently encroach upon them), we perceive the lines as existing on top of everything else. As we'll discover, Kandinsky plainly cultivated spatial ambiguities and reversals of this sort.

35. *KCW*, "Composition 6," 385. The whereabouts of the glass painting in question are unknown, though a black-and-white photograph can be found on p. 13, fig. 4, of the *Kandinsky: Painting on Glass* catalogue (as in n30, above).

36. *KCW*, 385.

37. Kandinsky (*KCW*, "Composition 6," 386) compared his inability to reproduce his mental image to a snake that couldn't quite fully slough its skin. "In the same way," he said, "for a year and a half, that element which was foreign to my inner picture of that catastrophe called the Deluge still stuck to me."

38. This is certainly how Kandinsky proceeded with *Composition VII* (November 1913), as is evident from the photographs Gabriele Münter took of the work in progress. It also accords with the recent scientific analysis of *Painting with White Border* (May 1913). For Münter's photos of *Composition VII*, see Magdalena Dabrowski, *Kandinsky: Compositions* (New York: Museum of Modern Art, 1995), 44; on the underdrawing in *Painting with White*

Border, see Elizabeth Steele, Gillian McMillan, Narayan Khandekar, and Erin Mysak, "Side by Side: The Technical Investigation of *Sketch I for Painting with White Border* and *Painting with White Border*," in Elsa Smithgall, ed. *Kandinsky and the Harmony of Silence: Painting with White Border* (Washington, D.C.: Phillips Collection, 2011), 116.

39. *KCW*, "Composition 6," 386.

40. *KCW*, "Composition 6," 387.

41. An early and exceptionally clear example of the phenomenon is provided by *With the Black Arc* (*Mit dem schwarzen Bogen*) (Figure 21) from the autumn of 1912. At the bottom of that painting are two explicitly opposed "centers": one dominated by Prussian blue, the other by a warmer reddish-orange. Their opposition is reconciled by not only the eponymous black arc but also the purplish shape that it fronts, insofar as that purple seems to be the product of an actual mixing of the blue and red-orange pigments below.

42. *KCW*, "Composition 6," 387. In the scenario I imagine, at some point, presumably during the autumn of 1912 (i.e., around the time he painted *With the Black Arc*), Kandinsky began to worry that, in the absence of an articulated third center, his compositions were vulnerable to the charge of being simply unresolved or incoherent. The third center, by negating the contradiction inherent in the other two, could explicitly demonstrate the sublation that was the work of the painting as a whole.

43. *KCW*, 387.

44. The linear "drama" of the right was itself the byproduct, Kandinsky says, of a confrontation between the "long, solemn lines" rising diagonally from the lower center of the composition outward and "the thicker lines running obliquely toward them in the upper part of the picture, with which they come into direct conflict" (*KCW*, 387). Significantly, the artist specified that those "long, solemn lines" had been borrowed from the "reclining figures" of *Composition IV*; once again, his concern was to underscore the continuities between paintings, to have us regard them all as part of a single, ongoing project.

45. *KCW*, "Composition 6," 387.

46. *KCW*, "Composition 6," 387. Specifically, Kandinsky says: "This apparent absence of surface, the same uncertainty as to distance can, e.g., be observed in the Russian steam baths. A man standing in the steam is neither close to nor far away; he is just somewhere."

47. *KCW*, "Composition 6," 387. The *Hinterglasmalerei*-effect of the earlier paintings was largely the product of the precision and opacity of their black lines, which caused those lines to be perceived as overlapping the other elements, as if they resided on a plane above. The third center of *Composition VI* involves instead an overlapping by semitransparent, "blurred" forms, their blurring and variable transparency no longer reading as features belonging to a planar surface but, instead, to a liquid or gaseous medium. We might say that, in this next turn of the dialectical wheel, a kind of "atmospheric spatiality" seems to be emerging from the opposition of "precise" and "blurred."

48. *KCW*, "Composition 6," 387. It should be said that this "toiling" seems to have been done only on the final canvas, since none of the preparatory sketches include anything resembling the "pink cloud" of the finished composition.

49. *KCW*, "Composition 6," 387. The relevant passage in the original German reads: "Gerade die minimalen Gewichte, die man hier braucht und die eine so starke Wirkung auf das ganze Bild ausüben, die unbeschreibliche Genauigkeit im Wirken eines verborgenen Gesetzes, das die glücklich gestimmte Hand wirken läßt und dem sie folgsam interliegt, ist

ebenso verlockend, wie das erste gewaltige Auf-die-Leinwand werfen der großen Massen" (*Kandinsky, 1901–1913*, 36; reproduced in Thürlemann, *Kandinsky über Kandinsky*, 222).

50. Similarly, in his Cologne Lecture, Kandinsky describes his artistic development as "a long path, which I *had* to follow":

> Apart from my innumerable experiments, I also spent much time in reflection, wishing to solve many things by way of logic. Yet what was logically so easy simply would not come in practice. As a rule it is not a difficult, but often an enjoyable task to get to the point at which one can say *ergo*. One knows much more often *what* one wants than how to attain it. This *how* is only and exclusively *good*, properly speaking, if it has come of its own accord, if the hand that has been blessed with the necessary gift is not dependent upon reason, but rather, contrary to the dictates of reason, often creates what is correct *of its own accord*. And apart from the satisfaction thus attained, only such a form can bring a kind of pleasure that is beyond comparison. [*KCW*, 393–394]

The point here, as in the essay on *Composition VI*, would seem to be that, although painting's "inner necessity" has a certain (dialectical) shape, and seems therefore to conform to a certain logic, that seeming is always an effect of hindsight. The specific movements of painting's dialectic are not predetermined, with the result that they can't be deduced by the artist or otherwise anticipated in advance.

51. It would also bring to an end the practice Kandinsky had used previously, of working up a composition in great detail before transferring it to the final canvas, point by point, by means of a pencil grid and extensive color notations. In the future, there would be considerably less correspondence between the preparatory sketches and finished composition— at least until 1921 or so, by which time Kandinsky's practice changed substantially again.

52. *KCW*, "Composition 6," 388 (emphasis mine). In the same essay Kandinsky also asserted that both yellow and (more surprisingly) green "animate" the "blunted, extremely abstract-sounding tone" introduced by the deep brown, even though in *Über das Geistige* he had characterized green as an inherently inert color. Nor was the general phenomenon limited to color. In his analysis of *Composition VI*, the artist reported that he "employed the same long, solemn lines [he] had already used in *Composition IV*," and was "pleased to see how this same device here produced such a different effect" (*KCW*, 387).

53. *KCW*, "Cologne Lecture," 398.

54. Because of the externality of the system used with those earlier paintings, Kandinsky could, and evidently often did, determine the placement of each color well in advance of its actual appearance in the composition. As noted earlier (Second Moment, Part 1, n65), in the Guggenheim sketch for *Composition II*, for example, color notations (such as "w" for *weiss*, "or" for orange, and even a non-abbreviated "blau") are still clearly visible beneath the corresponding pigments, suggesting something like a paint-by-numbers approach at this stage in the artist's working process. Admittedly, there are one or two places where Kandinsky departed from his penciled instructions, painting green, for example, where the notation called for white; but these are by far the exception to the rule during the period before 1913. On these matters, see Gillian McMillan and Vanessa Kowalski, "Kandinsky's Materials and Techniques: A Preliminary Study of Five Paintings," in Annegret Hoberg et al., *Kandinsky* (New York: Guggenheim Museum Publications, 2009), esp. 124–125.

55. *KCW*, "Composition 6," 388 (translation slightly modified), and Kandinsky, "Komposition 6," in *Kandinsky, 1901–1913*, 38. The original German reads: "So sind alle und

auch die sich widersprechenden Elemente in volles inneres Gleichgewicht gebracht," the emphasis on the fully *internal* (volles inneres) nature of the equilibrium underscoring its independence from any external system.

56. *KCW*, "Cologne Lecture," 397 (my emphasis). Kandinsky's growing interest in "composing" colors is clearly responsible for the vastly more varied and nuanced palette that he developed in 1913. Although I'm unaware of comparable analyses of the pigments used in *Composition VI*, recent scientific examinations of those in *Painting with White Border* have revealed an astonishing degree of complexity. The conservators report, for example, that the opaque green in the bottom left of the painting "is composed of two very thin layers; the darker green contains up to ten different pigments, and the lighter green over the top contains six or more pigments." See Steele, McMillan, Khandekar, and Mysak, "Side by Side," 118.

57. *KCW*, "Composition 6," 388.

58. *KCW*, "Picture with the White Edge," 389.

59. *KCW*, "Picture with the White Edge," 391.

60. This is the oil sketch now in the Phillips Collection in Washington. For a comparison of it with the finished painting, see Smithgall, ed., *Kandinsky and the Harmony of Silence*.

61. *KCW*, "Picture with the White Edge," 389. A "troika" is a characteristically Russian vehicle (with either wheels or sled-like runners) drawn by three horses harnessed abreast.

62. *KCW*, "Picture with the White Edge," 390.

63. *KCW*, "Picture with the White Edge," 390.

64. For an excellent discussion of *Painting with White Border*—including reproductions of all the preparatory sketches—see Smithgall, ed., *Kandinsky and the Harmony of Silence*.

65. *KCW*, "Picture with the White Edge," 390.

66. *KCW*, "Picture with the White Edge," 391. Lest we think that Kandinsky's reference to the "insistence" of his "inner voice" implies some personally expressive component (and the German is even more forceful: "diktierte mir meine innere Stimme gebieterisch"), we should note that the next sentence in the same paragraph, concerning the function of the *Quetschtechnik* within the larger composition, is rendered entirely in the passive voice: "Es ist sehr richtig und wieder zweckmäßig geschehen: wie nötig war diese technische Unruhe zwischen den drei beschriebenen Punkten." The beginning of that sentence, which Lindsay and Vergo render as "I used this technique quite correctly, and once again, with a clear sense of purpose," is perhaps more accurately translated as: "It appeared [or happened] correctly and, again, purposively"—*zweckmäßig* here carrying generally Kantian connotations of something created *as if* with a purpose but in the absence of any maker whose purpose it might be. There are as well other, comparably odd locutions within the essay. Earlier, when describing his use of "too much green," Kandinsky claimed that this excess occurred "quite unconsciously—and, as I see now, purposefully"—his pairing of these apparently contradictory adverbs (*unbewußt* and, in this case, *planmäßig*) suggesting less the involvement of *his* intentions than the suprapersonal logic of *Geist*.

67. *KCW*, "Composition 6," 388.

68. *KCW*, "Composition 6," 388.

69. I have chosen to use the Russian term *faktura* here and in subsequent descriptions

of Kandinsky's work rather than either of the English words "texture" or "facture" with which it is usually translated, both because the Russian places greater emphasis on the process of making (rather than merely its end result) and because the term was so crucial to artists of Kandinsky's generation and the generation following. On these matters, see Maria Gough, "Faktura: The Making of the Russian Avant-Garde," *RES: Journal of Anthropology and Aesthetics* 36 (Autumn 1999), 32–59.

70. Significantly, on the back of that same sheet of paper, Kandinsky made notes for an unnamed (and perhaps not-then-yet-painted) composition whose features he describes using terms, such as "inner boiling" (*inneres Kochen*) and "dissolution" (*Auflösung*), that reappear in his analysis of *Painting with White Border* (see *KCW*, 390–391). In fact, given the other references—to a "displaced center" (*verschobenes Zentrum*), "all kinds of movements" (*allerhand Bewegungen*), and even "inner totalization" (*inneres summieren*)—it doesn't seem too far-fetched to imagine that the notes were made in connection with *Painting with White Border* specifically. For a transcription of the handwritten portions of the drawing, see *KGS*, 565; the sheet is discussed as well by Matthias Haldemann in his essay "The Theater of Pictures: Kandinsky's Abstraction of Abstraction," in Hoberg et al., *Kandinsky*, 82.

71. *KCW*, "Painting with White Border," 391.

72. Clearly if we did retain the water references, we'd want to call attention to the way that, in the upper right-hand quadrant (and exclusively there), the main portion of the composition—everything, that is, that doesn't belong to the white border itself—appears to constitute a kind of land mass, an island, rising up from the waters of the "lake."

73. The illusion turns on the subtle brownish line, which, at the bottom of the painting (just below and behind "St. George") appears outside (which is to say, above) the edge of the white border—a subtle shadow cast onto the beige ground "underneath"—but that, further to the right and higher, seems to shift to the other side of the border's edge, the shadow it suggests now casting the white border itself into an imagined depth. (The illusion is cemented in the upper right corner by the orange, white, and red lines that extend beyond or "outside" the main body of the composition to apparently overlap the matte surface of the border, which now clearly reads as "below.") The reversal itself seems to occur somewhere near the point at which the border, having made its vertical ascent, turns the corner to head back leftward.

74. The first sketch for *Painting with White Border* (now in the Phillips Collection in Washington, D.C.) was 100.5 × 78.5 cm: a vertical canvas, about half the size of the finished painting. When Kandinsky made the decision to reorient the composition to the horizontal, most of the elements that had made their appearance in the earlier sketch wound up on the left-hand side of the painting, thereby creating a void on the right. Consequently, one of the primary functions of the white border was to fill in that otherwise empty space.

75. Indeed, it seems likely that Kandinsky's decision not to revise the essay for publication—specifically, to leave it in its present outline form rather than transforming it into prose paragraphs that would have brought it in line with the essays on *Composition VI* and *Painting with White Border*—was motivated by his desire to underscore the distinctness of the elements in *Composition IV*. Presumably the whole point was to contrast their separability with the greater interconnection among the parts of the later paintings.

76. For illustrations and discussion of the preparatory sketches, see Dabrowski, *Kandinsky*, 40–44 and 86–102.

77. See ibid., esp. plates 69–72.

78. For more on the inscriptions, see Jelena Hahl-Koch, *Kandinsky* (New York: Rizzoli, 1993), 210.

79. There is a sense in which this undecidability seems related to the figure/ground reversal that we experienced with *Painting with White Border*. Here, however, it has become a more concentrated phenomenon, the reversal happening not as our eyes move from the bottom of the painting upward (or vice versa) but, rather, simply as we shift our attention from one side of the "cut" to the other. The effect may be more localized, yet the oscillation is consequently more constant, the illusion now being relatively easily and frequently triggered.

80. The "trapezoid" in question is made up of the long, drawn orange line near the painting's left-hand edge; the right angle, surrounded by a halo of red, that abuts the bottom of the composition; the merely implicit, diagonal line constituted by the (approximately) aligned edges of a number of shapes both above and below the large, rounded blue form somewhat to the left of center; and pretty much any of the drawn lines in the upper left-hand corner. Our occasional uncertainty concerning the status of all of these contours is, as we will see momentarily, crucial to the overall effect of the phenomenon.

81. For the most interesting of these accounts, see Matthias Haldemann, *Kandinskys Abstraktion: Die Entstehung und Transformation seines Bildkonzepts* (Munich: Wilhelm Fink Verlag, 2002), 206–217.

82. Of the three square paintings from this period, *Picture with Red Spot* was exhibited most often during Kandinsky's life—six times, in fact, between 1914 and 1938—so that it would seem the one of the group the artist considered most successful. For a list of the exhibitions, see Hans K. Roethel and Jean K. Benjamin, *Kandinsky: Catalogue Raisonnée of the Oil Paintings* (Ithaca, NY: Cornell University Press, 1982), vol. 1: 483 (catalogue no. 486).

83. Of the sixteen paintings from 1916 catalogued by Roethel and Benjamin, *Kandinsky*, nine are highly representational works—mostly city views of Moscow—and all of the others, with the exception of *Painting on Light Ground*, either have been destroyed or their present whereabouts are unknown.

84. The most interesting of these—*Painting with Three Spots* (Museo Thyssen-Bornemisza, Madrid; R&B 490); *Red Border* (private collection; R&B 660); and *White Oval* (Tretyakov Gallery, Moscow; R&B 661)—as well as several others, were rightly included in the recent exhibition organized by the Phillips Collection and the Guggenheim around *Painting with White Border*. See the catalogue to that exhibition, Smithgall, ed., *Kandinsky and the Harmony of Silence*, which includes color photographs of all the extant paintings in question.

85. See Annegret Hoberg's entry on the painting in the catalogue of the 2009 Guggenheim exhibition, *Kandinsky*, 206.

86. As a measure of its significance for the artist, we should note that *In Gray* was exhibited on seven separate occasions during Kandinsky's lifetime—all of them between 1920 and 1925.

87. The illusion of overlapping is enhanced in the latter instance by the truncated white, black, and red-brown shapes that seem to slip beneath the leading edge of the gray plane to their left. The strategy is identical to the one used throughout *Composition VII*, even if, in this case, it is deployed only on one side of the line.

88. It seems telling that, shortly after he completed *In Gray*, Kandinsky produced another work on a predominantly gray field, which he titled *Black Lines II* (R&B 667); it is currently in the Georgian National Museum in Tbilisi. The first *Black Lines* (Figure 20), painted in 1913, explicitly juxtaposed the "bright-cold-sweet colors" Kandinsky used in *Compositions II* and *IV* with an array of fine, even brittle black lines.

89. In fact the effect is explicitly anti-naturalistic, in that the line marking the transition from a lighter to a darker orange exactly coincides with the seam between the green and white shapes behind. The coincidence once more gestures toward transparency, except of course that, if the orange band really were transparent, it would become lighter, rather than darker, as it passed over that divide.

90. Although Malevich himself would later criticize these works for their pronounced illusionism, it was, I tend to think, precisely the (non-sculptural) illusion of floating planar forms within them that Kandinsky found so exemplary.

91. Because the "ground" of *Picture on Light Ground* clearly evolved out of the border of *Painting with White Border*, that latter composition should probably be regarded as the pivotal one in this particular round of development. There the delicate sfumato that emerged with *Composition VI* began to be displaced by the different (and ultimately much longer-lived) technique of a precisely rendered but spatially reversible form.

92. Although the central area of *Red Spot II* appears monochromatic, it is only relatively so: the field is in fact variably colored by subtle chromatic tints, which, like the surface *faktura*, are evident on close inspection but largely disappear from view when the painting is seen from a distance.

93. The four mismatched corners of *Red Spot II* have a clear precedent in *White Line* (*Weisser Strich*) (R&B 673), a work done only a short time earlier. (It is number 232 on Kandinsky's handlist, while *Red Spot II* is number 234.) In *White Line*, however, the corners are much closer to one another in hue, saturation, and value, with the result that they're much more plausibly seen as constituting a single planar element: a solid frame through whose opening we view the main body of the composition. In that sense, *White Line* seems directly related to *Picture on Light Ground*—and serves as an obvious intermediary between that work and *Red Spot II*.

94. Here we might recall that Malevich frequently referred to the ground of his own paintings as a "white abyss." The four differentiated corners of *Red Spot II* seem to have been aimed at amplifying that same general effect. Evidently Kandinsky felt that, were the white field wholly coextensive with the surface of the canvas, the temptation would remain to see that white as itself simply surface, rather than succumbing to its illusion of depth. On Malevich's references to the "abyss," see Aleksandra Shatskikh, *Black Square: Malevich and the Origin of Suprematism*, trans. Marian Schwartz (New Haven, CT: Yale University Press, 2012), 93 and 252.

95. See, for example, Annegret Hoberg's description of the painting in the catalogue of the 2009 Guggenheim exhibition, *Kandinsky*, 219.

96. Although *Red Spot II* and *White Center* were done less than a year apart, and with only a single work intervening between them—again, they are numbers 234 and 236, respectively, on Kandinsky's handlist—*Red Spot II* was completed in Moscow, whereas *White Center* was done in Germany, after the artist had been invited to teach at the Bauhaus but before he had actually taken up his teaching position there.

97. The previous painting with that title, *On White I* (handlist 224, R&B 665), was done in February 1920, and is currently in the collection of the Russian Museum in Saint Petersburg. True to its name, the earlier painting is also done "on white," though—judging from the black-and-white reproductions I have seen—its ground is more painterly, and therefore less uniform, than that of *On White II.*

98. For more on the phenomenon of illusory transparence, see Josef Albers, *Interaction of Color* (New Haven, CT: Yale University Press, 2006 [original edition, 1963]), esp. 24–26 and plates IX-1, XI-1, and XI-3. It is, of course, relevant here to note that, from June 1922 on, Kandinsky taught the Theory of Form class at the Bauhaus, which included a component on color theory, and which was obligatory for all first-year students. Albers enrolled at the school in 1920; a short three years later, he would assume teaching responsibilities himself. Together with László Moholy-Nagy, Albers took over instruction of the Preliminary Course after Johannes Itten's departure in the early spring of 1923 (that is, exactly during the period when Kandinsky was painting *On White II*). It was in connection with his lessons for the Preliminary Course that Albers began to formulate the various color exercises that would eventually make up the core of his text, *Interaction of Color.* Although we have no record of conversations between Albers and Kandinsky on the subject of color—and the published correspondence is disappointingly thin in that area—it's hard to imagine that the exercises would not have been an at least occasional topic of discussion. Certainly many of the illusions analyzed by Albers have correlates, as we will see, in Kandinsky's paintings of the 1920s. The letters between the two men have been published as *Josef Albers and Wassily Kandinsky: Friends in Exile: A Decade of Correspondence, 1929–1940,* Nicholas Fox Weber and Jessica Boissel, eds. (Manchester, VT: Hudson Hills Press, 2010).

99. As Albers would explain in the *Interaction of Color,* the "foremost" of any two overlapping, transparent planes will be the one whose edges, around the area of intersection, present the strongest contrast. So, for example, in *On White II,* where the red triangle and olive green quadrilateral meet, producing an almost-rectangular area of deep purplish brown, the olive appears most proximate to us. This is the case because the uppermost edge of the purplish "rectangle" appears more sharply defined, the red offering a stronger contrast to it than does the olive green below. We thus infer that the quadrilateral is *on top of* the triangle, the triangle's lower edge having been rendered less distinct as it passes underneath the darkly transparent green. Of course, things become significantly more complicated if multiple apparently transparent planes are involved. On all these matters, see Albers, *Interaction of Color,* 96 and 102, as well as plates XI-1 and XI-3.

According to this same logic, the yellow-brown trapezoid in the lower center of *On White II* ought to be seen as similarly residing beneath the olive quadrilateral, since the olive green offers less of a contrast to the brown in the area of intersection than does the lighter yellow-brown of the trapezoid. That we are unable to read it that way—or at least to do so unproblematically—is a direct result of the small triangles, circles, and kidney-shaped elements present in this area, which appear as so much patterning on the surface of the trapezoid. Collectively they override the chromatic cues and push the olive-colored quadrilateral "unnaturally" into depth.

100. *On White II* might plausibly be seen as having arisen from an extension of the central area of *Red Spot II* (Figure 33 / Plate 11), the four complicating corners that framed that work having now been rendered unnecessary by the transparency invented for *White*

Center. (Even the title of *On White II* reads rather like a sublation of the titles of those other compositions, the preposition "on" hinting, ironically, at what has been won in the process: an illusory space deep enough to dispel Kandinsky's worries that the ground would simply be conflated with the canvas, the other pictorial elements taken to be directly residing on its surface.) The little bits of white in *On White II* that we perceive, at least intermittently, as positive shapes—the large red-dotted circle above and to the right of center or the middle wedge in the yellow-white-and-violet segment—might also be construed as carrying on, if a bit differently, the work of the corners in *Red Spot II*. For, like those corners, they heighten our uncertainty as to exactly where the white "ground" lies.

101. If this development toward regular geometries is unsurprising in one sense (i.e., insofar as the sharply articulated, transparent plane seems a reasonable outcome of the opposition between "precise" and "blurred" that had been playing itself out in Kandinsky's work over the past decade), it remains wholly unexpected in other respects. As recently as 1919, in his "Little Articles for Big Questions," written for the journal *Iskusstvo: Vestnik Otdela IZO NKP*, Kandinsky had minimized the possibilities inherent in "the triangle, the square, the rhomboid, the trapezoid, etc." Work that "speaks by means of these forms," he claimed, "belongs to the first sphere of graphic language—a language of harsh, sharp expressions devoid of resilience and complexity," one effectively "without declensions, conjugations, propositions, or prefixes" (see *KCW*, 425). We must assume either that Kandinsky's rhetoric—and the increasingly difficult position he occupied in relation to the younger members of the Russian avant-garde—simply got the better of him, or that he himself had been entirely unable to anticipate the path along which art's "inner necessity" would so soon thereafter lead him.

102. The format and overall composition are also clearly related to a number of the plates in the appendix to *Punkt und Linie zu Fläche*, on which Kandinsky was presumably working in 1923. Something of the text's didacticism seems to have carried over into *On White II* as well.

103. It seems to me especially illuminating in this context to also compare the tinted ground of *Composition VIII* with the similarly almost-monochromatic field of *In Gray* (Figure 32 / Plate 10). Whereas the value gradations inflecting *In Gray*'s ground inevitably invoke chiaroscuro modeling, and so impart to the surface an appearance of sculptural solidity and mass, the pastel tints of *Composition VIII* convey an airy ethereality—again, particularly when seen against the horizon of expectations set by Kandinsky's earlier paintings.

104. The color of the central quadrilateral in *On White II* varies considerably from one area to the next, and in a manner that seems largely unintentional. In some places it appears much browner; in others, it's a paler, purer green than is the norm. Evidently Kandinsky was mixing the color himself rather than using a single, store-bought tube. The resulting chromatic inconsistency is matched by the not-quite-straight edges and imperfectly rounded curves of the composition's geometric shapes. Perhaps the artist was slow to take up the ruler and compass—even when painting's "inner necessity" seemed to demand it—because he had so recently declared (in that same "Little Article" on line quoted above) that the ruler was the "most primitive of instruments" (see *KCW*, 426).

105. In conjunction with this thought, we might also observe that *Composition VIII* reinstates the opposition between (black) line and color that structured so much of Kan-

dinsky's early, Munich-period production. That opposition was itself deeply entangled with—in fact, might even be regarded as an extension or variant of—the dialectic between "precise" and "blurred" that emerged with *Composition IV*.

106. This dialectic, too, is plainly related to the opposition of line to color. For a discussion of Kandinsky's association of linear (and geometric) elements with materiality, as well as his belief in the essential immateriality of color, see "Second Moment, Part 2," 34ff.

107. *In the Black Square* (R&B 700) is number 259 on Kandinsky's handlist; it is in the collection of the Guggenheim Museum, New York.

108. Handlist 268a (R&B 711), Kunstmuseum Bern. According to most accounts, Kandinsky made *Backward Glance* "in order to give his young wife, Nina, an idea of a painting entitled *Small Pleasures*, which was done by him in 1913" (see Roethel and Benjamin, *Kandinsky*, vol. 1: 667). The two works are clearly compositionally related, but far from identical. At best we might say that *Backward Glance* represents a return at a higher—or at least a more objective/geometric—level of a content that first took form in *Small Pleasures*.

109. Like many of the other works Kandinsky painted during his tenure at the Bauhaus, *In Blue* is done on cardboard rather than canvas. In most cases, his choice of cardboard as a surface seems to have coincided with textural experimentation; presumably he felt that canvas would have been less receptive to the specific effects he was trying to achieve.

110. Additive mixing refers to the colors of the solar spectrum, which in combination produce white light. Material colors, such as paints or dyes, behave much differently. When mixed, they become darker instead of brighter, because they absorb or subtract wavelengths from the light as they reflect it. For this reason, a combination of differently colored pigments is referred to as *subtractive* mixing. For Albers's discussion of additive and subtractive mixing, see *Interaction of Color*, 27–28, and plate X-1. We find a precedent of sorts for the additive illusions of Kandinsky's *In Blue* in the upper right-hand quadrant of *Composition VIII*, where a light brown circle is overlapped by a dark yellow one, thereby producing a pale green; this is in explicit contrast to the intersecting green circle and yellow triangle in the lower right-hand corner, whose (subtractive) combination yields essentially the same light brown that colors the circle above.

111. Although it would probably require the intervention of a conservator to know for certain, one possible exception to this rule is *On White II*, the colors of whose areas of intersection may have been produced by an actual mixing of adjacent hues.

112. See Albers, *Interaction of Color*, 2; he lays out his rationale for preferring paper over pigments in section III, 6–7.

113. Evidently Kandinsky regarded the wholly fictional status of the situation as still too weak a declaration of the tableau's freedom from nature's determinacy. He made sure that the illusion of additive mixing gave way at either of its ends to a contradictory illusion of subtractive color, the orange bar reverting to a lighter shade as it passes beyond the external edges of the black shape "underneath." As a result, the play of colors in this central area is doubly impossible, which is to say again, possible only within the imaginary space of the tableau.

114. Kandinsky's ambition here—to make the pigments of his compositions behave as though they were colored *light*—resonates strongly with the views of Vladimir Soloviev, the nineteenth-century Russian philosopher who was the subject of Kojève's doctoral dissertation. (Interestingly, that dissertation was completed in 1926, the very same year that

Kandinsky painted *Several Circles*.) According to Soloviev, the Beautiful was, by definition, the "embodiment of Idea," just as light was "the elemental reality of Idea in its antithesis to solid matter." In his 1899 essay, "Beauty in Nature," Soloviev sought to explain why a diamond was beautiful, whereas coal, with a similar chemical composition, decidedly was not. "When a ray of light falls on a piece of coal," he wrote, "it is absorbed by [the coal's] material substance, and the black color of the latter is the natural symbol of the fact that light did not overcome the dark elements of nature here. . . . [In contrast,] a ray of light captured by the crystal body of a diamond obtains a new fullness of phenomenal existence in it and from it, and by refraction is broken up or separated into its constituent colors in every facet." In Soloviev's view, beauty inhered solely in those things whose material existence was able to merge with light, to both transform it and be transformed by it in turn. Of course, as I argued in the Third Moment, Kojève's claim that the Beautiful comprised the essence of art was strongly shaped by Soloviev's views on these matters. See Soloviev, "Beauty in Nature," in S. L. Frank, ed., *A Solovyov Anthology*, trans. Natalie Duddington (London: SCM Press, 1950), 127–138.

115. On Kandinsky's use of varnish in this area of *Several Circles* and its difference from the other parts of the painting, see Gillian McMillan and Vanessa Kowalski, "Kandinsky's Materials and Techniques: A Preliminary Study of Five Paintings," in Hoberg et al., *Kandinsky*, 126–127.

116. The illusion is strongest with the smaller, bright blue disk. The other—the one I'm tempted to describe as "violet"—presents a somewhat trickier case. We might imagine that the grey of the area it holds in common with the black circle suggests a semitransparent film, the disk being, then, rather like the milky center of *White Center* (Figure 35 / Plate 12). But that possibility is foreclosed by the uppermost, violet-magenta section of the circle, which seems more nearly to be passing underneath the edge of the large blue disk. Improbable though it is, the most consistent explanation for the multiple color changes that circle undergoes is that each of the larger disks is at least partially transparent, and that we're glimpsing the shape of the smallest of the three through their overlapping surfaces.

117. In the section on "The Absolute Idea," from his *Science of Logic*, for example, Hegel writes: "By virtue of the nature of the [dialectical] method just indicated, the science exhibits itself as a circle returning upon itself, the end being wound back into the beginning, the simple ground, by the mediation; this circle is moreover a circle of circles, for each individual member as ensouled by the method is reflected into itself, so that in returning into the beginning it is at the same time the beginning of a new member. Links of this chain are the individual sciences [of logic, nature, and spirit], each of which has an antecedent and a successor—or, expressed more accurately, has only the antecedent and indicates its successor in its conclusion." See *Hegel's Science of Logic*, trans. A. V. Miller (London: George Allen & Unwin, 1969), §1814. For further discussion of Hegel's figure of the "circle of circles," see Stephen Melville's "Plasticity: The Hegelian Writing of Art," in Margaret Iversen and Stephen Melville, *Writing Art History* (Chicago: University of Chicago Press, 2010), esp. 155ff.

118. The reference comes in a letter to Will Grohmann dated October 12, 1930; it is quoted in Angelica Zander Rudenstine, *The Guggenheim Collection: Paintings, 1880–1945* (New York: Solomon R. Guggenheim Foundation, 1976), vol. 1: 310.

119. Letter from Kojève to Kandinsky dated February 3, 1929. See Kandinsky, *Correspon-*

dances avec Zervos et Kojève, eds. Christian Derouet and Nina Ivanoff, *Les Cahiers du Musée national d'art moderne*, hors-série/archives (Paris: Centre Georges Pompidou, 1992), 129.

120. What Kojève actually wrote was that "the different elements of the tableau have a significance *if* they are tied together"—"les différents éléments du tableau ont une signification s'ils sont liés ensemble"—suggesting that his understanding of the work was driven more by a kind of iconographic recognition than an observation of the composition's subtle interplay of forms (ibid., emphasis added). One might well imagine that Kojève's letter, however positively intended, actually provoked worry on Kandinsky's part that the work's circles-within-circles structure was overly "iconographic," which is to say that it had emerged less out of his own practice than in response to Hegel's writings. In any case, very soon thereafter circles would start to play a much more subsidiary role within Kandinsky's compositions.

121. Ibid.

122. Like Hegel's "circle of circles," the Cusan circle stands as a figure for the Absolute. Certainly by 1932, Kojève would have been introduced to it through his studies with Alexandre Koyré at the École des hautes études; according to Dominique Auffret, Koyré taught two courses in that year, one on Nicholas of Cusa, the other on the religious philosophy of Hegel. Kojève regularly attended both. Even if those classes postdate Kojève's letter to Kandinsky, it seems likely that Kojève and Koyré had discussed correspondences between the philosophies of Nicholas and Hegel before, conceivably as early as 1929. See Dominique Auffret, *Alexandre Kojève: La philosophie, l'état, la fin de l'histoire* (Paris: Grasset, 1990), 312. Although that discussion is plainly somewhat peripheral to Kandinsky's painting, the role of geometrical form in Hegelian and Cusan thought has several interesting points of tangency with both *Several Circles* and the artist's larger project. This brief passage from Julián Marías's *History of Philosophy* will perhaps give us at least some idea of where they lie: "The Deity appears in Nicholas of Cusa's writings as *coincidentia oppositorum*, the coincidence of opposites. In this higher unity, contradiction is overcome: in the infinite all factors coincide. This idea has had its most profound repercussions in Hegel. Nicholas employs mathematical ideas to make this understandable: for example, a straight line and the circumference of a circle tend more and more to coincide as the radius of the circle is continually increased; they do coincide at the limit, if the radius approaches infinity. If, conversely, the radius becomes infinitely small, the circumference coincides with the center of the circle." See Julián Marías, *History of Philosophy*, trans. Stanley Appelbaum and Clarence C. Strowbridge (New York: Dover Publications, 1967), 198.

123. On these ideas as they pertain to Hegel, see Melville, "Plasticity," esp. 171.

124. *In Itself* (*In Sich*) is number 330 on Kandinsky's handlist (R&B 774), *Conclusion* (*Schluss*) number 360 (R&B 803). While the former work is composed almost entirely of circles, the latter juxtaposes a large circle (above) with an isosceles triangle (below), the triangle closely resembling many attempts to diagram the triadic structure of Hegel's system.

125. On the notion of "plasticity," see the following works by Catherine Malabou: *The Future of Hegel: Plasticity, Temporality, and Dialectic*, trans. Lisabeth During (London: Routledge 2005); *Plasticity at the Dusk of Writing: Dialectic, Destruction, Deconstruction*, trans. Carolyn Shread (New York: Columbia University Press, 2009); and *What Should We Do With Our Brain?*, trans. Sebastian Rand (New York: Fordham University Press, 2009). See also Melville, "Plasticity," 151–173. For Malabou especially, "plasticity" implies a process

of continual metamorphosis, Hegel's professed commitment to it thereby precluding any thought of a closed or finite system (of the sort that Kojève imagines).

126. We might also note that the colors of the composition are not only drawn from a specific segment of the color wheel—the portion running from violet through red and orange to yellow—but also that they are generally arranged according to that progression. *On Points* represents exactly the kind of contiguous-color harmony that Kandinsky had decried in *Über das Geistige*, and that his opposed-primary scheme of the early 'teens had been specifically designed to contravene. Despite its forced pairing of painterliness with precise geometry, the composition appears far less dissonant chromatically than most of the works produced either earlier or later in Kandinsky's oeuvre. I take this, too, as evidence of a general temptation by quiescence in the years surrounding *Several Circles*. If *On Points* was dedicated to reintroducing disturbance at the level of form (by sharply contrasting the apparent self-centeredness of the circles with the triangles' strong directionality, and by agitating the surface in the vicinity of both), the composition nonetheless remains fairly complacent in regard to color. That will change dramatically in Kandinsky's subsequent work—although the occasional overtly "harmonious" color scheme recurs as well.

127. I tend to think Clement Greenberg had *Composition VIII* specifically in mind when he complained that the surface of any painting by Kandinsky done after 1920 was "a mere receptacle, the painting itself an arbitrary agglomeration of shapes, spots and lines lacking even decorative coherence." See Greenberg, "Kandinsky," in *Art and Culture* (Boston: Beacon, 1961), 113.

128. As a result, we also become quite conscious that the color was applied in discrete layers or "levels," yielding an effect similar to what we find in several more or less contemporaneous works by Paul Klee. Nonetheless—I want to insist on this point—that effect is fully *prepared for* by and in Kandinsky's own previous production, from the subtly tinted background of *Composition VIII* to the thicker, more visible brushwork of *On Points*.

129. Between April 1934 and spring of the following year, sand found its way into roughly a dozen paintings by Kandinsky, most of them impressively large in scale. In addition to *Blue World* (Figure 44) and *Accompanied Contrast* (Figure 45), other significant sand-paintings include *Striped* (*Rayé*) (handlist 609, R&B 1047), *Two Green Points* (*Deux Points Verts*) (handlist 616, R&B 1054), *Relations* (handlist 604, R&B 1041), and *Division-Unity* (*Division-Unité*) (handlist 606, R&B 1044)—the titles of the last two works pointing toward the deliberate integration of individual, heterogeneous elements that was also at issue in Kandinsky's art of this period.

130. Masson's *Battle of Fishes*, for example, which is now in the collection of the Museum of Modern Art, New York, was in the possession of the Galerie Jeanne Bucher in Paris from 1930 until 1937. (Kandinsky himself would have four solo exhibitions at Jeanne Bucher, though the first was not until 1936, two years after the completion of his first sand-paintings.)

131. See McMillan and Kowalski, "Kandinsky's Materials and Techniques," esp. 126–127. As McMillan and Kowalski note in their description of his two-step process, Kandinsky recorded the medium of *Blue World* on his handlist as "oil *on* sand"—*huile sur sable*—rather than oil *and* sand. That wording functions a bit like Hegel's speculative proposition, in that it not only underscores the initial distinctness of the two elements, but also seems to place

the former—the oil paint (the color)—in the role of operative agent, acting on the sand so as to transform it into something else.

132. Kandinsky had, of course, produced a white monochromatic background previously—notably in his *On White II* (Figure 36 / Plate 13) of 1923. But he seemed to feel that white was more readily perceived as space than a colored ground would be. It was only much later, after he had developed various strategies (such as the addition of sand) for clearly detaching the "figures" from the ground, that he evidently felt secure enough to make that ground both colored and monochromatic.

133. Vivian Endicott Barnett, "Kandinsky and Science: The Introduction of Biological Images in the Paris Period," in *Kandinsky in Paris: 1934–1944* (New York: Solomon Guggenheim Foundation, 1985), 61–87. A slightly revised and shorter version of the essay appears under the same title in Oliver Arpad Istvan Botar and Isabel Wünsche, eds., *Biocentrism and Modernism* (Surrey, England: Ashgate, 2011), 207–226.

134. Barnett, "Kandinsky and Science," 63. Throughout her essay, Barnett refers to Kandinsky's "depiction" of this or that biological form, and generally considers these later paintings as having the same kind of "veiled" imagery found in the artist's work before World War I.

135. On the distinction between parts and members, see "Second Moment, Part 2," pp. 39–40.

136. "Purposiveness" indicates here, as it did for Kant, something adapted to a particular purpose or function, rather than something performed with conscious intention. For more on the purposiveness of natural beings and its significance in the writings of both Kant and Hegel, see James Kreines, "The Logic of Life: Hegel's Philosophical Defense of Teleological Explanation of Living Beings," in Frederick C. Beiser, ed., *The Cambridge Companion to Hegel and Nineteenth-Century Philosophy* (Cambridge: Cambridge University Press, 2008), 344–377.

137. One can, however, analyze scientific knowledge of mechanistic phenomena dialectically, which is precisely what Hegel did in the first chapter of his *Philosophy of Nature*.

138. *Aesthetics*, I, 145; and *Lectures on the Philosophy of Religion*, trans. by E. B. Spiers and J. Burton Sanderson (New York: Humanities Press, 1974), 17: 503/330. Both passages are cited by Kreines, "The Logic of Life."

139. *KCW*, 628. Barnett quotes this passage, too, in "Kandinsky and Science" (86–87), but misses its full significance because it has been excerpted or abstracted from the larger argument of which it forms an integral part.

140. Indeed the colors might be seen as simply lightened versions of those that had appeared in *Levels*, Kandinsky intent this time on holding them all to a similar degree of saturation and value.

141. Significantly, in his handlist, Kandinsky gave *Composition IX* the alternate title of *L'Un et l'autre—One and the Other*—perhaps in reference to the non-resolved opposition between the strongly colored ground and the painting's other figures.

142. Frank Stella, *Working Space* (Cambridge, MA: Harvard University Press, 1986), 123. The only things I think I can add to this description are relatively minor observations about the role that transparency plays in "interweaving" the figures and the diagonal backdrop with which they are fundamentally at odds. In several places, though especially near the upper center of the composition, the "figures" change color as they pass over the edge of one or another of the "rainbow" bands. As in the past, the illusion is often inconsistent,

so that the element that had at first seemed to be on top, subsequently appears behind. The result is an "interweaving" that insists on both the fictional status of the illusion and the space, however minimal, existing between the colored bands and figures.

143. Handlist 631 (R&B 1069), Solomon R. Guggenheim Museum, New York.

144. *Striped* (*Rayé*) is owned by the Guggenheim Museum, New York; *Delicate Accents* (*Accents délicats*) (handlist 624, R&B 1062) is in a private collection. There are also a number of later works—including *Sweet Trifles* (*Bagatelles douces*) (handlist 639, R&B 1077), and *Animated Stability* (*Stabilité animée*) (handlist 646, R&B 1084)—whose compartmentalized structure seems comparable to, and so derived from, that of *Thirty*. But *Sweet Trifles* clearly lacks the gravity of the earlier composition, and *Animated Stability* departs rather more (as its name perhaps suggests) from the regularity of *Thirty*'s grid. Also clearly related to *Thirty* are *Each for Itself* (*Chacun pour soi*) and *Division-Unity*, from April and October 1934, respectively (handlist 598, R&B 1035; and 606, R&B 1048). In those works, too, a collection of disparate organic and geometric forms is arranged in a grid-like structure. In *Each for Itself*, as the work's title implies, the emphasis is on the difference among the various parts: they appear relatively isolated from and independent of one another. In that regard, *Division-Unity* is much closer conceptually to *Thirty*, its title signaling the articulated unity-in-difference evidently at stake in both compositions.

145. Catherine Malabou describes "plasticity," a term that she derives from Hegel, as referring "to *the spontaneous organization of fragments*"—a description that seems particularly appropriate to the composition of *Composition X*. See Malabou, *Plasticity at the Dusk of Writing*, 7.

146. A more evenly distributed dissonance—such as we find in 1936's *Dominant Curve* (*Courbe dominante*)(Solomon R. Guggenheim Museum, New York; handlist 631, R&B 1069), for example—somehow seems less dissonant than the imbalanced variety of *Various Parts*.

147. Kandinsky's oeuvre of the late 'thirties and early 'forties seems to oscillate between compositions emphasizing system and others, such as *Reciprocal Accord*, oriented toward simpler or even singular instances of opposition. This alternation appears to have been yet another means by which Kandinsky sought to understand the relation of the individual part or member to the whole, and vice versa.

CONCLUSION

1. Theodor Adorno, *Aesthetic Theory*, trans. and ed. Robert Hullot-Kentor (Minneapolis: University of Minnesota Press, 1997), 87.

2. Ibid., 86–87.

3. On these matters, see Gregg M. Horowitz, "Art History and Autonomy," in Tom Huhn and Lambert Zuidervaart, eds., *The Semblance of Subjectivity: Adorno's Aesthetic Theory* (Cambridge, MA: MIT Press, 1997), 259–285.

4. As a discipline, art history has tended to focus on that moment in the early 'teens when representational content disappeared from Kandinsky's painting. That *Über das Geistige in der Kunst* coincided with—or, actually, slightly preceded—that moment, and offered some justification for its arrival, elevated the text to a status comparable to (perhaps even greater than) that of the paintings themselves.

5. Houlgate, "Presidential Address: Hegel and the Art of Painting," in William Maker, ed., *Hegel and Aesthetics* (Albany: State University of New York Press, 2000), 61–82.

6. Ibid., 72.

7. Ibid., 74.

8. Ibid., 75.

9. And, of course, even early on, the music Kandinsky saw as being mostly closely aligned with (his) painting was Schoenberg's atonal practice, a practice similarly difficult to characterize as oriented wholly toward the expression of some personal "inner feeling."

10. "Painting as a Pure Art" (1913), *KCW*, 350.

11. In the Preface to the *Phenomenology* (par. 17), Hegel says: "everything turns on grasping and expressing the true, not only as *substance*, but equally as *subject*." Donald Phillip Verene has glossed the passage this way: "Speculation requires us to approach the object as not substance but subject, as having an inner life—not simply, so to speak, as a body with anatomy but as a living body governed by spirit. Applicable here is A. N. Whitehead's concept in *Process and Reality* of 'vacuous actuality' (pp. 43; 253). Understood as substance, the object is vacuous in its actuality, a mere phenomenon for the knower to schematize in the production of judgments. Approached as subject, the object, like reason, is internally ordered, its actuality is not vacuous, not inert. It has an 'inside.'" See Verene, *Hegel's Absolute: An Introduction to Reading the Phenomenology of Spirit* (Albany: State University of New York Press, 2007), 7.

12. The full passage reads:

A work of art which has come into being in the way described [i.e., determined only by the "inner necessity" of its content/concept] is "beautiful." Thus a beautiful work of art is an ordered combination of the two elements, the internal and the external. It is this combination that confers upon the work its unity. The work of art becomes a subject. A painting is a spiritual organism that, like every material organism, consist of many individual parts. [*KCW*, 350]

13. In making each painting, in other words, Kandinsky was making (and was conscious of making) both a work of art and an art-historical claim—principally about the becoming-autonomous of modern art, i.e., its progressive turn from the determinations of nature toward ever increasing self-legislation.

14. Alexandre Koyré, "Hegel à Iena," in *Études d'histoire de la pensée philosophique* (Paris: NRF Gallimard, 1971), 148–149; cited in Catherine Malabou, *The Future of Hegel: Plasticity, Temporality, and Dialectic*, trans. Lisabeth During (New York: Routledge, 2005), 6.

15. See Michael S. Roth, "A Problem of Recognition: Alexandre Kojève and the End of History," *History and Theory* 24, no. 3 (October 1985), 293–306.

16. Jean-Joseph Goux, *Symbolic Economies*, trans. Jennifer Curtiss Gage (Ithaca, NY: Cornell University Press, 1990), 178ff. The section on Kandinsky and Hegel was originally published as part of Goux's *Les iconoclasts* (Paris: Éditions de Seuil, 1973).

17. Rather than the full (unpublished) text of "Les Peintures concrètes," Goux probably read the shorter published version, "Pourquoi concret," which appeared in *XXe Siècle*, no. 27 (December 1966).

18. Goux, *Symbolic Economies*, 180.

19. Alexandre Kojève, *Introduction à la lecture de Hegel* (Paris: Gallimard, 1947), 252.

20. Goux, *Symbolic Economies*, 181. If I understand him correctly, what Goux wants to show us about both Kandinsky's work and Hegel's is precisely the way they constitute self-sustaining systems, with no anchor or foundation outside of themselves. For him, both are

in that regard analogous to modern economic systems, which are driven by the "circulation of pure monetary signs" rather than being founded, as in the past, in the stable materialism of the gold standard. The terms of his analogy require him to emphasize the "abstraction and extreme detachment" of all three systems, and so also the "arbitrariness" of the signifying practices they comprise. As I have argued throughout my analysis, Kandinsky himself was deeply concerned that his work not appear arbitrary, that it be grounded, and show itself to be grounded, in its own past and the larger history of art—in their ongoing dialectical development.

21. Stephen Melville, "Plasticity: The Hegelian Writing of Art," in Margaret Iversen and Stephen Melville, *Writing Art History* (Chicago: University of Chicago Press, 2010), 165.

22. In the *Phenomenology of Spirit*, Hegel specifically identifies "plasticity" as the aim of his speculative method and the dialectical thinking on which it's founded: "only a philosophical exposition that rigidly excludes the usual way of relating the parts of a proposition [can] achieve the goal of plasticity." See *Phenomenology of Spirit*, 39.

APPENDIX

The original, handwritten manuscript of the essay "Les Peintures concrètes de Kandinsky," the document translated here, is preserved in La Bibliothèque Kandinsky at the Centre Pompidou in Paris. To date, it has been published (in the original French) three times. The first time was in 1985—thus nearly fifty years after it was written—by Michael Roth in the *Revue de métaphysique et de morale* 90, no. 2 (April–June 1985), 149–171; the second time was in a special issue of *Les Cahiers du Musée national d'art moderne* (hors série/archives) (Paris: December 1992), 176–193; and the third time as a slim paperback volume by the Belgian publisher La Lettre volée (Brussels, 2001). It's worth noting that Kojève had initially titled the essay "The Objective Paintings of Kandinsky" before changing his mind and replacing "Objective" with the word "Concrete."

1. The words "Table of Contents" ("Analyse de contenu") are actually written—lightly, with pencil—not in Kojève's hand but in Kandinsky's. The "table" itself, however, is by Kojève.

2. During revision of the essay, Kojève deleted "an animal" from his list of potentially beautiful things outside of art, and added the more Kantian (or Soloviev-inspired) "birdsong" in its stead. He also scratched the sentences that immediately followed: "Thus Beauty and Art are not the same thing. But the Beautiful—in all its specializations—is always beautiful; there is the beautiful, one and the same, in all that is beautiful, in Art or outside of Art." For Soloviev's understanding of the nightingale's song (as "the transfiguration of the sexual instinct, its liberation from the crude physiological fact— . . . the animal sex instinct embodying in itself *the idea of love*"), see his essay, "The Beauty of Nature," in S. L. Frank, ed., *A Solovyov Anthology*, trans. Natalie Duddington (London: SCM Press, 1950), esp. 129.

3. There is an interesting mistranscription of this sentence both in the version of the essay published by Michael Roth and, presumably as a result of that, in the small paperback edition released by La Lettre volée. In each, the sentence reads: "Un seul et même Beau s'incarne dans l'arbre réel et dans l'esprit peint." Kojève's handwriting could hardly be more legible: the penultimate word in the sentence is clearly *l'arbre* rather than *l'esprit*. The only explanation would seem to be that Roth—recognizing the generally Hegelian nature of

Kojève's argument, and anticipating (somewhat incorrectly) the distinction that Kojève would soon draw between Beauty-in-Art and Beauty-outside-of-Art—projected "spirit" onto the painted tree. Ironically, the mistranscription calls our attention to the surprising absence of any reference to "spirit" in Kojève's text, and so also to the complicated (if unarticulated) relation between Beauty and *Geist* implied by his argument.

4. Deleted phrase: "—like dirt on a table, which is there only by accident, insofar as it has not been mopped up, wiped away . . ."

5. The phrase that Kojève employs here, "étant 'en et pour soi,'" is a translation of *das An-und-für-sich* used by Hegel. For Hegel, Being that is "in-and-for-itself" is wholly complete and self-contained. To further emphasize its autonomy—that its existence is not determined through some other thing—Kojève will later add "by" (*par*) to the mix, referring to Being that is in-*by*-and-for-itself. Indeed Hegel himself used the phrase *Beisichselbstsein* (being self-sufficient, or at home with oneself), including in *The Philosophy of World History*, where he wrote: "spirit is self-sufficient being [*Beisichselbstsein*], and just this is freedom." See *Lectures on the Philosophy of World History: Introduction*, trans. H. B. Nisbet (Cambridge: Cambridge University Press, 1975), 48. For Kojève, then, following Hegel, the "in-by-and-for-itself" is yet another way of designating the Absolute.

6. The manuscript reads: "Il est évident que c'est seulement le *tableau* qui peut être en tant pure surface plane seulement, car la toile ne peut pas être *sans* profondeur"—rather than "*en* profondeur," as it appears in the Roth and paperback editions of the essay.

7. This entire paragraph (which may strike us as fairly digressive in the present context) picks up the thread of an argument about the role of line in painting that had animated much of Kandinsky's *Punkt und Linie zu Fläche*. See especially *PLP*, 634, where Kandinsky complains of a common "conceptual confusion," in which "what belongs together (in the present case, painting and graphics) is painstakingly divorced. Line is here reckoned as a 'graphic' element that may not be employed for 'painterly' ends, although no essential difference between 'graphics' and 'painting' can be found."

8. When the essay was published in *Les Cahiers du Musée national*, it included a mistranscription of this sentence. The "il n'y aura—dans tous ces types—des tableaux" of the manuscript was printed as "il n'y a âme dans tous ces types de tableaux." The mistake seems similar in kind to the one mentioned previously (see n3), in the version of the essay published in *Revue de Métaphysique et de Morale*—though now the result is rather less Hegelian. Presumably this projection of "soul" (*âme*) onto Kojève's essay is an indirect consequence of the strongly "spiritualist" cast of so much of the Kandinsky scholarship.

9. No doubt there is plenty to be said about Kojève's chosen example of the "nonartistically Beautiful": a woman's breast. Perhaps it will suffice here to say that the example is, obviously, highly overdetermined and, although clearly meant to demonstrate non-desirous contemplation (via the scholarly, authorial tone Kojève assumes throughout), somehow falls short of that goal.

10. Marginal note by Kandinsky: "Pure realism is abstract!"

11. The following section of Kojève's text, which seeks to differentiate among these four types of representational painting, echoes—and so seems to have been intended to rewrite—portions of Kandinsky's 1913 essay, "Painting as a Pure Art" ("Malerei als reine Kunst") (*KCW*, 349–354). There, the artist distinguished three distinct periods within the history of art, the first characterized by "Realistic painting," the second by "Naturalistic

painting (in the form of Impressionism, Neo-Impressionism, and Expressionism)," and the third, only then emerging, by "pure" (i.e., nonrepresentational) painting, which he designated as "compositional." The triadic form of Kandinsky's argument is perhaps more overtly Hegelian, yet Kojève apparently felt that it neither captured the full complexity of painting's historical development nor sufficiently emphasized the difference that had been achieved in and by Kandinsky's nonrepresentational painting.

12. Alongside the subtitle—(The Art of Kandinsky)—in the original manuscript, someone—the handwriting doesn't seem to be Kandinsky's, although it also looks a bit different from most of Kojève's—wrote (in pencil) "≠ *constructivisme*." In all of the previously published versions of the text, the symbol is mistakenly given as an equals sign, but the diagonal bar is plainly visible (if somewhat faint), and the clear intention seems to have been to differentiate Kandinsky's paintings from the work of the Russian constructivists, who had claimed the language of "concrete objectivity" for themselves.

13. At this point in the manuscript there is a word written in Kandinsky's hand— "POVTORENIE" (repetition)—and then a passage struck out. The deleted passage reads:

In effect, the tableau "Tree"—and its Beauty—are abstract because the real tree is tall, deep, fragrant, hard, useful, resonant, etc., etc., whereas the "represented" tree is none of that. Now, the tableau "Circle-Triangle" *is* the circle-triangle, which is *nothing* outside of the tableau. Said otherwise, the circle-triangle is "itself" nothing more than its flat, visual aspect: "it" has no depth, "its" size is exactly the one it has in the painting, it is neither fragrant nor hard, useful nor resonant—in a word, "it" possesses no qualities other than those it has in the tableau. Thus, if the real tree has an infinity of visual aspects, while the tableau "Tree" "represents" only one of these aspects, the circle-triangle is nothing other than the visual aspect that the tableau "Circle-Triangle" presents, which "represents" nothing. The tableau "Tree" shows us the "front" of the tree but hides what's "behind"; in contrast, there is nothing "behind" the aspect presented by the tableau "Circle-Triangle" (or, if you want, there is a behind: what you can see by looking at the tableau in a mirror, or the drawing through [its] transparency). The tableau "circle-triangle" and its Beauty are thus just as real and complete, that is, concrete, as the real tree and its Beauty.

14. In this passage, Kojève is clearly working to shield Kandinsky's art from any claims of subjectivity. He does this by distinguishing two separate moments within the making of a representational painting: an initial moment, when the artist imaginatively extracts or abstracts the Beautiful of the nonartistic object; and a second moment, when he or she successfully incarnates that "extracted" Beautiful in a tableau. The latter moment, Kojève insists, involves no abstraction whatsoever and is therefore also free from any subjectivity. By extension, because Kandinsky's art avoids that initial moment of "extraction," his works are wholly objective. We should also note, however, that in referring to each of the two differentiated moments as moments of the tableau's "birth" (rather than, say, its "creation"), Kojève seems to be alluding to a well known if enigmatic passage from the Introduction to the *Aesthetics* in which Hegel asserts that the "beauty of art is beauty *born of the spirit and born again*" (*Aesthetics*, I, 2). Kojève's argument effectively makes sense of the "born again" part of that passage by explaining how the creation of a representational image involves two separate moments of "birth"; of course, in doing so, it also subtly insinuates that representational art was foremost on Hegel's mind when formulating the *Aesthetics*, his (fairly cursory) treatment of music not withstanding.

15. I take this comment to have been intended to answer to the charges, frequently heard throughout the 1920s and '30s, that Kandinsky's art was overly theoretical or intellectual, and therefore insufficiently artistic.

16. Marginal note by Kojève:

People of late are trying desperately to create "objects." What is true and serious in this movement is the desire—unconscious or misunderstood—for concrete and objective, that is, total and absolute or "nonrepresentational" art, which—in the form of painting—is represented by Kandinsky. But one must not forget that it is not enough to pile up real, nonartistic objects in order to create an artistic one. In the vast majority of cases, the creation of objects called "surrealist" has nothing to do with Art in the standard sense of the term, but at the very most with the art of deception, the art of those who succeed—in a pinch—at passing for mad—and even then only with the gullible (to be polite)—without really being mad (since the absence of common sense is simply foolishness, which is quite different from madness).

17. Kojève condensed—and substantially clarified—this argument in the shorter essay published in the journal *XXe Siècle*:

Art is thus the art of producing beautiful objects. If the object produced also has a value other than its beauty, the art is an *applied* art: the artist "decorates," "embellishes" a thing (natural or fabricated). If beauty is the only value of the object produced, the art is *autonomous* (or "pure," as is generally said). It follows from this definition that, if God is an Artist, his art is necessarily "decorative" or "applied," whereas Kandinsky's art is autonomous, in that the objects made by him would be "without value" if they were not beautiful (their economic value then being "negative," since the producer will have "wasted" canvas and colors). [Alexandre Kojève, "Pourquoi concret," *XXe Siècle*, no. 27 (December 1966), 65]

18. In Kojève's handwritten manuscript, the headings underlined here—"art," "autonomous art," and "art of sight"— were underlined with blue pencil, while the word "painting" was underlined in red. The Roman numerals and accompanying letters that differentiate among the various types of painting were also written in red pencil.

INDEX